The Management of Human Services

THE MANAGEMENT OF HUMAN SERVICES

ROSEMARY C. SARRI
AND
YEHESKEL HASENFELD
EDITORS

NEW YORK   COLUMBIA UNIVERSITY PRESS   1978

Library of Congress Cataloging in Publication Data

MAIN ENTRY UNDER TITLE:

THE MANAGEMENT OF HUMAN SERVICES.

PAPERS PREPARED FOR A CONFERENCE ORGANIZED BY THE
LOIS AND SAMUEL SILBERMAN FUND AND THE JOHNSON FOUNDA-
TION, AND HELD IN RACINE, WIS., JUNE 27–30, 1977.

INCLUDES BIBLIOGRAPHIES AND INDEX.

1. SOCIAL WORK ADMINISTRATION—CONGRESSES.

2. SOCIAL SERVICE—CONGRESSES. I. SARRI, ROSEMARY C.

II. HASENFELD, YEHESKEL.

HV41.M276   658'91'361   78-9083

ISBN 0-231-04628-6

COLUMBIA UNIVERSITY PRESS

NEW YORK   GUILDFORD, SURREY

Contents

Foreword

THIS VOLUME is the product of a project initiated by the Lois and Samuel Silberman Fund with the objective of bringing together some of the most recent and, it is hoped, forefront theoretical and empirical studies of the issues inherent in the management and administration of human services, and providing the forum through which they can be communicated to those concerned with the future of human services. The issues clearly transcend this field and are equally pertinent to other social institutions such as government, éducation, and culture.

A word about foundation grants in general and this grant in particular. Every legitimate grant seeks a public benefit. The role of a foundation is catalytic. The most any foundation can do is recognize a need and stimulate those who are able to address the problem through personal encouragement coupled with financial support. The willingness of Rosemary Sarri and all of the participants to make themselves available on relatively short notice, submit themselves to a self-imposed discipline as to quality of effort and timetable for completion is a testament to the fact that no project is a product of a foundation, but rather belongs to those who produce it. The Johnson Foundation which generously made its Wingspread conference facility available for this project shares this thinking.

And so, I have asked the editors, and they have agreed to dedicate this volume

TO THE THOUSANDS OF CREATIVE INDIVIDUALS
ENGAGED IN FOUNDATION PROJECT GRANTS. THEIR
COMMITMENT OF TALENT, INTELLECT, EFFORT, AND TIME
HAS MADE THE PRIVATE FOUNDATION A UNIQUE AMERICAN
INSTITUTION,

SANCTIONED TO ENTER THE PUBLIC FORUM WITH PRIVATE
INITIATIVE
TO STIMULATE EXCELLENCE, INNOVATION, AND BETTERMENT
OF HUMAN WELFARE.

Samuel J. Silberman
President
The Lois and Samuel Silberman Fund

Acknowledgments

PROBLEMS in the management of human services have long been an important concern of the editors of this book—in our research and consultative
work with these organizations, in our own practice as administrators, and in
the training of social work professionals for management positions. Administration of these organizations is becoming increasingly complex, but
our knowledge of the necessary strategies and technologies is quite inadequate to meet the ever-increasing demands. Moreover, there are high levels
of dissatisfaction expressed by clients, staff, and the community about the
rigid and ineffectual bureaucratization of human services. Thus, it was a significant opportunity when Samuel J. Silberman approached the senior editor
indicating that the Silberman Fund was interested in sponsoring a series of
projects to aid in the improvement of administrative management capabilities of human service organizations. In our case he asked her to consider the
preparation of a book for senior level administrators, policy makers, social
work educators, and students which would deal with some of the critical
issues for public and private agencies in the 1970s. When we accepted his
offer we decided to focus our attention particularly on the management
issues as related to service delivery to clientele.

As a result of the Silberman Fund's interest and support along with that
of the Johnson Foundation a conference was held at Wingspread conference
facility in Racine, Wisconsin, June 27–30, 1977. Participating in the conference were the authors of papers presented in this book and nine social work
administrators, social scientists, and educators who served as discussants
(see Appendix A for list of participants).

To each and all of these distinguished colleagues we are deeply appre-
ciative of the way in which they completed their work and complied with
deadlines.

The Wingspread setting on Lake Michigan provided a most pleasant setting for three stimulating days of discussion of issues in the delivery of human services. It was particularly stimulating because of the frank candor among social scientists, administrators, and educators. Since then it has occurred to us that each of the respective professional groups has much to gain from similar opportunities of this type.

Without the stimulation and support of Samuel Silberman it is doubtful that this effort could have come to fruition as quickly as it did. Moreover, he used his not inconsiderable management skills very effectively to facilitate the entire project. We also wish to acknowledge the generous support of the Johnson Foundation, especially Mr. Leslie Paffrath, President, and Mr. Richard Kinch, Program Associate. Everything was done so well by them to provide an environment conducive to creative discussion.

The cooperation of Dean Philip Fellin of the University of Michigan School of Social Work is gratefully acknowledged. He relieved the editors of regular assignments and without that, the project could not have been completed. We also wish to acknowledge a special debt to Ms. Christine Sherman, who assisted in arranging and managing the Conference and in the subsequent preparation of papers for publication. Her dedication to the success of the effort merits our deep gratitude.

We were greatly stimulated in the activities associated with producing this book by students, colleagues, administrators, and others. We hope that the book will in turn stimulate others as they cope with the management of human services. If it does, then clients of human service organizations should benefit significantly and a major objective for all of us will have been achieved.

Rosemary Sarri
Yeheskel Hasenfeld
University of Michigan
February 1978

The Management of Human Services

ONE

The Management of Human Services—
A Challenging Opportunity

IN THE evaluation of social welfare institutions in the United States the seventies will undoubtedly be characterized as the decade during which the management of human service organizations became of paramount concern. The preoccupation with the development of management tools and techniques to increase the effectiveness and efficiency of human service organizations may be seen, in part, as a reaction to the wide-spread disillusionment with the efforts at social service reforms in the 1960s and early 1970s. The issues evolve less around the extension of citizenship rights and social service entitlement to disenfranchised social groups, and more in checking the rise of welfare expenditures, reduction of waste and service duplications, and efficient use of existing services.

It is widely acknowledged that social welfare institutions in the United States are facing a growing crisis in terms of their societal legitimation, allocation of resources, public expectations and demands, and administration and management. Several factors may have converged to produce this sense of malaise. First, there has been an unparalleled expansion of federal expenditures on social welfare in the years following World War II, from 8.9 percent of the Gross National Product in 1950 to 17 percent of the GNP in 1973 (Janowitz, 1976). At the same time, however, as Janowitz cogently points out, this expansion has been accompanied by deficit spending, which at times of declining economic growth and especially of reduced economic surplus creates severe pressures on the economy.

Second, there has been a tremendous rise in the expectations and demands of various social groups to have a share of the "human services pie."

Many of these groups have been previously denied access to adequate health, education, and welfare services, while others received services under highly restrictive and degrading conditions. Titmuss (1969), in writing about attitudes toward welfare in the United States, notes that most people have a "public burden" notion of the welfare state. In contrast, in Europe welfare is more often synonomous with well-being and certainly is not a popular "bad word." He further refers to the United States as the "diswelfare state" and documents the fact that many of our so-called welfare programs benefit the total society despite the popular view of being for the undeserving, deviant, poor, or handicapped population. This clash between greater demands for human services and the predominant public attitudes toward welfare has created a crisis in the societal legitimation of these institutions. This is exemplified in what Wilensky (1975) terms the revolt of the middle mass against the welfare state.

Third, the expansion of human services was coupled with an accelerated bureaucratization of the system. There has been a vast proliferation of new human service bureaucracies, regulatory agencies, and an ever-increasing array of administrative bodies. The bureaucratization of the human services had introduced powerful new interest groups, namely the bureaucracies themselves (Wilensky, 1975; Alford, 1975). As each human service bureaucracy pursues its own self-maintenance and self-expansion, fragmentation of services, lack of coordination, zealous defense of domain, and rejection of "undesirable" clients are the frequently observed consequences. The public outcry as to the increasing inhumaneness, rigidity, and lack of responsiveness by human service organizations may be anchored in the sense of loss of power in controlling one's fate vis-à-vis these bureaucracies (Coleman, 1973).

THE NATURE OF HUMAN SERVICE ORGANIZATIONS

It is within this context that the management issues of human service organizations must be addressed. In particular, we must identify and develop an organizational theory that is applicable to this set of organizations and that can inform us about the parameters that control their functioning. Until recently, most of the theory of organizational behavior was based on the study of business and industrial organizations. It was assumed that the constructs and propositions useful in understanding the behavior of these organizations could be applied to understanding the behavior of the human service agencies. In fact, in a recent series of essays Richard Cyert argues that there are more similarities than there are differences between profit and non-profit organizations, as he defines them (Cyert, 1975). Although he presents a convincing set of arguments, adequate comparative research about the similarities and differences remains to be completed before one can accept Cyert's assertions. In fact, he himself acknowledges some of the profound differences with respect to defining and increasing productivity, controlling resources and budgeting, and performance evaluation. Whether one conceptualizes human service organizations as a distinct and unique set of organizations depends on the importance attached to the following attributes which characterize them.

First, human service organizations work on people by processing and/or changing them individually or collectively. The persons directly handled by these organizations are simultaneously their input, raw material, and product. As Perrow (1965) notes, people are vested with values and have definite social position and location which the organization must respond to. Thus, every decision and action undertaken by these organizations involve moral evaluation and moral judgment of people and have consequences to their normative and social standing (Hasenfeld and English, 1974; Freidson, 1970). As a result, human service organizations must adopt ideological systems to justify their activities, yet always face the risk that these ideologies will be contested by various social groups.

Second, and related to the above, human service organizations are characterized by a precarious domain consensus. Since these organizations intervene in the lives of people, they confront multiple expectations and conflicting demands in a pluralistic society. For example, on the one hand there is an expectation that welfare departments respond in a humane way and provide for the needs of the poor. On the other hand, there are persistent demands to reduce the welfare rolls and force the poor into the labor market. Similarly, juvenile courts are simultaneously pushed to pursue a "law and order" goal and a "social rehabilitation" orientation (Sarri and Hasenfeld, 1976). The lack of domain consensus is intensified as these organizations serve populations perceived or defined as deviant. In order to accommodate to multiple and often conflicting demands, human service organizations are likely to develop ambiguous and often contradictory goals. Therefore, the issues concerning who should be served and what services should be provided are never fully resolved, nor can clear goal priorities be established.

Third, human service organizations, particularly in the public sector, acquire very limited autonomy in relation to their task environment. In particular, these organizations are highly dependent on resources controlled by other organizations and are often subject to extensive regulations by various legislative and administrative bodies. Dependency on the task environment constrains the ability of these organizations to develop service modalities which reflect the actual needs of the population. Rather, these tend to reflect the constraints and contingencies imposed by external units. Helfgot (1974) showed, for example, how a reform organization established to promote structural changes in social service agencies on behalf of the poor has transformed its goals to treat the personal and social pathologies of the poor as a consequence of the pressures by the funding and regulating agencies. Warren, Rose, and Bergunder (1974) arrived at a similar conclusion when assessing the impact of Model Cities programs. Similarly, Hasenfeld (1975) noted that the employment placement services serving the poor are more likely to heed the needs of the potential employers than the job seekers.

Put differently, in many instances, human service organizations become captives of external units and thus come to serve their interests rather than the interests of the population they were established to serve. Moreover, being dependent on other organizations reduces the incentives of such organizations to innovate, for there seem to be little real payoffs in developing new programs unless they are clearly underwritten by public funds.

Fourth, despite the increase in the variety of new service technologies, a major characteristic of human service organizations is the lack of determinate and effective technologies. With few exceptions, particularly in the health field, most human service technologies are based on limited and fragmentary knowledge bases while having to deal with complex human behavior. As a result, most fail to meet the attributes of a technology as defined by Perrow (1965). In particular, few of these technologies can be shown to be effective (see, for example, Segal, 1972). Consequently, human service organizations develop ideological systems in lieu of technologies which guide and justify the behavior of staff. The lack of coherent and determinate technologies generates a great deal of internal ambiguity and inconsistencies in response to client needs. Specifically, indeterminate technologies generate a great deal of staff discretion and lack of any service capabilities of quality control. Development of explicit criteria for performance assessment and measures of accountability become highly problematic.

These forementioned characteristics indicate that, at the very least, organizational and management theories must incorporate them into their explanatory models and prescriptive paradigms in order to be of any relevance to human service organizations, particularly as these confront current challenges and problems.

PROBLEMS CONFRONTING
HUMAN SERVICE ORGANIZATIONS

The manifestations of the crisis in our welfare institutions are readily apparent in the pressures, dilemmas, and problems facing the administrators of human service organizations. We shall note some of them briefly.

ENVIRONMENTAL UNCERTAINTY

It is already apparent that human service agencies face serious problems in this time of stable or declining resources and growing demand. The social service agency is in a peculiar dilemma because resources are stable or declining in some areas, but demand generally continues to rise. As Cyert (1975) notes, problems for non-profit and human service agencies are particularly significant in this regard, since these organizations place little emphasis on generating new resources; instead they see the solution in the allocation of resources provided to them by the environment through governmental agencies, members, or clientele. The persistent problems of high inflation coupled with high unemployment that plague society pose significant problems for human service agencies which rely so heavily on public resources.

It is difficult to determine whether environmental uncertainties and rapid social change are the key factors producing the crises for social service administrators or whether these are the results of development in administrative practice itself. Not long ago Herbert Simon recapitulated developments in public administration that seem equally applicable to administrators of social service agencies.

If a science has been culture bound—and public administration has been through most of its history—it becomes difficult to distinguish between progress in the science, on the one hand, and changes in the social institutions they purport to describe, on the other—The developments taking place in public administration theory and practice are, to a considerable extent, consequences of modifications of the social environment of governmental organizations. (Simon, 1967, p. 89)

In either case, the ability of these organizations to plan for the future is highly curtailed in the face of such uncertainty, resulting in a reactive and passive posture to changing human needs. Similarly, there are increasing and unrelenting pressures on human service organizations to become more efficient and cost-effective (Rivlin, 1971). It is clear that, in the face of shrinking resources, human service organizations must readdress themselves to fundamental policy questions regarding the setting of service priorities and populations to be served. There is a serious danger that in doing so, these organizations will succumb to the pressures of the more articulate and resourceful social groups, while abandoning their commitment to the disenfranchised, the dependent, and the weak.

PLANNING SERVICE DELIVERY SYSTEMS

The diversity, complexity, and apparent fragmentation of the human services has created pressures toward increased coordination and integration of social services. Human service organizations are asked to participate in multi-organizational planning systems and are frequently required to give up some of their autonomy in planning for the future. Increasingly, the planning functions of human service organizations are made contingent upon conditions set by coordinating bodies of various jurisdictions, by pressures to affiliate with networks of organizations, and by demands to cooperate with other service agencies. This has resulted in a far greater intervention of governmental bodies in the planning process. In fact, it seems that one of the unanticipated consequences of the greater involvement of multi-systems in the planning process is to reduce significantly the probability of actual program implementation (Pressman and Wildavsky, 1973; Williams and Elmore, 1976). In the same vein, services integration has been a federal priority of HEW since the mid-1960s, and progressively the concern has been directed toward integration of various political and horizontal units with the assumption that effectiveness and efficiency would thereby be enhanced. Primary attention has been directed toward program planning and management at the state and regional levels with little explicit reference to the "frontline" problems of designing, organizing, and delivering services to clients in relation to their immediate situation and needs. Encouragement has been given to reorganizing state agencies into large health and welfare conglomerates, as in Georgia, Florida, Washington, Arizona, North Carolina, and other states. In fact, about half of the fifty states now have some form of comprehensive human service agency and it seems rather clear that this is at least partially a result of the federal priority and guidelines. As a consequence, more attention has been directed toward linking providers and service programs at the administrative level to improve management. However, as Morris and Lescohier note in a subsequent chapter of this volume, assessment of the results indicate that there is little concrete evidence of significant measurable change, and even less evidence of more effective service delivery to clientele.

ORGANIZATIONAL RESPONSIVENESS

With preference for centralized planning and management by governmental bodies and the need for human service organizations to handle high degrees of dependency on the task environment, the issues of organizational responsiveness to citizens—potential and active clients—becomes problematic. In a very fundamental sense, the question becomes: Whose interests does the organization serve? Perrow, in a provocative essay in this volume, asserts that the interests of clients are least likely to be represented in the organization as compared to the interests of elites, professionals, and the like. The various experiments in citizen participation during the sixties certainly produce a note of pessimism regarding the ability of social service organizations to allow effective participation of clients in decision making (Moynihan, 1969).

Nevertheless, there is a growing and insisting pressure by various social groups to have some control over the very organizations that intervene in their lives. These groups include not only actual clients, such as welfare recipients, patients, inmates, and students, but also other groups whose interests were seldom considered, such as ethnic minorities, women, parents of the mentally retarded, and the like. Most frequently, the only vehicle open to these groups to attain some degree of organizational responsiveness has been through litigations or disruptive tactics. Yet, it is clear that other, less conflict producing mechanisms must be developed.

Paradoxically, as human service organizations become more responsive to multiple client demands, they are more likely to become immobilized and torn by conflicting and contradictory pressures, unless social integration mechanisms are developed to reach consensus over goals. This problem is clearly demonstrated in the attempts to develop community-based treatment programs that are thus responsive to local needs. Neighborhood groups organize to block the establishment of group homes, day treatment centers, and the like, thus depriving other citizens of needed services. At a more general level, Janowitz (1976) argues that this leads to the weakening of parliamentary institutions, and the paper presented by him and Suttles in this volume suggests new forms of citizen participation in the decision-making process about their welfare.

MEASURING EFFICIENCY AND EFFECTIVENESS

Contemporary definitions of effectiveness and efficiency pose another set of problems that have long resisted solution for these organizations. They continue to be present despite vast efforts and resources devoted to their examination in program evaluation design, in policy formulation, in program budgeting, and in benefit-cost analysis. Part of the reason for this situation is the fact that most attention has been focused on outcome variables for individual clients, such as recidivism, permanent remission of mental illness, and so forth. Far less effort is devoted to assessing organizational outputs or organizational performance that is related to stated and expected goals.

Social service administrators today face conflicting demands that they meet new requirements for managing and reporting social services, and for being accountable to provide information about the effectiveness of their services to clients, taxpayers, legislators, and peer professionals. The solution to these conflicting demands, if there is one, seems to lie in the ability of agencies to move from information and evaluation systems at the "case level" to information and evaluation systems at the "operations" level (Rossi, 1976; Rossi and Williams, 1972). That is, criteria for evaluation of efficiency and effectiveness must be developed in relation to identified social problems and needs of client groups which are within the scope of the organizational mandate. Operational goals for resolving these problems must be determined along with the objectives for achieving these goals. These objectives must be stated in quantifiable terms for specific programs and services. Measures of effectiveness need to be related explicitly to these objectives. Moreover, the measures of effectiveness need to consider not only individual client performance, but also organizational performance, including both process and effort variables (Suchman, 1967; Sarri and Selo, 1974). Unless effectiveness measures concentrate on the results of the program rather than its activities or attributes of individuals, it's doubtful that they will be useful in modifying organizational behavior.

BUREAUCRATIZATION AND PROFESSIONALIZATION

Finally, human service organizations seem to experience a simultaneous increase in bureaucratization and professionalization. This phenomenon is very apparent in human service organizations where social work as a profession has grown very rapidly since World War II. As a professional group, it now evidences many of the attributes associated with the more traditional professions. Street (in press) charges, in a recent provocative paper, that bureaucratization and professionalization have interacted in social service organizations to perpetuate poverty, inequality, and injustice. This is a disturbing charge, but his analysis of public schools and public welfare shows that there has been tremendous growth of bureaucratization of inequality through the extension and elaboration of governmental services which define, but do not change, the procedures under which inequality is maintained. He goes further to describe and document the professionalization of reform efforts whereby social workers and other human service professionals have defined social problems as a special province of the profession. They assess poor persons and their behavior to provide additional social definitions that catch the poor in a web of multiple reifications, but they provide no means for "diversion" or movement out of the status of being poor, criminal, handicapped, or labeled deviant. Wilensky (1975) comes to a similar conclusion in his re-analysis of the welfare state. Social work professionals have received broad discretion to define and implement their own interpretation of reform proposals. Needless to say, society seldom has provided the necessary resources for those programs, perhaps because so many of the persons to be served are disesteemed or disadvantaged with respect to the characteristics valued by the majority. Nevertheless, the technologies of the profession have been insufficient to modify the perceptions and values of the majority. For example, the perceptions of the problems of poverty, illness, and criminality as individual pathologies have been largely accepted by the profession, and correspondingly technologies have focused on change targets for individuals. Understanding of this perception is critical to understanding the operations of social service agencies in the United States today.

How can the problems of human service organizations be approached and resolved, if at all? One can identify two diametrically opposing approaches to the problems of human service organizations, both in the public discussion and the professional literature. The first approach can be termed the "scientific management" approach as advocated by Cyert (1975). The second can be termed a "political economy" model as proposed by Zald (1970), and implicitly used by such researchers as Warren, et al (1974), Alford (1975) and Perrow in this volume. Both approaches are reflected in the various essays in this book and we shall outline each briefly.

SCIENTIFIC MANAGEMENT FOR SOCIAL WELFARE

It is argued that many of the problems encountered by human service organizations can be handled effectively through the adoption of modern management tools originally developed in the business sector, such as Management by Objective, Management Information Systems, and Operations Research.

A recent Task Force of the National Conference of Social Welfare (1976:12–15) presented a detailed set of proposals for enhancing technologies with the explicit goal of delivering services more effectively to clients. In other words, as they state, management for more effective "front line performance." Although their proposal has not been empirically tested, it does depend on an assessment of available research. They propose a "human resources model of management," emphasizing rational strategies and strong management approaches. Their model identifies the following elements as critical preconditions:

1. Clearly articulated and operationalizable goals based on valid data, staff participation, and client needs.
2. Enforcement of worker accountability for achieving results, not merely performing activities.
3. Facilitation of staff behavior and implementation activities which involves discretion and flexibility in means to achieve results.
4. Implementation of objective methods of evaluation linked to goals, with rewards to staff and clients for successful output.
5. Securing of necessary resources for ongoing activities and also for innovations and experimentation.

6. Facilitation of personal and professional growth in staff, including career development for new managers.
7. Simplification of bureaucratic procedures and reduction of paper work.
8. Developing ongoing problem-solving and change mechanisms.
9. Goal-oriented case management as a basic strategy of programming for workers.
10. Creation of ongoing mechanisms for effecting sound interorganizational relationships.

The utility of an approach such as that developed by the Task Force can be seen in the research findings of Stein and Gambrill (1976) regarding the administration of foster child-care programs in California and in the New York City model case management for children in residential care outside their natural home.

This model of rational management has come under considerable criticism. First, it has been argued that managerial decision making in actuality follows a "garbage can" model, whereby problems are sought for solutions at hand rather than the other way around (Cohen, March, and Olsen 1972). Second, the model is oblivious to the socio-political milieu in which these organizations are embedded and to the influence it exerts over them. Third, the model undervalues the particular attributes of human service organizations. Drucker (1973), a noted business management expert, argues that borrowing from either business or industrial administration, or both, is quite inappropriate for human service organizations because of important qualitative differences in the essential characteristics of these organizations. Among the differences which he identified are the intangibility of goals and objectives, criteria for determining efficiency, basis for budgetary allocations, indeterminacy in the measurement of both outputs and outcomes, and the criteria for successful performance.

THE POLITICAL ECONOMY OF SOCIAL WELFARE

The political economy approach starts with the fundamental assumption that the organization is embedded in a larger social system in which the allocation of power and resources determine the goals of the organization. Put differently, the objectives pursued by the organization are determined by those interest groups within and without the organization who have control over critical resources. Thus, the service delivery system developed by the agency will reflect the political processes among these interest groups, organizational access to resources, and their internal allocation.

For example, although the relationship between unemployment and crime has long been documented in a number of studies, the dominant political interest groups permit the highest rates of unemployment to exist in the age group that is responsible for most of the crime. However, they are then willing to spend billions of dollars on law enforcement, courts, prisons, and parole programs for these same persons who have been denied access to legitimate social roles. Moreover, these resources are spent despite repeated evidence of the relative ineffectiveness of these programs in resocialization of these same young persons for desired social role behavior.

Similarly, Alford (1975) argues that no amount of rational planning and management of our medical care services is going to improve the system so long as the existing structural institutionalization of the interests of medical care providers remain intact.

Following this perspective, then, changing human service organizations and improving their effectiveness must take place in the political and economic arena. Taken to its extreme, such a model tends to trivialize societal commitments to social welfare. Moreover, it fails to acknowledge that the failures of human service organizations may indeed be due to lack of know-how and inadequate administrative skills. Certainly, one could list numerous examples of such instances.

To sum up, the development of a more adequate theoretical framework and knowledge base for administration deserves serious attention today. That framework should assist in selecting out critical variables, propositions, criteria, and so forth, which are necessary to direct management decision making behavior. The literature is filled with many sophisticated models developed to explain limited aspects of organizational behavior, but they do not provide the components for a general theory of management. Also required for an adequate theory are the results from comparative studies across organizations, institutions, and national boundaries if we are to be able to assess adequately the similarities and differences within and among different types of organizations. Verification of similarities, differences, and patterns among apparently diverse organizations is urgently needed and would be most helpful in the utilization of a substantial set of research which is already developed. Regardless of the organizing rubric that is used, there seems to be little doubt that the management of human service organizations urgently needs and could benefit substantially from more work devoted to the development of a systematic theoretical framework.

FORECAST OF THE BOOK

This volume does not purport to deal with all the critical issues facing social welfare in the United States in the late 1970s, but it does attempt to analyze some of the more critical issues which have not been fully examined and it proposes some alternatives for future policy and program development. Although the papers are not limited to the administrative management of social service agencies, we have tried to keep this as a primary focus so that the book may be of particular value to social welfare administrators and educators.

The book is organized into three parts. Part I deals with macro-level issues affecting the management of human service organizations. Robert Morris and Ilana Lescohier cogently analyze some of the problems and results which have been achieved thus far in several efforts at services integration which were initiated by the Department of Health, Education and Welfare. They properly argue that "integration" and "coordination" should not be treated as synonomous. Moreover, they assert that given the governmental structure in the United States, more attention should be paid to policies which facilitate limited coordination among existing networks and services. Howard Aldrich examines the consequences of centralized and decentralized structures for service delivery, giving particular attention to manpower services organizations. He also points to some of the variable characteristics of the advocates of these two strategies and shows the utility of organizational analysis for tracing the implementation of these in manpower programs. He concludes that a decentralized or "loosely coupled" approach maximizes service delivery to heterogeneous clients, situations, and demands.

Gerald Suttles and Morris Janowitz present a model for the development of local community participatory groups to enhance welfarism and parliamentary democracy. They point to some of the factors which have led to the deterioration and, sometimes, demise of these groups in the recent past and claim that the environment is more receptive to their development at the present time.

Charles Perrow's paper provides the bridge between the macro and micro levels. He begins by asking why there has been so little impact from the developments in mainstream organizational theory on the behavior of human service organizations, despite the fact that a vast amount of knowledge is available for application. He suggests that in attempting to answer these questions, one inevitably raises a more fundamental inquiry and he proposes that constructs at the fringes of organizational theory rather than in the mainstream provide more fruitful avenues for research and theory development. He then considers what our understanding and expectations about these organizations would be if peripheral ideas were treated as mainstream constructs.

Part II, the micro section, opens with a paper by Eugene Litwak, in which he presents an alternative conceptual formulation of the development of organizational theory. He builds his "multi-model theory" around the nature of the task situation and suggests that this provides the basis for determining optimal organizational structures. Epstein and Conrad raise a series of questions about the descriptive and predictive validity of the concept of professionalization within social work. They challenge the claim to professionalization within social work and critique the limited predictive value of professionalization as a variable. They further suggest some ways in which professionalization would have to be specified further if it were to be useful in predicting different levels of effectiveness and service delivery and they conclude with recommendations for a de-professionalized conceptual model of social work which they argue would enable us to identify more readily factors which facilitate or obstruct social service delivery. Hasenfeld formulates a comprehensive framework for the study of client-organization relations, based on concepts from systems theory. The client and the organization are both viewed as open systems, each with analogous sets of subsystems. The interaction between the client and the organization is conceived as an exchange of energy—information, whereby each system attempts to obtain the needed resources from the other system, in a manner that optimizes payoff and minimizes costs. This model is then used to generate hypotheses focusing on three components of interaction: initiation, power-dependence, and trust. Utilization of social exchange theory enables one to generate specific hypotheses about causal relationships between client attributes, organizational variables, and components of client-organization interaction. Concluding this section is a paper by Perlmutter and Alexander in which they examine racism and sexism in social service agencies. Human services, they assert, were organized in the homogeneous manner until the 1960s, reflecting the cohesive monolithic arrangement. Assumptions underlying services reflected not only the ideological thrust of the poor law, but also conceptions of the dominant professions concerning both the constituents to be served as well as the nature of the services provided. Perlmutter and Alexander examined a vast amount of social work and social welfare literature to identify the times and mechanisms through which new voices emerged, reflecting a variety of interest groups in American society. They use a social movement analysis in their examination of these social changes, considering how these emergent interest groups reflected new values, new assumptions, new leads, and how they demanded new strategies. Although the data for this purpose were less than that which the authors desired, they attempt to use it to assess the organizational responses to these new pressures and to ascertain whether or not these movements were effective in improving social services.

Part III of the book presents a series of papers dealing with prescriptive strategies for the management of human service organizations where the goal is enhancing service delivery. Peter Rossi considers some of the issues in the evaluation of human service organizations. He suggests that the nature of service delivery in these organizations is of paramount importance in any understanding of them because it is highly operator dependent, difficult to standardize, and therefore subject to considerable agency situation and deliverer variation. He further asserts that it is often difficult to say that a particular service is being delivered when the service itself is subject to such wide variation. As a result, one of the main issues in evaluation is defining, measuring, and describing the services actually being delivered. Implementation research becomes a critical aspect of evaluation activity for these reasons. Rossi also goes on to point out that service delivery has to be considered as a total complex of services, including the deliverers and the administrative apparatus surrounding the delivery, because each of these has significant effects on output measures. Lastly, he examines some of the issues of statistical inference that arise from the nature of human service delivery. Rino Patti presents a model for developmental administration. He asserts that much of the existing literature on administration is organized around some taxonomy of management functions, such as planning, budgeting, and so forth. These functions tend to be treated as discrete steps in a linear process that unfolds systematically over time. Patti argues that administrative practices can be more productively conceptualized in terms of stages or phases of program development, each of which involves characteristic issues and problems requiring purposeful intervention by organizational leaders. Patti focuses particularly on several phases of program development—design, initiation, implementation, and evaluation—with particular reference to the critical tasks that must be addressed if the agency is to develop and maintain effective service delivery capability. Arnold Gurin then examines the commonly held assumption that social service programs are not well managed. In doing so he points out the need to distinguish problems of management from issues of policy choice. Comparisons are analyzed about the similarities and differences in the management problems and processes of human service organizations. Gurin concludes that the management of human services is still at a relatively primitive stage. Existing management theory could be utilized far more extensively to provide sensitizing concepts and approaches for staff to consider in solving problems in new ways. However, he emphasizes the need for a more positive approach to careful experimentation rather than blind application of knowledge from one field to the other. Delbecq provides a model for introducing innovation into human service organizations, taking into consideration social and political factors which affect this process. He directs his remarks to the administrator who will play the advocate role in introducing innovation. The paper focuses upon idea generation, solution development, and the implementation of programs, not so much from the standpoint of technology as from the standpoint of "politicking" through bureaucratic systems. Delbecq uses a normative framework developed from his interpretation of findings about organizational change and development, needs assessment, program planning, and so forth. In the last chapter we have attempted to present the conference in perspective, drawing extensively from the critiques of several discussants and from the conference discussion of the papers.

REFERENCES

Alford, R. 1975. *Health Care Politics*. Chicago: University of Chicago Press.

Coleman, J. 1973. "Loss of Power," *American Sociological Review,* 38:1–17.

Cohen, M.D., T. G. March, and J. P. Olsen. 1972. "A Garbage Can Model of Organizational Choice," *Administrative Science Quarterly* (March), 17:1–25.

Cyert, Richard. 1975. *The Management of the Non-Profit Organization,* Lexington, Mass.: D.C. Heath.

Drucker, Peter. 1973. "On Managing the Public Service Institution." *The Public Interest* (Fall), 33:43–60.

Freidson, E. 1970. *The Profession of Medicine.* New York: Dodd, Mead.

Hasenfeld, Yeheskel. 1975. "The Role of Employment Placement Services in Maintaining Poverty," *Social Service Review,* 49:569–87.

Hasenfeld, Y., and R. A. English, eds. 1974. *Human Service Organizations.* Ann Arbor: University of Michigan Press.

Helfgot, J. 1974. "Professional Reform Organizations and the Symbolic Representation of the Poor," *American Sociological Review,* 39:475–91.

Janowitz, Morris. 1976. *Social Control of the Welfare State.* New York: Elsevier.

Moynihan, Daniel P. 1969. *Maximum Feasible Misunderstanding.* New York: Free Press.

National Conference of Social Welfare. 1976. Task Force on Expanding Management Technology and Professional Accountability in Social Service Programs, 103rd Annual Forum, Washington, D.C.: June 14.

Perrow, Charles. 1965. "Hospitals: Technology, Structure and Goals," In J. G. March, ed. *Handbook of Organizations, pp. 910–71.* Chicago: Rand McNally.

Pressman, J. L., and A. B. Wildavsky. 1973. *Implementation.* Berkeley: University of California Press.

Rivlin, A. M. 1971. *Systematic Thinking for Social Action.* Washington, D.C.: The Brookings Institution.

Rossi, Peter H. 1976. *Reforming Public Welfare.* New York: Russell Sage.

Rossi, Peter H. and W. Williams, eds. 1972. *Evaluating Social Programs.* New York: Seminar Press.

Sarri, R. C. and Y. Hasenfeld, eds. 1976. *Brought to Justice.* Ann Arbor, Mich.: National Assessment of Juvenile Corrections.

Sarri, R. C. and E. Selo. 1974. "Evaluation Process and Outcome in Juvenile Corrections: Musings on a Grim Tale." In P. Davidson, F. C. Clark, and L. W. Hamerlynck, eds., *Evaluation of Behavioral Programs.* Champaign, Ill.: Research Press.

Segal, S. P. 1972. "Research on the Outcome of Social Work Therapeutic Intervention," *Journal of Health and Social Behavior,* 13:3–17.

Simon, Herbert. 1967. "The Changing Theory and Changing Practice of Public Administration." In J. de Sola Pool, ed., *Contemporary Political Science,* pp. 86–120. New York: McGraw-Hill.

Stein, T. J. and E. D. Gambril. 1976. *Decision Making in Foster Care: A Training Manual.* Berkeley: University of California Press.

Street, David. In press. "Bureaucratization, Professionalization and the Poor." In K. Grønbjerg, D. Street, and G. Suttles, eds., *Poverty and Social Change.* Chicago. University of Chicago Press.

Suchman, Edward. 1967. *Evaluation Research.* New York: Russell Sage Foundation.

Titmuss, Richard. 1969. *Commitment to Welfare.* New York: Pantheon.

Warren, R., S. Rose, and A. Bergunder. 1974. *The Structure of Urban Reform.* Lexington, Mass.: D.C. Heath.

Wilensky, H. L. 1975. *The Welfare State and Equality.* Berkeley: University of California Press.

Williams, W. and R. E. Elmore, eds. 1976. *Social Program Implementation,* New York: Academic Press.

Zald, Mayer. 1970. "Political Economy: A Framework for Comparative Analysis." In M. N. Zald, ed., *Power in Organizations,* pp. 221–61. Nashville, Tenn.: Vanderbilt University Press.

THE MACRO LEVEL

TWO

Service Integration:
Real Versus Illusory Solutions to Welfare Dilemmas

ROBERT MORRIS AND ILANA HIRSCH LESCOHIER

THE INTEGRATION of human (or social) services is a hardy, perennial issue. It received major attention as early as the late nineteenth century in the United States, when community organization societies were first considered the remedy to fragmented and disorganized welfare activities of voluntary groups of that era. It is a subject that has continued to attract significant interest and attention fueled by the growing complexity of social welfare organizations. Unfortunately, throughout a hundred years, the subject has been plagued by ambiguity as to terminology and concept, by a confusion among problems, aims, and remedies. The more complex our welfare systems become, the more we seek to bring order into their relationships, although this goal consistently eludes our grasp.

This paper is another attempt to understand the confusions which have clouded the subject, to assess the results of recent efforts to secure more effective integration of services, and to reach some conclusion about approaches that might fruitfully be taken in the near-term future.

We want to resist a common tendency to reconstruct the entire human services system in the image of an idealized perfect state. Rather than striving for a friction-free network of social services, we will look for specific defects which integration or coordination might reasonably be expected to improve. We approach this task from a position outside of any one service provider unit; our focus is on the potential for integration or coordination of independent service units. Such an approach necessarily requires the introduction of influences from outside the structure of individual service organizations.

Our analysis leads us to the conclusion that integration and coordination are often turned to because the real problems of social organization and social distress are too difficult to deal with frontally or directly. Inequity, inequality, serious deprivation, and disability are impossible to overcome without serious expenditure of resources, energies, and emotions, but such expenditures are often resisted consciously or unconsciously. Integration is then seized upon as a less painful way to make the existing welfare system function more efficiently by presumably stretching its resources further. The reasonableness of such an assumption needs to be examined.

MEANINGS OF THE TERM INTEGRATION

Dull and difficult though it be, it is useful to understand the sense in which the term is being used in this paper. Integration is often considered in current literature as akin to coordination and the two words are frequently used interchangeably, although they have distinct origins and differences in meaning.[1] A common dictionary definition defines integrate as "to put or

1. Definitions of services integration used by other students of the subject are worth noting. Some examples:

Gans and Horton (1975): "The linking together by various means of the services of two or more service providers to allow treatment of an individual's or family's needs in a more coordinated and comprehensive manner."

Mittenthal et al. (1974): "Services integration is preeminently a process. Especially it is a goal-directed process whose objective is the establishment of an operating, integrated human services system that addresses a range of an individual's needs and contributes to his status of personal independence and economic self-sufficiency. An integrated system is simply one whose effects and cost performance are likely to be superior if based on a specification that packages the related needs of whole individuals and families."

Harbridge House (1972): "Services integration is defined as improvement in the delivery of human services to facilitate access to and use of all needed services, to improve the effectiveness of those services and to make the most effective use of service resources."

Lucas (1975): "A service integration project is defined as an organizational innovation seeking to coordinate or consolidate human services activities at the client or local level in two or more traditional agencies as a means of enhancing the effectiveness, efficiency or continuity of service delivery."

Gardner (1971): "A service delivery system which can provide all those services needed by a given client or community—constrained only by the state of the art and the availability of resources."

bring together parts or elements so as to form one whole; to combine into a whole.'' An integrated element is one which is united or undivided. By contrast, coordinate means "to place or arrange things in proper position relative to each other; to bring into proper order.'' This paper will consider both subjects. Integration will be used to mean that action which brings previously separated and independent functions and organizations (or personnel, or resources, or clientele) into a new, unitary structure; whereas coordination will be used to describe various efforts to alter or smooth the relationships of continuing, independent elements such as organizations, staffs, and resources.

BACKGROUND FOR RECENT INTEGRATION EFFORTS BY DHEW[2]

Recent federal activities to extend integration efforts have, by and large, been undertaken without much scrutiny of the long antecedent history, perhaps due to the fact that current efforts differ from those of the past in that they deal primarily with large and numerous governmental elements to be related to each other, whereas earlier efforts dealt primarily with voluntary organizations which are now minority partners in a vastly enlarged enterprise. It remains to be seen whether the principles involved differ in any material way.

During the 1960s, several federal programs sought to encourage voluntary coordination at the local community level: Mobilization for Youth, Community Action Agencies of the Office of Economic Opportunity, the Model Cities Program, and pilot Neighborhood Service Centers. Various federal entities were involved to encourage collaboration and to reduce the distance and fragmentation among local service-providing organizations. Each of these programs has been carefully studied, and the results are relevant to the recent efforts undertaken by DHEW.

The impetus for integration carried on with direct HEW support, beginning in the early 1970s, was stimulated by a variety of influences:

1. The income strategy of the Nixon administration, which separated more than before the provision of income from services, sought to shift certain choice responsibilities to state and local governments (the new federal-

2. This section is based upon impressions conveyed by services integration literature and, in particular, discussions by Henton (1975), Lynn and Seidl (1976), Brown (1976), and Gans and Horton (1975).

ism), was supported by various forms of revenue sharing and attempted to combine categorical programs into block grants.

2. When Elliott Richardson was Secretary of HEW, he brought with him an appreciation of the fragmentation of categorical grants as they were applied and utilized through state and local governments. His concern extended to the incapacity of state and local governments to plan and manage this congeries of categorical programs. As Secretary, he sought, therefore, to use the instrumentalities of HEW for strengthening state government capacities to bring order into the existing fragmentation.

3. By the 1970s, the significant expansion of state, local, and federal grant programs and the increase in the number of categorical programs administered by HEW (106 in 1961—280 in 1973) produced uncertainty about how to accommodate that growth.

4. A number of federal officials, as well as professionals and legislators, became concerned about the gap between the promise of what can be achieved and the performance of the programs which all of them had supported.

5. In recent years, the offices of the White House, the Office of Management and Budget, and the Offices of the Secretary of HEW were affected by a succession of reorganizations which brought into prominence a variety of "generalists" in public management, who were more concerned with the pattern of public programs than with the technical details of specific services. One expression of this "generalist" approach began to make its appearance in support for a variety of demonstration programs to test integration of services at the state and local levels and in the preparation of federal legislative plans such as the Allied Services Act. Over the early 1970s, strategy shifted between an attempt to design or redesign service delivery patterns through the instruments of the federal government and an alternative approach, called "capacity-building," whereby the management capacity of general purpose governments was to be strengthened.

The activities and strategies which ensued produced a variety of objectives and approaches, not all of them compatible. Problems were defined at the federal level in ways different than at state and local levels. Federal strategy may have considered various SITO projects (Service Integration Targets of Opportunity) as pre-tests for a national Allied Services Act, but local jurisdictions had other contending priorities which each jurisdiction sought to reconcile.

These differences accounted in part for the lack of clarity as to the definition of the problems to be tackled, the objectives to be achieved, and the selection of services integration or coordination as the preferred means for achieving these ends.

The problems most frequently identified by these federal acts were fragmentation of the service delivery system as a result of the categorical approach to funding and authorization, the failure of the service "system" to develop a capacity to treat the "whole" person or family, and the presumed irrational, inefficient, and costly use of resources as reflected in assumed duplication. The task to be dealt with by integration has variously been presented in terms of effectiveness (or quality), efficiency (or economy), or accountability of service delivery. In addition, concern about the confusions, which a complex and rapidly growing system presents, reinforced the belief that the system was out of control because it was difficult for experts as well as for consumers and ordinary citizens to find out what services were available for particular human needs or to secure access to wanted services in any timely fashion.

THE ELUSIVE NATURE OF THE CONCEPT

If it is reasonably concluded that the interest in integration came variously from a concern that the human services were either inefficient, ineffective, or confusing and wasteful, it is important to ask why integration or coordination were chosen as prime means with which to resolve such difficulties. It will be the main burden of the authors' argument that, while integration may conceivably provide relief from some problems, it is clearly an inappropriate or least desirable means for the solution of other problems, and that failure to make these distinctions accounts for the lack of progress to date.

AMBIGUITY AS TO FUNCTION AND CONCEPTS

The subject is elusive in part because general terms are used by almost all students of the subject without adequately identifying the tangible content of these terms or concepts. If one looks back to the definitions which have been used (see footnote 1), it will be noted that such concepts as services and needs are so broad that frequently they are given contradictory meanings. Much of the time, "integration" or "coordination" is used in the definition of the term itself.

In a practical sense, the common usage makes it difficult to distinguish between: (1) attempts to reorganize service delivery patterns directly as, for example, the attempts to pull together into a unified administration, hospital in-patient, hospital out-patient, ambulatory, and home personal care services for the severely ill; and (2) coordination which seeks to persuade organizationally and administratively independent in-patient, out-patient, ambulatory, and home care service delivery components to cooperate more fully with one another.

The subject is further confused by many difficulties which beset the human services field. Even if we cannot conceptualize what we mean by human services, they can at least be listed; but having listed them, we are still not altogether clear about the functions they are to perform. Any review of Title xx "services" will identify some reasonably discrete functions such as homemakers and foster care, but almost half of the so-called "services" are identified by the populations to be served without specifying what is to be delivered to them (for example, mental health services or child welfare services).

WHAT IS COMPREHENSIVE SERVICE ORGANIZATION?

Another difficulty stems from the lack of clarity about what is meant by a comprehensive or accessible system—do we mean that the almost infinite variety of wants expressed by clients are to be responded to, or only "needs" which are identified by professional providers? When providers identify needs, it often means the provision of a narrow range of services which they are capable of giving or prefer to give without full attention to the other wants or conditions for which those services are also presumed by the public to be intended.

The provider system has also introduced further complexities into the debate by raising the question of improvement in client life conditions as the necessary outcome of any integration. However, measures of improvement of life condition are often unclear, and the relationship between a particular service and a particular change in a client's life condition has hardly been established except in a few rare cases.

PRIMARY versus POLICY LEVELS OF COORDINATION

In addition, both the literature and program efforts have often dealt not only with alterations at the end of the delivery stream to the client, but have also addressed themselves to higher organizational and administrative levels where authority and financial allocation are determined. Integration efforts taking place at these higher levels of system structure are narrowly concerned with redistribution or consolidation of control over the flow of funds to a variety of service-providing components (either governmental or voluntary, funded through contract or subsidy) in an attempt to centralize more substantial authority at the higher level. But change in the pattern of direct service delivery to users is not immediately attempted in the hope that the centralization will bring in its wake changes in the future in the frontline delivery pattern noted above.

RELUCTANCE TO CONFRONT INHERITED PATTERNS

Perhaps the subject has remained in this state of confusion because of a reluctance (or an inability) to confront the hard task of altering a deeply-rooted if loose system of social organizations' special interests and constituencies in order to produce a "more rational" arrangement of human services in relation to needs. The old adage that you cannot make an omelet without breaking eggs may be apt. Because of the difficulty inherent in trying directly to challenge or change a set pattern of organizational and constituency relationships involving innumerable laws, groupings of interest, and formal organizations, the push for integration has sought to modify the front-end delivery of services by providers without significantly modifying the host of conditions which have accompanied the evolution of the existing state of affairs. To mention but a few constraints: categories of mandated programs are retained; fund allocations and services to categories of users have not been significantly altered; attempts to loosen up and make somewhat more flexible the use of categorical funds through such devices as block grants and waivers have been marginal at best. Block grants at best represent perhaps 10 percent of all funds allocated to any one function and are, therefore, subject to the very resistant pressures of the remaining 90 percent of categorical allocations (Stenberg, 1977).[3]

In addition, service organizations and professional providers have over the years developed their own priorities, which represent the things those professions consider themselves capable of doing, and the kinds of activities

3. In 1976, $59 billion of federal grants to state and local governments consisted of categorical grants to 79 percent of the total. Block grants represented 9 percent and revenue sharing or general support represented 12 percent of the total. (Stenberg, 1977).

they prefer to engage in. At the same time, the persisting dissatisfactions appear to require that these professions and service providers somehow behave differently than they have in the past and, therefore, alter or violate the principles of service provision which they have painstakingly built up over previous decades. Many integration efforts seek to resolve this contradiction without confronting the conditions which permit it to persist. No superordinate authority exists to force the confrontation.

SCOPE OF CLIENT DISSATISFACTION: PLURALISM versus HEGEMONY

Is the present complex system really all that unsatisfactory to most of the users? Critics too often assume that dissatisfactions voiced by some reveal widespread dissatisfactions with existing arrangements. But is this necessarily true? Good data are lacking, and the lack of overwhelming evidence to the contrary leads some critics to argue that consumers do not press for significant changes because they do not know what better arrangements might be developed. A contrary interpretation is just as reasonable—that most consumers are fairly well satisfied with the present system and are reluctant to force a major change which may, at best, benefit a relative few—and that that benefit is not certain. Clearly there has been no overwhelming pressure by citizens for National Health Insurance or for welfare reform, although critics abound.

One conclusion is that a multiple provider, pluralist system with many relatively small units may meet the innumerable wants and needs of a large and diverse population much more satisfactorily than a large hegemony of integrated or tightly controlled coordinated subunits. Good data is simply lacking to decide when small units may be more flexible, effective, and responsive, and for what conditions of distress, and when large units can overcome the cumbersomeness of size through mobilization of resources. Efforts have been made to isolate and define conditions suitable for large-scale human service organization and conditions favorable for small-scale organization, but convincing evidence for or against any one paradigm is lacking. There is conflicting evidence as to whether a plural system stimulates more resources and greater readiness to identify minority and specialized needs than does a more monolithic system that places a cap on the total volume of resources finally allocated. These assertions regarding plural and integrated systems of organization can be reversed and evidence can be adduced for either view.

An example may illustrate why the satisfaction/dissatisfaction ratio with present arrangements is hard to establish and even more difficult to use as an argument for more integration than we now have. Consider the field of medical care. While it is a difficult task to relate the services provided by a large medical center, a small community hospital, outpatient clinics, neighborhood health centers, the private physician, and visiting nurses services, patients seldom use all of them simultaneously. As a result, it appears that each of these service provision elements may do a reasonable job for a large part of its clientele. Patients at a neighborhood health center may be unhappy with the private physician but not with their own center; patients at a community hospital may complain about lack of access to a teaching hospital without complaining about their community hospital. Others may be dissatisfied with medical care in general but, lacking knowledge about better alternatives, these patients appear reasonably content with the major medical service available to them. It is probable that only a minority of clients or patients require the use of all of these services simultaneously or sequentially, and there is little evidence that most patients have major difficulty negotiating this complex system. What the majority may complain of is high cost, or impersonal treatment, or waiting time—none of which is necessarily overcome by service integration.

However, the minority who do have difficulty should cause real concern. This minority, usually poor, may not get access to all services as readily as the majority; it may be treated even more impersonally than is the majority. The minority may also have such problems as poor nutrition, concern over drug addiction and unsanitary housing, low income, or unemployment, none of which are within the competence of medical agencies established to treat disease. The contradiction is resolved not by coordination, but by a fresh look at service functions in relation to the needs of specific populations. The difficulty arises not so much because of fragmentation but because the eligibility requirements, wants, or needs of this minority do not fit into the functions the various health service providers deliver satisfactorily to the rest of their clients.

If we turn to fields other than medical, the situation is more confusing because other human service areas are even less well-defined. A fine example is found in a recent report of the General Accounting Office. A Report to Congress (1977) of the wants of the elderly and of the services of voluntary agencies in northern Ohio found that the high priority wants of the aged were for services to which voluntary agencies assigned a low priority. The contradiction did not arise because the agencies failed to coordinate their work, although there was clearly a lack of congruence between provider and user perceptions about what is required by this population.

Since there are such complexities in trying to coordinate the efforts of units within a specific human service subsystem, it would not be surprising if more ambitious efforts to coordinate efforts between overlapping subsystems should encounter even more serious difficulty. In the interests of orderliness and efficiency, each provider agency fixes boundaries around what it will do to separate itself from what it will not or cannot do. Activities which, by self-definition, are external to the main interests of the agency can be readily ignored as "belonging" to some other agency. For example, the aged or the chronically ill of any age are difficult to accommodate fully in a medical system, and they are treated almost as an "externality" to health provision. They represent a problem of flow between this health system and an abutting and only slightly overlapping system of personal care or community care. Some of this population requires income from the income system, or personal care services from the community social welfare system, and the flow between and among these slightly overlapping systems for such clients is admittedly uneven.

What is the basic question posed by the foregoing issues: lack of integration and coordination as an organizational matter; difficulty in relationship among these systems due to differing definitions of eligible populations, often embedded in legislation and in categorical programs; preference, capacities or incapacities of service providers to be of much help anyway; simple lack of information and mechanisms for transfer; or differences of view about priorities in allocating funds among the various systems?

For these and for other reasons, the subject remains confusing and ambiguous.

FINDINGS FROM RECENT EXPERIMENTS AND STUDIES

HEW has supported services integration since 1971 by awarding demonstration grants (SITO) and later Partnership Grants to a large number of projects on the state and local level. The continuing support of these projects has been viewed by HEW as a way to accumulate experience and knowledge in preparation for the passage of an Allied Services Act. However, documents which have accompanied the successive attempts of the Department to introduce the Allied Services Act have not brought forward new information or concrete findings that document the achievements of services integration as a superior strategy. What evidence has research produced about services integration as a strategy?

Descriptions of individual services integration projects have appeared in a variety of publications during the last few years. These descriptions, together with annual reports prepared by the projects themselves, provide some interesting detail about a local experience. They offer neither hard data nor common conceptual framework with which to evaluate the achievements of services integration efforts. Attempts to evaluate many services integration projects, and in particular those supported by HEW, were commissioned by the Department and most often conducted by consulting firms. These evaluation reports, while using different methods and analytical frameworks, share a common frustration in attempting to aggregate the experiences of uncomparable services integration projects.

The most frequent complaint of the evaluators is lack of concrete and useful data. Services integration projects differ by program and demographic characteristics and could not be clustered into meaningful categories on these dimensions. Furthermore, the projects were not set up from the start to provide information amenable to evaluation. The lack of baseline data and "outcome" measures is particularly noted by evaluators as a serious deficiency.

Given these circumstances, the bulk of the evaluation material is devoted to case descriptions of the projects studied, while general conclusions are cautious and qualified.

Most evaluations focus their analysis on a particular aspect of the projects, namely, the linkage mechanisms utilized to promote integration or what we would call coordination—not integration. The classification of linkage mechanisms and the analysis of their relative power in promoting cooperation may shed some light on the *process* of coordination but is insufficient on its own. Too little has been done to relate such instrumental means to firm outcome measures to permit any systematic conclusions about coordinating efforts. One of the reasons for this lack is the absence of consensus about service integration objectives.

As a result, conclusions about the overall effort are more often phrased in terms of what the experience has not demonstrated; and the few general conclusions offered relate primarily to specific conditions, circumstances, and mechanisms which the evaluators believe (but cannot prove) inhibit or promote coordination without reference to outcome measures.

The following section summarizes what has been learned from studies of local organization as a first step in understanding whether or not the ambiguities and difficulties can be diminished.

1. *Gans and Horton* (*1975*) reviewed thirty projects supported by HEW. Their study found that, generally, integration is not extensive even in the demonstration projects that were identified as successful by HEW. No one best model was identified, and there was little difference among projects in the impact as measured by the three criterion measures (accessibility, continuity, and efficiency). Although there were some gains on each of these measures, it is unclear whether the gains are attributable to the integration experiments or not. The authors conclude that it is probably impossible to convert the current, diffused, and variegated picture of human services into a unitary system because of the great variety in approaches, the variety of funding sources, the lobbies of various constituencies, the absence of strong consumer pressure for a unitary system, and so on.

2. *The Human Ecology Institute* (*Mittenthal et al., 1974*) studied twenty-two Services Integration Target of Opportunity projects. No evidence was found that any of the experiments could yet be defined as a "system," being instead a composite of administrative reorganizations and operations research. None of the projects was able to define the effects they wished to achieve as regards clients served.

3. *ABT Associates* (*1971*) evaluated twelve integration projects. Since this evaluation was conducted at the beginning of the twelve projects, it was not possible to assess any results; rather the processes set in motion were simply described.

4. *Harbridge House* (*1972*) sampled the opinion of officials in state and local organizations and found that service integration was not considered a high priority and that improvement in delivery system could be achieved through other strategies.

5. *Rand* (*Lucas, 1975*) is less a study than a proposal to aggregate findings from a variety of other studies. Instead of answering questions about in-

tegration, it proposes a census of programs, concluding that "there is little hope that reliable organizational data can be gathered from written materials available."

6. *Henton* (*1975*) reviewed thirty-four demonstrations and produced a typology of integration models. The only types found clearly feasible were state-sponsored projects operating in a stable, rural environment and locally sponsored projects in medium-sized cities relying primarily on information linkages (not integration, but coordination through informational systems).

Another set of studies or analyses is concerned not with the local delivery of services, but with the creation of state-level human service agencies in an attempt to achieve state-level integration.

1. *Kathleen Heintz* (*1976*) reviewed twenty-six Comprehensive Human Resource Agencies (CHRA) and concluded: "it is now generally agreed that no immediate savings can be realized through the creation of a CHRA." Such a state-level umbrella agency *may* create a more responsive and effective service delivery system, but details are not provided.

2. *Gans and Horton* (*1975*) conclude, on the basis of a study of six state agencies, that there is insufficient or untraceable involvement of state-level reorganization with local-level delivery, and no capacity at the local level to reorganize services comprehensively along the lines postulated in the Allied Services Act.

3. Numerous case reports are available from state agencies which have reorganized state programs in various forms. These reports are not evaluations and some may be reviewed with an open mind, since they represent the claims made by the persons currently responsible for administering the state programs.

RE-ANALYSIS OF PROBLEMS AND AIMS OF INTEGRATION

In an attempt to move beyond the state of affairs as understood by the authors in the foregoing sections, we propose to approach the subject with more modest aims and with the use of less extensive analytic frameworks.

We will consider integration and coordination as defined at the beginning of the paper, but limited to expression at the local delivery of services. Attention may be given to either integration or coordination at higher structural levels, but only where the discussion can be directly traced to some alteration in the final delivery pattern itself. Reorganization of higher levels of bureaucracy, in an attempt to acquire control over a system as a first step in bringing about changes, will be deferred.

ASSUMPTIONS

This analysis assumes that strong, authoritative, and controlling action is unlikely to be taken by any national or state administration in the recognizable future to *force* any wide variety of institutions or organizations into a unitary mold, which is the definition of integration, and in which personnel, funds, and other resources of several independent categories are put under a single administration with an altered set of eligibility criteria and an altered mandate. We further assume that the very intricate network of service providers, numbering in the many thousands, perform acceptable functions for a large part of their clientele and their staffs despite dissatisfactions or imperfections. Because of this, the existing complex of organizations is considered to represent a loose, relatively intractable system of service providers whose established patterns of professional behavior, of eligibility, and of fund allocation, cannot be significantly modified without powerful overriding authority imposed from without. It is further assumed that these organizations carry out their daily activities in the context of an interlocking nest of exchange relationships (Levine and White, 1961). In such an exchange relationship, agencies at the margins complement one another's activities by a process of referral and cross-referral in which they, in effect, exchange clients, personnel, and services in such a manner that each of the service delivery partners derives some reciprocal benefit.

AIMS OF INTEGRATION

Beyond these assumptions, however, it is also recognized that a number of very troublesome problems still exist which have immediate policy relevance. Each of these problem areas will be examined briefly in order to test the extent to which integration or coordination is necessarily the only or, primarily, the preferred remedy.

1. Accessibility: Limited access to service is a common criticism. Accessibility has two dimensions. It may involve impeded access for some clients in some jurisdictions to some services which do *exist* elsewhere. These limitations may be due to an inadequate volume of available services, to low density populations insufficient to support a service network, racial or ethnic discrimination, and professional preference. The other dimension involves access to services which do not exist at all but which are either desired by clients or recommended by professional providers who do not wish to provide certain services themselves. An example is the provision of personal care and home care services for the physically disabled independently of medical prescription and treatment and providing such services for extended periods of time.

For the first of these, accessibility to services which do exist somewhere, it can be seriously questioned whether integration or coordination are the only or the most effective strategies. Eligibility limitations built into legislation or built into agency practices can be modified by de-categorization in a fashion which will increase access without altering the formal pattern of organizational structure. Similarly, access which is limited because there is an insufficient volume of certain services (renal dialysis, day care, group homes for disturbed adolescents, and so on) can be remedied by increasing the flow of funds to permit existing agencies which do provide these services to simply increase their volume. Administrative arrangements by service providers as they are now organized can alter the location of services, the hours and eligibility in a fashion to reduce access limitation due to discrimination or provider preference. Ethnic discrimination is better confronted by legal action.

The second aspect of access, access to services which are not anywhere provided by the existing network, is unlikely to be remedied by any attempt at integration or coordination. Instead, what is required is action that will fill the gap either by persuading providers to add these functions to their existing battery of services, or by creating new arrangements to provide the missing services. These actions can be achieved by increased allocations or by administrative shifts in priority use of existing resources or by policy action to create a new agency. Such steps are probably more powerful than coordination to overcome access limitations.

2. *Continuity of Service—The Reject Syndrome:* Given the initial set of assumptions, it remains true that numbers of clients or patients have difficulty in maintaining continuity in services they want or require. Fundamentally, the problem of continuity is a matter of linking specialties coherently so that there are no disruptions. A common example lies in the provision of after-care services for patients discharged from acute hospitals with continuing chronic illness or disabilities which cannot be cured or removed. Similar

problems in continuity are encountered when mentally ill patients are discharged from hospitals to communities, when the retarded are discharged from state schools, and when prisoners are discharged from penal institutions.

In all these cases, discontinuity involves the disruption between institutionalized and community care activities. This discontinuity is sometimes due to professional and agency selectivity in the kinds of patients or clients it chooses to care for. Some hospitals and agencies will take only certain kinds of physical, psychological, or social cases and will keep them for only limited periods when the therapeutic potentials of the staff are presumed to be effective. When maximum effectiveness in in-house treatment is reached, patients or clients are discharged and the discharging institution has little formal responsibility for after-care unless it can succeed in bringing discharged patients back for periodic ambulatory attention.

But the problem is not solely one of organizational selectivity. Many major institutional programs have become, over time, the responsibility of one level of government—often of the state or county—whereas other forms of ambulatory or community care services are frequently the fiscal and sanctioned responsibility of local governments. For example, mental hospital patients have had not only their mental treatment, but their total financial and personal care needs assumed by the state as long as they are retained in state-financed institutions. When such patients are discharged to their own homes or to community residences, it means that the costs of room and board, as well as therapeutic services, must be paid for and absorbed by their local communities. This set of problems is compounded by the powerful emotions generated in neighborhoods about criminals, the mentally ill, the retarded, and the chronically ill. As a result, local jurisdictions are often reluctant to underwrite community services essential for continuity of care between institution and home. They are also reluctant to sanction half-way houses, nursing homes, and the like.

Integration or coordination to overcome this problem is not a simple matter of meshing together the functions of the home care and the institutional programs; what is involved is a major task of reallocating resources as between institutions and community care, reassigning personnel—to say nothing of reversing long-standing community prejudices which, in the first instance, produced the development of institutional programs. Arrangements for referral or for case managers are likely to have limited impact in securing coordination and integration. Substantial modification of institutional programs is necessary if their resources are to be divided differently between the management of institutional programs and the delivery of after-care services by the discharging institution itself. This would seem to involve either a substantial increase in fund allocation in order to create a missing after-care service or provision of incentives to the existing agencies to modify their service priorities so that they will actually provide the after-care for discharged patients themselves. The absence of such arrangements is encountered everywhere as existing local service providers resist the introduction of new groups which would compete for services with their current clientele. The arguments with which to persuade existing providers to abandon some clients in favor of others have not been overpowering so far.

Aside from this institutional/community problem of continuity, the problem of linking a variety of community specialist functions remains. To a large extent, specialist services are linked to one another by a variety of referral mechanisms. This existing system breaks down, however, when one specialist service is reluctant to assume responsibility for certain clients, and instead identifies a service which "should be" provided by another agency. Numerous examples can be brought to mind: the slow-learning child in the classroom; the aged and feeble person who finds it difficult to come to the outpatient clinic and, when there, does not arouse the interest of specialists who are unable to help with chronic conditions; the aggressive, acting-out adolescent who cannot be reached in the customary mental health center; the run-away foster child; the AFDC mother with limited education, no skills, a desire to work, and small children.

The problem of continuity here is primarily how best to handle rejects of existing service providers. Rejects often represent problems and persons not attractive to the existing service system, not likely to respond readily to existing measures, and demanding an inordinate investment in time and resources which agencies are reluctant to give, because of other demands which they believe they can meet more fruitfully. For this dilemma in continuity, coordination seems an unlikely solution. Rather, powerful incentives sufficient to encourage agencies to assume responsibility for this rejected class seem to be necessary, or a new set of services created that would be devoted primarily to these rejected groups on a no-reject basis.

3. Fragmentation: The fragmentation of services may be a special case of continuity. There is widespread belief that a variety of specialized services are now so selective that attention to the whole person or the whole problem is virtually impossible to achieve. The case is further argued that, because of these many specialties, there are so many doors through which clients could enter a service system that confusion can not only be frustrating, but also that the feeble and the poorly motivated may find it impossible to negotiate the complex maze. Closer examination of this complaint about fragmentation forces us to ask: to whom is it a problem? Undoubtedly, clients may be confused about the best place to start, although limited studies of clients suggest that most clients are able to make use of existing information systems to find their way to some service provider (these information systems may be neighbors, family members, agencies which they try, city hall, information services, newspapers, magazines, television, hotlines, and the like).

If this is accurate, then it seems likely that there is a *minority* of clients who may be lost because they are not sufficiently assertive, are reticent, or are realistically confused. It must be asked whether an improved system of information, supplemented by some guidance program whereby the reticent and reluctant person can be helped by another person (such as the outreach worker) to go to a service provider, would not be fully as effective as any attempt to introduce a more systematic order into the variety of specialized programs now in place. Clearly, coordination is not the only feasible solution.

A special case of fragmentation may be presented by the multi-problem family. It has long been argued that some families have multiple needs, and that it is very difficult to find arrangements whereby any one agency assumes responsibility for the complex. It is important to stress, however, that the proportion of multi-problem families has been found to be very small in almost all studies. The original St. Paul studies (1960; 1961) which first identified the problem, found that only about 5–6 percent of the client population could be so identified. A more recent study by Perlman (1975) found that at least three-quarters of the population applying to a multi-purpose center brought a single problem for attention, and that for most of this population there was no increase in the number of problems that emerged as it continued to be in touch with the multi-purpose center. The evidence is reasonably clear that the multi-problem situation, troubling as it is, represents a relatively small proportion of the total potential client population. For this problem, some limited form of coordination would seem to be the remedy, a form that does not destroy nor disrupt the rest of the provider complex that seems to be appropriately designed for clientele seeking help with a single problem.

It is not certain, therefore, from available evidence whether the attempt to clear up the fragmentation is a response on the part of generalist managers in the human service system who seek to "tidy up" the arrangements for service delivery because it makes the entire system more amenable to centralized planning and control, or whether the tidying-up does in fact produce any results for the multi-problem family. Coordination might seem to be appropriate in a limited fashion for a select population by such devices as multi-provider teams organized for specific groups of cases. However, the costs of such limited coordination (and they are likely to be very large costs, indeed, on a per case basis) need to be weighed against the possible costs of disrupting a reasonably functioning service system for the majority of clients in order to better meet the needs of a minority defined as a multi-problem case.

4. Efficiency and Cost: A recurrent and powerful argument for integration is found in the concern over welfare costs. The enormous escalation in the cost of providing human services has led to a belief on the part of many citizens, legislators, and higher-level administrative officials that somehow the increase in costs must be attributable to waste in the system and not to the increases in demand or the increase in the range of services provided. The assumption further is made that these increases in cost are unnecessary, that there is substantial slack in the present system which could absorb either more or different kinds of clients; or, alternatively, that integration can assure efficiency through reduction in administrative costs in multiple small agencies and in a more efficient use of existing personnel.

The studies to date, including those cited above, have not yet been able to identify savings in any of the integration or coordination experiments undertaken. The few reports which claim several million dollars in savings as a result of state-level reorganization are dubious examples. The cuts in administrative personnel of Human Resource Agencies in Florida and Georgia seem to have resulted from arbitrary political decisions rather than increased efficiency in the use of existing staff. In the case of North Carolina, no evidence has been adduced to counter the charge that the savings are a result of reduction in volume and range in services rather than by innovative management techniques. Furthermore, these claims do not trace out the extent to which certain costs may have been transferred to other budget lines and are, therefore, obscured in the final presentation.

If cost savings are the primary reason for integration, it is clear that costs can also be cut by reducing the volume of services, by reducing the quality of services, or by other means. On the other hand, all known forms of integration or coordination in themselves involve additional costs. It is commonly reported that attempts to create a higher-level reorganization in comprehensive human service agencies have resulted in a significant increase in the total number of central office personnel as compared with those on the front line. Whether integration or coordination will actually reduce costs remains a hypothesis which is yet to be tested empirically. There is some justification for doubt; for example, recent evolution in programs for the aging has assumed a hierarchical attempt to coordinate services from Washington down through the lowest district level in states by a process of decentralization. However, this process has involved the maintenance of a Washington staff, the maintenance of a regional office staff for Aging, the creation of new personnel at the state levels of Aging Administration, the creation of a new layer of Area Agencies for the Aging to facilitate service coordination and delivery and, finally, the untraced cost of administration in voluntary and proprietary service providers securing contracts through the Aging apparatus. A minimum of five layers of administration can thus be traced in a system committed to the process of coordination, not integration.

No systematic analysis has been conducted of the price paid for large-scale coordinating efforts between levels of government due to the layering of non-service administrative costs. Beatrice (1974) found that regional overhead or support or administrative costs for the mentally retarded, in our present loose system, come to 13.5 percent of all regional expenditures; and the administrative costs of state schools for the retarded come to 32 percent. Similar figures were reported for programs for the aging in Virginia (Morris, 1974). It is doubtful that the proportions will be reduced by increasing administrative mechanisms necessary for either coordination or integration although, admittedly, no real study of the subject has been completed.

If costs are not reduced, it is argued that at least the rate of increase can be controlled by integration. It is suggested that, somehow, integration would make it possible for agencies to meet growing demands with a level-state of funding—in other words, be a means with which to control inflating service costs. Instead of integration, policy choices about who is to be served, for what needs, and with what services would be a more appropriate solution. Such choices are not necessarily made by the integration device.

5. *Better Care with the Same Funds:* It is finally argued, wholly apart from matters of access, continuity, disorganization, and cost that coordination and integration will produce better results in the treatment of a variety of social problems. The only thing that can be said at this point is that such an aim and assertion remains an article of faith unproven by any studies to date. It is not so much a matter that coordination has not been tested but that, for the kinds of complicated human problems with which this field deals (deviance, dependency, illness), there is woefully little evidence that the treatment and therapeutic resources which we have available alter the incidence of these conditions in any substantial sense.

However, the modest gains from treatment represent a humane commitment to continue the search for improved ways of dealing with troublesome human needs. Better care is sought more productively through improvement in professional skill, better knowledge about social problems and better administration at the delivery end of the service system. In this situation, it compounds the difficulty to argue that some integration or coordination of ill-tested therapeutic services or human services will further enhance the conditions of the clientele being served. This is not to argue that the claim should not be given attention, but merely to state there is no evidence on which to make strong assertions and no evidence upon which to build a clear model for either integrating or coordinating services in a given situation.

POSSIBLE COURSES OF
ACTION IN THE NEAR-TERM FUTURE

The foregoing analysis leads to some modest alternative approaches to the future for integration or coordination in the human services. It suggests that our national size and diversity, the intricate accumulation of organizations, services, and professions, the relative satisfaction found for a majority of system users (if matters of cost are omitted) argue against any attempt to remake the entire human service system into any kind of more simplified and rationalized structure at this time. Instead, the problems can be more sharply delimited and coordination furthered for some of those problems for which it is relevant.

If integration is not appropriate for correcting inequity and if one big system is not always better than many small units, what is the proper role for an integration strategy? We suggest that integration (or coordination) may be a proper remedy for reject policies of agencies where the proportion of rejects is small against the total numbers served by any provider system; it serves well the needs of cases with multiple complex problems which require simultaneous attention; and it can ease the path for those who need extra help in connecting with a too complex network of services.

Two models are proposed.

A LIMITED COORDINATION MODEL— ATTACKING THE CLIENT REJECT SYNDROME

The major deficiencies, other than rising costs, in the existing system appear to be either an absence of certain services or an organizational tendency to reject difficult and unattractive clientele.

In an attempt to tackle such deficiencies, several options usually proposed are rejected. These options could be characterized as: (a) comprehensive linkage; (b) voluntary coordination; (c) comprehensive planning. Our preceding analysis leads us to consider these strategies as the least promising. Instead, we propose a model of *limited coordination control* having the following characteristics.

1. Reserve and limited control of a proportion of flow-through funds: A mechanism is required outside of the direct (worker-client) service frontier, capable of *marginally* altering the flow of resources into the provider units. This control is essential to introduce incentives that will encourage organizations to reduce the number of case and problem rejections, or to reserve funds for the financing of services not now provided by any units in the provider system. This marginal control over some funds can be used either to alter incentives to agencies or to create new agencies with available funds reserved for the purpose. The volume of reserved funds needs to be settled either by legislative mandate or by executive negotiation.

Centers to allocate or reallocate resources do exist in many forms, but their effectiveness (offices of management and budget, state planning offices, planning bureaus in comprehensive human resource agencies) have been diminished by the obligation to plan or manage or change the total functioning of the entire delivery system. It is here suggested that this centralized "resource-control" be limited; that it accept the major operations of service provider units and avoid interrupting the major flow of resources which underpins these operations. Some proportion of the flow of funds needs to be reserved, however, to achieve the purposes mentioned above.

2. *Monitoring gaps and rejections:* To use reserved funds effectively, the centralized unit requires a minimum capacity to monitor and evaluate the reject tendencies or the service gaps. This can be achieved by some combination of assessing professional views, evaluating referral and eligibility patterns, and probing consumer wants. This monitoring-assessing capacity would be limited to identifying services that are wholly lacking or services that do not reach clients because of the reject tendencies. The reserved funds would be utilized with some flexibility either to modify agency practices through incentives or to create new services.

This central capacity to assess will not be easy to develop, but it can be developed more readily than any attempt to impose a comprehensive control mechanism over all the operations of all the providers. A capability limited to identifying gaps in service and reject tendencies in the existing system does not threaten the heartland of service providers' interests, but rather touches upon the marginal difficulties that emerge between elements of the provider system. Thus focused, the generalist or overview capacities are concentrated in the control unit. Here the generalist is free to foster less subjective approaches to service gaps and reject policies, rather than being burdened with the charge to impose or introduce a generalist service doctrine upon the entire service system that violates the specialist competences that have been developed through experience and evidence over the years.

3. *Control location:* This mechanism for limited, specially focused coordination at the resource allocation level can be organized either across the board for all human services, as in an office of management and budget or a planning office of comprehensive human resources agency at the state level; or it can be organized along separate functional lines that conform more or less satisfactorily to the loose service provider subsystems that have grown up: the mental health, physical health, housing, correctional, and income maintenance subsystems.

In practice, regrettably in our view, many of the experimenting programs have opted for the approaches that we have rejected. The development of comprehensive linkages through the customary mechanisms of case management, of central location, and of single-point entry, have not been adequate or sufficient for the identified problems. The voluntary coordination approach relies upon the unguided cooperation of the service providers through case conferences, teams, co-location of offices and case managers. All are without authority to persuade service providers to alter their practices and to reallocate their own resources on the basis of mutual consent. While this is not an unreasonable approach, it has not been notably successful in dealing with the problems we have here isolated for attention.

The proposed limited coordination model does, of course, set up a tension between the service providers and some unit controlling the flow of resources to them. However, the stalemating tendencies of past efforts in this direction will be avoided, we believe, if the control is limited explicitly to a relatively small proportion of the fund flow and is focused on specific problem areas which can be recognized by service providers and clients alike.

This model has, we believe, the additional advantage of preserving another tension at the interface between the consumer and the provider. Numerous service providers are likely to deal with relatively distinct client groups, each of which may be able to bring its distinctive pressures for attention to an agency roughly devoted to meeting their needs. Integration is likely to move the tension away from the client interface and to submerge many distinctive client groups and their needs into some more generalized category in which the differences have difficulty finding expression. Ethnic and racial groups, various categories of disadvantaged persons (the disabled, for example) should be able to concentrate their energies on securing proper attention from agencies concerned explicitly with their needs; putting all of them into a more general client category forces them to compete with each other for the attention of the same administration which administers the integrated program.

There remain, of course, those other problems for which coordination and integration are often (erroneously) considered a solution. We believe that alternative remedies for such problems do exist. The obstructing effects of categorical eligibility limitations can best be handled by abolition of categories at the federal level. Difficulties inherent in insufficient financing to produce the requisite volume of services clearly require more finance, and this surely requires policy decision at the appropriation level of government, not coordination. Problems which involve linkage of various specialty services for clients whom the service providers are able to and wish to serve is best secured through more forceful use of existing exchange mechanisms between independent providers. Concern over the mounting cost of human services requires public executive and legislative understanding and judgment about why the total sums are needed and what the appropriation action should be. Coordination and integration mechanisms do not touch the central problem of cost control *except* as an administrative constraint imposed by the sums made available to service providers.

Finally, the argument that human services can be more effective as well as more efficient through a substantial recasting of relationships among service providers remains a belief and, possibly, a hypothesis for which no evidence is as yet forthcoming—as discussed above. It is, therefore, argued that no basic policy premised on such a hypothesis is worth attempting on any national scale at the present time. None of the experiments funded in recent years have introduced any criterion measures whereby the outcomes of the supposed integrated programs have affected the lives of their clientele. Lacking such measures, and lacking such evidence, it is argued that more modest aims be reserved for coordination efforts.

Any attempt to recast delivery systems more thoroughly than is here proposed can, of course, be useful but, in the present state of knowledge, is best limited to experiments in which the changes in the delivery system are clearly identified as measurable independent variables, and in which the outcomes in the lives of clients are also measurably identified as dependent variables.

A PUBLIC INTEGRATION MODEL

A truly integrated human service system represents an alternative to the modest approach proposed. We have argued that integration which requires a major reconstruction of the entire human service system is not feasible and lacks supporting evidence. However, two more manageable forms of integration (as distinguished from coordination) may be more feasible and may also have some empirical experience upon which to draw.

It may be feasible to bring into one administration a number of *publicly* funded social services now administered by several public administrations. Such services are now scattered through public health, mental health, public assistance, and youth service agencies as support services to those agencies. If a purpose can be defined, this personnel—or some part of it—could be detached from the existing host agencies and assigned to a new unitary public social services agency.

The success of such a move would depend first upon identifying a reasonable task within the scope of resources assembled in the new agency.

One such function might be to provide alternative care arrangements for clients discharged from institutions (medical, mental health, correctional). Other possible functions are: to provide personal counseling for those rejected or not covered by existing aencies; to provide community care services to reduce the volume of unnecessary institutional admissions; to strengthen family life; or to mainstream the severely disabled.

Such a limited integration would not of course fully consolidate all programs that seek to combat poverty, or to reduce delinquency, or to foster mental health. Such an ambitious integration would require that large professional empires be merged, and we have already argued that this is neither feasible nor likely to improve the present state of affairs. But a more limited merger of resources to accomplish limited ends has some justification.

An alternative to this integration is to attempt a new form of *vertical integration* in selected areas. An example would be the merging of responsiblity for intitutional and community care under one administration and one budget. This could be attempted in mental health, corrections, juvenile delinquency, developmental disability, chronic illness, or aging. Instead of having institutional and community services managed by separate agencies with separate authorization and funding, often at different levels of government, the full stream of responsibility for clients sharing a common condition would be consolidated and the traditional buck-passing and discontinuity of the present might conceivably be reduced. Whether or not the elements of personnel, mandates, and resources can be blended, and whether the tasks to be performed can be adequately delimited so that the combined resources are suitably related to the new mandate, represents a question difficult to answer. The complexities of the American scene, already noted, make such an approach unlikely in the near future. Still, integration could be experimented with.

Such integration in regard to the *social services* (excluding education, income, medical care, and housing) has been attempted in the United Kingdom with modest success and some difficulty. It demonstrates clearly that allocating resources among various wants (institutional care, sheltered workshops, counseling, employment, home care) could be shifted to a single administration which internally allocates its resources among a variety of demands. What is characteristic of the English system, however, is that these decisions are primarily off-loaded on to the local level of government and at the level of service delivery itself rather than being retained as decisions at a higher authority.

Some modest attempts have also been identified in the United States which approximate this approach. One of the more interesting examples is found in Wilkes-Barre, Pennsylvania, where a variety of staff members, funded by categorical programs, have been brought together into a single United Services Agency with unitary administration. The unified agency is responsible for a broad range of services previously offered by all of the categories which fund the consolidated staff. It has an open charge to meet human needs whenever they are uncovered and where populations are "eligible" for public services. However, the personnel continue to be paid out of categorical funds, a process legalized by complex accounting within the unified agency.

There have been similar demonstrations of vertical integration, at least in the mental health field, where area mental health agencies consolidate responsiblity for both in-patient and outpatient care and treatment for the mentally ill. Some hospitals and some homes for the aged have also begun to organize home care delivery of services to persons not living in these institutions, although the span of population covered by the home care service is limited.

SUMMARY

To sum up this discursive review, we conclude:

1. The most promising future lies in the direction of a *delimited coordination,* which relies upon the following components: (a) reinforcing the existing loose network of service providers through improved information and referral mechanisms; (b) a limited external control over the flow of resources to this network, by empowering a central unit to reserve a marginal proportion of the total flow of funds; (c) the reserved funds kept within the authority of the central control to be used to fill gaps and to induce agencies to reduce their rates of client rejection; (d) the development of a capability at the central control level to identify and monitor cient reject patterns and service gaps.

2. The alternative model of limited *integration* would seem to be feasible for a limited number of publicly administered social services now scat-

tered in several large bureaucracies with extensive missions. Some of these social services could be merged under a unitary administration to carry out limited functions clearly in the domain of public service and complementary to the large bureaucracies from which they are drawn.

3. Numerous other difficulties with the delivery system which have been referred to integration for solution—access, continuity, cost control— would seem to be better resolved by other means, such as alteration of categorical eligibility regulations imposed from above, changes in appropriations or allocation, or changes in public policy.

4. The conventional mechanisms of case management and of information and referral systems and office co-location, the major coordinating devices developed to date, seem to be of limited usefulness as regards the problems of service gaps and case rejection, but may be of value in facilitating the normal exchange process which goes on among independent units in complex but loose subsystems of service providers. These devices are most needed for a minority of service users who have multiple problems needing simultaneous attention or who are confused by the current pluralist service system.

5. Perhaps the major difficulty with a modest approach is that it does not deal with the difficulties found in the flow between service subsystems. Deficiencies in income maintenance create ripple effects through health, mental health, and delinquency programs and, conversely, deficiencies in these service subsystems create serious difficulties for the income maintenance system. However, our technology and conceptual strength have not yet developed means whereby these cross-system difficulties can be controlled. Conceptually and theoretically, it would be possible to develop a wholly controlled system of planning, beginning in HEW and the level of the Cabinet in Washington, and working its way down to the states, whereby these cross-system difficulties could be addressed. However, such a capacity would require the kind of control over our service system and our decision-making processes in the legislatures thus far alien to the American tradition.

Negotiation to be carried on voluntarily at all levels of government between various service systems is costly and is carried on in an atmosphere in which subsystems and providers are focused primarily on the maintenance of their own interests and priorities and are subject only marginally to modification in their service programs. It is because of the potential for affecting the margins of interest among service providers that we have recommended the modest approach towards coordination outlined above.

REFERENCES

ABT Associates. 1971. *A Report of Findings and of Specific Integrating Techniques in Twelve Services Integration Projects.* Cambridge, Mass.: ABT Associates for DHEW.

Beatrice, Ellen. 1974. *State Services for Mentally Retarded Citizens.* Boston: United Community Planning Corporation.

Brown, Bertram. 1976. "Conversation Contact-Polcy," *Evaluation,* 3:15–20.

Gans, Sheldon, and Gerald Horton. 1975. *Integration of Human Services: The State and Municipal Levels.* New York: Praeger.

Gardner, Sidney. 1971. "Services Integration in HEW: An Initial Report." DHEW Internal Departmental Memorandum.

Harbridge House. 1972. *Survey of Services Integration.* Boston: Harbridge House.

Heintz, Kathleen. 1976. "State Organizations for Human Services," *Evaluation,* 3:106–10.

Henton, Douglas. 1975. *The Feasibility of Services Integration.* Berkeley: University of California Press.

Levine, Sol, and Paul White. 1961. "Exchange as a Conceptual Framework for the Study of Interorganizational Relationships," *Administrative Science Quarterly,* 5:583–601.

Lucas, William. 1975. *Aggregating Organizational Experience with Service Integration: Working Note 9059.* Santa Monica, Calif.: Rand Corporation.

Lynn, L., and J. Seidl. 1976. "The Mega-Proposal," *Evaluation,* 3:111–14.

Mittenthal, S. J., et al. 1974. *Twenty-Two Allied Services (SITO) Projects Described as Human Services Systems.* Wellesley, Mass.: The Human Ecology Institute.

Morris, Robert. 1974. *Toward a Caring Society.* New York: Columbia University School of Social Work.

Perlman, Robert. 1975. *Consumers and Social Services.* New York: Wiley.

Report to the Congress, Comptroller General of the U.S. 1977. "The Well-Being of Older People in Cleveland, Ohio."

Stenberg, Carl W. 1977. "Block Grants: Middlemen of the Federal Aid System," p. 8–13, in *Advisory Commission on Intergovernmental Relations,* ed. Intergovernmental Perspectives, Volume 3.

St. Paul Minnesota Community Chest and Council. 1960. "The Multi-Problem Family," pp. 166–79, in *Social Welfare Forum 1960.* New York: Columbia University Press.

—— 1961. "The Family-Centered Project," Mimeo, St. Paul: Community Chest and Council.

THREE

Centralization Versus Decentralization in the Design of Human Service Delivery Systems: A Response to Gouldner's Lament*

HOWARD ALDRICH

Goulder's Lament
A commitment to a theory often occurs by a process other than one which its proponents believe and it is usually more consequential than they realize. A commitment to a theory may be made because the theory is congruent with the mood or deep-lying sentiments of its adherents, rather than merely because it has been cerebrally inspected and found valid.

So too is it with the theory of organization. Paradoxically enough, some of the very theories which promise to make man's own work more intelligible to himself and more amenable to his intelligence are infused with an intangible metaphysical pathos which insinuates, in the very midst of new discoveries, that all is lost. For the metaphysical pathos of much of the modern theory of group organization is that of pessimism and fatalism. (Gouldner, 1955: 498)

A DIALECTICAL tension exists in social service delivery systems between advocates of a strongly centralized structure and advocates of a strongly de-

* As usual, Pat Reeves provided phenomenal last-minute assistance in the preparation of this paper, making possible its completion. In drawing up these arguments, I have been heavily influenced by Banfield and Grodzins' (1958) discussion of arguments concerning metropolitan reorganization. This paper builds upon ideas originally developed in a paper given at the International Institute of Management, Berlin, June 1975, and published as Aldrich (1977). I am indebted to Charles Perrow and Jane Weiss for their critical comments on an earlier version of this paper.

centralized structure. Neither party has managed a clear-cut victory, and the strength of each has led to systems containing an unstable mixture of centralization *and* decentralization. Government agencies and other funding sources typically display an overarching policy concern for "interorganizational coordination" and elimination of "duplication of effort," and they are often joined by professionals and administrators in dominant agencies. Clients and local interest groups typically argue against the degree of centralization sought by the former, but there are many exceptions. I have investigated one system that has swung back and forth between the two positions and embodies characteristics of both—the manpower services system.

In 1973, the federal Comprehensive Employment and Training Act (CETA) upgraded the role of local communities in allocating funds for manpower training and substantially reduced the role of *direct* federal control. Categorical programs were eliminated in favor of local determination of services required, with local elected officials given control over the service delivery systems in their jurisdictions. The delegation of authority from the national to the local level was part of the general package of revenue sharing items enacted by the Nixon administration and proved very popular with local officials. Whether the changes created a more effective and efficient manpower training system is difficult to determine, as evaluations are still in progress. Nevertheless, it seems clear that program designers have concentrated on the technology of delivering and administering services, while ignoring the impact of organizational-level factors on the distribution of benefits.

I will review the centralization versus decentralization issue from the perspective of organizational as well as client needs. All human service delivery systems are products of compromises between centralizing and decentralizing forces, and I emphasize the contradictions structured into systems because of the irresolvable nature of the arguments. Examples are taken from a comparative field study of manpower organizations in New York State communities, as well as from the literature on social service organizations.

LEVELS OF ANALYSIS AND EVALUATIONS

Social service organizations face a situation of uncertain technologies, few resources, demand overload, and constant pressures from other organizations and groups to modify their activities in one way or another. Debates over the appropriate design for human service delivery systems are quite confusing because multiple constituencies, technologies, and operating paradigms are involved. Such issues come to the surface whenever authorities attempt to reorganize social service systems or to coordinate the actions of organizations to improve general public welfare. Authorities cannot escape the questions of relative power and resource allocation among organizations in these situations, although the fundamental issues are sometimes obscured because of the rhetoric used.

A central question in system design is the degree to which a population of organizations should be tightly or loosely coupled internally, with the major determinant of coupling being the degree of hierarchical control exercised by a central authority. "Coupling" refers to the strength of vertical or horizontal ties between organizations, to the generality or specificity of policy guidelines, to voluntary or mandated relations, and to the number of direct and indirect ties between organizations. Interorganizational systems are dynamic in part because of the mix of centralization and decentralization on the different dimensions of coupling.

Observers often mistake the new programs, new relationships, and new technologies in a system as indicating chaos or disorder. "Yet, when viewed from the inclusive level, the major domains, the division of labor, the legitimated technologies, the basic orientations to the social problems of the inner cities—all have shown, in their total configuration, an identifiable and specifiable stability" (Warren et al., 1974: 154). Choosing appropriate levels and units of analysis is thus a critical step in examining the coordination issue.

Three units of analysis in social services systems differ markedly in their roles and in their vulnerability to outside interventions: clients, organizations, and the interorganizational field. Clients are the raw material for people-processing and people-changing organizations, and they confront service bureaucracies as isolated individuals against powerful and professionalized staff. Organizations develop and apply service programs, and require an administrative structure organized according to a logic all its own. Access to external resources is an especially critical problem for social service organizations, as their market on the output side is not clearly defined and their product is difficult for consumers or supraorganizational authorities to evaluate. Most organizations are thus oriented toward the acquisition of resources through various forms of subsidization—the so-called "grants economy"—and varieties of interorganizational coordination. The resource dependence perspective has emerged as a conceptual scheme that incorporates these assumptions into a theory of administrators' behavior (Aldrich and Pfeffer, 1976).

The interorganizational field consists of the population of social service organizations, their organization sets, and the linkages among organizations and agencies. A comprehensive view of interorganizational fields includes not only organizations in local communities but also their links to state and federal agencies. If the vocabulary agency administrators use in describing their operations sounds slightly alien to clients caught up in local programs—"universe of need," "placements," "outreach"—that of system-level planners is even more bizzare. Planners are concerned with "delivery agents," "target populations," "prioritizing," and "trainable occupations."

Two criteria appear in most social service evaluations, whether made by agency administrators or system planners: Who benefits from programs, and the degree of adaptiveness and innovativeness of programs, given changing local needs. The distinction between the three units of analysis is manifestly apparent in the differential way benefits are distributed across clients, organizations, and fields by various structures. Adaptiveness and innovativeness are assessed in terms of a program's fit with target population needs and its ability to function effectively as needs change. I am assuming that meeting local needs is a high priority in the American political system.

The strength of arguments on both sides of the centralization-decentralization debate, and the discovery of structures that provide examples of each, shows the complexity of the design issue. Just as organization theorists have reconciled themselves to the realization that there is no "one best way" to organize, given the extent to which environments and tasks vary across occasions, so planners have discovered there is not one best way to design a "coordinated" human service delivery system. General points can be made about the tendency of centralization (tight coupling) or decentralization (loose coupling) to produce particular kinds of benefits, but master plans are beyond our comprehension or competence at this point. In reviewing four arguments on each side of the debate, I will introduce elements of the resource control and population ecology models of organizations.

ARGUMENTS FOR CENTRALIZATION/TIGHT COUPLING

Arguments in support of centralizing planning and control in human service delivery systems assert that tight coupling and hierarchical control must be used to negate the tendencies of organizations to pursue narrow sectarian interests. Services benefiting socially and economically heterogeneous populations are possible only in structures where special interests are held tightly in check. The equitable distribution of benefits is treated as more important than the adaptation of programs to local needs. Arguments for decentralization, on the other hand, emphasize adaptiveness and innovativeness while arguing that loose coupling is the most efficient way of allocating societal resources.

INDIVISIBLE PROBLEMS
REQUIRE A CENTRALIZED STRUCTURE

Social service programs require extensive involvement with clients, long-term followup, contain unanticipated side-effects, and possess other complicating factors that make large-scale action necessary. The treatment of multi-problem families, the crime problem in metropolitan areas, and the provision of health care facilities cannot be carried out by small organizations acting on their own. If these large-scale problems are broken down into separate pieces and different organizations are allowed to work on problems from their own perspectives, the result is a series of incomplete solutions. Resources are wasted because each organization duplicates work done by others: in-take, processing of clients, record or account keeping, revenue raising, and so forth.

The most common variation on the theme of indivisible problems is the argument for economies of scale. Advocates of centralization assert that it is uneconomical to attack certain problems on other than a tightly coordinated multi-organization scale. Planners contrast the wasted resources and duplication of effort resulting from market transactions with the efficiency and speed of transactions internalized under one hierarchical structure.

Whether defined as unemployment or underemployment, problems in the manpower sector are too widespread to be dealt with by small organizations. Manpower planners argue that coping with an unemployment rate of more than 6 percent requires the redistribution of massive resources. Without a large scale commitment of funds, local organizations only scratch the surface of the problems. For example, in one county manpower planners drew up a plan of service for 1976–77 that identified areas of need and what the local program could do. The resulting plan resembles a David and Goliath scenario: there were 5,800 welfare recipients with 165 to be served; 4,200 veterans in need of service were identified, with 38 to be served by the program, and so forth. The surge in unemployment in the past few years has swamped even the largest manpower services organizations.

The major reasoning behind the 1973 Comprehensive Employment and Training Act was that the resources of a local community would be assembled into one operation. The resulting organization would combine all the functions previously distributed among the autonomous manpower programs, each funded under its own categorical grant from the federal government. Local programs were sponsored by Community Action Agencies, Model Cities agencies, local school districts, associations of businessmen, and the Employment Service. Also, state Departments of Labor mounted their own programs. The new structure would combine the functions of intake, placement, counseling, and so forth in the same office; one administrative staff would be used to cover all sub-programs. The scale of the resulting organizations would allow new procedures to be introduced that could not be implemented in smaller organizations. For example, small organizations had great difficulty in coping with the problem of following up their clients; that is, what happened to clients after the processing period was over. Large operations were able to create specialized recordkeeping divisions to keep track of clients, with some information systems automated and computerized.

To counter arguments by decentralization advocates that the resulting structure was unwieldy and too far removed from local conditions, planners pointed out that a centralized structure still allowed for specialization within the system. Large corporations, especially multinationals, use a divisionalized structure that permits the adaptation of specialized divisions to local environments while at the same time retaining a centralized accounting and control structure. Divisions are guided by headquarter's policies, but have enough autonomy to respond to specialized opportunities. Planners argued that these same principles were applicable to the public sector.

Manpower regulations can be written to allow local flexibility and staff discretion. For example, one CETA operation uses the Employment Service to screen everyone for eligibility, the Urban League to recruit blacks and other minorities, an association of the aged to recruit older workers, and the community action agency to recruit and place low income and rural persons. All this is done through a series of subcontracts with the main CETA office.

The reasoning behind the CETA bill was that large metropolitan areas or rural counties comprise a single employment catchment area, and planning on a smaller level would fragment and damage the delivery of manpower services. Whether a problem is, in fact, "indivisible" depends upon the extent to which its causes are understood and an appropriate technology is available. A common characteristic of problems defined through the public policy-making process is that their boundaries are often arbitrary and are determined through bypassing technical analysis. Some problems are so complex as to defy reasoned analysis, such as the "poverty problem" of the 1960s in the United States. In these cases, the critical point is not in the structuring of a solution, but rather in defining a problem's boundaries.

ORGANIZATION AUTONOMY IS A BARRIER TO SYSTEM-WIDE SOLUTIONS

Advocates for centralization assert that the existence of autonomous organizations and agencies, each with its own protective boundaries, fragments problems and creates nearly insurmountable obstacles to coordination. Administrators defend their agencies' domains and seek preservation of the integrity of their own organization's boundaries. The vested interests of administrators take precedence over any sentiments embodied in abstract declarations concerning interorganizational cooperation. A strong centralized authority is needed to override individual organizational boundaries. This is, of course, the familiar problem of the rationality of collective action. A mechanism has to be found to force organizations to cooperate, thus solving the "hold-out" problem. The hold-out problem can occur only when organizations have the autonomy and separate authority to reject proposed system-wide solutions.

Most social service agencies face demands far greater than they can possibly meet with their limited resources. A central characteristic of the services sector is that demand is nearly infinitely expandable because of subsidized costs and the lack of client contributions. Thus, faced with a potential overload of clients, staff can practice "creaming" and exercise their discretion in ways that benefit the agency but not necessarily the total system or clients in need. Attacks on the creaming process can be repelled by pointing out that, of course, clients *are* being served. It is, therefore, hard to fault an agency unless a critic can come up with a rigorous ranking of clients by priority of need.

A number of studies have shown the insidious effects of staff discretion, given agency autonomy and client overload. Gordon's (1975) research on the use of administrative discretion in welfare agencies found that staff were able to reward clients who had knowledge of the bureaucratic ropes and caused fewer problems than ignorant clients. Discretion was exercised in ways that favored the outcomes desired by knowledgeable clients. Roth (1972) found that medical practitioners systematically discriminated against certain classes of patients for purely organizational reasons. These same tendencies are also present in centralized structures, but they can be controlled through central monitoring and auditing units. A "welfare inspector" empowered to intervene in local agencies' operations has more influence than external resource groups not part of the authority structure.

In the manpower training sector, public service employment is rapidly becoming the largest single component. This component recruits and places individuals in jobs requiring a fairly high degree of competence in local government and non-profit agencies. Since training and socialization of underskilled employees is not a main orientation of the recipient departments and agencies, it is understandable that they seek the most competent and highly skilled clients. One consequence has been that manpower programs have moved away from service to the unskilled and disadvantaged populations originally served in the 1960s. Perhaps a stronger regional or national auditing agency is needed to reassert service priorities.

Autonomous agencies and organizations can use their autonomy to "hide" from public scrutiny. There is little need for them to advertise their existence, given the tremendous demand for their services and the fact that agencies can rely on other organizations for referrals. A common strategy is to lay low and avoid attracting attention. Experience with CETA shows that even "centralization" at the community-level may be too much "decentralization" if administrators aren't committed to a concern for constituency assessment of their program. A central component of the CETA program is the local Manpower Planning Advisory Council (MPAC) made up of representatives from the various important segments of the community. This body was designed as a review and consultation group giving advice to the CETA staff, suggesting new programs, and in general overseeing the policies of the program. Rather than serving as a review and advisory body, however, the

MPAC has *internalized* the potential *external* evaluators of the program and thus coopted them. "Voice" has been muted by encouraging loyalty among persons and representatives who at one time might have been critical of CETA operations (Hirschman, 1972).

Some planners assert that a decentralized system fragments the client population and encourages agencies to deal with clients on a "professionalized" one-to-one basis. The large number of agencies and their autonomous status make it difficult for external pressure groups to mount an effective counter pressure. Opponents have to fight many small skirmishes instead of several big battles. A possible remedy to client powerlessness is the centralization of programs thus facilitating the formation and effectiveness of external pressure groups.

The MPAC, for example, is hampered because its members have an ideological commitment to the program but little time to follow up on issues. As non-paid, part-time members, they can't hope to compete with the full-time staff of CETA. If centralization were used to provide funds for pressure groups and organizations of clients, then perhaps the balance could be righted. At the very least, one could argue that the MPAC deserves a professional planning staff of its own. At present, under the decentralized CETA operation the major evaluator and pressure organization maintaining standards is the federal Department of Labor, by default. In spite of the fact that the system is much more decentralized than previously, a powerful central agency still plays a significant role, reinforcing the point that most delivery systems are a dynamic mix of centralized and decentralized components.

Information impactedness and opportunism are major problems in interorganizational fields organized on market principles (Williamson, 1975). Planners, wishing to take a system-wide view, can't get the accurate and timely information they need to draw up useful plans. Autonomous agencies withhold information or release inaccurate and misleading information. Centralizing a system by bringing agencies under one hierarchical structure internalizes former market transactions and substantially lessens the problems of acquiring valid information.

The resource dependence model treats authority as a resource that is sought by organizations seeking to control their environments. Authority over other organizations is sometimes achieved through deliberate strategies and tactics, but in the social services sector it is most often achieved through legislative mandates or bureaucratic directives from supraordinate authority. Research on the manpower training system has shown the importance of mandated relationships in bringing organizations together that otherwise would deal with each other only at arms length. Prior to the 1973 reorganization, the Employment Service occupied a central role in manpower training systems because many manpower organizations were mandated to use it for referrals and placements. Research showed that the scope and intensity of relations between the ES and manpower organizations formally linked to it were much greater than for organizations whose ties to the ES were based only on needs generated by the interorganizational division of labor.

Formalization of ties enhanced the prospect of complementary relations and increased the volume of contact, thus moving clients between organizations that had different services to offer. Formalization also smoothed interorganizational contacts, as interaction was more likely to be standardized and interagency rivalries were lessened (Aldrich, 1976a, 1976b). Research on relations between the ES and Social Services Department uncovered similar processes, as mandated interaction led to more intense interaction and an imbalance in favor of the ES, but lower perceived cooperation. Currently, mandated interaction between social services departments and the ES exists in the 131.5 Program, under which employable welfare recipients must pick up their checks at Employment Service offices. This brings clients into periodic contact with another important agency, even though in most cases this is a rather perfunctory visit.

Perhaps theorists have overlooked the importance of manipulating authority in interorganizational systems because they have taken it as one of the fixed parameters of a system. The resource dependence perspective, however, warns us that such relations should not be taken for granted. Mandating relations may be the only way to bring agencies together with complementary services to offer.

NORMAL INTERORGANIZATIONAL RELATIONS FOCUS ON ORGANIZATIONAL RATHER THAN SYSTEM NEEDS

The resource dependence perspective posits that administrators seek their own organization's survival, privileged position, or dominance of the field. Such objectives would seem to be incompatible with the system-wide perspective that centralization is designed to achieve. Normal interorganizational transactions are conducted on too issue specific a level to allow the achievement of coordination among organizations at the population level. The divergent objectives of organizations within decentralized systems mean that some attend closely to clients whereas others do not, resulting in inequitable treatment of the client population. There are exceptions—agencies where "client concern" shines through—but they don't cumulate to have system-wide consequences.

The behavior of social service organization administrators can be characterized in three empirical generalizations (Benson, 1975). First, administrators attempt to fulfill program requirements justifying their organizations' claims to a supply of funds and authority. This requires action with *visible* consequences, such as a high number of referrals, a large number of clients served, or the manipulation of a measurement and accounting system. Interorganizational behavior thus reflects a concern for the intensity of interaction with other organizations; that is, with the amount and frequency of resource flows.

Second, administrators attempt to maintain a clear domain that is societally legitimated. Given the general acceptance among organizations of the social service paradigm, there are few conflicts over domains. Thus, the extended application and defense of an organization's domain occurs sporadically and does not figure very heavily in day-to-day activities.

Third, administrators seek to maintain an orderly, reliable pattern of resource flow as free from uncertainty as is organizationally and technologically possible. The drive toward reducing uncertainty often takes the form of standardizing transactions to make them more predictable and manageable. Standardization can be achieved either by segmenting organizations into separate functional units, with each assigned a limited portion of a transaction, or through routinizing procedures and allowing them to be invoked upon recognition of a relatively small number of cues.

The resource dependence perspective's prediction that administrators will show a high concern for the volume of resource flows and attempt to routinize transactions is supported by several research findings (Aldrich, 1976a, 1976b). The greater the flow of resources between two social service agencies, the more likely transactions are to be standardized and the less likely it is that agency heads will desire still greater standardization. A high volume of interaction leads to a positive evaluation of the cooperativeness of another agency, and a high degree of standardization in transactions has a similar effect.

Minimizing uncertainty by standardizing transactions allows staff members to become skilled in the offering of certain specialized services and may free them from the needless duplication of effort occurring when each transaction is begun anew. The danger is that staff will become inflexible and unresponsive to the specific needs of clients not fitting into prestandardized categories. Centralization partly overcomes this danger by allowing a high enough degree of internal differentiation to permit separate standardized and unstandardized boundary routines. Thus, in large organizations, staff members who cannot cope with a particular client's needs are able to route the client to the appropriate routine or unit. The small size of organizations in decentralized systems means that many of them are crisis oriented and are more vulnerable to short term environmental fluctuations than larger organizations. Large, centralized organizations can differentiate internally, not only to offer a mix of standardized and unstandardized routines, but also to allow the creation of a planning department which enables them to avoid a crisis mentality.

DOMINANT ORGANIZATIONS BENEFIT THE MOST FROM DECENTRALIZATION

Some theorists argue that, in the absence of authoritative and planned coordination, the flow of resources benefits the already dominant organizations in a system. Loose coupling favors the groups and organizations with the most resources and strongest lobbying efforts. They can push aside the smaller organizations and gain access to resources which they use to enhance their dominant position. New programs are simply absorbed by the pre-existing system, aided by the presence of an institutionalized thought structure (Warren et al., 1974).

Perhaps the already dominant organizations in a community *should* benefit because they are less parochial or particularistic than others. However, research on social services organizations is not cause for optimism in this regard. Agreement among dominant organizations on a common paradigm generally ensures that new organizations will not radically *challenge* existing ones. Powerful organizations subscribe to a shared paradigm that defines the nature of community problems and the form of acceptable solutions. For example, Model Cities organizations in the 1960s made little progress in changing patterns of interaction among social service organizations because the shared interorganizational paradigm diagnosed social problems as a failure of the individual rather than the social system.

The population ecology model of organizations posits that in loosely coupled interorganizational networks, a key role is played by linking pin organizations (Aldrich, 1979). Linking pin organizations have extensive and overlapping ties to different parts of a network and play a key role in integrating the population. Having ties to more than one subset or subnetwork, linking pin organizations are the nodes through which a network is loosely coupled. Three functions of linking pin organizations are particularly important: (1) They serve as communication channels between organizations; (2) They provide general services that link third parties to one another by transfering resources, information, or clients; and (3) If they are dominant or high status organizations, they serve as models to be imitated by other organizations or use the dependence of other organizations on themselves to actively direct network activities. Linking pin organizations help preserve the complexity of networks that would otherwise decay into isolated subnetworks.

Dominant or high status organizations would be expected to occupy the roles of linking pin organizations, as they achieve their position in the organizational hierarchy by strategic maneuvering into central positions and by manipulating interorganizational relations as a means of retaining power. Dominant employers in a local economy, for example, exercise power in a variety of contexts, with their influence extending from setting standards for wages down to the very subtle level of providing much of the leadership for voluntary associations. The community power literature emphasizes the coordinating role of organizations representing vested interests—such as the Chamber of Commerce, country clubs, or local economic development associations (Freeman, 1968)).

Despite all the attention paid to "domains" and "domain consensus" in the social service organizations literature, it is difficult to find evidence of overt conflict in the field. Consensus, albeit implicit, reigns supreme. A multi-city study of the Model Cities program found so little evidence for domain conflict that it was hardly worth analyzing (Warren et al., 1974). In my own research I found a high incidence of perceived domain overlap between manpower programs and the Employment Service with no apparent ill effects (Aldrich, 1976a, 1976b). Out of 48 manpower organizations, only 4 instances of genuine domain conflict in the previous year were recorded. In another study of 249 social service organizations, only two directors named the local Employment Service office as duplicating their own function. There was no overt evidence of any manifest battles over domain control in spite of the fact that the ES was the most visible target for critics of the manpower training system in the 1960s and early 1970s.

The resource dependence perspective predicts that these findings should be typical, as the network of interorganizational relations evolving at the community level is highly stable. Stability is promoted and conflict inhibited because of three factors. First, stability is supported at the level of individual agency administrators seeking certainty in relations with their environments. Second, vested interests are characteristic of relations between pairs of organizations through authoritative dominance, resource dependence, or complementarity of needs. Finally, at the level of institutional legitimacy, the overarching normative and legal order is supported by state and federal laws and by local community support from institutional elites. Thus, new programs placed in local communities can be expected to have little impact in terms of either increasing innovativeness or altering the existing distribution of benefits. Only a large scale centralized structure can overcome the bonds of dependence and dominance joining the components of the existing system.

Some evidence for these propositions may be found in comparing the pre- and post-CETA manpower systems in New York State communities. Under the old manpower system, funds for on-the-job training were provided to employers who could take a fairly large number of trainees, thus minimizing counseling and overhead costs. Expenditures for both on-the-job training and classroom training represented, to some extent, the externalization of the training function by large firms in the private sector. Private employers had their training costs subsidized by public funds. Perhaps this would make sense for jobs in the secondary labor market, where there is a high level of turnover and a great deal of mobility between fairly low skilled jobs. However, it makes less sense for jobs in the primary sector, which relies heavily upon training persons in highly firm-specific skills and promoting them up through an internal labor market. Turnover is much lower and skills are not as transferable between firms as in the secondary labor market. Under the new system, large employers are not as favored and some prime sponsors have a rule that only one training slot will be allocated to each employer. Others require firm evidence that a person taken on is being trained and that funds are not being used to substitute for the firm's normal training costs.

Centralization may protect programs that would otherwise face a debilitating opposition from special interest groups. Organizations that oppose social services such as "free" health clinics, legal aid, and abortion referrals are organized on a national scale and disseminate information about opposition tactics to their local affiliates. If social service programs are not partially insulated against these external pressures through their incorporation into a hierarchical structure, they are quite vulnerable. Thus there must be structural congruence between social service programs and their opponents, as in the labor relations sector, where unions attempt to organize on the same scale as employers.

SUMMARY OF ARGUMENTS FOR CENTRALIZING

1. Indivisible problems require large-scale planned interaction of a magnitude not possible if social service organizations interact only to satisfy their own requirements.

2. The autonomy and separate authority of organizations impedes the development of a more encompassing solution to clients' problems, as parochial interests take precedence over system-wide interests. Differences in organizational objectives and commitment mean that a market solution at the organizational level may result in an inequitable distribution of benefits at the client level.

3. Normal interorganizational relations are focused on specific organizational needs rather than the common welfare. This leads to a concern for standardized and routinized transactions which may not be in the clients' best interests.

4. In a decentralized, loosely coupled system, the flow of resources tends to benefit the already well-off organizations.

ARGUMENTS FOR DECENTRALIZATION/LOOSE COUPLING

Most of the arguments for decentralization emphasize the increased adaptiveness and innovativeness that result from decentralization. Advocates argue that loose coupling is a more efficient means of allocating societal resources and that although equity is an important issue, a centralized system is inappropriate in situations where goals are ambiguous, technologies uncertain, and environmental conditions constantly changing. The four arguments reviewed below are not simply attempts to refute arguments for centralization. They stand on their own as substantive assertions of the benefits of decentralization and, by implication, the costs of centralization. Indeed, the arguments are so persuasive that planners who on one occasion argue strongly for centralization find themselves on other occasions defending the benefits of decentralization. Such is the appeal of the arguments that most human service delivery systems ultimately are designed with both sets of principles underlying them. These built-in contradictions manifest themselves in numerous ways, some of which will be pointed out in the examples given. The strength of arguments advanced for decentralization may mean that a resolution of conflicting stands—if such a result is desired—may be achieved only on a case-by-case basis, and then only after an explicit recognition that many design questions actually concern fundamental values rather than technical procedures.

DECENTRALIZATION ALLOWS FOR MAXIMUM ORGANIZATIONAL RESPONSIVENESS

One implication of highly centralized systems is that problems are indivisible and much the same for all the clients involved. A contrary argument, positing that many problems are not the same for all clients, is one basis for arguments in support of decentralization. An implicit assumption of this argument is that planners should place as high a value on allowing localized choice of means to ends as on the quality of outcomes themselves. The superiority of loosely coupled systems in an evolving environment lies in the freedom individual units have to adapt to local conditions.

Arguments for maximum responsiveness underlay the movement in the 1960s for community control and in the 1970s for governmental decentralization and revenue sharing. Advocates of decentralization argued that money saved by coordination and consolidation of individual agencies did not offset the costs added when additional layers of authority were imposed between decision makers and local environments. This was the basis for the argument over decategorization under the 1973 CETA bill. The Department of Labor Manpower Administration in Washington was attacked for being too far from local labor markets to design programs for them. Centralized coordination had made administrators unresponsive to idiosyncratic needs. It was assumed that local leaders with an ear to their political constituency know what's happening in their environments and what local needs actually are. Planners were frustrated over their inability to alter centralized regulations concerning how resources should be used. The inability of local planners to design unique programs reinforced a particular way of dealing with manpower services that critics saw as outdated.

Loose coupling is especially important in manpower planning, where information on labor market conditions is difficult to obtain. Federal and state data are often out of date and not detailed enough to be of much use for local planning. Instead planners rely on "general community knowledge" and informal sources. They still have access to federal and state information, but they supplement it with their own knowledge of the local community. In fact, the manpower planning system is remarkable for the large amount of money spent in an area with so little information available about existing conditions or the consequences of treatments used. This has changed very little since 1973 and probably won't until local planners are given enough resources to create community-based information systems.

Decentralization brings local *accountability* to systems by making visible the local leaders and administrators responsible for programs. Centralized and categorical programs, while allowing for centralized accountability, make administrators invisible to local populations. Under these conditions, it is not clear who should be held accountable for expenditures and the quality of services. Increased accountability is promoted only if a feedback mechanism is provided linking constituency evaluations to organizational rewards. Because of the non-market nature of most organization-client transactions and the tenuous link between individual citizen evaluations and agency funding, it has proved extremely difficult for planners to design effective feedback mechanisms.

Decentralization does not mean the absence of ties between organizations or the breakdown of delivery systems into chaos. Indirect ties— through third parties—serve a very important function in coordinating the behavior of independent organizations. Research on the manpower training systems of local communities prior to the 1973 act found that indirect ties between organizations increased the intensity of interaction between them over and above the level expected on the basis of individual organizational characteristics. For example, the greater the number of indirect linkages between social service organizations and local Employment Service offices, the larger the two-way flow of referrals. At that time the Employment Service stood near the center of the manpower training system referral process and had many direct ties to manpower programs. Therefore, it also had many indirect ties to social service organizations that were linked to manpower programs. These indirect ties were a link that drew the organizations closer together. These findings as well as others demonstrate the potential of network analysis for understanding relations within social service delivery systems (Aldrich, 1979).

Advocates assert that a loosely coupled structure is most appropriate under conditions of environmental change where decisions must be taken rapidly and where a high degree of responsiveness to citizen demands is desired. Advocates of centralization attack these arguments on the grounds that a decentralized system caters to local interests at the expense of societal interests and is more costly to administer because of duplication of administrative overhead across many semi-autonomous organizations.

DECENTRALIZATION ALLOWS MAXIMUM BENEFITS FROM THE INTERORGANIZATIONAL DIVISION OF LABOR

In a decentralized system, each organization can respond to a unique set of needs and can carve a niche for itself in an area where it is most competent. When problems are divisible, establishing centralized structures amounts to administrative overkill. Centralized structures are attacked for being only loosely tied to their markets and thus pursuing goals that are relevant to various internal procedural and administrative needs rather than client needs. Centralized structures wipe out the subtle differences between specialized organizations that are preserved in decentralized systems.

Centralization inhibits innovation by subunits if guidelines for regulations are tightly written or if innovation is not in the interest of dominant organizations. Extreme centralization thus prevents specialization and the division of labor from taking their natural course. The benefits of specialization and the division of labor have been commented upon by a number of investigators. Aiken and Alford (1970), in their study of innovation in urban renewal and public housing programs, argued that "The greater the number of centers of power in a community, and the more pervasive and encompassing the interfaces, the higher the probability of innovation in a given issue area." A large number of power centers in frequent interaction with one another lead to the introduction of innovations as the by-product of competitive strategies. The separate and autonomous power centers are quick to imitate their rivals' innovative behaviors or to join coalitions to support their own programs.

Advocates of centralization argue that allowing free reign to the division of labor and specialization will result in chaos and disorder at the interorganizational field level. However, decentralization proponents counter with the argument that a number of factors prevent chaos from resulting. First, there is a high degree of consensus among agencies and professionals on the service paradigm and this guides most organizational and staff actions. Radical departures from the paradigm are infrequent. Second, there is an extremely high degree of interchange of personnel between social service organizations. Quite a few boundary spanning personnel in the various agencies have extensive contacts with other social service organizations. For example, many CETA staff were taken from the Employment Service, Community Action Agencies, and other social service agencies concerned with manpower in one form or another.

Maximizing responsiveness to local conditions and reaping the benefits of specialization are interrelated arguments. If local populations vary sufficiently in their needs, then programs tailored to those needs will eventually become highly specialized. Similarly, specialized programs linked to target populations by effective feedback procedures should become quite responsive to local needs. Whether either of these sequences develops in a particular program depends upon the ability of planners to establish a link between client satisfaction and organizational rewards.

DUPLICATION AND OVERLAP
INCREASE SYSTEM RELIABILITY

Redundancy in human service delivery systems increases the possibility of detecting system errors and of occasionally hitting the target. The simplest way to grasp the importance of duplication or redundancy in a complex system is to consider the interpersonal communication process. If I avoid all repetition and redundancy in speaking to you, my message will be short but there will be no way for you to assess its reliability or whether you have truly understood it. It is only when I repeat the same message in different ways—speak in a redundant fashion—that the detection of error or misunderstanding is possible. A message with zero redundancy would not allow for the detection of error. This argument can be generalized to the situation of interorganizational relations in a complex system (Landau, 1969).

Traditional theories of public administration call for "each role to be perfected, each bureau to be exactly delimited, each linkage to articulate unfailingly and each line of communication to be noiseless—all to produce one interlocking system, one means ends chain which possesses the absolute minimum number of links, and which culminates at a central control point" (Landau, 1969: 354). In systems terms, this is a highly centralized, hierarchical, richly coupled system. This model is clearly a high risk one because the failure of a single component could shut down the entire system. A single failure breaks the system, just as a failure in an electrical circuit connected in series shuts down the entire circuit. Error introduced at one point is sent unchecked throughout the entire system.

The most appropriate environment for a richly coupled, highly centralized system appears to be one where the environmental conditions producing the problem treated by the social service agency are fully known and therefore uncertainty is low, where the goals of all the components are fixed and widely accepted, and where the technologies of the various components are well understood. Needless to say, these conditions don't obtain very often in most social service delivery systems. Economists are still trying to untangle the link between inflation and unemployment and educators still aren't certain why Johnny can't read. Most recent organizational research calls into question the usefulness of static models for understanding interorganizational relations.

One of the objectives of the redesigned manpower training system under CETA has been to eliminate redundancy. Under the old system, even though programs were categorically determined from Washington, a number of options were open to the unemployed. Each of the various programs had its own intake and placement operation. Now these functions are all centralized under CETA, although in many cases CETA has delegated them to other organizations. Nevertheless, the delegation process has generally been one of finding a single subcontractor to take a single function. A systems theorist could argue that eliminating all duplication and overlap may lead to lessened system performance in the long run.

Under certain conditions a system with individual elements that are unreliable can be formed into a system with a fairly high degree of reliability. Two conditions are that the failure of component parts must be random and statistically independent of one another. In such a system the probability of failure of the whole system decreases exponentially as redundancy factors increase arithmetically. For example, assume that in a metropolitan area there are three organizations performing roughly the same function. Each has a probability of failure of .20 over some specified time period. Failures occur at random and are not related. The probability of two organizations failing at the same time is .20 X .20 or .04. The probability of all three organizations failing at the same time is only .008. Thus, a one unit increase in redundancy from one to two or from two to three leads to a geometric increase in the system's reliability. This example is admittedly over-simplified and one would have to consider how rapidly the surviving organizations could expand their operations to take in the clients of failed organizations. Nonetheless, the general point is well taken: in an environment that is uncertain and somewhat unpredictable, where technologies used are incompletely understood, and where objectives are still evolving, duplication of effort and overlap between goals and domains is one way of increasing the probability of some organizations accomplishing their tasks.

CENTRALIZATION AND "COORDINATION" TEND TO REINFORCE PRIOR PATTERNS OF DOMINANCE

Decentralization advocates argue that centralization or "coordinated" strategies are thinly disguised attempts to further the interests of dominant organizations. They point out that if a coordination plan is administered by or through existing organizations, they gain a predominant voice in what is to be done (Warren, 1973). Gaining a major voice, in turn, benefits dominant organizations in several ways. The social service "problem" is defined in the organization's own terms, allowing it to use its existing staff and technology. Dominant organizations can reduce the threat of competition from new organizations in the name of "avoiding duplication of services." The problem can be defined as one requiring more services, especially of the kind offered by existing organizations. Defining the problem of poverty, medical care, legal services and manpower services, and so forth, as a problem of coordinating the behavior of existing organizations enables the affluent and influential sectors of the population to avoid more drastic change. In short, it enables the privileged to retain their positions.

The effect of turning CETA over to local governments has been to redistribute benefits into local government agencies and bureaus. The work experience program, designed to give disadvantaged and unemployed persons a taste of a real work experience, has become a supplemental labor force for local governments. This is in addition to the public service employment component which was explicitly designed to aid the public sector. Attaching CETA to existing political units has meant that in some cases it is nearly inseparable and indistinguishable from existing city or county departments. In these situations it is treated as simply another departmental resource. Continuing a trend apparent under the old system, the private business sector has been relatively neglected in favor of the public and non-profit sectors. The benefits to local non-profit agencies in particular have been phenomenal.

Indeed, one issue not raised explicitly up to now is the question of why programs are so seldom evaluated in terms of their benefits to the other organizations in a community. In the case of CETA, local CETA operations provide part and full-time employees to dozens and in some cases hundreds of local non-profit agencies, such as the Red Cross, Salvation Army, YMCA, day care centers, alternate education operations, programs for the aged, and just about every social service imaginable. This is in addition to the employees provided to governmental bureaus and departments. Curiously enough, the program is never described in these terms. Rather, it is described in terms of benefits to clients in the program and in terms of a reduction in the unemployment rate resulting from trainees finding jobs in the private sector. It would seem equally important to point out the tremendous supplement that these subsidized workers provide to the social services sector.

Centralization in the manpower training system has meant that the allocation of manpower training funds has not become an issue in "partisan politics." Some planners see this as a decided plus for the system, while others decry the passing of an opportunity to debate crucial political priorities. For the latter group, the issue has become a "non-issue" (Bachrach and Baratz, 1962).

The issue has been de-politicized for a number of reasons. First, there is consensus on the social services paradigm. Neither major political party advocates major institutional change in the United States. Second, most staff positions within the various agencies are allocated on a merit basis. Thus, neither party sees any gain to be had from taking over the programs. Third, the program is designed so that issues can be defined as "getting more for our local constituency in the contest with other localities." This unites the two parties in the community against the other communities in a region. Finally, the public has no alternative source of information about programs and must rely upon announcements by public officials and administrators. The effect of these factors has been to keep CETA remarkably conflict free, at least with regard to the political arena.

Centralization allows dominant organizations to deal with potential dissent from community groups by coopting them. Establishing new plans or councils to achieve "better coordination" is a way of coopting protesting clients and interest groups. It gives the appearance of change and responsiveness to "voice" without requiring major changes in the traditional definition of problems or their solutions. Moreover, the resource pot available to centralized agencies is sizeable, and their legislatively enforced central position gives dominant organizations the right to distribute benefits so as to reward "cooperative" organizations.

In the 1960s, Community Action Agencies were among the most vocal critics of local social services operations. Many were highly critical of the way manpower programs were run, arguing that the poor and minority groups were being systematically neglected in favor of more skilled workers. Both Community Action Agencies and Model Cities agencies adopted what Warren et al. (1974) referred to as "Paradigm II." This is a paradigm which says that more services are not enough, and that major institutional change is required to improve the position of the poverty stricken and disadvantaged in American society. Many Community Action Agencies were funded under the old manpower training system, but they received money separately through the Office of Economic Opportunity HEW program for youth. In the reorganized system, Community Action Agencies have been coopted by CETA administrators giving them major roles to play. In a number of the cities studied in New York State, Community Action Agencies play important roles in running CETA programs. They have subcontracts to do intake counseling, placement, and in at least one large city, they run the entire program under subcontract from the county government. For example, in one county 25 percent of the Community Action Agency's budget comes from CETA and 30 of its staff positions are CETA funded. In another large upstate city, the CAA is the single largest contractor under CETA, with more than a million dollars in grant funds. Other groups and organizations that were potentially problematic for CETA have been coopted either by giving them subcontracts and placements or by their being given advisory voice: educational organizations, Chambers of Commerce, social service departments, organizations of minority groups, and so forth.

Centralization makes it easier for existing programs to survive *if* they're supported by major interests in a community. However, it is also easier to omit those not supported by major interests. What's difficult is the creation of new programs that go outside the existing set of services offered.

Centralization not only reinforces prior patterns of dominance, but also reinforces the trend toward the over-bureaucratization of social service organizations. Human service organizations lack a market test and tend to be over-administered, as authorities search for ways to control the behavior of staff members and administrators. Positions proliferate on the basis of *internal* evaluations of need and professionals lobbying for more of their own kind. Centralization simply enhances this tendency. Advocates of decentralization argue that instead of economies of scale resulting from centralization, what in fact happens is that centralization leads to an administrative explosion. It is better, they assert, to fund smaller organizations with one or two people performing a large number of functions and getting most of them right.

Given the different pattern of subcontracting among the CETA operations of the various cities studied, it is difficult to make direct comparisons of staff size, but some differences were striking. One county has 20 CETA staff and their plan of action for the last fiscal year said that they would achieve 83 direct placements (this means persons placed without going through training), 108 indirect placements (after training), with 28 clients obtaining their own placements in the course of a year's budget. Might it not be better to distribute these 20 staff positions across 5, 6, or even 9 separate organizations? In an adjacent county that is quite a bit larger and serves quite a few more clients, the CETA staff consists of only 13 persons, but this is partially due to the fact that this CETA agency uses the Employment Service and Community Action Agency extensively, whereas the first county does not. Thus, one agency has used its power and discretion to grow internally, whereas another has a relatively smaller staff and has subsidized other major community organizations.

The argument that centralization tends to benefit the already well off organizations could, of course, be used to argue for either greater centralization or decentralization. Advocates of still greater centralization argue that centralized control should be strengthened, perhaps by giving higher authorities more control, so that dominant organizations are forced to subordinate their goals to those of a larger plan. Public choice theorists and system designers who value citizen autonomy and the benefits of a market mechanism might interpret the fourth argument to imply that small, less powerful, and unrepresented groups and organizations should be assisted and given preferential treatment so they can compete on an equal basis with dominant organizations. I am unsure as to how one would resolve debate of this kind by relying solely on technical analysis.

SUMMARY OF ARGUMENTS FOR GREATER DECENTRALIZATION

1. Decentralization allows organizations to be maximally responsive to heterogeneous client demands and to innovate when local conditions demand.

2. Decentralization allows the maximum benefits of the interorganizational division of labor and specialization to be realized.

3. Duplication and overlap of functions and domains increases overall system reliability.

4. Centralization favors the already well-off organizations and decentralization is a way of breaking up the existing flow of benefits.

CONCLUSIONS

Advocates of centralization and decentralization both claim that the "other" structure benefits dominant and well-established organizations. Both sets of arguments are compelling and it may be that this result—elite domination—is inescapable. The manipulation of authority to gain a dominant position or to avoid dominance by others in a network is a common tactic in interorganizational networks. Some centralized systems are obviously a result of such strategic moves by dominant organizations. Whether anything could or should be done about this is not obvious from the research findings available at present. Answering such questions requires research that correlates interorganizational system outputs with system characteristics, and knowledge on this score is woefully deficient. Moreover, undoubtedly the "best" systems combine elements of centralization *and* decentralization, and most of us are simply not clever enough to design such systems in the abstract.

Considering organizations as the relevant units of analysis and evalua-tion, it may be that smaller organizations actually benefit more from a cen-tralized than a decentralized system. This seems to have been one result of the reorganization of manpower training under CETA. Programs are more visible in large centralized structures and the scale of administration is such that administrators can devote resources to assisting smaller organizations. In decentralized systems, it is probable that innovation is greater in response to specialized needs and organizational technologies, but smaller organiza-tions have much more difficulty in gaining access to resources to follow up innovations. In centralized systems, new programs are sheltered from buffet-ing forces by protection under the wing of dominant organizations.

Richly coupled systems that are *not* hierarchies are inherently unstable (Simon, 1962), and heavy environmental pressure is required to preserve them. The failure of many voluntarily constituted richly coupled systems, such as coordinating councils, clearing house agencies, or human service co-alitions, is due to the lack of either external pressure *or* an authority struc-ture that could preserve the system. It is also easy for dominant organiza-tions to sabotage such systems through non-cooperation. Planners desiring highly decentralized systems with weak central authority may have to accept a high degree of isolation of key units as the cost of local autonomy and responsiveness. Alternatively, planners concerned with the equitable treat-ment of clients may have to accept a high degree of centralization at su-praordinate authority levels—state and federal—and also accept the inevita-ble marginality or demise of small local organizations.

A major problem in designing a human services delivery system lies in defining the boundaries of an ideal decision-making unit. Such a unit should include the causes of problems, the victims, and related externalities. In the social services sector, the focus of problems and the relevant catchment areas are ambiguous and open to manipulation. For example, in the manpower training realm, is the relevant unit a city, county, metropolitan area, region, or the entire economy? When technical analysis is unable to supply answers to these questions, the resulting uncertainty is resolved by turning to other bases for decision making: the prestige and power of per-sons or organizations proposing solutions, the convenience of using existing solutions, and so forth (Pfeffer, 1977).

Regardless of the boundaries of a system, the relation between benefits to component organizations and benefits to individuals is not obvious. Planners sometimes assume that any structure efficient in saving resources, by eliminating duplication of effort or administrative overhead or other means, results in more resources for clients or at least for other programs. However, social service organizations are labor intensive and it's very easy to add more persons to a staff. There is little or no investment in fixed assets and budgets can expand very quickly with little advance planning. This shows up in two ways in the manpower planning system. First, local CETA administrators are asked to respond very quickly to requests for proposals from the Department of Labor, sometimes within thirty days, and many of their proposals contain allotments for new staff to be recruited in a very short period of time. Second, several times in the past few years money has been made available on very short notice for public service employment positions, and local governments as well as non-profit agencies have suddenly found room for new personnel as if by magic. My impression is that personnel sections of social service budgets have voracious appetites all their own which can greedily devour funds saved from other activities.

The biggest gap in assessing whether organizational advantages translate into benefits for clients is the tenuous link between clients' evaluations and organizational fate. Assessments of benefits to clients are usually made by professionals who have a vested interest in the survival of their programs. The manpower training system, for example, has not been able to work out a satisfactory evaluation system that includes clients. Manpower Planning Advisory Councils have not lived up to the expectations expressed in the 1973 legislation, as they've been dominated by CETA administrators and their staff.

The title to this paper was left deliberately ambiguous, reflecting my own feelings regarding Gouldner's lament:

Wrapping themselves in the shrouds of nineteenth-century political economy, some social scientists appear to be bent on resurrecting a dismal science. Instead of telling men how bureaucracy might be mitigated, they insist that it is inevitable. Instead of explaining how democratic patterns may, to some extent, be fortified and extended, they warn us that democracy cannot be perfect. Instead of controlling the disease, they suggest that we are deluded, or more politely, incurably romantic, for hoping to control it. Instead of assuming responsibilities whenever they can, many social scientists have become morticians, all too eager to bury men's hopes. (Gouldner, 1955: 507)

On one side, I think the problem is more severe than Gouldner recognized, as I've tried to point out in these conclusions. On the other side, I think many social scientists are as eager as ever to make positive contributions. The question is, is anybody listening?

REFERENCES

Aiken, Michael, and Robert Alford. 1970. "Community Structure and Innovation: The Case of Urban Renewal," *American Sociological Review,* 35:650–65.

Aldrich, Howard. 1976a. "Resource Dependence and Interorganizational Relations: Local Employment Service Offices and Social Services Sector Organizations," *Administration and Society,* 7:419–54.

—— 1976b. "An Interorganization Dependency Perspective on Relations between the Employment Service and Its Organization Set." In R. Kilmann, L. Pondy, and D. Slevin, eds., *The Management of Organization Design,* pp. 231–66. Amsterdam: Elsevier.

—— 1977. "Visionaries and Villains: The Politics of Designing Interorganizational Relations," *Organization and Administrative Sciences,* 8:23–40.

—— 1979. *Organizations and Environments.* Englewood Cliffs, N.J.: Prentice Hall.

Aldrich, Howard, and Jeffrey Pfeffer. 1976. "Environments of Organizations." In A. Inkeles, ed., *Annual Review of Sociology,* 2:79–106. Palo Alto: Annual Reviews.

Bachrach, Peter, and Morton Baratz. 1962. "The Two Forces of Power," *American Political Science Review,* 57:947–52.

Banfield, Edward and Morton Grodzins. 1958. *Government and Housing in Metropolitan Areas.* New York: McGraw-Hill.

Benson, J. Kenneth. 1975. "The Interorganizational Network as a Political Economy," *Administrative Science Quarterly,* 20:229–49.

Freeman, Linton. 1968. *Patterns of Local Community Leadership.* Indianapolis: Bobbs-Merrill.

Gordon, Laura. 1975. "Bureaucratic Competence and Success in Dealing with Public Bureaucracies," *Social Problems,* 23:197–208.

Gouldner, Alvin. 1955. "Metaphysical Pathos and the Theory of Bureaucracy," *American Political Science Review,* 49:496–507.

Hirschman, A. O. 1972. *Exit, Voice, and Loyalty.* Cambridge: Harvard University Press.

Landau, Martin. 1969. "Redundancy, Rationality, and the Problem of Duplication and Overlap," *Public Administration Review,* 39:346–58.

Pfeffer, Jeffrey. 1977. "Power and Resource Allocation in Organizations." In B. Staw and G. Salancik, eds., *New Directions in Organizational Behavior.* Chicago: St. Clair Press.

Roth, Julius. 1972. "Some Contingencies of the Moral Evaluation and Control of Clientele: The Case of the Hospital Emergency Service," *American Journal of Sociology*, 77:839–56.

Simon, H. A. 1962. "The Architecture of Complexity." *Proceedings of the American Philosophical Society*, 106:284–315.

Warren, Roland. 1973. "Comprehensive Planning and Coordination—— Some Functional Aspects," *Social Problems*, 20:355–64.

Warren, Roland, Stephen Rose, and Ann Bergunder. 1974. *The Structure of Urban Reform: Community Decision Organizations in Stability and Change*. Lexington, Mass.: D. C. Heath.

Williamson, O. 1975. *Markets and Hierarchies: Analysis and Antitrust Implications*. New York: Free Press.

FOUR

The Social Ecology of Citizenship

MORRIS JANOWITZ AND GERALD D. SUTTLES

THE EXPANSION and intensification of industrialization in Western Europe and the United States have been accompanied by repeated forecasts of the disappearance of the local community and most forms of primary association. From Durkheim to the prophets of mass society, the most available image of the emerging present has been that of an atomized society in which the most durable units of solidarity are social classes linked by economic interests.[1] Most sociologists have been especially inclined to accept this perspective along with its central proposition that new social forms arise by replacing older ones.[2] *Gesellschaft* replaces *Gemeinschaft*, organic solidarity replaces folk society, rationalism replaces traditionalism, and universalistic associations replace particularistic ones. In their subsequent elaboration,

1. Kornhauser (1959) and Arendt (1951) have both used the concept of "mass society" to indicate an atomized society in which the individual is uprooted from primordial and primary associations and prone to involvement in popular enthusiasms. Shils (1975) has seriously and effectively questioned this conception of modern society and pointed to the broadening participation provided by modern societies. Nonetheless, the concept of mass society has continued to have a negative connotation and, for most readers, to imply a fragmented or atomized society. For analyses which run in somewhat the same direction, see Nisbet (1953), Stein (1960), and Webber (1961).

2. Some recent enthusiasts have drawn upon the work of Thomas Kuhn (1962) and see in his analyses of scientific revolutions a paradigm for all social change. Such a proposition seems not only premature, but embraces the implausible proposition that all forms of social change are shaped by cognitive considerations parallel to those which have developed in academic physics. The limits to this approach to even academic disciplines are only beginning to be worked out in an empirical fashion; see Stephan Cole (1975).

these ideas have become so embedded in the vocabulary of sociological analysis that it is necessary to make a special intellectual effort if one is not to assume that new social forms invariably replace old ones.

There is, of course, a lesser but persistent counterstream of sociological writings that offers a more differentiated "philosophy of history," one that is more cumulative and more closely attuned to contemporary, empirical findings. Certainly the growing scale of territorial units, especially the nation-state, modifies and refashions groups like the local community, the family, and the peer group. Yet, despite competing loyalties and the emergence of more inclusive intermediary social groupings, the smaller and older social forms seem to have survived in Western Europe and the United States.[3] The process of social change appears to have been less one of replacement than one in which older, local, and provincial social forms become more specialized and more delimited in their social claims. At new levels of socio-cultural integration (Steward, 1955), such groups usually develop specific links which relate them to the wider society in a mutually supportive manner. Thus, while the family has lost many of its economic functions, it has become the central institution providing support for economic activity (Schumpeter, 1942: 160), educational attainment (Coleman, et al 1966), and a generalized form of patriotism to the nation-state (Coser, 1951). Similarly, the widely hailed militancy of local control groups and ethnic groups probably represents less an outright effort at separation than a visceral urge to create some reciprocal avenues of influence between themselves and the centralized bureaucracies of the wider society.

The popular idea that new social forms replace old ones has not only confused the intellectual work of social scientists, but it has also had negative consequences in the management of public affairs, particularly in our ideology guiding the organization of partisan politics. Of course, the nation-state has become the dominant social form in the contemporary societies of

3. This is so much the case that some sociologists are regularly required to hail the "reemergence" of pre-modern social forms. Thus, in the last decade and a half we have had the "resurgence of ethnicity," an "emergent" local control movement, a "back to Jesus movement," and a "withdrawal" to communitarian social life. There is little doubt that some of these social movements involve a genuine increase in public interest, but by and large they are continuations of past forms of social affiliation and activity. Much of the surprise registered by some authors is due to a premature belief that such groups were moribund. Studies documenting the continuity of primary and primordial relations have regularly provided an available counterbalance (Janowitz, 1967; Shils, 1957).

Western Europe and the United States. But this has not meant the loss of their local communities, their families, their religious congregations, and the like. Nor has it meant the clear formation of the population into contending social classes with a stable identity and a persistent recognition of their unitary interests. Confrontation and outright efforts at secession are present, but in general the contest between sub-national and national groups has been resolved by clarifying and narrowing the respective responsibilities of local communities and those of more widely based institutions. Indeed, the general pattern seems to be one where the older, more localized social forms retrench their holistic claims on the loyalty of members and maintain their vitality both by specializing and by forging new reciprocal links to the wider society.[4] The local community remains a primary catchment area within which many national organizations attempt to recruit and mobilize their memberships. The church congregation may retain only delimited liturgical forms, but it has become a major institution in shaping the delivery of social work services. While most ethnic groups retain some distinctive celebrations and consumptory practices, they also find occasion to honor national values and symbols (Thomas et al. 1921; Warner, 1959; Herberg, 1955; Glazer and Moynihan, 1963).

Current political debate tends to pass over these persistent accommodations between national and local forms and to beguile us into a "crisis of legitimacy" in which the Local Control Movement and the resurgence of primordial groups is seen as a profound and possible terminal confrontation with the nation-state. This is particularly the case with the Local Control Movement whose demands are usually juxtaposed to the powers of the central government and most other nation-wide organizations including those representing broad social classes (Lowi, 1971). In the case of the local community this preconception seems especially misleading to us and in this article we will attempt to recast this issue in different terms. In our own view the major issue is not a final solution to the competing claims of the local community and the nation-state, but a profound disarticulation between the "natural" territorial groupings of the local community and the more con-

4. Some of the followers of Mills and Hunter have chosen to work with such an undifferentiated notion of "power" that the qualitative dominance of the nation-state is seen as totally one-sided (Domhoff, 1971). Such an undifferentiated and qualitative conception of power is useful only if one wishes to slide over the distinction between totalitarianism and social democracy. Lasswell (1958) pointed out the difficulties inherent in this approach as early as 1958.

trived ones of political and administrative hierarchies. There is strong evidence that the natural community survives in the continuing effort of residents to conceive of themselves as belonging to small neighborhoods, or what we will call the *social bloc*. These social blocs, however, are frequently embedded in at least two other levels of geographic mobilization: an *organizational community* which adopts explicit goals and strategies on behalf of local interests and the *aggregated metropolitan community* which is an attempt to aggregate diverse organizational communities on behalf of the political economy of the metropolis. In the contemporary metropolis, then, community is a diffuse form of social organization, and in fact the citizen finds himself involved in multiple communities. Properly conceived, the local community is a staging area in which diverse interests are mobilized and joined in an aggregative political process that can shape, strengthen, and legitimize the actions of political and administrative hierarchies. The failure to see this is attributable in part to the "decline in community" approach but is also due to an overly simple and reified conception of local communities.

THE LOCAL COMMUNITY AND CITIZENSHIP

According to democratic theory the most rudimentary social responsibility of local communities is to transform the ideals of citzenship into effective and self-governing action. The idea of citizenship centers on political rights in the first instance but has gradually come to include economic and social rights as essential to a competitive parliamentary democracy. Political rights, such as free speech or enfranchisement, have become the basis for arguing for economic and social rights. In turn, the latter (that is, the right to essential economic security) have come to be seen as requisites to the exercise of political rights. Each affirmation of citizenship leads to a general claim for the extension of rights—political, economic, and social. The classic analysis is that of T. H. Marshall (1964) and his ambitious efforts to understand the broad extension of citizenship in the parliamentary democracies of Western Europe, the United States, Canada, Australia, and New Zealand. His analysis, like that of others, focuses on the manner in which industrialization transforms the criteria of social mobility and as a result bureaucracy provides a more "rational" and "impartial" judgment of individual prerogatives.

We accept this line of argument, but it is partial and far from complete.

The extension of rights—political, social, or economic—presupposes an effective extension of obligations or voluntary stewardship. Rights or "freedom" can be extended only when and where there is some assurance that citizens and the smaller groups to which they belong will accept their newly won liberties with circumspection and self-imposed responsibility.[5] Parliamentary democracies, then, are workable only when they maintain a delicate balance between the extension of individual freedoms and the willingness of subgroups to become contributors to the maintenance of social order. By themselves, bureaucratic norms, universalistic standards, and the civic ideals of democracy seem uncompelling unless they are endorsed and given exemplary weight in the smaller confines in which individuals can feel the consequences of their action by "taking the role of the other." Except in rare instances, it simply seems impossible for individuals to internalize directly the impersonal aims and rules of administrative hierarchies. To the extent that such norms are incorporated into the personality, they must be experienced as consequential for others who are sufficiently close to arouse "empathy."[6] Necessarily, then, it is primordial and primary relations such as those in the family or the local community that translate to the individual the reciprocities which go with nationally declared freedoms and make people more or less willing and responsible citizens whose self-regulation replaces the need for repression by the central state (Janowitz, 1975).

The survival of parliamentary democracies, then, depends heavily upon how nearly its separate, local parts—its more intimate circles—relate to and interpret the larger movements of the wider society. Here, the local community seems to have a central, if not unique, role. Where the family, the peer group, and the church congregation tend to be very homogeneous and to have very narrow interests, the local community creates a potential interface between diverse interests and the opportunity to debate, sort, sift, and balance each against the other. This potential is of extraordinary importance, for while it is the habit of sociologists and most contrived groups to speak of narrowly defined interests, real individuals are the repository of an aggregate of interests, most of them poorly represented by the formal groups that cur-

5. See Shils (1957) for his observations on how the failure of subnational groups to accept such responsibilities retards the development of social democracies and favors authoritarian governments in the developing nations.

6. Our statement on this matter is necessarily brief, but it follows the durable analyses of Cooley (1902), Mead (1934), and Dewey (1922).

rently have an acknowledged role in the political process. It is in the local community that individuals have the opportunity—by no means always realized—both to internalize and aggregate the diverse gains and costs of public policy.

Understandably, macrosociology has been predominantly concerned with the impact of the global processes of urbanization, industrialization, and bureaucratization. As a result it has given only sporadic attention to the infrastructure of lesser groups which can play either a supporting or corrosive part in the maintenance of total societies. Our intent is to examine the local community—the neighborhood as it is commonly understood—in terms of its continued role in modern parliamentary democracies, including both its existing limitations and its potentialities. In our view modern societies suffer especially from an "irresponsible" citizenry, a citizenry which is able to represent its interests primarily through narrow and mutually exclusive interest groups. Thus, despite widespread evidence of public feeling, people find themselves impotent at conserving national resources, enforcing frugality in public expenditures, or accepting responsibility for the excesses of the past. The fault lies not so much with the citizenry itself, however, as the lack of any systematic structure for articulating grass roots sentiments with policies of national leadership.

THE MORAL AND POLITICAL FUNCTIONS OF LOCAL COMMUNITIES

We do not insist that the local community is an especially vigorous or simply indestructible social unit in contemporary society. Journalistic and sociological writers have overburdened it with a sentimental obituary. Local leadership is frustrated and prone to accuse all national organizations as the cause of their weakness. Some local spokesmen have retreated into utopianism, demanding complete local control in a nation heavily dependent on the central management of national accounts (Janowitz, 1975). Other spokesmen have deliberately followed a "beggar your neighbor" strategy trying to shift unattractive installations (power plants, public housing) to other areas while they benefit from the benign placement of clean industries,[7] golf

7. Universities continue to be popular although medical centers with their detoxification centers and emergency wards are encountering resistance. Even parks, which tend to attract unruly youngsters, seem to be running into some opposition. There seems to be a heightened

courses, luxury housing, and homes for the elderly. It is easy to dismiss these demands for local control as a fatal weakness of the local community or to conceive of them as only segregationist efforts to obtain the best for oneself to the disadvantage of others. But the outcry for local control is not just a sign of community disorganization nor is it individualism writ large.

The Local Control Movement reflects a real concern with territorially based or locational decisions made by regulatory, administrative, and public service agencies that affect both public finances and the quality of life in the broadest sense. On the financial level, the movement reveals a chronic discontent with access to employment and the disparate pattern of local taxation and municipal finances. Despite expanding employment and welfare services during the 1960s, financial advantages continued to shift to suburban communities and even this pattern was highly selective and partial (Kain, 1975). At the public service level, the failure of the mass urban educational system to respond to changing occupational requirements was a core issue but the debate over public management was easily extended to include health services, transportation, and access to cultural institutions.[8] The demand for community control was not merely an expression of a dying social group, but a public judgment on the shortcomings of centralized and bureaucratic arrangements which were thought to be a rational means of serving local populations.

One group of sociologists, economists, and political scientists have responded by arguing for another increase in the scale of urban organization, essentially some kind of metropolitan government which would extend to include, in effect, entire SMSA's (Hawley and Rock, 1975; Committee for Economic Development, 1970).[9] Undoubtedly, this strategy would balance

---

awareness of the costs associated with public installations and a growing pattern of segregation in which facilities low and high income communities are willing to accept. This seems to be particularly true in the suburbs (Logan, 1976). But in general, the lack of any systematic review process vastly prolongs the development of such installations and increases their costs as well.

8. This diffusion of discontent, as every minority increased its demands, seems to have confused public leaders who seemed unable to distinguish between issues that were of widespread concern and those urged upon them by a tiny number of partisans.

9. We do not disagree with these supporters of metropolitan government, but we do recognize that one of the main sources of resistance to metropolitan government is the absence of any rational and systematic structure within which the residents of local communities can separately manage their own affairs or have a say in the management of metropolitan governance. In this instance as well as many others the drive for centralization does not exclude that for decentralization (Suttles, 1975).

some of the inequities so apparent in the local tax structure and the quality of public services. However, metropolitanization has not been a popular or effective success in the United States (Campbell and Dollenmayer, 1975). The few urban areas which have implemented it seem to have experienced only modest gains in improving the equity of their delivery of services or the imbalance in their collection of revenues. Metropolitanization is a defensible organizational effort. It is not a panacea and, in our view, it must be accompanied by an articulate structure for aggregating grass root opinions so that local and provincial views are included in the council of government and responded to in such a manner that local groups rightfully feel that they are a party to municipal decisions.

Similarly, the hope of restoring local control by fragmenting existing jurisdictions into small, sometimes overlapping units seems fraught with difficulties. This counter proposal to metropolitanization takes its most explicit form in the public choice literature (Ostrom, 1974; Bish, 1971; Bish and Ostrom, 1973) which argues that government services are most responsive when residents can vote with their feet among many relatively independent territorial units. The central problem, of course, is that family income is a heavy determinant in who can vote in this scheme by changing their residence. Such a pattern of jurisdictional fragmentation may only worsen the discrepancy between have and have-not residential groups, since agencies would be responsible primarily to those with a great deal of discretion in where they choose to live. More importantly, perhaps, a further fragmention of metropolitan jurisdictions—turning the central city into something like the suburbs—seems likely to only reinforce provincialism and reduce the necessity for trade-offs between groups competing for social services. The "toy governments" of suburbia not only trivialize civic life (Gottdiener, 1977), but fail to attach leaders and citizens to broad based conceptions of social welfare. Clearly there is a need for including the demands of small scale local groups, but they must be aggregated in some larger system that permits debates, trade-offs, and transfer payments among diverse groups.

During the later 1960s and early 1970s there has been some recognition of the need for local participation in an increasingly metropolitanized society.[10] Both those advocating metropolitanization and those advocating local

10. Considerable metropolitanization has already taken place in the form of port authorities, transportation authorities, regional water and sewer districts, and a variety of federal agencies (health, welfare, and pollution) which have regional jurisdictions. As A. Hawley (1971:

control have refined and sharpened their objectives and their rhetorics. Participants in community organizations have become more oriented toward metropolitan organization while reform politicians have come to realize the advantages of appealing to local community organizations—not only to capture office but also to reshape the distribution of public services and urban policies. Some community groups have shifted away from lobbying exclusively for "their share" to a demand for more direct and continuous participation in the operation of administrative and service agencies. There has also emerged a number of national groups, such as the National Association of Neighborhoods, National Peoples Action, and National Neighbors, which have begun to link groups from different metropolitan areas. A much larger number of metropolitan-wide citizen groups have developed as some specialized public services have achieved metropolitan scale (environmental, sanitation, water) and attracted the attention of citizens hoping to exercise influence in limited areas (pollution, transportation, consumer protection).

Despite these realignments, it would be a grave error to say that broadened community participation or a heightened awareness of localism have been substantial steps toward an effective representative structure for making both leaders and citizens more responsive to some shared conception of public welfare. The politicization of submerged and marginal groups has broadened participation, but their increasing demands for participation have not been matched by institutional guarantees to insure that new rights would be weighted by assured duties. Indeed, the general tendency of local community organizations has been to heighten fears of irresponsibility and lend additional credibility to the image that all cities are "rip-off cities"— localized, limited liability corporations in which each gets without giving, or the more frequent complaint, gives without getting.[11]

The mechanisms by which the local community can aggregate both public demands and social accountability are varied. Residential areas are above all the social site within which the family life cycle is given moral and

---

262) has pointed out, these authorities actually reduce potential political participation since their administrators are not subject to direct election, review, or recall. An example of how the administrators of such authorities may avoid popular consideration is contained in Robert Caro's (1974) biography of Robert Moses.

11. The recent recession and financial crisis in the urban heartland has also made many city dwellers conscious of the balance between what they contribute in taxes and what is returned to them. This was especially evident during the efforts to get the federal government to help finance deficit spending for New York City.

symbolic content. It is the locus within which each generation is called upon to invest in the next generation, to transcend generational and territorial existence and expend resources—material and psychic—on the fate of another person. The local school is its most obvious and natural repository of sacred involvement, the core institution by which one generation gives without immediate expectation of repayment. It is both the long-run hope for familial advancement and of one's hope to cross into *la vie serieuese* (Shils, 1975). The neighborhood school, then, is a precious institution and we should not be too surprised that it is so ardently defended as in South Boston and other locales.

The local community also has a caretaker function, and one that is not easily transferred to other groups. Much, if not all, of the physical plant of human society is sessile; that is, most of our public possessions must be located where they can be guarded, cared for, kept clean, or at least left unharmed.[12] Those who live around these sessile resources are necessarily public custodians; people who look out for school windows, the disposal of wastes, and the informal surveillance of street life. In the diurnal cycle of the citizen, a set of norms emerges—or does not emerge—for disposing of discarded cigarette butts, mowing one's lawn, helping a neighbor in distress, or in the governance of local policy.

The local community, then, is a catchment area in which accountability is identified and made collective; a bounded group in which responsibility is joint, yet so narrowly circumscribed that its members can realistically contribute to the task of self-regulation. Collective investments in the future of children and the caretaking of the nearby physical environment dramatize its moral and political functions. Its more general function, however, is to allow people to internalize the costs and benefits of collective life through face-to-face relations that extend beyond narrowly defined primary groups. If responsibility (and correspondingly guilt) are extensively diffused and circulated throughout a total society, they tend to cancel themselves out, making no one in particular responsible. Diffusion of responsibility relies

12. As Anthony Downs (1970) comments, home ownership is the main way in which Americans experience and involve themselves in capitalism. The value of a home is so dependent upon the maintenance of surrounding property that we need not expand on the importance of local caretaking in this respect. Among some Americans, for instance low-income blacks and youths, the automobile seems to be their only secure investment. Such a mobile stake in the society has little consequence in promoting a sense of collective responsibility and a care for long-term aspirations.

upon ineffective self-judgment and leaves everyone able to point the finger of blame at everyone else. Put simply, there must be someone innocent enough to accord blame; conversely blame must be so segregated or delimited as to shame the culprit before an audience that is yet a part of his larger social world.

One can summarize these functions by asserting that the local community aggregates and internalizes both public demands and their costs; that its primary functions inevitably involve it in the management of total societies. Its capacity to promote primary relations across diverse groups is its outstanding and distinctive feature. Most other sub-national groups are either very homogeneous or unable to capture more than a narrow aspect of the individual's identity. Labor unions and professional groups have come to be seen as bargainers for higher wages and little else, as if their members were not taxpayers, mortgage holders, welfare recipients, or investors.[13] The heads of industrial enterprise and corporate executives are viewed in the same way and cannot act in a credible manner on behalf of the wider community. Through continual reform or bureaucratization, even the big city political parties have lost their direct and intimate contacts with precinct level demands (Lowi, 1971). Despite their recent prominence, ethnic and racial groups have been especially narrow in their demands upon the wider society, arguing for their share of benefits rather than pressing for a general reconsideration of the relationship between the political economy of public and private services and the balance between expenses and social benefits.

Because members of different households share a single territory, each of their special interests—those of housewives, taxpayers, union leaders, public employees, activists, parents, and the like—are brought together so that their relative merit can be debated and transformed into some effective image of "the public interest." Thus, the local community is one mechanism—maybe the only one—in which the diseconomies of a highly differentiated society come into a single social account which weighs both

13. This is evident not only in the very limited participation in most labor unions, but also in the frequent dissatisfaction of their rank and file over working conditions while their leadership continues to lobby for higher wages alone. The failure of American labor unions to grow much over the last two decades also indicates their inability to enlarge their popular appeal. In turn the growth of municipal employee unions has resulted in an escalation of their wages with no apparent increase in their morale or productivity.

gains and losses. Parliamentary democracy rests on those institutions that reconcile diverse interests and provide a voluntary rather than a coercive social order. Our political parties have the same tasks, but they presuppose a prior sifting and sorting of public opinion—a sifting and sorting that will give political leaders a clear sense of the drift of grass roots feeling.

It is clear from recent examination of the political parties that they are inadequate as the sole mechanism for discovering the collective demands of the American people. The decline in party loyalty and the rise in voter distrust (Janowitz, 1975) document the weakness of the party system as a sufficient means for finding a shared set of objectives within the "regular political process" (Broder, 1972). Correspondingly the rise of community groups, which explicitly aim to replace the political party or which claim a special legitimacy for their representational powers, is evidence of the limitation of the party system. Not only are our political parties weak, but they are being challenged in their own strongholds—the local community, the ward, the precinct, or the election district. Neither the Local Community nor the political parties seem to be fully able to accept their responsibility to reach or develop centers of power that are regarded as effective or legitimate. Neither seems to be sufficiently self conscious to recognize the need for a social reconstruction of the local community or the political parties. Our analysis suggests a mindful attempt to do both.

SOCIOLOGICAL AND POLITICAL CONCEPTIONS OF THE LOCAL NEIGHBORHOOD

There has been a long-term effort in sociology to define the "local community." The first was an attempt to designate "natural communities"; self-designated and self-generated communities which were thought to be a subsocial construction rather than an intended product. This model was promoted most effectively by Ernest W. Burgess (1929) and his followers who sought to identify communities which were the product of ecological processes such as proximity, frequent interaction, and the spatially determined traffic patterns which brought local residents into a shared life around common facilities like the school, local shopping facilities, play lots, and local centers for the delivery of social services. In this view, the patterns of socio-economic, ethnic, and racial segregation were an unintended, crescive

way of distributing people so that they could form communities—impersonal, subsocial forces which made population aggregates into
communities whether or not they liked it.

Following the work of Burgess (1929), the concept of the natural community became progressively less persuasive, and to a considerable extent it
was replaced by the concept of the community of limited liability (Janowitz,
1967). The community of limited liability emphasized the voluntary character of personal ties to the local community. On the one hand, residents were
seen as having a choice about where they could live and how much they
would participate in the local community and in designing the nature of their
own schools, convenience shopping centers, play lots, or local services. On
the other hand, the community of limited liability emphasized the instrumental momentum of local community relations, the purposeful creation of a
community which provided a common way of life to people living in close
proximity.

Still again, the community has been viewed as a contiguous clientele
for a constellation of public services. In this conception the community is
mainly an area of service delivery, some locale large or small, but separated
out by the fact that its residents are common consumers in a school district,
sanitation district, police district, or the like. Not only do the heads of these
public service agencies persistently refer to their district as a "community,"
but the resident consumers have often mobilized themselves around the same
imagery in an effort to control or shape the services they receive (Barsky,
1974).

Each of these conceptions of the local community should not be considered as if it captured, or at least approximated, the full reality of the community. Much debate has gone into the decision as to which is the "true"
basis for the local community formation; whether it is a subsocial product,
whether it is a construction of individual or group decisions, or whether it is
merely a collective consumer. In effect, however, urban residents have
drawn upon all three lines of community formation in their efforts to achieve
accountability and to aggregate competing self-interests into stable political
preferences.

To insure accountability, citizens in the United States, with the aid of
the housing market, have tended to segregate themselves into small, homogeneous groups who are relatively well acquainted with one another and can
presume mutual trust. These local units range from ethnic enclaves to the

well-fenced suburban estate. The social processes which give rise to these territorial units is similar to that which Ernest Burgess (1929) attributed to the natural area segregation, invasion, and succession. However, the social bloc is probably a more appropriate descriptive term for these population concentrations.

Such small residential groups, however, have found it impossible to avoid encroaching on one another's social space; shared schools, shopping areas, parks, local traffic arteries, and the like. Thus, while people have tended to withdraw into provincial enclaves, they have been drawn simultaneously into more encompassing voluntary associations to achieve broader, more integrative goals. Their commitment to such associational forms was always limited and frequently rather instrumental, even downright selfish. However, as de Toqueville first documented, the vitality in American communities rested not on the coercion of the residents into a single territorial unit, but on the flexibility of developing and settling upon rather pragmatic boundaries and organizational forms. The community of limited liability, then, was founded largely on secondary and voluntary associations aimed to aggregate public opinion across many social boundaries for the purpose of self-help, self-regulation, and negotiation with the wider community. Necessarily, such communities often had shifting boundaries and changing organizational forms. With the increasing scale of most public agencies, community organizations tended to shift the scale of their own organizations as well, creating in many instances yet another tier of organizational life through federations and metropolitan-wide social movements (Hunter, 1974). These organizations are often the most visible forms of community in contemporary America, and they are among the most militant in the demand for decentralization or local control. Typically, however, they represent a loosely coordinated federation whose cohesion rests upon some degree of territorial unity and local leaders concerned to influence specific administrative centers. Such federations, then, tend to move toward a more professional staff and a more self-conscious effort to contrive communities and to enlist support.

It is our contention that each tier to this hierarchy of community organization is an authentic form of the local community and that they represent elaborations of the concept of community rather than the replacement of one concept of community or the replacement of one social type by another. We are not alone in this observation. Greer (1962: 90–91) has offered elements in a similar argument. More recently Hunter (1974) has amply documented the persistence of Burgess' (1929) symbolic designations for Chicago's community areas as well as both their division into smaller social blocs and their inclusion in larger areas through linked social organizations. Similar findings can be drawn from other research on community areas (Kornblum, 1974; Molotch, 1972). Even in his 1929 work, Burgess' notes reveal that he was aware of this type of tiering of community areas, although he did not emphasize it in his published work and instead sought to define "self-sufficient" communities as relatively isolated, self-contained entities. It was the community, not the tier of communities, which captured his attention.

Most citizens have a similarly limited perspective on community organization: they can usually identify the parts to the tier of community areas but they do not perceive the tier itself. As a result, community groups become inconsistent and incoherent when they try to define the "right" or the "true" community. Jurisdictional disputes between community organizations abound, and there are persistent difficulties in deciding who should represent whom. The Civil Rights Movement, by its necessary focus on the spatially contained black ghetto, has moved ahead our limited awareness of the scale of the black community and its existence beyond the social bloc. Also, the War on Poverty, despite its excessive aspirations and administrative weaknesses, has dramatized the problematic definition of the local community and its scale of operation. The Local Control Movement seems to be even more widely based and a stubborn declaration of the need to face the division between the social bloc and its necessary involvement in the wider, metropolitan community.

The fundamental division between the very localized neighborhood or social bloc and the institutional linkages which draw the citizen into the metropolis represents a persistent and enlarged pattern. Under appropriate leadership and conditions, this division might become the dynamic by which competing interests are aggregated and brought to legitimate resolution while also preserving the accountability which is integral to the social bloc. Local demands are the launching platform for demands to intervene—to meddle, if you wish—in the affairs of other communities. In an articulated debate of this variety, it is always a two-way process, one in which narrowly based, often rather homogeneous residential groups get and give. This is so whether the issue is pollution, school finances, gun control, or public housing. However slowly, the popular debate pushes forward a broader geographic perspective on civic responsibility.

Yet, the contemporary popular debate about community participation has become unusually tardy and unproductive.[14] Much effort is wasted on what is the true community, and social policies are distorted by efforts to arbitrate among competing claims as if one or another community level were more genuine than another. Both local leaders and political aspirants are relieved of responsibility when public officials insist that their administrative districts take precedence over the territorial boundaries promoted by local residents or when the opposite occurs. Even more destructive is the shifting of political decisions from one level of the tier to another, so as to work a persistent bias against one faction or to avoid the aggregation of diverse interests in reaching a resolution that might be defended on the grounds that it is instrumental to the long-term welfare of the larger community. Stalemate and counter accusations of "conspiracy" are a common product. An "ecology of games" without any moral claim for the need for restraint or compromise in the interests of a larger collectivity is one way of portraying this outcome (Long, 1958).

Thus different proponents of the local community, as well as those who openly discount it, tend to embrace a common outlook, attributing both responsibility and power to a vaguely defined "they" who are outside the practical management of local affairs. As a result highly centralized authorities such as the Supreme Court or federal regulatory agencies are frequently called upon to adjudicate local disputes. The frequency of federal cases has grown rapidly and it has become a common practice to initiate community controversies with the hope that they will reach the higher courts or federal regulatory agencies.

But the federal courts and federal regulatory agencies have had only a most limited impact on disputes which continue to unsettle local communities. Federal directives on school busing, on public housing, on group living quarters, as well as local taxation, are examples of federal intervention which have resulted in continuing controversy and tension. Federal origination or intervention does not insure public acceptance. But it is also clear

14. Such a debate also tends to discredit the proponents of local community control and lead to Lowi's (1971: 65–80) conclusion that the local control movement is only an opportunistic effort to press narrowly based social interests.

that we have not made adequate provision for the effective development of local consultation and debate which might contribute to new solutions or at least give those proposed by the federal authorities the necessary legiti-macy.[15]

Both community leaders and those attempting to respond to them gen-erally operate with overly primitive notions about the nature of the local community. Typically they are locked into an inarticulate test of strength with the local community proclaiming its popular mandate, while central, governmental agencies issue formal directives and elaborate plans based on constitutional and legal authority. Neither demonstrates sufficient enlighten-ment about the potentials of parliamentary democracy, but they do demon-strate the need for a more differentiated conception of the local community and its potential capacity for assuming the burdens of a society that aims at high levels of participation and low levels of coercion. The initial step toward rational change is to identify the levels of the local community and to link each part of this tier to the functions and responsibilities of the public hierarchy which parallel it.

The social bloc or natural community is a persistent and ongoing struc-ture in American life. The social bloc itself is frequently represented or em-bedded in formal associations which link it to other social blocs and munici-pal agencies. These formal associations themselves are frequently combined into a web of inter-organizational relations whose natural boundary seems to be the metropolis itself. The first of these levels—the social bloc—arises primarily from the indigenous processes usually associated with the local community—propinquity, homogeneity, natural boundaries, and a diffuse pattern of interaction. The other two levels, however, are much more ob-viously instrumental efforts to link up local residential groups with the bu-reaucratic order of urban government and they are often initiated by govern-ment agencies specifically for this purpose (Taub, 1976). While each of these forms is relatively distinct and only partially coincides in the persons who participate in each, they seem to represent a growing division of labor in which there is considerable potential for coordination.

The social bloc is basic to the structure because it provides people with

15. Although the resolution shown by the federal government is clearly important in reconciling some communities, notably those in the South, to school desegregation, it is also clear that school desegregation has been accompanied by less friction where local community groups have been active in developing community acceptance as in Detroit and Charlotte.

a sense of joint responsibility and some measure of mutual control and access. Relations within it tend to be intimate and diffuse in character. The reciprocities which are expected within this territorial unit, however, tend to be limited and relatively uncontroversial—the informal supervision of one another's children or pets, taking in another's mail, driving someone to the hospital, or lending a cup of brandy—all the little emergencies that allow us to appeal to proximity as the cause for available kindness. The social bloc tends to be very homogeneous, or it is unstable. People simply move out once differences in ethnic, religious, or other primordial guarantees of trust become imperiled. It is also the level of community within which strong differences of opinion are difficult to broach lest they endanger the limited and diffuse consensus of the co-residents. Typically small and homogeneous, its demands on government tend to be fairly narrow and unmindful of the counterclaims of other social blocs and groups.[16]

For all these reasons the *social bloc* is not the appropriate unit for direct political debate or for formal negotiations with administrative hierarchies. Above all it needs to be given recognition as a natural unit with its own informal processes of developing leadership. One of the great shortcomings of the U.S. Census Bureau and other data-gathering agencies is that they have failed in their original responsibility to report reliably to such small areas on their social health, composition, and the impact of social programs. The failure to report on such areas diminishes the stability of their identity and reduces the likelihood that their leadership will be able to play a role in higher levels of community organization. For this reason the social bloc is most often left out in community-wide decisions and this leads to both a sense of estrangement on the part of its residents and an inability to call upon the natural leaders it produces. The leadership of the social bloc, however, is one of its most valued assets since it may have the ability to open up the channels of communication between it and other levels of community organizations. Indeed the distinctive feature of all the community levels we are

16. Obviously there are exceptions to this, particularly where the homogeneity of the social bloc remains uncontested and such areas grow to the point that they include an entire complement of social services—a school district, a political ward, or a historic enclave that is widely recognized, such as our "Chinatowns," "Little Italys," "Bohemias." It is our impression that such enlarged social blocs tend to be remnants of the old ethnic colonies, high-income inner-city areas, or satellite communities which have retained their identities despite suburbanization.

proposing here is not their self-contained unity, but their tendency to enlarge their ambitions and their membership.

It is the organizational community that typically makes a much more explicit bid to involve itself in controversies and to shape the delivery of municipal services. The organizational community may range from a very formal association which has an elected body of officers and staff and publicized procedures for participation to little more than a persistent group of "concerned citizens" who meet at the local school, church, or wherever they can find space. Although much of its leadership is voluntary and informally selected, the organizational community usually aspires to a name and to some limited presence in the form of a list of officers, mailing list, and flyers for publicity. The organizational community arises in part from the persistent effort of residents in the social bloc to involve themselves in a larger territorial framework and to enlist allies to shape or redirect the policies of local service agencies in their districts. But the organizational community is also often a response to external demands for "community representation" and its formation usually draws in additional leaders, especially advocates from welfare organizations, the church, and the school (Taub, 1976). Its natural tendency is to form around the district level delivery of services and to focus on episodic, "crisis" issues that afflict more than one social bloc. It is a purposeful organization, but its ability to mobilize concerted action still depends heavily upon broad support from its constituent social blocs and an informal consensus among its leaders.

The organizational community, however, is continually frustrated by the expanding scale of urban organization and the fragmentation of most municipal delivery systems. If the school district, local ward, police district, and other delivery units roughly coincide, efforts to influence the day-to-day operation of municipal agencies can be effective. But in most cities these delivery districts are badly fragmented (Hunter and Suttles, 1972) and this fragmentation has been accompanied by the growth of super districts— federal, state, and local—which makes decision making very remote from the organizational community. Thus, despite the ability of the organizational community to enjoin controversial issues and to develop a more instrumental leadership, its aims are frequently frustrated by an inability to reach the metropolitan-wide administration that increasingly makes policy for district level agencies.

It is to this changing scale of urban organization that Hunter (1974) attributes the growth in confederations of community organizations. This *aggregated metropolitan community* is obviously incompletely formed in our major cities, however, many of its distinctive features are apparent. It tends to have at least some full-time professional staff, to be able to publicize its own efforts and organization, and to acquire sufficient visibility to bring some municipal officials to the bargaining table. So far, such federations have tended to have a rather narrow focus on community-wide services like transportation, housing, or sewage disposal, which are organized on a regional basis. But the ability of these federations to catch the attention of the press and to dramatize gross malfunctions have given them considerable political leverage and they have been able to put together razor-thin majorities to authorize mass transportation in Chicago and to help elect the mayor of Gary, Indiana.

Nonetheless these federations seem to be weakened by their narrow focus on services which have a regional base. They are also weakened by the clash—exacerbated by different racial concentrations—between the interests of the inner city and those of the suburbs. Yet even here there are attempts, weak and fragile as they may be, to create some overarching level of community participation. The central issues which have promoted this suburban-city level of cooperation is the mangement of the transportation system because of the energy crisis and the rapidly growing costs of services in the suburbs. Obviously a metropolitan level of government would facilitate the expansion of effort by the aggregated metropolitan community.

It is our argument that these three levels represent the natural or functional division of labor in the search for community in parliamentary societies. Their importance lies not so much in their self-announced presence—although that element should be given due weight—but in their capacity to address the problems of accountability and the management of the new urban *oikonomus*. The issue is more than merely a matter of resolving competing interests, although that is essential. Rather the basis for this selective tier lies in its internal dynamic, the persistent efforts of the social bloc to reach outward through voluntary organizations to meet the administrative levels of the central city and the metropolis. In turn, the sense of participation and the more systematic debate permitted by this tier of community levels provides a responsible role for community groups. This role, then, not only makes them party to municipal decision-making, but reinforces their obligation to bear its costs as well as its benefits.

Certainly we do not mean in these comments to elaborate a structure through which the local community can be co-opted as a passive partner to existing administrative hierarchies. Taken together each of these community levels has real influence under even present circumstances and their aspirations seem to be well justified. Undoubtedly, each level is weakened by the complexity and haphazard contrivances of municipal agencies. The *social bloc* usually lacks any explicit form of recognition and is seldom systematically included in collective efforts to provide an account of its collective welfare. The organizational community is continually frustrated by the fragmentation of district level delivery systems and the rigidity of bureaucratized and unionized city services agencies. The *aggregated metropolitan community* faces the serious barrier of suburb-city separation and some of the same types of rigid bureaucratization. All of these community levels are overshadowed by the widespread tendency either to dismiss the community as a viable collectivity or to juxtapose its continued existence to that of centralized government. The missing element in the analysis of the local community remains the clarification of the scope and hierarchy of the territorial units appropriate in a differentiated conception of community responsibilities. If the local community is to contribute to citizen accountability and to citizen participation, however, it is obvious that two or more levels are necessary. Localism, in this view, is not provincialism, but potentially an incentive to cosmopolitanism—or, at least, metropolitanism.

Such a perspective gains weight when we consider the likely issues that will face out metropolitan centers over the next decade. The great spurt in economic growth that occurred in the post-World War II period seems to be drawing to a close. It would appear that a limited quantity of resources growing slowly must be divided among competing groups without much hope that a sudden increase will make it possible to satisfy all groups. The uneven pattern of urban growth, with the sunbelt increasing and the urban heartland declining or remaining stable, will exacerbate the friction of competing claims (Janowitz, 1976: 41–71). Leaders at all levels of the society must be prepared to offer only marginal gains in public services and expenditures. Acceptance of such appeals will not be forthcoming unless there is an articulate debate among the various interest groups and a more genuine appreciation of the realities of limited growth and how it affects people of diverse statuses. The community structure which we can dimly outline seems to have this capacity to internalize and balance the sacrifices and marginal gains that are possible. For this reason it seems especially important to us that sociologists recognize the vitality of local communities without romanticizing them or without discounting them as dying collectivities. Both folk images and the urge to publish "sociological news" tempt us to a revolutionary perspective in which the past is replaced by the future. By now, however, there are sufficient empirical findings to argue that social change is seldom so drastic and that the usual practice is for old social forms to adapt themselves to new, more inclusive social forms. Intellectual efforts to appreciate this sort of social adjustment are important, because a failure to perceive them may limit our alternatives and reduce the choices that are essential to a non-authoritarian or democratic management of public life.

Our intention, then, has been to draw attention to the tiering of community groups and their potential contribution to develop citizenship in a parliamentary democracy. In our view the local community is a multi-level structure which aggregates public opinions and makes available to the individual a realistic appreciation of the condition of others like and unlike himself. It mobilizes and balances contending claims and makes more evident the limits to which they can be pursued. Thus, in a society as diverse as the United States and one that depends so heavily upon self-regulation, the local community, is an essential structure if governmental actions are to be widely regarded as legitimate and the cooperation of most citizens is to be enlisted. The ability of the residents of the local community to internalize both the costs and benefits of public undertakings is vital where there are strong, contending interest groups and a limited consensus on national purposes. Even more important may be the local communities' ability to enlist people into the day-to-day responsibility of effectively monitoring one anothers behavior so that it subscribes to some rudimentary sense of collective responsibility. Many of the major tasks of citizen participation are quite primitive in the sense that they demand little more than a concert of individual actions: the maintenance of housing, the survelliance of children, the reporting of violence to the police, or the participation of people in voter registration drives. A large volume of social science research has shown that these are tasks which can best be effected between intimates in a context of continuing relations. It is becoming increasingly clear that the courts and bureaucratic authorities cannot dictate to people to accomplish these rudimentary but essential responsibilities. These failures of bureaucracy and administrative direction give increased weight to the essential role of the local community and its elaboration.

REFERENCES

Alinsky, Saul. 1971. *Rules for Radicals*. New York: Random House.
Arendt, Hannah. 1951. *The Origins of Totalitarianism*. New York: Harcourt, Brace.
Barsky, Stephen. 1974. "Representations of Community," Ph. D. Diss., University of Chicago.
Bish, Robert L. 1971. *The Public Economy of Metropolitan Areas*. Chicago: Markham.
Bish, Robert L., and Vincent Ostrum. 1973. *Understanding Urban Government: Metropolitan Reform Reconsidered*. Washington, D.C.: American Enterprise Institute for Public Policy Research.
Broder, David S. 1972. *The Party's Over*. New York: Harper.
Burgess, Ernest W. 1929. *Urban Areas of Chicago: An Experiment in Social Science Research*. Chicago: University of Chicago Press.
Campbell, Alan K., and Judith A. Dollenmayer. 1975. "Governance in a Metropolitan Society." In A. Hawley and V. Rock, eds., *Metropolitan America in Contemporary Perspective*, pp. 335–96. New York: Halsted.
Caro, Robert A. 1974. *The Power Broker*. New York: Knopf.
Cole, Stephan. 1975. "The Growth of Scientific Knowledge." In L. Coser, ed., *The Idea of Social Structure*, pp. 175–220. New York: Harcourt, Brace, Jovanovich.
Coleman, J., et al. 1966. *Equality of Educational Opportunity*. Washington, D.C.: U.S. Government Printing Office.
Committee for Economic Development. 1960. *Guiding Economic Growth*. New York: Committee for Economic Development.
——1970. *Reshaping Government in Metropolitan Areas*. New York: Committee for Economic Development.
Cooley, Charles H. 1902. *Human Nature and the Social Order*. New York: Scribners.
Coser, Lewis A. 1951. "Some Aspects of Societal Family Policy," *American Journal of Sociology*, 56:424–37.
Dewey, John. 1922. *Human Nature and Conduct*. New York: Holt.
Domhoff, G. William. 1971. *The Higher Circles*. New York: Random House.

Downs, Anthony. 1970. *Urban Problems and Prospects.* Chicago: Markham.

Glazer, Nathan, and Daniel Moynihan. 1963. *Beyond the Melting Pot.* Cambridge: Harvard-M.I.T. Press.

Gottdeiner, Mark. 1977. *Planned Sprawl.* Beverly Hills, Calif: Sage Publications.

Greer, Scott. 1962. *The Emerging City: Myth and Reality.* New York: Free Press.

Hawley, Amos H. 1971. *Urban Society.* New York: Ronald Press.

Hawley, Amos H. and Vincent P. Rock, eds. 1975. *Metropolitan American in Contemporary Perspective.* New York: Halsted.

Herberg, Will. 1955. *Protestant, Catholic, Jew.* Garden City, N.Y.: Doubleday.

Hunter, Albert. 1974. *Symbolic Communities: The Persistence of Change of Chicago's Local Communities.* Chicago: University of Chicago Press.

Hunter, Albert, and Gerald D. Suttles. 1972. "The Expanding Community of Limited Liability," pp. 44–81, in *The Social Construction of Communities.* Chicago: University of Chicago Press.

Janowitz, Morris. 1967. *The Community Press in an Urban Setting.* Second Edition. Chicago: University of Chicago Press.

—— 1975. "Sociological Theory and Social Control," *American Journal of Sociology,* 81:82–108.

—— 1976. *Social Control of the Welfare State.* New York: Elsevier.

Kain, John F. 1975. *Essays on Urban Spatial Structure.* Cambridge, Mass.: Ballinger.

Kasarda, John D. 1972. "The Impact of Suburban Population Growth on Central City Service Functions," *American Journal of Sociology,* 77:1111–24.

Kornblum, William. 1974. *Blue Collar Community.* Chicago: University of Chicago Press.

Kornhauser, W. 1959. *The Politics of Mass Society.* New York: Free Press.

Kuhn, Thomas S. 1962. *The Structure of Scientific Revolutions.* Chicago: University of Chicago Press.

Lasswell, Harold. 1958. *Who Gets What, When, and How.* New York: Meridian.

Logan, John. 1976. "Suburban Industrialization and Stratification," *American Journal of Sociology,* 82:333–48.

Long, Norton. 1958. "The Local Community as an Ecology of Games," *American Journal of Sociology,* 64:251–61.

Lowi, Theodore J. 1971. *The Politics of Disorder*. New York: Basic Books.

Marshall, Thomas H. 1964. *Class, Citizenship, and Social Development*. Garden City, N.Y.: Doubleday.

Mead, George Herbert. 1934. *Mind, Self, and Society*. Chicago: University of Chicago Press.

Molotch, Harvey Luskin. 1972. *Managed Integration*. Berkeley: University of California Press.

Nisbet, Robert A. 1953. *The Quest for Community: A Study in the Ethics of Order and Freedom*. New York: Oxford University Press.

——1962. *Community and Power*. London: Oxford University Press.

Ostrom, Vincent. 1974. *The Intellectual Crisis in American Public Administration*, University, Ala.: University of Alabama Press.

Schumpeter, Joseph A. 1942. *Capitalism, Socialism and Democracy*. New York: Harper.

Shils, Edward. 1957. "Primordial, Personal, Sacred, and Civil Ties," *British Journal of Sociology*, 8:130–45.

——1975. *Center and Periphery*, Chicago: University of Chicago Press.

Stein, Maurice. 1960. *The Eclipse of Community*. Princeton: Princeton University Press.

Steward, Julian H. 1955. *Theory of Culture Change*, Urbana: University of Illinois Press.

Suttles, Gerald D. 1968. *The Social Order of the Slum*, Chicago: University of Chicago Press.

——1975. "Community Design: The Search for Participation in a Metropolitan Society." In A. Hawley and V. Rock, eds., *Metropolitan American in Contemporary Perspective*, pp. 235–97. New York: Halsted.

Taub, Richard, George P. Surgeon, Sara Lindholm, Phyllis Betts Otti, and Amy Bridges. 1977. "Urban Voluntary Association, Locality Based and Externally Induced," *American Journal of Sociology*, 82:425–42.

Thomas, W. I., Robert E. Park, and Herbert A. Miller. 1921. *Old World Traits Transplanted*. New York: Knopf.

Warner, W. Lloyd. 1959. *The Living and the Dead*. New Haven: Yale University Press.

Webber, Melvin M. 1961. "Order in Diversity: Community Without Propinquity." In R. Gutman and D. Popenoe, eds., *Neighborhood, City and Metropolis*, pp. 792–811. New York: Random.

FIVE

Demystifying Organizations

CHARLES PERROW

IT IS A mystery why the many advances in organizational theory have not had an appreciable impact upon health service organizations. Wave on wave of sophisticated theory, from human relations techniques to the latest in contingency theory have been applied, proved to have a small effect in research studies, and virtually no effect in actual usage. They all *should* work, if we know anything at all about human behavior organizations. But none seem to work well. Why?

It seems possible that an extreme answer is worth pursuing—our theories are mystifications of reality and need to be demystified. The theories are mystifications because they are designed to disguise what I will claim are the real functions of organizations and to assert a counter reality. The reality being asserted in mainstream theory is that organizations are, or can be, rational instruments of announced goals. Of course some mainstream theories such as systems and human relations theories oppose a mechanical, rationalistic notion of organizations when they stress natural adaptations, human needs, informal groups, and so on. But these natural characteristics are perceived as constraints on the organization, as problems to be overcome, or opportunities to be utilized in making the organization more effective (rational) in achieving its legitimate, announced goals. The hospital should cure, the training program train, the prison reform, the welfare program help people to become independent. Deviations from these goals are due to such things as poor motivation, faulty communications, misperceived goals, poor coordination, inadequate resources, poor management, or faulty structures, according to most theories.

No doubt these play a role. But an alternative position is worth exploring: announced goals are one of the least important constraints on organizational behavior; organizations can be rational instruments of announced goals only to a very limited extent. They have more important things to do. Instead, organizations are resources for a variety of group interests within and without the organization; they are used by a multitude of interests, and the announced purposes, while they must be met to some limited degree in most cases, largely serve as legitimating device for these interests, or a mystification of the reality.

There is nothing novel in the view that organizations serve many functions; what may be novel is to take this view so seriously as to put it at the center of our theory, rather than leave it as a peripheral routine observation or qualifier while we vigorously explore the impact of technology on structure or leadership on productivity. To expose these uses and the low priority of legitimate goals is a part of the demystifying process. To stop there would merely be sophisticated muckraking. To complete the demystifying process means to present an alternative definition of organizations and explain how well-meaning people and institutions participate in the fiction of intended rationality in the service of official goals.

Demystification does not take place because of new knowledge or new insights—all that I will say has been said before, often by mainstream theorists, and most of it will not surprise you. But these observations in the literature are generally routine qualifications and disclaimers. Some are inserted at the beginning of our publications—"We will ignore X, though it obviously is important"; "the phenomenon of morale (or whatever) is, of course, complex, but we will use the concept of Professor Y as operationalized by Professor Z." Others come in at the end—"Together these explain 32 percent of the variation in the dependent variable; given the complexity of this phenomenon this is substantial, though, of course, there are numerous other influences at work." These disclaimers are part of the "fringe" of theory. Demystification takes place when we place them at the center, and push the notion of intendedly rational instruments of announced goals to the periphery.

We can also utilize another part of the fringe of theory—those notions that run counter to mainstream cosmologies. I am particularly intrigued by developments in cognitive psychology that question the validity of concepts such as personality, norms, and values; in ethnomethodology, which emphasizes the everyday construction of reality; and in radical and neo-Marxist theory which emphasizes the reproduction of divisions in society. Although I will not be able to bring these into this essay in any thorough way—I intend to in a planned volume, "A Society of Organizations"—some loose connections will be noted.

Since I am still very much a mainstream theorist, the reader should bear with me in the quite painful process of trying to think oneself out of a paradigm one has lived with, even contributed to. It is difficult to think that one's work on, say, goals or technology, while not wrong in any normal sense, is largely irrelevant in the face of notions that were dimly recognized but put aside.

First, I will examine the environment of human service organizations, then the participants, and finally those processes labled coordination, control, change, efficiency, and technology.

THE ENVIRONMENTAL USES

I will utilize a commonplace distinction between the functions of an organization and its goals. By functions I mean the actual services the organization performs for interested groups outside of the organization (we will examine functions for the members later). They may be consistent with the official goals, irrelevant to them, or in conflict with them. We can identify them by noting when, if these services were to be changed or challenged, significant sectors of the environment would protest in some effective way. "I couldn't do that; the X group would be on my neck," would be a typical indicator from an executive. For human service organizations (HSOs), it seems to be typical that (a) failure to supply unofficial benefits to the environment will be greatly resisted; (b) the large majority of these benefits are inconsistent with official goals and detract from their realization, but (c) the failure to meet official goals meets with very little resistance because the constituency is poorly organized and/or the goals themselves are recognized as unrealistic. (Peter Rossi, in his contribution to this volume, gives ample indication of the last problem here: we often do not know whether the "treatment" is effective; if effective whether it can be delivered; if it can be delivered, whether it will be delivered.)

Recent work in an area that touches on organizational theory—the labeling theory of deviance—has highlighted an important function of

HSOs, that of regulating the behavior of people that become classified as deviants, ostensibly in their own interests. At least three aspects of regulation are important. (1) HSOs seek to isolate "clients" from positions of potential influence by placing them in a dependent status where they must conform to survive. Were they not in job training programs, asylums, prisons, rehabilitation centers, summer work programs, on welfare rolls and the like, they might organize protests or disrupt the system individually. (2) Deviants are bought off by some of these programs through material aid. (3) HSOs (and other organizations) segregate deviants from our view so that their wretched state will not visibly affront us. I am not thinking only of leper colonies here, or of their modern equivalents, the nursing homes, nor even such obvious examples as mental hospitals, prisons, and reformatories, but of agencies for the blind, redlining programs of banks, urban renewal and interstate highway programs, welfare hotels, ghettos, and segregation practices in general. (A recent cartoon by Auth in the *Philadelphia Inquirer* shows two wealthy people in their highrise apartment. The wife looks sadly out at the steaming ghetto, below in the distance, while the indifferent husband says "The problem of the ghettos? The ghettos, my dear, are a solution, not a problem.")

(For a general statement of labeling theory see Scheff [1966]. For an interpretation of control and buying-off see Piven and Cloward [1971]. Although I find their position extreme and the evidence for their grand theory equivocal—see the critique of Muraskin [1975] and of Ryan [1977]—there is certainly some truth in their view. Regarding job training, see Perrow [1972: 32–47, 209–23]. The literature in this area is considerable and I do not claim to have mentioned the best or most representative pieces.)

Now in the course of regulating the behavior of deviants it is possible that they will be helped with advice, psychotherapy, training, protection from themselves and from each other, and with money. But these aides are *contingent* with their being forced to conform, being bought off to prevent protest, or their remaining hidden. The latter functions are essential; the aid the deviants get is not essential and may be quite small or even nonexistent. When the poor receive welfare checks but still show themselves in middle-class hospitals, middle-class shopping or recreational areas, like any other person, or if they show themselves in marches or protests outside of the slums, there is a feeling that something is wrong with the system because they still look poor (deviant) and are still visible.

The implication of this view that I wish to draw out is not that society is mean or capitalism exploitative, or that organizations are poorly functioning and their goals are displaced. All that may be true. But the important point for organizational theory is that it is on the basis of the regulatory functions that organizations are judged, not their announced service goals. Wardens are not fired for not rehabilitating prisoners; psychiatric administrators or therapists for not curing the insane; welfare administrators for not getting people to work or mending broken homes or raising their allotments. The criteria is more likely to be "how many people did you regulate at what cost per person." The effective administrator knows that failure to meet announced goals will not mean his or her demise, and certainly not the demise of the organization. But failure to control, buy off, or segregate his or her charges will bring trouble. Furthermore, the administrator knows that announced goals are hard to achieve, because of poor technologies, poor organizational structure, inadequate training facilities, low quality employees, inadequate budgets, or recalcitrant charges. Therefore, it is not worth much effort to attempt to achieve them; no one really expects much. He or she will be interested in improvements that make life easier or more predictable for the staff, or that increase the degree of regulation, if that is called for. But the announced service goals are primarily legitimating devices for regulation and serve their purpose even if unmet.

A second function of HSOs is to absorb a part of the work force of the nation. It is not a function that organizational theory recognizes and takes into account, although certainly it is on the minds of politicians and government officials at all levels. It is quite clear that the private sector of business and industry cannot absorb the daily increases in those seeking employment; all firms prefer to maximize capital and minimize labor, and our tax laws favor that. Thus, the public sector has been forced to grow rapidly to absorb the worthy job seekers. Presumably, at some time there will be what James O'Conner (1973) calls the fiscal crisis of the state that will force elites to confront this inherent dilemma of advanced capitalism. The growing role of for-profit firms in the public sector (the "welfare-industrial complex") will ease the crisis somewhat, but the public sector must continue to grow. To do this, we need public facilities that employ a lot of people. Using public funds, we train large numbers of people to be clerks, social workers, psychiatrists, judges, hospital administrators, and so on.

The emerging field of organization-environment relations is silent on this function, but one example should indicate its importance. It would be a disaster for New York City if the public welfare department found some social scientist who could simplify and reorganize that mess so that half of the twenty to thirty thousand employees could be laid off. Large amounts of federal and state funds would be lost, the retail economy would suffer, and large numbers of generally vocal and politically mobilizable people would be protesting the lack of jobs. It would be as if the Man in the White Suit, having invented an indestructible garment, sought the capital to produce the garment from cotton growers, textile firms, and retail clothing stores. Inefficient public organizations have always been a part of a continuing war on poverty and will continue to be so. Current proposals to subsidize labor intensive firms in the private sector to discourage the substitution of capital for labor indicates how severe the problem is.

A third function of HSOs that is not placed at the center of organizational theories is the most important: to provide resources for other organizations. These resources are provided at the public expense but are not calculated as such in the balance sheets. They also have the advantage of being easily accessed, have little accountability in their use, and much flexibility to meet changing situations. Lloyd Ohlin (1960) drew attention to this some years ago in a piece about the environment of HSOs. In one example, he described the attempt of an economy minded executive to close down a quarry that was losing money for the prison. But the quarry, worked by the prison, provided free construction materials for private firms in the area, and so it was kept. The example could be multiplied a thousand times. The Mafia is reportedly well into the New York school system, which purchases hundreds of millions each year in supplies and contracted services and has been under no realistic constraint to save money; the hospital equipment industry and supply industry, not to speak of the drug companies, could not survive without extravagant waste, duplication, and inefficiency in hospitals; land holders and real estate firms have enjoyed considerable largess through New York City's poverty programs and day care centers with twenty-year leases at several times the market value; the political system evades civil service regulations to staff HSOs, and sometimes extracts kickbacks and campaign contributions; a substantial number of legitimate organizations benefit from police corruption and inefficiency; private employees found the agencies serving the handicapped a convenient reservoir that they could dip into in times of labor shortages and then could discharge the handicapped back to the agencies in times of labor surplus, thus smoothing production and retaining their normal workers; job training programs proved to be a bonanza to private employers, the more so the more inefficient the programs were, and so on and on. I recommend this as a central topic for those studying interorganizational relations. To my knowledge, it has not been accorded more than a footnote in the major statements.

The message here is not that private business, politicians, and so on are corrupt and indifferent to the needs of the poor and the stigmatized, or that agency executives should have more guts. As true as that might be, it tells us little about organizations. What these examples do tell us about public organizations is that they must be viewed as resources for other groups, groups with more well organized and powerful members or constituencies. If this view is moved to the center of organizational theory, rather than being a footnote offering some unknown degree of qualification to all that follows in the study, then variations in efficiency or official goal achievement can be moved to the periphery. The footnote would then read: "Of course there are some variations in performance depending upon leadership techniques, the fit between technology and structure, innovations in technologies, number of shared programs or telephone contacts between organizations, and so on. But these are quite minor and we need not spend much time studying them. The way the organization is used by other interests is much more important for understanding internal efficiency or organizational networks."

HSOs are created at public expense (or in the case of private ones, with significant tax benefits for the organizations and the donors which amounts to a public subsidy). Once created they can be used by a variety of groups. Executives prosper in proportion to this use, not in proportion to service to clients. The use value may well be inversely correlated with efficiency or achievement of official goals. Use value increases as the organization is more accessible to outside interests, has little performance accounting, and is flexible enough to change its operations to generate valuable usages. Mainstream theory emphasizes organizational autonomy, credibility, and clear direction as values. But they are not values the organization should maximize in the demystified view. Dependency, duplicity, and opportunism are more appropriate. Mainstream theory seems to have stood the priorities on their heads, mystifying organizations.

Let me emphasize again that I am not taking a muckraking line and talking about particularly corrupt sectors of society which might be cleaned up in some fashion. Organized crime is, by definition, corrupt. But the drug companies, supply companies, medical profession, legal profession, large firms such as Litton Industries and banks such as Chase Manhattan are not, by definition anyway, corrupt. They are, on the whole, rather public-regarding, some even politically moderate parts of the whole system. It is because they are doing what they are supposed to do in our system that they find HSOs useful. We have a society of organizations and this means that the interpenetration of organizations is much more dense, self-sustaining, and gratifying than it has ever been in the past. There are few resources other than other organizations. HSOs are relatively powerless, and thus are particularly attractive resources for more powerful and well organized groups or organizations, but the point is also easily applied to the private sector. Most discussions of goals, effectiveness, and so on do not place this observation at the center of their enquiry.

But on the other hand, one might reply, these organizations do cure the ill, succor the disturbed, deter the criminal, and sometimes make life somewhat easier for the poor, the retarded, and the maimed. Of course they do. It is one of their many outputs. It is a constraint upon the use of these organizations by other organizations that these public-regarding service goals cannot be completely neglected. But it is also a constraint upon the service goals of HSOs that outside interests can't be neglected. I think the conventional phrase, multiple goals, does not capture this reality at all. I prefer the phrase multiple usages, and I would stress the adjective "multiple." There are many more usages than conventional theory will admit. Each group's usage is a constraint on each other group; in such a situation, power—group power—is likely to play an important role. Organizational theory is shy of the word power, preferring to mystify it by calling it authority, but it should be one of the key words in the perspective I am trying to develop.

THE INTERNAL USES

Turning inward, what do we find? First let us examine the leaders of the organization, those "fulminators of purpose" as Chester Barnard was wont to call them. Their objectives are many, and in the case of HSOs, meeting official goals is likely to be rather far down on the list. First, as Yuchtman and Seashore (1967) point out, a crucial objective of the executive is to exploit the environment as much as possible to secure resources.

They do not draw out the rapacious implications of this in their famous article, but the implications are clear. It is more important to get funding, elite support, elimination of competitors, favorable contracts with suppliers, favorable contracts with unions, or low wage scales for employees, than to provide services. If there is a conflict between the two—securing resources and providing services—the first must take precedence. As Scott (1967a and b) notes in his well-known pieces on agencies for the blind, the need is greatest for the unattractive blind—the 80 percent or so who are old, handicapped, black, female, or whatever—but the source of funding and elite support comes from servicing the attractive blind—the children and the presumably employable. (Although as he also points out, to find them employment is to lose them as fund-raising resources, so an ideology is developed that they do better in the sheltered workshops than outside.) These are oft-cited research articles, but Scott's (1967) work is treated as an extreme case, and not used to illuminate all organizations. Yuchtman and Seashore (1967) are a footnote in the endless debate about goals. (It is only occasionally noted that public service organizations especially should seek to use as few as possible of the precious resources available to them to do their job, rather than be judged on their ability to get and consume.) We need a theory of organizations that puts these observations in a central place, for all organizations, not as curios.

Can they be generalized? I certainly think so. The successful executive is judged on the basis of the growth of her or his organization, the size of the budget, the contacts with elites, the accomodations it has with other powerful organizations, and the number of programs it has. We admit that it is very hard to measure the effectiveness of the programs, or the quality of the care; but it is easy to measure size and even clout. The executive knows this also. Why should she or he not act accordingly?

Another objective of the executive is to conform to the expectations of the environment of organizations and class relations. As Warren, Rose, and Bergunder (1974) try to demonstrate (it is a point that, by its very nature, is extremely difficult to demonstrate), the problem the organization is mandated to deal with, and the methods of dealing with it, are formulated on the basis of elite consensus about how the system should work. Poverty is the responsibility of the poor; deviant behavior is defined as such by elites even if the deviants do not see it as deviant; solutions must come from help to the poor, rather than a restructuring of society, and so on. It would not do for the executive of an agency that purportedly is helping the poor to seek a massive redistribution of wealth in the community by taxing the rich heavily and giving it to the poor, or cutting the salaries of highly paid officials and using the money to create jobs for the poor, in, say, renovating slum housing; to investigate inefficiency and corruption in other agencies so that they might give more help; or organize the poor into an effective political force that would remove elected officials or even restructure the government. These are all possible solutions to the problem, but they would not conform to the expectations of the present system. Thus, solutions, such as they are, must not disturb the system, even if the system might help cause the problem. The sensible executives know this quite well; indeed, so well that they often are not aware that they know it.

Another objective is to maintain internal stability in his or her organization. There should be no conflicts that might get outside of the organization and into the press, or to overhead agencies. There should be a reasonable degree of rectitude so that scandals do not embarrass legislators, mayors, boards, and the like. Note that the scandal is not bad because it shows that official goals are not being achieved; studies showing that abound, but do not cause embarrassment, because everyone knows that problems are complex, clients recalcitrant, and so on. Scandals are bad because they unmask some of the uses to which the organization can be put. We as social scientists participate in the gentle conspiracy of pretending that organizations are designed to achieve legitimate goals and are funded for that purpose. Were we to say too openly that organizations are not designed for that to any greater extent than they are designed to make life easier for executives and management, other organizations, and various elites, we would be turning the exception (the scandal) into rule, and all legitimacy would be lost. This is perhaps why the endless uncovering of scandals in big cities like Chicago and New York and big organizations such as General Electric, Gulf Oil, the Pentagon, or the FDA causes so little change. Too many important people use too many organizations to allow our view of them to change. Public officials had been told of the nursing home scandals for about ten years, but did nothing beyond an occasional study commission, which in turn did nothing but make recommendations. When political fortunes could be made by using the unsavory aspects of the industry—another use of organizations—the scandals became headlines. But even that is not likely to change things. So, the executive must beware of scandals, but she or he may well survive them; the organization, at any rate, will. The Penn-Central survives in another form.

In all this, then, the usual functions of the executive that we find in organization texts, management programs, social work schools, and so on, loom rather small. It does not take a great deal of "organizational skill," in the sense of ability to plan ahead, formulate goals, make wise decisions on technical matters, summon the energies of the staff, and so on to be a successful executive. Perhaps you have noticed that many of them do not seem to be too bright, or energetic, or dynamic, or considerate. But it does take consummate political skills in extracting resources from a sometimes stingy environment, delivering goods to interested parties without having scandals, and meeting at a minimal level—the going rate for the locality—the official goals of the agency. But even this is too rationalistic a view; later I will argue that much of this success is due to sheer luck and accident.

Turning now to managers and workers in the organization, mainstream theory tells us they must be motivated, informed of the goals, shown their part in the process, properly trained, rewarded, and punished. Our surveys test their understanding or commitment to the goals of the organization.

Were we to take seriously some of the marginal or incidental observations about employees, we might have a survey that would ask: the extent to which they support their superiors in covering up scandals, conform to political directives, service suppliers and others that make use of the organization, falsify records in subtle ways, and generally behave as loyal vassals of the executive irrespective of official directives or goals. We should also ask, not "how is your morale," or how satisfied are you with professional advancement opportunities, but can you minimize the personal costs of working in this place; can you manage to make the work fairly light; can you avoid unpleasant duties or clients; can you find time for relaxing conversation with friendly co-workers; can you exercise some of the skills or knowledge you laboriously picked up so as to make it seem worthwhile and give you some sense of control over your work; can you daydream and withdraw if you feel like it; can you manage to pick up office supplies or food from the kitchen or pieces of furniture for your own use; does the organization provide good cheap lunch facilities, recreation center, a retirement plan, credit union, counseling services, and so on? Can you get your friend or relative a job here? Most important of all, can you be sure of having a job here as long as you need it?

Such an "employee commitment," "employee motivation," "participation scale," or whatever would be unthinkable in the normal survey. As I
have noted elsewhere, high morale means that people find it gratifying to do
what the organization wants them to do, not what they want to do (Perrow,
1977). But there are enough good ethnographic accounts of organizations, to
suggest that the goals of the organization, or efficiency, effectiveness, uni-
versalism, and so on are not what is on the workers mind. Or the minds of
most managers. Why do we not have such a scale? Because, despite our
asides, we do not take seriously the notion that employees too use the organization. We assume they are a part of it, or are it, and therefore, if organizations have goals, they must share them. If they don't, it is a pathology and
should be corrected. But it is not a pathology. It is a fundamental characteristic of organizations that employees too use them for their own ends. Why
should they act differently from other groups?

Of course, executives, and superiors in general, do a great deal either
to minimize this usage or to find some way to make sure that the ends of the
employees and their own ends coincide. There may not be a great deal of
conflict if we recall that executives are not particularly weighed down by a
commitment to the official goals, so common ground can be found wherein
employee comfort and security is not too inconsistent with survival and a
little growth. Where there is conflict between the uses to which the employees wish to put the organization and those the executive wishes—and
there will be some—the executive does his best to manipulate, threaten, and
punish. She or he can manipulate more effectively than she or he can punish
or threaten. Civil service regulations (and political patronage positions
where there is no effective civil service) effectively remove the threat of dismissal for cause. The lack of power the executive has over the daily running
of the organization, of which we will speak shortly, makes threats of poorer
jobs, harder work, no raises, no promotions, and so on fairly ineffective.
Anger—direct, personal anger and hostility—is the best she or he can do,
and while it works for a while, as with one's children, it invites retaliation
and loses its effect after a time.

Note in all this that performance indicators, the structure of authority,
the difference between routine and non-routine technologies, Theory X and
Theory Y, and so on, play no role. They have some effect, of course; let us
assume they account for up to 20 percent of the variance. But why develop
theories that deal with that amount of variance and keep on the margins

perspectives that might account for three times as much? Ah, we might say, we can do little about the political environment or human nature, but something about structure, leadership, planning, coordination, delegation, standardization, and so on. These are key terms in mainstream theory. What might we perversely say about them?

A curious convergence of Marxist and ethnomethodological theory would tell us to beware of putting much weight on these terms. A standard qualifier of mainstream theory would also have that effect if it were taken seriously. The qualifier is that organizations are ever-changing, dynamic, even living things. The Marxist and the ethnomethodologists would remind us that people create their own reality and that what we see as structure is only the trace of past movement, but is continually changing because people have to affirm it, act it out, and they never do so in the same way. We can go further, and draw upon people like Karl Weick (1969) and James March and Johan Olson (1976), who note that situations are inherently ambiguous, decisions are made with highly imperfect knowledge, motives are unclear, effects of actions are unpredictable. Planning is more or less an illusion in this view, an imaginative reconstruction of the past, so that we forecast and plan for the future in ways that are most convenient for justifying the present. "Life," the novelist says, "is something that happens to us when we are busy making other plans."

It gets worse. According to Weick (1969), the deed is father to the thought; that is, motives, values, ideologies, and so on stem from actions, not the other way around. This is consistent with arguments in cognitive psychology that question the usefulness of the constructs "personality," "values," and "norms," and consistent with some brands of operant conditioning theory. Add to these developments, the emerging notions about systems—organisms differentiate in highly stable environments, not turbulent reactive ones, and become simpler in turbulent ones; successful systems are those that are loosely coupled overall, with weak ties binding reactive tightly coupled sub parts—and our rationalistic theories of organizational behavior, and even our human relations modifications, are greatly misleading.

Why do we have these rational theories and humanistic codes? Because of a passion for giving accounts, for believing in order, for justifying behavior, for escaping the actual turbulence of social systems that are created anew each moment by all actors in the system.

But if all actors are powerful, what happens to notions of "they"—the elites, executives, or of power in organizations, and so on? The answer seems to be that elites simply have more resources and thus more power than others. But they are to a large extent also victims of the world they and others have created and are unable to achieve even a moderate degree of effectiveness in realizing their goals. They have an edge and are more effective than non-elites, but it gives them considerable trouble to get their way, even in part. In a complex, post-industrial society, that may be all that is allowed them. Furthermore, the non elites, and especially the working class and the poor and the minorities, are no better and a bit worse at establishing what their own priorities should be, formulating their own goals, and realizing their own inherent powers in the system. Much of what they get may come as a result of accident. They too are subject to random events, unpredictable collisions of poorly articulated subsystems, only more so than the elites.

Thus, in this view, we should expect little out of our Human Service Organizations. In a society of organizations, they are part of the resources of other organizations, of elites, and of employees, and the complexity, uncertainty, and ambiguity of all organizations are visited on them at least at full measure. Only minimal functioning, in terms of our extravagant expectations, is to be expected. As users, we are all prone to ask all organizations to be more goal oriented (to our own goals), efficient (for us, in terms of the resources we put in) and rational (in terms of our own interests only) than they can ever be. Thus, organizational reform is transitory even if not misdirected. The State Department, Warwick (1975) tells us, eliminated several "superfluous" levels and specialized units and decentralized; a few years later all the levels and units had mysteriously appeared again. He notes that the bureaucrats need bureaus, even as they inveigh against bureaucracy.

The executive who finds social science theory unrealistic is correct. Explaining a tiring day to his wife or his sociologist, he stresses the enormous complexity and unpredictability of his organization, its uniqueness, the role of individual peculiarities, its ability to exasperate and veer off in unpredictable directions, and he is correct in his own constructed world. We press him and he offers to us explanations we consider simplistic—people are like that; individuals make a big difference; leadership counts, or dedication, hard work, intelligence, or loyalty, or whatever. We find these things elusive or impossible to measure, or commonplace, and offer him alternative concepts we have taken decades to formulate. We test them, constructing measures which are largely self-confirming, predicting relationships that are nearly tautological (group cohesiveness is associated with value homopholy, for example), and still find that when we move beyond a small sample that the variance our loaded dice explains is still only 20 percent. Worse still, we are gratified by this result, even though our conclusions are largely irrelevant to the executive. (Perhaps it is well that we do not work for the worker or the poor; our conclusions would be even worse for them.) We have constructed our own social reality, and are wounded when men of practical affairs don't recognize it, and won't use it. They are correct not to use it. We are just one other group trying to use a multi-use collectivity, getting paid to do so, and building our careers on it.

Is all this a counsel of despair? It certainly is in terms of our usual expectations as citizens, and certainly in view of our advertisements for ourselves as craftsmen and our use of public funds for research and consultation. But suppose we took the periphery seriously and placed it at the center. We then would ask, not why nothing works, but why anything works. Why have the elites not walked away with everything, instead of just a good deal more than the non-elites? Why do people in institutions get any care at all? Why do we have public-regarding foundations? Why don't we just shoot juvenile offenders instead of allowing them to live so that most of them will become adult nonoffenders? True, the poor suffer more from juveniles when they are offending than the rich suffer, but they are still of some inconvenience to the rich. Why do we have retirement programs, dental plans, fair employment laws, and so on?

We might, in discovering the answers to these questions, discover a capacity for constructing social structures that we have taken for granted, and thus little explored. As we did make that discovery, we could explore that capacity more and think of ways to increase it manyfold. What is problematic for mainstream theory is the best way of organizing to meet official goals—what kind of leadership, structure, communication, training, and so on. If we took for granted that official goals were not that important, only one constraint among many, and a weak one at that, and that the organizational variables should be seen as constructions to mask what was really going on, then we might better find out why anything at all is achieved. As we do that, we are free from our own constructions, and can ask ''how might it otherwise be done?''

I can't even phrase that last question well enough to direct my inquiry as yet. It will take me a very long time to get out of the box I have so willingly let myself into and worked so long in trying to tidy up. If many of us tried to redirect our inquiry, we might really have a paradigm shift in organizational theory.

REFERENCES

March, James and Johan Olson. 1976. *Ambiguity and Choice in Organizations*. Bergen: Universitetsforlaget.

Muraskin, William. 1975. "Review of Piven and Cloward," *Contemporary Sociology* (November), 4:607–13.

O'Conner, James. 1973. *The Fiscal Crisis of the State*. New York: St. Martin's Press.

Ohlin, Lloyd. 1960. "Conflicting Interests in Correctional Objectives." In R. Cloward et al., eds., *Theoretical Studies in the Social Organization of the Prison*, pp. 111–29. New York: Social Science Research Council.

Perrow, Charles. 1972. *The Radical Attack on Business*. New York: Harcourt, Brace, Jovanovich.

—— 1977. "Three Types of Effectiveness Studies." In Paul S. Goodman, Johannes M. Pennings, and Associates, *New Perspectives on Organizational Effectiveness*. San Francisco: Jossey-Bass. pp. 96–105.

Piven, Frances Fox and Richard A. Cloward. 1971. *Regulating the Poor*. New York: Random.

Ryan, Michael. 1977. "Mass Movements, Political-Institutional Strategy, and American Welfare Institutions: 1950–1972." Sociology Department, State University of New York at Stony Brook. Mimeo.

Scheff, Thomas. 1966. *Being Mentally Ill: A Sociological Theory*. Chicago: Aldine.

Scott, Richard. 1967a. "The Factory as a Social Service Organization," *Social Problems*, 14:160–75.

—— 1967b. "The Selection of Clients by Social Welfare Agencies: The Case of the Blind," *Social Problems*, 14:248–67.

Strauss, Anselm, et al. 1964. *Psychiatric Ideologies and Institutions*. New York: Free Press.

Warren, Roland, Steven Rose, and Ann Bergunder. 1974. *The Structure of Urban Reform*. Lexington, Mass.: D. C. Heath.

Warwick, Donald P. 1975. *A Theory of Public Bureaucracy*. Cambridge: Harvard University Press.

Weick, Karl E. 1969. *The Social Psychology of Organizing*. Reading, Mass.: Addison-Wesley.

Yuchtman, Ephraim and Stanley Seashore. 1967. "A Resource Approach to Organizational Effectiveness," *American Sociological Review*, 32:891–903.

II   THE MICRO LEVEL

SIX

Organizational Constructs and Mega Bureaucracy

EUGENE LITWAK

IN THIS paper an attempt will be made to outline the basic propositions of organizational theory that have emerged over the last twenty years.[1] This theory will be referred to as the multi-model contingency theory. It rests on the assertion that different organizational structures are most effective for different organizational goals. In addition, it provides a few basic dimensions that enable students of organization to classify a very large number of organizational structures and goals. It suggests that such seemingly diverse schemes or organizational analyses as Perrow's (1967), which rests on technology, Thompson's (1967), which stresses interdependencies, Blau's (1970), which emphasizes size, and Etzioni's (1969a), which stresses compliance structures, share in common the idea that different structures are best for different tasks, and that tasks are defined in terms of contingencies.

Major attention will be given to stating the underlying logic and the propositions of the multi-model contingency theory. Limits of space permit only a brief statement as to why the seemingly diverse theories indicated above really share the same framework.

MONOCRATIC BUREAUCRACY

To highlight the theoretical argument, I shall first discuss one of the major single model theories of organization: that which Weber (1947) re-

1. I should like to express my appreciation to Cecilia Falbe for her comments on this paper, although she cannot be held responsible for the statements herein.

ferred to as the monocratic bureaucracy. Next, the other major single model theory called the "Human Relations" structure will be discussed (Whyte, 1956). Given these extremes, the multi-model theory of organizational structure will be developed.

LOGIC OF EFFECTIVENESS—TECHNICAL KNOWLEDGE AND ECONOMIES OF LARGE SCALE

Weber's monocratic bureaucracy was presumed by him to be the most effective form of organizational structure in a market economy, because it maximizes the use of technical knowledge and large scale resources. The monocratic bureaucracy permits the development of knowledge through specialization. This process operates in any one of the following ways. By narrowing the scope of activity an individual undertakes, the individual can become more proficient in that activity than those who have to deal with many different activities. This is the logic which says a thoracic surgeon who performs cardiac surgery on 100 patients a year will be more knowledgeable and proficient than the general surgeon who performs such surgery only five times a year.

Sometimes specialization leads to economies of large scale but not necessarily to increased knowledge. For instance, by breaking a complex task down into many components it may be possible for each component to be handled with greater speed and accuracy. This is the assumption of the assembly line. This form of specialization often leads to replacement of people by machinery that requires highly technical knowledge to design and build. It should be noted that with the concept of detailed specialization suggested by Weber, there is an assumption of large size. Thus, if a task has 100 components and each is specialized, then at least 100 people are required as well as a sufficient volume of work to support this labor force.

Weber, in his analysis, also points to another dimension of monocratic bureaucracy that encourages technical expertise. He suggests that organizations appoint, promote, and fire people on the basis of merit, that is, their demonstrated ability to perform the given tasks.

COORDINATION OF LARGE GROUPS

Once the organization utilizes detailed specialization it is confronted with the problem of coordination. How does one insure that the right specialist will be at the right place at the right time? In Social Security, if one person establishes the eligibility of the client and another maintains that information on records, and a third collects funds from the employers and employees, a fourth checks for fraud, and a fifth banks the money, how are we to insure coordination of all the tasks so that the proper person receives the correct amount at the right time?

If Social Security consisted of only a handful of people, five or six, and they lived in the same community, the answer would be simple. They would just get together every time a payment had to be made and decide if the person were still eligible. However, if the Social Security system consists of thousands of employees and has several million recipients, then it is difficult, if not impossible, for them to get together every time they have to make a report. The question arises, what alternatives are there to face-to-face meetings? The three basic alternatives that most people consider are: 1) use rules for coordination; 2) internalize the goals of the organization in all members; and 3) delegate the task of coordination to a few.

The rationalistic organization uses a combination of the first and third procedures. It suggests that the bulk of tasks be coordinated by rules. Implicit is the assumption that the bulk of the tasks involve repetitive and continuous decisions. In its most extreme form, a machine operator in a plant turning out an order of 100,000 quarter-inch bolts is making a decision each time he makes an individual bolt—that is, 100,000 decisions. If he had to stop each time he made a bolt to have a meeting with the total factory, or if he had to stop each time to consult the head of his factory, it would clearly be time-consuming. By contrast, if he has a work order (a written rule) which states that he is to turn out 100,000 bolts, he could work continuously with occasional glances at the work order.

The option to internalize policy and have each person make his own decision based on a common policy has one drawback. Weber implies that internalization is often a difficult and slow process. It assumes that people are motivated by normative identification with the organization. If there is a rapid and continuous shift in tasks of the organization, management is faced with a costly resocialization process. For example, in Social Security a very precise amount of money must be paid to a very specific person, for a very specific time. However, there are constant changes in these details. A change in the law may change the amount paid; a death of a spouse may alter the payment; a change in technology may produce a different check-writing machine that alters the form of the check; a change in legislation may permit direct mailing of the check to the banks. If coordination is being managed through normative incentive, that is, internalization, then each aspect of coordination must be internalized. That is, the amount paid, the check-writing machines, the mailing of the check to the client, and the division of labor, would be considered as highly valued (that is, sacred) objects. Insofar as these details change continuously it would call for continuous resocialization for the entire labor force—a costly and very slow process.

As a consequence of reasoning of this kind, Weber suggested that the majority of activities and the majority of the labor force not be coordinated by normative modes (that is, internalization). Rules were the ideal way of coordinating most of the behavior in organizations. Weber suggested that, in addition to rules, a need for hierarchy as a coordinating device exists. Rules could not be used in situations that were unpredictable. How would one write rules about an event that is unknown? The entire staff cannot meet to make decisions where it is large or geographically scattered, and decisions must be made quickly. The only possibility in such a situation is delegation of the authority to make decisions. A number of assumptions are made with this argument. One is that the persons at the top are making the decisions with organizational goals clearly in mind. A second is that they have as much, and, it is hoped, greater, knowledge for making such decisions than others in the organization.

It is not necessary that the person at the top make all decisions in the organization or be the most knowledgeable about all aspects of the organization. Many decisions in the organization might involve only the worker in his job and have no implications beyond that level. Still other decisions might involve two units but not the rest of the organization. For all these decisions, someone on the lower level might be more knowledgeable and might make the decision without reducing effective coordination. A chemist working in a laboratory of the Ford Motor Company may to a large extent determine which experiment will be run, the nature of chemicals used, and the chemical implications of the results. In such matters the chemist is far more knowledgeable than the heads of the company. Insofar as these decisions do not significantly affect other units, there is no negative consequence to coordination in having these decisions made at a "lower" level.

I emphasize these points because it should be understood that the head of the organization in a rationalistic bureaucracy neither makes most of the decisions nor is the best educated man in terms of college degrees in the organization. This is sometimes implied by students of organizational theory (Etzioni, 1969b). Researchers who try to measure hierarchy by asking staff who makes decisions on their job might reach erroneous conclusions if they assume they are measuring hierarchy in rationalistic structures. Such questions would have to differentiate clearly between decisions that affect the entire organization versus those that refer specifically to a given position.

The above justification for hierarchy assumes a very large organization. If the organization consisted of only five to ten people, then it would be reasonable to convene the total group to make decisions.

MOTIVATION

Thus far Weber's formulation suggests how one can organize work to maximize and coordinate knowledge. The question remains: how does one motivate people to work for organizational goals? Weber deals with this issue in two ways. First, an individual's personal goals should be prevented from interfering with organizational goals. In a normal everyday interaction between two or more individuals, likes and dislikes will arise. Such likes and dislikes in a work situation will often lead individuals to evaluate others on the basis of their interpersonal attractiveness rather than work performance. To try to prevent such irrelevant evaluations, Weber argued that bureaucracies should stress impersonal ties among staff members.

Still another way in which personal goals may interfere with organizational ones is through those at the top of the hierarchy, who use their positions of authority for personal gain at the expense of the organization. To prevent this, Weber suggested that organizations must have strictly delimited a priori rights and duties. Thus hierarchy in the rationalistic organization is not unlimited but is exercised only in certain work areas. The organization may have rules that state it is wrong for the head of Social Security, who is not an auditor, to insist on auditing procedures that violate those recommended by the professional auditor. The head of a business corporation may be prevented by organizational rules from requesting work by his employees on his house as a condition of promotion. It is the imposition of these limits on authority and the distinction between work and non-work situations that clearly differentiate the monocratic hierarchy from the authoritarian hierarchy. In designing research on organizations it is therefore necessary not only to measure hierarchy, but also to measure the extent to which that hierarchy has a priori delimitations.

There are a series of implications which evolve from the notion that rights and duties are a priori delimited.. One is that individuals who are subordinates must have some procedures for appealing violations of the rules. Such procedures may be internal to the organizations—like the Army's Office of Inspector General or the Social Security appeals procedures. On the other hand they may be external, such as the ability of women and blacks to take their cases to human rights commissions and the courts if they feel they have been discriminated against on the job. An even more general case in point is the use of unions to act as external appeals procedure with the threat of strike the ultimate mechanism to enforce employees' views. Any measure of organizational delimitation of rights and duties should include some measure of appeal procedures for enforcing these rights and duties (Michels, 1949; Lipset, Trow, Coleman, 1956).

On the more positive side of human motivation, Weber argues for what Etzioni (1969b) calls instrumental rewards. However, he further specifies that these instrumental forms of compliance must be monetary ones in a society dominated by a market economy. In such a society money is a generalized means to most goals. By paying people money, one can insure that they will reach their goals without having to know these goals. This capacity to reward without knowledge of specific goals is important. It permits the organization to maintain a separation between the personal life of the staff and its work life. As such, it lessens the chance that individual goals will interfere with organizational goals. For instance, Weber suggests that if staff members used a barter system as a mode of instrumental compliance, they would need a very close and intimate knowledge of one another's non-work lives to insure that the right goods were available for optimal trading. Such intimacy in the non-work situation increases the probability of favoritism and nepotism in the work situation. Thus the utilitarian reward system requires an impersonal mechanism (that is, money rather than barter) to be used successfully by a monocratic bureaucracy. It has already been suggested above that normative modes of motivation could not be used as a general means for motivating people in a bureaucracy because it could not handle rapid everyday changes in work situations.

Finally, the use of physical force as a mode of influence is ruled out on both moral and expedient grounds. Because of its alienating character, individuals motivated by coercion must be kept under constant observation or they will flee (Etzioni, 1969b). To keep people under constant observation at a reasonable cost requires a task that is highly predictable, with everyone doing the same thing at the same time. One person can watch many. However, the more complex the division of labor and the more uncertain the task, the more observers are needed and the more costly and ineffective coercive modes become (Sykes, 1958). Given that Weber saw major economies arising from detailed division of labor it is clear that coercion would not be an effective mode for motivating people.

PROBLEMS OF DEALING WITH CHANGE

The Weberian formulation can deal with problems of change as long as people will work for economic incentives. However, there are certain problems of organizations, for example, the problems of setting organizational goals, which demand some normative forms of compliance. Should a social work agency use its resources to reach many people with minor problems, or a few with serious problems? Should a business concern seek to maximize short-term or long-term profits? Such decisions often reflect value orientations. Who will make these decisions? If everyone in the organization participated, it is implied that they share some common value position. If the larger society decided to alter the policy of the organization, the staff would have to be resocialized or replaced. Either alternative would be expensive and time-consuming, particularly if the staff was very large.

Thus Weber suggests that those functions which depend on normative compliance (goal setting) should be explicitly identified, isolated, and handled by a small group at the top of the organization.

The majority of the staff is hired knowing that policy issues are not part of their job. If a change in goals is necessary, it is comparatively easy to remove the few people at the top without disrupting the entire organization. The American governmental civil service is a classic example of this rationale. The top positions are filled by political appointees who can be fired or removed by election to change policy. The majority of the staff remains. Thus Weber suggests that normative modes of influence can be used in rationalistic organizations, but only at the very top. The majority of employees must separate policy from administration and be motivated by utilitarian modes of influence. This combination permits organizations to deal with problems of technological and policy changes without having to deal with costly and slow processes of resocialization.

It is important to understand that Weber presents a series of interrelated hypotheses covering the development of expertise through differentiation and merit appointments, the coordination of this expertise by rules and hierarchy, the motivation of people to work so as to maximize this expertise, and the processes for handling change.

HUMAN RELATIONS STRUCTURES AS AN ALTERNATIVE TO MONOCRATIC ONES

Although Weber's propositions do have some face validity, a group of organizational theorists said he was wrong. Often they did not try to deal with the theoretical assumptions of the Weberian formulation but rather rested their arguments on empirical grounds. For instance, a series of studies argued that the modern army (the epitome of the rationalistic bureaucracy) actually seemed to operate best when it had primary group-like enclaves working within it (Shils and Janowitz, 1948; Shils, 1951; Whyte, 1956). Somewhat the same implications arose in mental health (Hamburg, 1957), in government (Blau, 1955), in mass media (Katz and Lazarsfield, 1955), and in education (Coleman et al., 1966). Many studies on factories pointed out the same phenomena and formed the basis of "the Human Relations" school of organizational theory (Whyte, 1956). This theory posited the most efficient organization as one that was diametrically opposed in many key respects to that of the Weberian monocratic model. It suggested that generalists were more effective than detailed specialists, collegial committees and internalized norms were better than heirarchy and rules, warm personal ties rather than impersonal ones were preferred, diffused relations were superior to detailed specifications of rights and duties, and internalization of organizational goals by the entire staff was better than the separation of policy and administration.

However, the authors of this approach often did not work out in any systematic fashion their specific hypotheses. It is important to see whether they explicitly contradicted Weberian formulations or simply specified some circumstances under which their formulations might be superior to those of Weber. This theoretical investigation becomes necessary because investigators found, after the first blush of discovery of the superiority of human relations organizations, that the empirical evidence became increasingly in-conclusive (Whyte, 1956).

THE ROLE OF TECHNICAL KNOWLEDGE

If the Weberian formulation is to be questioned, one must ask, "What are the circumstances under which technical knowledge and economies of large scale are *not* superior to everyday knowledge and small groups?" By technical knowledge, we mean knowledge which requires training above and beyond that of everyday socialization. Obviously there is a continuum of technical knowledge, with some occupations, such as that of physician, requiring ten to twelve years of training, while others may have only six months of specialized training. It would seem at first that technical knowl-edge would be superior to everyday knowledge in all circumstances. How-ever, there are some obvious cases where technical knowledge is not supe-rior. First, there may be frontier areas where there is no technical knowledge, or areas where tasks are intrinsically simple. Advanced training under such circumstances adds to the cost of the problem solving but does not add to the effectiveness of solving problems. Technical knowledge would not add greatly to such tasks as driving a car, putting on clothes, purchasing food, calling the police to report a crime in progress, taking aspirin for a tension headache, or running home appliances.

A second case where technical knowledge may be of little use is when the situation is so unexpected that technical people cannot be brought to the situation in time or when technical knowledge cannot be developed in time to make a difference. A person hit by a car and hemorrhaging from a rup-tured artery requires attention from a doctor. However, before a doctor can reach him, he may bleed to death. The accident victim would benefit imme-diately from an ordinary passerby who knew how to apply a tourniquet. This is simple knowledge, not much beyond that of everyday socialization. Faced with the alternative of a doctor who is better trained but unavailable, and a passerby with less training but available, the passerby is clearly superior for immediate assistance than the doctor. In a similar way, a passerby is supe-rior to a policeman for snatching small children out of the way of au-tomobiles, reporting a crime in progress, calling an ambulance service for a person collapsed on the street.

Somewhat related to these circumstances are situations in which there are so many contingencies that experts cannot be trained for all contingencies, or experts cannot be coordinated if they are trained. This point was made in a very interesting way by Bradley Buell (1957), who pointed out in a study of people on welfare that the multi-problem families might be related to as many as twenty agencies. The advice given by each to the client often had contradictory implications. There were so many it was difficult, if not impossible, to coordinate them.

To summarize, I am suggesting that Weber's assumption that technical knowledge would *always* be more effective for solving problems is not in principle correct for all situations. The circumstances under which these hypotheses fail are: 1) where frontier areas of knowledge are prevalent; 2) where tasks require little knowledge; 3) where situations are unpredictable; and 4) where situations have many contingencies. We will henceforth refer to all of these situations as non-uniform situations. The term non-uniform is not precisely accurate, since some of the situations which require low levels of knowledge (such as getting dressed) might be repetitive. However, with this exception, the above term is adequate.

With regard to these non-uniform tasks, we have three points to make. First, there is not a simple dichotomy between uniform and non-uniform, but a continuum. Tasks handled by doctors or engineers may involve much in the way of technical training. A typist's tasks also require training, but far less. To be a semi-skilled laborer might require even less training, while to learn to drive a car may require even less training, and so on.

The second point is that non-uniform tasks appear in every area of life. As examples elaborated above they may involve the areas of physical protection, medical attention, everyday household tasks, or daily religious behavior such as obeying dietary laws. In some sense every business and scientific activity has frontier areas.

The third point is that the logic of science and technology suggests such non-uniform tasks will be with us for the foreseeable future (Litwak and Figueria, 1968). In the past many analyses have sought to show how science and technology can reduce uncertainty; for example, developing computers for dealing with many contingencies, or increasing productivity by substituting experts for non-experts (Ogburn, 1953). However, it is apparent that science and technology can do the opposite as well (Foote and Cottrell, 1955). Thus, the flying of airplanes, the use of computers, the taking of various blood tests, are now all handled by trained experts. However, there is no reason in principle why science and technology might not lead to inventions in the future that would make it possible for the ordinary individual with modest, if any, training, to do all of these things. In a similar fashion it is important to understand that scientific inventions like the automobile lead to so many unanticipated consequences as to introduce even more uncertainties than they close down.

Many organizational theorists are absolutely convinced that uncertainty and turbulence characterize the future and therefore tend to argue that a human relations type of structure is ideal (Bennis, 1966; Emery and Trist, 1965; Terreberry, 1968). I would argue that the logic of science and technology can cause it to move in the direction of either increasing or decreasing uniformity; therefore I would hypothesize that at any given time there will be pressures for automation and a monocratic structure in some areas of life (Sheppard, 1972), while at the same time, in other areas, there will be the introduction of uncertainty and pressures for a human relations structure (Bennis, 1966).

Thus far I have suggested that there are situations where economies of large scale and technical knowledge are not central to effective problem solving. What must now be demonstrated is the nature of organizational structure that will best solve such problems.

ROLE OF SPECIALIZATION AND MERIT

With these thoughts in mind, Weber's basic hypotheses can be addressed directly. For instance, his hypothesis on specialization can be questioned. It has been suggested above that there are three circumstances in which breaking things down into simpler components will not increase effectiveness. In frontier areas of knowledge there may be no knowledge of how to break things down effectively into simpler components. Such differentiation only leads to costs of coordination (for example, unnecessary communications or the cost of training unnecessary specialists) and no benefits. Similarly, specialization is ineffective where there are many contingencies. In such situations one cannot train enough specialists to cover all the contingencies, so there are "gaps in service" (Wilensky and Lebeaux, 1958). As Buell's (1957) material suggests, it is often difficult if not impossible to coordinate many specialists. Given the handicaps of specialization in such situations, it is hypothesized that the most effective way to handle un-

certainty and contingencies is to stress the generalist rather than the specialist. In medicine, the movement towards the family practice as a "specialty"
has behind it much of the rationale just discussed.

What must be understood is that a theoretical alternative has been given
for Weber's formulation that specialization leads to increased technical
knowledge and efficiency. This alternative, however, is not a universal refutation of Weber. It holds only insofar as the situation is a non-uniform one.
Weber's formulations would still be true where the task is of sufficient regularity and where knowledge is sufficiently developed so that the situation can
be split up into simpler components.

If we examine the second basis for introducing technical expertise into
the organization: the selection, promotion, and dismissal of people on the
basis of merit, we find that objective and comprehensive measures are difficult to develop for uncertain and unpredictable situations. In fact, one may
be unable to measure or specify in advance the qualities necessary for effective performance under these conditions. It is hypothesized that members
may best be selected on the bases of trust and ease of communication when
dealing with non-uniform events, i.e., no clear evaluation criteria.

HYPOTHESES ON COORDINATION—
RULES AND HIERARCHY

Most people who attack Weber's position immediately leap to a criticism of rules. As indicated, Weber recognized that rules could not work
well in situations which involved great uncertainties, great contingencies,
and frontier areas of knowledge. As such, he foresaw much of the criticism
currently directed his way. However, Weber made the assumption that the
majority of situations with which organizations must deal will be uniform
ones. He implicitly assumed that science and technology operated only with
economies of large scale. As a consequence, Weber's assumption that the
uncertain tasks in all organizations can be handled most effectively by hierarchy is also incorrect. Theoretically, hierarchy can handle uncertain tasks
as long as they constitute a small percentage of the tasks of the organization.
When there is much uncertainty, the hierarchy quickly becomes over-
whelmed. This leads to choked channels of communication and intolerably
slow decision processes (Franklin, 1955); or to the application of inappropriate rules in order to make quick decisions (Selznick, 1949); or to the introduction of personal values which may not necessarily coincide with orga-

nizational policy since people are hired without attention to their values (Selznick, 1949). Thus, in situations of widespread non-uniformity, the use of a combination of rules and hierarchy tends to be ineffective.

What are the optimal alternatives in such situations? Where the organizational size can be kept small, coordination can be handled by group meetings and collegial structures. Rather than one person making all decisions involving uncertainty, such decisions can be allocated to different people and coordinated through group meetings, thereby speeding up the process. When people cannot meet in groups to coordinate, either because there is not sufficient time or because of geographic spread, they must coordinate by internalizing the policies of the organization and thereby providing a common basis for decision making.

The internalization of policy (but not everyday work procedures) by the entire staff does permit coordination of non-uniform everyday work activities. However, as suggested above, it does not permit the organization to change organizational policy or goals very rapidly. Where this is necessary, such merger of policy and administration is ineffectual. The Human Relations school does suggest a logical refutation of Weber's assumption that rules and hierarchy are always the most effective way of coordinating behavior in a large organization. However, the refutation is a conditional one. It holds only when most organizational tasks are non-uniform. Otherwise Weber's formulations are still correct.

MOTIVATIONAL ELEMENTS IN FORMAL ORGANIZATIONS

Another crucial area of attack on Weber's position centers on his arguments for impersonality. Generally, two counter arguments are made. One, which was most clearly developed by Blau (1955), points out that under conditions of uncertainty people will communicate only with those whom they can trust. Trust is in turn related to personal liking. Therefore, positive affect is crucial to insure proper communication under conditions of uncertainty.

Another consideration concerns the difficulties of supervising individuals in uncertain settings. As was suggested above, if employees are motivated by expedient modes of influences, such as economic utilitarian ones, and they cannot be observed, they may not bother performing the tasks for which they are being paid. Therefore, it becomes important to induce members to internalize the values of the organization in order to get their commitment. This kind of internalization generally requires the development of warm positive ties. Therefore, ties of a positive and affective nature are often very functional when dealing with highly uncertain contingent situations.

Thus it is hypothesized that impersonal work norms, economic payments, and a priori elimination of rights and duties would not lead to effective problem solving when dealing with unpredictableness, many contingencies, and tasks requiring few resources. As suggested above, favoritism, which the bureaucratic mechanisms of impersonality and a priori limits were designed to curb, is not as serious a problem in dealing with non-uniform situations.

The Human Relations hypothesis that positive affective ties and internalization of policy are most effective for handling non-uniform tasks is a partial refutation of Weber's hypothesis on impersonality and economic motivation. However, Weber's hypotheses continue to hold when tasks are uniform.

MULTI-MODEL THEORY

With these thoughts in mind, a generalized statement can be made about the respective positions of the Weberian monocratic organization and its opposite number—the Human Relations school. It is that each is right for different tasks. The monocratic structure can maximize technical knowledge and large scale human resources. The latter are good for solving problems in uniform situations. The human relations structures (and in the extreme, primary groups) are more effective for handling non-uniform tasks. These propositions are derived from the dimensions of organizational structure elaborated above (for example, merit, specialization, rules, hierarchy, impersonal ties, a priori limits on rights and duties, and separation of policy from administration).

It is very important to follow the argument of the above analysis. It says nothing about the source of the uncertainty or the contingencies. They could come from the nature of technology, from the outer environment, from the personalities of the staffs or clients; they could come from the nature of interdependencies with other organizations, or from the forms of compliance organizations use. We have used the term "task" or "situation" to cover all sources of uncertainty. For some purposes, knowing the source of non-uniformity is very useful. However, to focus on the difference in source of non-uniformity, without realizing the common consequences of all forms of uncertainty for organizational structure is an impediment to intellectual clarity. This error has contributed to the feeling of intellectual disarray.

The central idea that different types of organizations are necessary for different types of uniform and non-uniform situations is what is meant by the "multi-model contingency theory." So far only two types of formal organizations (the monocratic and the human relations) have been discussed.

What I would now like to do is show how using these units and principles makes it possible to derive an almost infinite number of organizational types. However, that does not mean one is faced with great indeterminacy. If the prior speculations are correct, the theoretical properties of any given type can be quickly specified. To make this point clear we will show two types of generalizations and indicate the principles governing them.

GENERALIZATION THROUGH THE CONCEPT OF ORGANIZATIONAL CONTINUUM

One way by which the framework can be generalized is to suggest there is a continuum of tasks going from the extreme of uniform to the extreme of non-uniform. On one extreme are the repetitive tasks which also require great knowledge and large numbers of people; such tasks are illustrated by the semi-automated procedures used by electric and gas utilities to bill their customers. Following in order on the continuum might be the task of establishing eligibility for Social Security benefits, establishing eligibility for welfare, doing psychotherapy for neuroses, teaching first aid classes, organizing groups of neighbors into "block watcher" clubs, and finally, at the other end of the continuum, informal neighborhood cooperation such as calling the doctor if one of the neighbors falls down.

Given such a continuum of tasks we would like to suggest there is a continuum of organizations. For the purpose of clarity we have spoken about rationalistic and human relations structures. However, in principle there is a continuum of organization structures.

To present this idea systematically it is only necessary to take each of Weber's dimensions of organization and to point out that they might cover all or only part of the activities of an organization. Thus, in Social Security, somewhere between 90 and 100 percent of the activity might be covered by objective rules of merit, while in welfare organization the range may be between 70 and 80 percent, and in a 24-hour small therapy home as described by Jules Henry (1957), 50–60 percent. As one moves to voluntary associations, such as a charity fund-raising organization (a mixture of professionals and non-professionals), one might have something like 30–40 percent of the behavior covered by rules of merit, while in the small neighborhood block association it might be that only 10–20 percent, and in the family only 10 to 0 percent of the activities can be evaluated by merit.

In a similar way, one can speak about the number of activities covered by detailed specialization, the number of activities covered by rules, the number of activities characterized by impersonal relations, and so on. Chart 6.1 presents this idea.

Once the principles of the theory we have raised have been absorbed they provide statements in theory as to which of the organizations on the continuum is best able to handle which of the tasks on the task continuum. Because we do not as yet have precise measurements of tasks or organizational structures, it is often possible to provide only limited empirical tests of these ideas. However, such limited tests are often very useful to practitioners. It turns out that for many decisions practitioners have a limited option. Thus, they are often confronted with a given task and a choice of one or two organizational styles—more rationalistic or less rationalistic. For such decisions the above conceptual approach and limited tests would be very useful. It predicts the direction of change.

GENERALIZATION TO MULTIPLE TASK
ORGANIZATIONS—COMPARTMENTALIZED

Yet another form of generalization is that which points out that organizations often have multiple tasks and the question arises as to what kind of administrative structure evolves where one has multiple tasks. Let us take up the type of multiple task most difficult to deal with. These organizations have tasks drawn from different points on the task continuum mentioned above. For instance, a welfare center might have as one of its functions the regular payment of income to those who have already been declared eligible—those who fall below a certain income level. Part of what is involved is a highly standardized task. Once eligibility has been established, the process of payments follows a regular routine, that is, being sure the payment goes to the person with the same name, the same address, and in the same amount, each pay period. The same center may have a home adoption unit for hard-to-place children, that is, children who are older, who may be suffering from mental illness or who may have some physical deformity. By comparison, this is a highly non-uniform task, because there is no standardized or predictable way of locating adoptive parents for such children.

Our theory would suggest that the highly standardized tasks of income maintenance would require a more rationalistic form of organization, while the highly non-standardized task of finding a home for hard-to-place children would require a more human relations structure. Specifically, the workers in the income maintenance section can have most of their activities evaluated in objective terms as to whether they are "goofing off" or really working. Their task can be broken down into detailed components, and job descriptions which cover 80 to 90 percent of their activities can be stated. Work and non-work activities can be clearly delimited, as can supervisors' authority. The general policy of the organization is set by legislation and people at the top, and the worker is expected to go along with each change in policy, such as liberalized or constricted views of eligibility.

By contrast, the work of a child placement staff can be only partially evaluated in terms of merit. Often the only thing that can be evaluated is the outcome: was the child placed or not? Even here it may be difficult to evaluate, because success or failure may come either as a result of the workers' ability or from community resources. Measures of merit used are often indirect: does the worker have educational credentials (e.g., M.S.W.) or an appealing personality? However, there is often no way of insuring that these measures are in fact related to job performance. There is no detailed division of labor. The worker might recruit parents by sitting in the office, going to various organizations and speaking, writing a news release, or visiting key people such as ministers and asking for references. The parents are evaluated as to their capacity to love the child, their economic state, their health, their mental state. Workers have only general rules governing their behavior. Often the hours of work cannot be clearly stated—they may sometimes work evenings or weekends. The daily routine varies as contingencies arise.

In short, the two tasks in the welfare center (income maintenance and adoption) require a somewhat contradictory structure. It is not the task but the structures which are contradictory. For instance, the person in the income maintenance department can generally lay out his day with a five to

Chart 6.1 TASK AND ORGANIZATIONAL CONTINUUM

Task Conformity	Extreme Uniformity[a]	Predominate Uniformity
	e.g., Social Security in U.S. or automated utilities	e.g., Establishing eligibility for welfare payments or unemployment insurance, custodial care of aged and mentally ill
Organizational Dimensions	Extreme Rationalistic[b]	Predominate Rationalistic
% of tasks eval. by objective merit	90–100%	80–90
Degree to which job broken into small component for indiv. or machine specialization	90–100%	80–90
Length of Authority Ladder	very long	long
% of activities governed by rules	90–100%	80–90
% of activities governed by inpersonal norms	90–100%	80–90
% of activities having a priori rights and duties	90–100%	80–90
% of activities where administration and policy separated	90–100%	80–90
Need for balance linkages	Minor	Minor

[a] These are only points on the task continuum. There are presumably many more if we wanted to make even finer distinctions.

[b] These are only points on the organizational continuum. At the very end we have included the compartmentalized which in turn can combine any two points on the task continuum. In addition, it is possible that the dimensions of organization will not vary together in which case we get even more organizational types.

ten minute tolerance, while the person in the foster care unit may require several hours of leeway in appointments. The problem of scheduling appointments between the two if they should need to meet would be difficult. The income maintenance person would feel the appointment was canceled if the foster home person was more than ten minutes late, while the foster care person might tolerate an hour's delay before canceling. If in the course of the meeting the income maintenance person should happen to strike some

Moderate Uniformity	Moderate Non-Uniformity	Predominate Non-Uniformity
Psychotherapy of Freudian or neo-Freudian or provision of direct family services like employment training	Running of half-way homes or group homes, use of volunteers in fund raising	Running of alcoholics annonymous, running small block clubs, or intimate social clubs
Moderate Human Relations	Strong Human Relations	Proto Primary Grp. Vol. association
70–80	60–70	30–50
70–80 shorter	60–70 some collegial	20–50 collegial
70–80	60–70	20–50
70–80	60–70	20–50
70–80	60–70	20–50
70–80 Minor	60–70 Minor	20–50 Minor

continued on p. 142

ambiguity not covered by the rules, she would say, send it to the top. By contrast, the adoption staff person would say, let's settle it ourselves. The foster care person might suggest meeting in the evenings or on weekends, while the income maintenance person would insist on a time between 9 a.m. and 5 p.m.

In short, the very structure of their different administrative styles would force them into conflict in a given meeting no matter how congenial they were personally. Thus, one of the basic problems that emerges when dealing with multiple tasks from different parts of the task continuum is how to co-

Chart 6.1 (continued)

Task Conformity

	Extreme Non-Uniformity	*Multiple Tasks Uniform & Non-Uniform*
	Every-day activities such as driving, cooking, dressing, housekeeping, disciplining small children, etc.	Organization with income maintenance and family counseling or hospital with big housekeeping and billing departments; also large treatment clinics, mental hospital with strong custodial/treatment goals, prisons with strong custodial/treatment goals

Organizational Dimensions

	Family, Neigh. & Friends-Primary Grp.	*Compartmentalized Organizations*
% of tasks eval. by objective merit	0–10	Sub-unit 90–100 Sub-unit 60–70
Degree to which job broken into small component for indiv. or machine specialization	0–10	Sub-unit 90–100 Sub-unit 60–70
Length of Authority Ladder	very collegial	Sub-unit long Sub-unit collegial
% of activities governed by rules	20–50	Sub-unit 90–100 Sub-unit 60–70
% of activities governed by impersonal norms	20–50	Sub-unit 90–100 Sub-unit 60–70
% of activities having a priori rights and duties	20–50	Sub-unit 90–100 Sub-unit 60–70
% of activities where administration and policy separated	20–50	Sub-unit 90–100 Sub-unit 60–70
Need for balance linkages	Minor	Major

ordinate contradictory administrative structures within the same organization.

COORDINATION OF CONTRADICTORY STRUCTURE

If it can be solved, it is possible to think of organizational structures with almost any kind of shape. One of the most obvious solutions would be to isolate the contradictory groups as much as possible. One way of considering the problem of isolation is through people; another way is through place (Goode, 1960; Merton, 1957). With these two variables in mind we can conceive of situations where all the people in one place do one task and are physically separated from people doing different tasks. We will call this a department. The staff of each unit would have its own set of offices, physically located on different floors, in different buildings, or in different parts of the city.

Sometimes different people can be isolated for different tasks, but must work in the same place. Thus, an adoption staff person, an income maintenance person, and a doctor might meet together to discuss a given adoption problem. We shall refer to this as a "team" situation. Still a third solution is one in which the same person has two different tasks which have to be performed in the same place. In this case the only thing separating the two tasks is an internalized role division. Thus, a staff person at a welfare center may be simultaneously responsible for checking out welfare eligibility and providing services to the same client at the same time.

Insofar as there is an option in organizational design, it is generally best to keep tasks from radically different parts of the continuum, and their resultant contradictory structures, in autonomous departments. However, this is not always possible. There is no way the surgical team of surgeon, anesthesiologist, and nurses can be in different places when an operation is underway. It is often not possible to separate contradictory structures because the units may have other interdependencies which require close contact.

Thus, in developing principles for coordination between sub-units, one must take into account all forms of interdependencies—from those which involve separate departments, to teams, to those which involve one person with segregated roles.

It is also necessary to consider that the separate departments have to exchange despite their contradictory structures. If there were no need for exchange at all, then generally both units need not be in the same organization. In addition, what uniquely characterizes the contradiction between units is that the organization can never hope to resolve it completely without failing at one of its major tasks. That is, if the organization would make the structure of the child placement unit more monocratic, it would eliminate the conflict between it and the income maintenance unit. However, it would also lead to the failure to locate parents for the children. Therefore, the conflict can never be fully resolved on behalf of either party if the organization values its multiple tasks. In such circumstances the best procedure is to minimize the conflict sufficiently so that the two units still communicate with each other, and yet not moderate the conflict to the extent that one or the other is destroyed.

In a situation where there are inevitable and unsolvable conflicts, I see three considerations. First, there must be some way to stop discussion and agree to action. Because the two units are in a conflict that cannot be resolved, discussion after a point cannot expect to achieve anything but waste time. Therefore there must be a procedure by which the two units can agree to an action despite their differences. The general principle guiding such adjudication procedures is that neither party will consistently win. For instance, two people who have trouble making appointments because of conflicts in their structure might devise a conflict rule which alternately asks each one to bend his organizational structure to the needs of the other. That is, in one case the income maintenance person will waive his ten-minute rule, while in the other case the foster placement person will waive his one-hour rule. Another procedure might be a principle that one unit will win the dispute if the decision against that unit would be more damaging to it than to the opponent. To assess potential damage, a third party might be appointed with no vested interest in either group but with an understanding that both groups must survive in strong form if the larger goals of the organization are to be met. Often, the third party is a supervisor.

Second, each unit must operate on the principle of confidentiality of files. The assumption of such conflict situations is that each unit must protect its own interest, given the conflict between them. As part of that protection it should present only its strongest side. The opponent will be motivated to present the negative side. If both organizations were to be responsible for presenting both the strong and the weak sides of their case, then the first to present its strong side only would win the dispute.

Finally, as noted above, the decision-making process must be weighted so that neither group has an undue advantage over the other insofar as both goals are equally important. If one goal is more important than the other, then the decision-making process should reflect that fact as well.

In addition to the above considerations, there must be some assessment of the volume of exchange and the extent to which the object being exchanged involves a uniform or non-uniform task. In general the principle would be that the greater the volume, the more formalistic the exchange process should be, the assumption being that high volume of exchange is not accompanied by increases in staff necessary to deal with the increased complexity. All things being equal, complexities generally increase geometrically with number of exchanges while organizations cannot afford to add staff at that rate. Therefore, the only way large numbers of exchanges can be handled is through the arbitrary elimination of contingencies or through economies on a large scale.

In a similar way, it can be argued that where one is dealing with a highly uniform task (for example, providing names of eligible clients) that has to be exchanged between the two sub-units, it can generally be handled more effectively by use of formal procedures or rules (for example, printed lists), the logic being the same as that developed at the beginning of the paper. If all these factors are considered together, that is, degree of interdependence in place and person; the volume and the degree of standardization; and it is remembered that the exchange must always be carried on within an adjudication and confidentiality framework, then some of the major elements for a theory of optimal exchange between organizational sub-units can be stated. (For a more complete statement of all the variables see Litwak et al., 1970.) The hypothesized forms of optimal exchanges under all combinations of elements are presented in Chart 6.2.

If the readers examine the column under Departmentalization on the chart, they can see where the department has to exchange a standardized object in great volume. Then the scheme suggests a written statement with specific decisions under all alternatives. For instance, between payroll and social service, there might be a form which indicates the names of those who according to service criteria are no longer eligible for payment and a form which reports who is being paid and a rule that states if there is any difference the payment should be cancelled. The main point is that the adjudication principle can be embodied in a written document that indicates in all possible cases how the differences between the two units are to be

Chart 6.2 LINKAGE PROCEDURES BETWEEN SUB-UNITS IN THE SAME ORGANIZATION WHERE THERE ARE DIFFERENT STRUCTURES— ADJUDICATION MECHANISMS

Form of Interdependence between Sub-Units

Frequency or Volume of Exchange	Uniformity of Task Exchanged	Internalized Role (Same Person and Same Place)	Team (Separation by People but not Place)	Departmentalization (Separation by People and Place)
High Volume	Uniform Task	1. Written job description indicating which role has priority, and specialized supervision (e.g., systematic checks of decisions on random base.)	1. Written rules for settling disputes, but in addition, regular short, factual meetings. Use of many abbreviations in conversation.	1. Written rules which state, in case of dispute, who wins or to whom does one go for decision, or what process to follow to get decision.
High Volume	Non-Uniform Task	2. Consultations (regular length but informal) with peers on how to handle role conflicts; early job rotation to occupations which have more consistent roles.	2. Specialized Committees for settling disputes. In addition, there must be some procedure for preventing conflict from spreading because of daily contact (e.g., convention not to discuss potential conflict; temporary agreements that one person wins until final decision is worked out). Special committee must work faster than interdepartmental committees. Systematic meetings with non-team peers to maintain role. Regular job rotation between teams so team identification is not too strong.	2. Specialized committee set up to settle disputes between sub-units.

Low Volume Uniform Task	3. Use job traditions which are not written down for settling role conflict. Each department may have its own procedure for settling role conflict. Short, limited ad hoc consultations with peers on role conflict.	3. Short, factual meetings, very quickly convened, with procedure (often informal) for settling disputes.	3. Departmental procedures, not necessarily written down but in oral tradition, for settling disputes. Exchanges between departments may be short memoranda.
Low Volume Non-Uniform Task	4. Ad hoc, informal and lengthy consultation with peers on how to settle role conflicts: Later job rotation to occupations with fewer role conflicts.	4. Dispute given to single individual to settle. Must act quickly and must have procedure for isolating areas of dispute (e.g., conventions permitting one to carry on all other activities) while dispute is being negotiated. Ad hoc meetings with non-team peers and ad hoc rotation to other teams to maintain occupational identity.	4. Single individual used for settling disputes. If volume moderate then he may spend full time. But if volume is very low it may be only part of larger job, e.g., interdepartment meetings.

resolved. Classic in this case would be the cost-of-living clauses in union-management contracts.

By contrast, if there is a high volume of exchange but a non-standardized task has to be exchanged, it may be difficult to write rules for settling the dispute. There must be face-to-face contact to deal with contingencies. However, the high volume suggests that the adjudication is a full-time job requiring a specialized group, something like a specialized committee for adjudication. If the volume were extremely high it could even be a specialized department; if less frequent, then maybe one individual or a part-time job represented by periodic inter-staff negotiations.

If we now consider those situations which involve an exchange of standardized things, but which are infrequent, it may be too costly to prepare a priori written rules for infrequent occurances. However, there are no great complexities to be negotiated that would require special committees. Under these circumstances the scheme would suggest something like a series of short memos to be exchanged as a way of settling a dispute. It may also be a meeting between the two groups but one characterized by an agenda that can be set ahead of time, so that the meeting can be short and factual. It may also be true that although there are no company-wide rules, each department may have its own procedures, which may be given to its members either through oral tradition or in some mimeographed form. We present these procedures as though they are dichotomies, but they are clearly continua.

These procedures operate on the assumption that there is some separation between members of the group by place and by people. If we now consider the concept of a team (that is, separation by people, but all must work together in the same place), a further complication is introduced. The complication results from the fact the team members are in everyday contact with one another. Any dispute that arises between them may have a special urgency not necessarily felt where departmentalization occurs. The team procedures may have exactly the same set of adjudicatory mechanics that characterize the department. But, in addition, some mechanisms are needed to prevent these disputes from leading into immediate interpersonal conflict. Some method must be set up so that team members involved in a dispute agree explicitly not to discuss the dispute while it is in the process of being settled. This may mean that the issue in dispute will either have to be set aside or, alternatively, there may have to be some specialized rules which permit one party or the other to win temporarily, until the dispute is settled.

On the other hand, members of a team are subject to somewhat unique pressures to make friends and to replace professional identity with team identity. To counteract this pressure, team members might have to be given a much greater opportunity than those in departments to attend meetings with their own professional groups. If at all possible team members might have to be continuously rotated to other teams.

In contrast to the departmental and team forms of interdependency, the role-segregated approach has the unique problem of trusting one individual to be judge and jury. This problem arises because one individual has to recognize the area of dispute and employ the machinery of adjudication, but in such a way as not to destroy either group. Because the individual is being asked to preserve a conflict that is a daily irritant, there is considerable pressure on the individual psyche. In this regard the more informal the adjudication procedure becomes (that is, in situations that are frequent and non-standardized), the greater discretion is given to individuals to invoke the decision-making process and the greater the psychic strain.

It would seem especially important for those involved in jobs that encompass conflicting roles to be selected on the basis of their ability to handle ambiguity. In addition, they should be rotated as early as possible into jobs which have minimal conflict, as well as being given every opportunity to consult in informal meetings with others having the same type of conflict.

VARIETY OF STRUCTURES

The problem of coordinating sub-units is a central one for organizational theorists and practitioners. The formulation suggested herein has been elaborated elsewhere (Litwak et al., 1970; Litwak and Rothman, 1970).

If conflicting structures can be coordinated, then the implications for organizational form and structure are substantial. It opens up a wide range of organizational structures for consideration. Rather than the limited formulation of a monocratic bureaucracy and a human relations bureaucracy, we now have a concept of organizations with a variety of sub-units—some human relations, others rationalistic, and varying in the extent of human relations and rationalistic. When the structures are contradictory they are "glued" together by mechanisms that permit conflict. What they reflect is a variety of tasks the organization must perform. Yet, despite the bewildering variety of forms suggested by this multi-model orientation, there is no chaos in understanding or even designing the structure. For each sub-unit can be tied to a given task and the rationale of the relationship can be specified—using the concept of an organizational continuum and a task continuum already given. At the same time the logic of the mechanisms connecting them can be understood as well. What might look like a "garbage can" type of structure and decision process lends itself to systematic analysis once these underlying principles are understood. I will call organizations which have conflicting sub-structures "compartmentalized" organizations. This replaces an earlier term, "professional" organization (Litwak, 1961), and overlaps with the term "matrix" organizations.

CONFLICTING TASKS, CONSISTENT TASKS, AND DEPARTMENTAL SUBDIVISIONS

It is necessary to consider forms of departmentalization that arise when tasks do not come from different parts of the task continuum and the structures of the sub-units are not in conflict with one another. There are two general bases for division of labor. One derives from a concept of competitive interdependence while the other involves facilitative interdependence.

Competitive interdependence means that the more successful one unit is, the less successful the other. However, if one unit tries to destroy the other, it will suffer. For instance, a social work agency might have two programs involving non-uniform tasks. One might be a group work therapy program and the other might be a casework therapy program. Both tasks might be non-uniform and both might require human relations structures. However, the two tasks might be in conflict with each other. Sometimes the conflict might be a logical one. Thus, in the instance of the casework and group work conflict, some of the participants might view them as alternatives to each other and not as different techniques to be used for different purposes. On the other hand, the conflict may be indirect in that the agency has to support both but has limited funds. The more it gives to one, the less it has for the other.

In either case the agency might want to maintain both. They might want two competing techniques to establish which is superior, or they might want two complementary techniques because they want to deal with different but equally necessary tasks. The coordination of the sub-units would follow the same logic as that developed for conflicting administrative styles. We bring this case up to sensitize the reader to the notion that there is a need for mechanisms of coordination for situations of structural conflict and those of goal conflict.

By facilitative interdependence we mean there is no way two units can each gain its own goals without helping the other. In social work, the faster and more efficient the payroll department is in getting out its checks to foster parents, the better the social worker can deal with them. The promptness with which the social worker keeps the payroll department informed about who is legitimately in the program and who is not, the easier the payroll department's task to prevent fraud can be accomplished.

When Weber wrote on monocratic bureaucracy, it is hypothesized that what he had in mind was a series of sub-units, each organized along a rationalistic basis and facilitatively interdependent. Although Weber is not explicit on this matter, it also seems to be implied that these sub-units exchange around uniform tasks with a high volume. That is in part why Weber stressed rules. He saw a very small percentage of the exchange involving non-standardized tasks. He suggested they could be handled by individuals.

It is important to recognize that there might be a parallel mode for human relations structures as well. That is, settlement houses and many multi-purpose agencies may have several programs, each involving non-uniform tasks, which are facilitatively interdependent with one another. They differ from Weber's formulation in that much of their exchange involves non-uniform tasks and therefore requires face-to-face contact to coordinate them.

The logic for the development of sub-units because of facilitative interdependence in a monocratic organization has already been developed (this is Weber's rationale, that tasks broken into components permit more focused training, fewer errors, and more rational use of time). The human relations theorists's rationale for splitting organizations into sub-units has not been developed but is easily derived. The point has been made that the need to coordinate by committees, the need to develop positive affect and normative compliance, all require small size. Therefore, wherever a unit grows because of increased clientele or because it performs multiple non-uniform tasks, there is an incentive to split off into semi-autonomous sub-units to minimize administrative costs and to protect its effectiveness.

The mechanisms of coordination for sub-units not in conflict would bear a resemblance to those in which they would be in conflict, the basic difference being that where there is facilitative interdependence, the stress would be on consensual decision-making rather than adjudicative, and scientific open communication rather than confidentiality. It is assumed that when the other unit can only help, there is no reason to withhold the information it wants and the two units would continue to talk until one finds a solution to which both parties agree.

Thus, where sub-units are organized as two separate departments and have a high volume of standardized elements to communicate, the most effective mechanisms are likely to be highly formalized procedures in which all alternatives are written out. For instance, in a business concern, the office staff might have an order form upon which all office supplies are listed and the staff might check off the volume needed and send it to the warehouse or purchasing department for action. The order form is the coordinating device. The optimal linkages are presented in Chart 6.3. It differs from Chart 6.2. in that coordination does not involve adjudication or confidentiality. Otherwise the underlying logic is the same.

Having made this point, another complexity arises. What happens if the two sub-units have competitive interdependence in some areas while facilitative in others? If that is the case, the two processes can be isolated from each other by having different people handle them. Insofar as the isolation can be complete, the two processes might be treated as though only one were involved. This is quite clear when one is speaking about interorganizational relationships. Social work agencies might be facilitatively interdependent when lobbying with Congress to support social programs, but competitively interdependent over clients when requesting funds to run programs for a city agency. These two processes can often go on virtually autonomously, because they are carried out by different people in different places.

However, it is not always possible to keep competitive and facilitative interdependencies separate. This may be especially true where one is dealing with sub-units of the same organization. Insofar as it is impossible to keep them separate, then the organization must choose which should be given preference and how much. If one is given 100 percent backing and the other none, then it is simply a matter of choosing one procedure over the other. If equal weight is to be given to each, the solution might be arrived at by utilizing an exchange procedure somewhere in the middle between adjudicative and consensual decision-making. Alternatively, it may be possible to organize two different processes but permit each to operate only 50 percent of

Frequency or Volume of Exchange	Uniformity of Task Exchanged	Internalized Role (Same Person and Same Place)	Team (Separation by People but not Place)	Departmentalization (Separation by People and Place)
High Volume	Uniform Task	1. Written job description indicating different roles, systematic evaluations but for eyes of workers alone.	1. Printed forms, but, in addition, everyday contact with language sprinkled with abbreviations for consensual agreements.	1. Printed form for exchange, such as order forms, application forms, lists of names and addresses. Stress on consensual agreement.
High Volume	Non-Uniform Task	2. Systematic consultation with peers (e.g., regular group meetings) and supervision but as consultants and not "inspectors."	2. Regular meeting, not structured with general agenda. No need for adjudication but procedures emphasize consensual agreements.	2. Specialized committee to handle exchanges between units with the assumption of no intrinsic conflicts (i.e., stress on consensual agreement and open communication).
Low Volume	Uniform Task	3. Use of job traditions (i.e., not written down). Short factual contacts with peers and supervisors around consensual roles.	3. Short factual memorandum, but more likely short factual conversations or meetings which are ad hoc for consensual agreement.	3. Use of short factual memorandum and well recognized norms to communicate.
Low Volume	Non-Uniform Task	4. Ad hoc consultations with peers and supervisors around consistent roles.	4. Ad hoc meeting with general agenda and consensual decision, little formal structure.	4. Liaison person to communicate. Does not act as arbitrator mediator, but more as communicator link. If volume is low may be part-time job.

the time through the use of various rules that insure that both would continue to be operative. A more complete analysis of this problem has been carried out elsewhere (Litwak et al., 1970; Litwak and Rothman, 1970).

MULTI-MODEL ORGANIZATIONS AND MEGA ORGANIZATIONS

I have spoken thus far of compartmentalized organizations dealing with multiple and contradictory tasks. It was also suggested that tasks may have differential degrees of interdependence. In fact, the argument has been made that it is sometimes functional to put as much distance between some units of the organization as possible. The concept of organization begins to take on curious formulations with the assertion of the latter approach. A business conglomerate like General Electric is recognized as one organization despite the fact that the firm makes a wide range of products. Similarly, under the U.S. Office of Health, Education, and Welfare, there are a series of giant sub-units, such as Social Security, Office of Education, and Institute of Mental Health. Alternatively, one looks at price setting and wage negotiations in an industry like steel, where basic patterns are often set by the largest unit, U.S. Steel, and the others follow. The question arises, in what sense are the former one organization and the latter separate?

In the classical sense of organization, one had in mind a group with one goal which had the highest priority—all other tasks were seen as being in the service of that goal. In addition, that organization had a single authority structure with the various sub-units highly interdependent. Thus, one could have a shoe factory whose major product was shoes, with a profit as a goal. To achieve this, some additional tasks are necessary, such as union negotiations, the support of a lobby to deal with tariffs on foreign shoes, influence on local tax structures, a concern for local hospitals and education, in order to attract able management. All of these subsidiary tasks are geared to the objective of making profits through the manufacturing of shoes. By contrast, if we look at a business conglomerate, it is often made up of a series of products, each having equal priority and each related to profit in the same way. Thus, in General Electric, the television division may be as important as the refrigerator division. Moreover, the divisions may not be interdependent in terms of lobbying, tariff, raw materials, or customers. They are interdependent, however, in that they all draw on common capital for long-term investment and are assessed against one another in terms of their profit-making abilities. In the investment area they may be subject to centralized authority, while for the bulk of their operating decisions they may be autonomous. Government agencies such as HEW have the same structure. However, instead of being judged on the basis of profit, each unit is judged by its political accountability. Thus, if one unit fails politically, the Secretary of HEW might be moved to alter its leadership.

It is argued that organizations characterized by relatively equal goals with equal sub-units which are semi-autonomous is what people have in mind when they speak about mega bureaucracies. Such organizations can grow to enormous size because they generally do not have the coordination problems of an organization with highly interdependent subunits and a single authority structure. The analysis of these mega bureaucracies or conglomerates involves the same set of variables as one would use in traditional organization theory. However, the weights given to these variables differ. The single biggest difference is the lack of a single autonomous center, except in a few limited areas of activity. This type of analysis is something organizational theorists call interorganizational analysis (Litwak et al, 1970; Litwak and Rothman, 1970). The logic of that analysis is the same as that used to describe the relationship between sub-units in a given organization. However, in an organization with a well-defined authority structure and heavily interdependent sub-units, there is always the option to get things done by going to the central authority structure, which often has the power to force changes in the sub-units. As one approaches the mega bureaucracy, the ability of the central administration to enforce decisions becomes less and less. When one reaches true interorganizational relations it is often non-existent. That means that getting such organizations or their sub-units to cooperate often requires a different emphasis. In mega bureaucracy the subunits' awareness of their interdependency is a major factor in determining the form of coordination, while in a traditional organization, the sub-units' self-awareness might be a negligible factor, as long as those at the top of the hierarchy are aware of it. In a mega organization, the potential for fatal conflicts between sub-units is possible because ultimately no single authority can arbitrarily terminate them; in the traditional organization, the possibilities for such fatal conflicts would be far less. If it is necessary to get the entire mega bureaucracy to cooperate on a given issue, then it is important to have a linkage mechanism which has a scope wide enough to reach each sub-unit of the mega bureaucracy. In a regular organization it is often necessary to persuade only the people at the top, who, in turn, can persuade the sub-units. In the mega bureaucracy there is a much greater need to understand and make use of linkages which open, as well as close, distance in order to maintain the semi-autonomous state. In the traditional bureaucracy, such semi-autonomous states can rely on the power of the single authority figure. In the mega bureaucracy the autonomy of the sub-units tends to make an inward merger much less probable, while in a traditional organization with a single authority head, it is always possible, if one unit or the other captures the central authority figure, to force the merger of various sub-units.

The differences between the traditional organization and the mega bureaucracy and ultimately the semi-autonomous coalitions of organizations can be located on a continuum. When dealing with single organizations, the theories of organizations we have presented would more than suffice. When dealing with semi-autonomous organizations coordinating with one another, then interorganizational theory would be the tool for analysis. When dealing with mega bureaucracies, which are single organizations for some purposes and separate units for others, it is often necessary to utilize different modes of analysis to understand their different structures. As suggested above, the problem is not so much difference in variables, but in the weight given these variables.

ORGANIZATIONS WITH INDEPENDENT DIMENSIONS

Thus far the assumption has been made that all dimensions of organizations change together. However, it is also possible for the dimensions to act independently. For instance, it is possible for an organization to have all of the dimensions of a rationalistic structure except that there may be no a priori limits on rights and duties—this defines an authoritarian structure.

Obviously there are as many logical possibilities of organizational models as there are possible combinations of eight dimensions. This line of analysis will not be explored in this paper because of limitations of space. There is some danger in studying organizations by concentrating on each dimension only. The danger is that the investigator may fail to realize that organizations may have multiple tasks and multiple structures. As a consequence he may seek to average each dimension over the entire organization and thereby eliminate all forms of compartmentalized structures.

ALTERNATIVE FORMULATIONS OF MULTI-MODEL
THEORIES AND CONCLUSION

There are several formulations of multi-model theories very close to the ideas presented herein. However, because different language was used and because the authors had a somewhat different purpose, they are often viewed as competing formulations. Perrow (1967) develops a version of the multi-model theory very close to that presented herein. He uses the term "technology" in a way that overlaps with the terms uniform and non-uniform tasks. Technology is characterized as having "a number of exceptions or few exceptions" or being "analyzable" or "non-analyzable." The idea of "exceptions" overlaps with the idea "unpredictable," while "non-analyzable" is the same as "frontier areas of knowledge." Perrow's definition of organizational structure has similar parallelisms, as does his conclusion that different types of technology (tasks) require different types of structure.

Thompson (1967) tried to show how the nature of interdependencies between units were related to organizational structure. Thompson suggests that pooled interdependency is related to rules and hierarchy, while reciprocal interdependency is related to face-to-face coordination and the need for autonomous decisions. Sequential forms of interdependence come between these two extremes as does the form of coordination. Why does Thompson argue that the form of interdependence will lead to either rules or committees? He writes, "The three types of interdependence are increasingly difficult to coordinate because they contain increasing degrees of contingencies." In other words, it is not the interdependencies *per se* which explain why one must use rules or committees, but the contingencies which are associated with them. The more contingencies, the more one must use committees. This is precisely the rationale used by Perrow and developed in this paper.

By contrast, Blau's (1970) suggestion that size is the key factor affecting organizational structure seems to contradict the view that characteristics of task and structure are related to each other. However, when Blau seeks to explain his major finding (that with increasing size, the administrative-staff ratio shrinks, but at a decreasing rate), he utilizes the same rationale as the multi-model theorist. He suggests that with increasing size there is a need for less supervision within units and more supervision between units. An analysis of Blau's reasoning suggests that supervision across departments involves many contingencies, while supervision within departments involves few contingencies. It is the number of contingencies which determines whether size will lead to more or less supervision, or to other structural features. Put somewhat differently, the effect of size on structure depends on the task (that is, internal or external supervision) and the task in turn is defined in terms of contingencies. If Blau's logic were to be followed to its conclusion, he would come to a position very close to that of the multi-model contingency theorist. Furthermore, Blau's view that size is related to organizational structure would receive support from multi-model contingency theory. As indicated above, human relations structures cannot effectively coordinate structures with large numbers, while monocratic bureaucracies require large numbers for a detailed division of labor.

Etzioni (1969b) is clearly one of the first to point out that different goals are best implemented by different organizational structures. However, his stress on compliance and his way of describing goals as cultural, economic, and order seem to suggest an analytic scheme that differs from the contingency models described in this paper. But, as suggested above, Etzioni's modes of compliance are heavily related to task contingencies. For instance, coercive modes of influence can be used only where those being coerced can be kept under constant observation and is possible only in situations where the task being performed has few contingencies and is highly predictable. By contrast, normative modes of compliance can be used where there are many contingencies as long as the norms are constant. Normative modes, because they are internalized, require no external supervision. Remunerative modes of compliance are not as alienating as coercion, so they can be used where there are a moderate number of contingencies. They do not require internalization of organizational goals but only generalized internalization of larger social norms, such as "honest day's work for an honest day's pay." As such they can deal with substantial changes in organizational goals which normative modes of influence cannot handle. However, they cannot deal with extreme numbers of work contingencies, since remunerative modes do assume some expediency and therefore require some observability. I would suggest that such an analysis underlies much of Etzioni's formulation and that it would be highly related to the key elements of multi-model contingency theory.

It is my feeling that the so-called "garbage-can" concept of organizational process simply reflects the realization that single model theories are inadequate. It also reflects the fact that the author does not see any multi-model theory as providing an adequate explanation and therefore has concluded that investigators must use ad hoc eclectic approaches to understand organizational behavior properly. I would argue that current multi-model theory is capable of handling such complexities.

The remarks about these alternatives are necessarily cryptic because of limited space. As such they do not give the full import of the contribution each of these writers has made to organizational theory. Rather what has been stressed in this paper is that there is a common framework which in fact encompasses them all. This common framework is stressed, because the diversity of theories and finding suggests much greater disarray in the field than in fact now exists. It not only leads to confusion on the part of the neophyte, but also leads many able students to misinterpret their empirical data. Thus Pennings (1975) suggests, on the basis of a study of forty brokerage firms, that the human relations structure may always be more effective. Not fully taking into account the rationale behind the multi-model theory, he never asks himself how the human relations structure could, with its stress on committees as a mode of coordination, deal with highly repetitive tasks, such as a machinist stamping out 100,000 quarter-inch bolts. In a monocratic bureaucracy this type of decision is handled by a rule. If one had to hold a committee meeting for each bolt, it would clearly be impossible and inefficient. Pennings does not consider such obvious objections, because he has not fully immersed himself in the underlying rationale for the multi-model approach. His findings on the forty brokerage firms would be completely consistent with the multi-model approach if the assumption could be made that, in fact, his measures of complexity are attenuated. All brokerage firms deal with enormous amounts of uncertainty.[2] He is in fact testing the proposition that human relations structures are best able to handle non-uniform tasks and not testing the proposition that rationalistic organizations are best able to handle uniform ones.

2. If one wants to see the relationship between task and structure it is necessary to have tasks that range over a substantial part of the continuum. Thus, Lawrence and Lorsch (1967) contrasted the plastic plants having two new products a year with the bottling plants which had only one or two new products a year. When these extremes (the bottling plant and the plastic companies) were compared, then the multi-model theory was indeed demonstrated. In other words, Pennings (1975) and Mohr (1971) did only one part of the Lawrence and Lorsch study. They studied the equivalent of the plastic factories.

To conclude, it is suggested that despite the seeming diversity of organizational theories, a multi-model contingency theory has emerged that tends to be common to most of these organizational formulations. This paper has sought to outline the basic premises of such a theory, and, it is hoped, that it will provide the policy makers with a general guide to the principles of organizational structure and indicate to the social scientists where they share the same framework, in addition to pointing out future lines of research.

REFERENCES

Bennis, Warren G. 1966. *Changing Organizations*. New York: McGraw-Hill.

Blau, Peter M. 1955. *The Dynamics of Bureaucracy*. Chicago: University of Chicago Press.

—— 1970. "A Formal Theory of Differentiation in Organization," *American Sociological Review*, 35:201–18.

Blau, Peter and W. Richard Scott. 1962. *Formal Organizations*. San Francisco: Chandler.

Buell, Bradley. 1957. *Community Planning for Human Services*. New York: Columbia University Press.

Coleman, James et al. 1966. *Equality of Educational Opportunity*. Washington, D.C.: U.S. Government Printing Office.

Cooley, Charles H. 1955. "Primary Groups." In P. Hare, E. Borgotta, and R. Bales, eds., *Small Groups,* pp. 15–17. New York: Knopf.

Emery, F. E. and E. L. Trist. 1965. "The Causal Texture of Organizational Environments," *Human Relations,* 18:21–32.

Etzioni, Amitai. 1969a. "A Basis for Comparative Analysis of Complex Organizations." In A. Etzioni, ed., *A Sociological Reader on Complex Organizations,* pp. 59–76. 2d ed. New York: Holt, Rinehart and Winston.

—— 1969b. *Modern Organizations*. Englewood Cliffs, N.J.: Prentice-Hall.

Foote, Nelson and Leonard S. Cottrell. 1955. *Identity and Interpersonal Competence*. Chicago: University of Chicago Press.

Franklin, Julian. 1955. "Bureaucracy and Freedom," pp. 941–42. In Contemporary Civilization Staff, eds., *Man in Contemporary Society,* pp. 941–42. New York: Columbia University Press.

Goode, William J. 1960. "Theory of Role Strain," *American Sociological Review,* 25:483–96.

Haas, Eugene, Richard H. Hall, and Norman S. Johnson. 1968. "Toward an Empirically Derived Taxonomy of Organizations." In R. Bowers, ed.,

Studies in Behavior in Organizations. Athens: University of Georgia Press.

Hall, Richard H. 1972. *Organizations: Structure and Process.* Englewood Cliffs, N.J.: Prentice-Hall.

Hamburg, D. A. 1957. "Therapeutic Aspects of Communication and Administrative Policy in the Psychiatric Section of a General Hospital." In M. Greenblatt et al., eds., *The Patient and the Mental Hospital,* pp. 91–107. Glencoe, Ill.: Free Press.

Henry, Jules. 1957. "Types of Institutional Structures." In M. Greenblatt et al., eds., *The Patient and the Mental Hospital,* pp. 73–90. Glencoe, Ill.: Free Press.

Katz, Elihu, and Paul F. Lazarsfeld. 1955. *Personal Influence.* Glencoe, Ill.: Free Press.

Lawrence, P. R., and J. W. Lorsch. 1967. Organization and Environment. Cambridge: Harvard Graduate School of Business Administration.

Lipset, Seymour M., Martin Trow, and James Coleman. 1956. *Union Democracy.* New York: Free Press of Glencoe.

Litwak, Eugene. 1961. "Models of Bureaucracy Which Permit Conflict," *American Journal of Sociology,* 67:177–84.

Litwak, Eugene et al. 1970. *Toward the Multifactor Theory and Practice of Linkage Between Formal Organizations. Washington, D.C.: U.S. Department of Health, Education and Welfare, Social and Rehabilitative Services Department.*

Litwak, Eugene and Josefina Figueira. 1968. "Technological Innovation and Theoretical Functioning of Primary Groups and Bureaucratic Structures," American Journal of Sociology, 73:468–81.

Litwak, Eugene and Jack Rothman. 1970. "Toward the Theory and Practice of Coordination." In W. Rosengren and M. Lefton, eds., *Organizations and Clients.* Columbus, Ohio: Merrill.

Merton, Robert K. 1957. "The Role-set: Problems in Sociological Theory," *The British Journal of Sociology,* 94:106–20.

Michels, Robert. 1949. *Political Parties.* Glencoe, Ill.: Free Press.

Mohr, Lawrence B. 1971. "Organizational Technology and Organizational Structure," *Administrative Science Quarterly,* 16:444–59.

Ogburn, William F. 1953. "The Changing Family." In R. Winch and R. McGinnis, eds, *Selected Readings in Marriage and the Family,* pp. 75–77. New York: Rinehart and Winston.

Ohlin, Lloyd, Herman Piven, and Donnell Pappenford. 1965. "Major Dilemmas of the Social Worker in Probation and Parole." In M. Zald, ed., *Social Welfare Institutions,* pp. 523–38. New York: Wiley.

Pennings, Johannes. 1975. "The Relevance of the Structural-Contingency Model for Organizational Effectiveness," *Administrative Science Quarterly,* 20:393–410.

Perrow, Charles. 1967. "A Framework for the Comparative Analysis of Complex Organizations," *American Sociological Review,* 32:194–208.

Selznick, Philip. 1949. *TVA and the Grass Roots: A Study in the Sociology of Formal Organizations.* Berkeley: University of California Press.

Sheppard, Harold. 1972. *Where Have All the Robots Gone?* New York: Free Press.

Shils, Edward. 1951. "The Study of Primary Groups." In D. Lerner and H. Casswell, eds., *The Policy Sciences,* pp. 44–69. Palo Alto Calif.: Stanford University Press.

Shils, Edward, and Morris Janowitz. 1948. "Cohesion and Disintegration in the Wehrmacht in World War II," *Public Opinion Quarterly,* 12:280–315.

Skinner, C. William and Edwin Winkler, 1969. "Compliance Succession in Rural Communist China: A Cyclical Theory." In A. Etzioni, ed., *A Sociological Reader on Com,ex Organizations,* pp. 410–38, 2nd ed. New York: Holt, Rinehart and Winston.

Sykes, Gresham. 1958. *The Society of Captives.* Princeton, N.J.: Princeton University Press.

Sykes, Gresham and S. Messinger. 1960. "The Inmate Social System." In R. Cloward et al., eds., *Theoretical Studies in Social Organization of the Prison.* New York: Social Science Research Council.

Terreberry, Shirley. 1968. "The Evolution of Organizational Environments," *Administrative Science Quarterly,* 12:590–613.

Thompson, James D. 1967. *Organizations in Action.* New York: McGraw-Hill.

Weber, Max. 1947. *The Theory of Social and Economic Organization.* A. Henderson and Talcott Parsons, trs.; Talcott Parsons, ed. Glencoe, Ill.: Free Press.

Whyte, William F. 1956. "Human Relations: A Progress Report," *Harvard Business Review,* 34:125–32.

Wilensky, Harold and Charles N. Lebeaux. 1958. *Industrial Society and Social Welfare.* New York: Russell Sage Foundation.

SEVEN

The Empirical Limits of Social Work Professionalization

IRWIN EPSTEIN AND KAYLA CONRAD

TWO DECADES ago, just a few years after the formation of the National Association of Social Workers (NASW), sociologist Ernest Greenwood (1957) pronounced social work a profession. He based this assertion on his *perception* of the degree to which social workers adhered to five criteria often used as distinguishing marks of professionalization: (1) the extent to which the knowledge social workers employ is based on a systematic body of theory; (2) the degree of development of and commitment to professional authority; (3) the attainment of community sanction for what social workers do; (4) the ethical code of social work; and (5) the values, norms, and symbols of a professional community of social workers. Naturally, social workers were pleased to receive what was considered Greenwood's "scientific" support for their claim to professional status; and his article, as might be expected, is frequently cited as offering proof that social work is indeed a profession.

Without questioning Greenwood's conclusion, Meyer (1966), another sociologist of social work, went on to ask whether the "community" or the "process" model of profession best describes social work. Viewing these two approaches as complementary rather than as conflicting, Meyer applies them to the problems of recruiting, training, allocating, and organizing professionals. Finally, he concludes that professionalization of social work "constitutes one safeguard against untempered bureaucratization of service programs and agencies" (Meyer, 1966:80).

Other proponents as well as critics of social work professionalization have at any rate given great significance to the concept. Those in favor of professionalization view it as enhancing organizational rationality, effectiveness, efficiency, innovation, and responsiveness (see, for example, Blau and Scott, 1962; Etzioni, 1969; Halmos, 1970). Those opposed to it view professionalization as reinforcing bureaucratic oppression, as a conservatizing force, and as a self-serving device for achieving power and prestige at the expense of the underclass and the "uncredentialed" (see, for example, Cloward and Piven, 1977; Galper, 1975; Reissman, 1977). Proponents want more professionalization. Opponents prefer de-professionalization. Nevertheless, both groups seem convinced of the conceptual significance of this analytic dimension.

Despite the virulence and occasional viciousness of this debate, Greenwood's (1957) assertion has never been challenged *within* the ranks of social work. Moreover, in the literature on the sociology of the professions, his paper is frequently reprinted, cited, and offered as a prototype of the "attribute approach" to the study of professions (Roth, 1974). Recently, however, in an article entitled "Professionalism: The Sociologist's Decoy," Roth (1974:7) described his sociologist/colleague Greenwood's article as "the epitome of misdirected zeal and even misunderstanding concerning professionalism."[1] Employing his own "everyday experience" and a knowledge of the empirical literature concerning *other* occupational groups, Roth systematically challenges Greenwood's approach and conclusions. One example should suffice to acquaint the reader with the character of Roth's attack. Thus, in challenging Greenwood's claim that professional social workers "convene regularly in their associations to learn and to evaluate innovations in theory" (1957:47), Roth (1974:8) remarks:

Does this describe any professional meeting you have observed or heard about? We are all familiar with the function of conventions as a job market, as a place to meet friends and make useful contacts, and as an opportunity for ritualized whoopee. Evaluation of innovations in theory has little chance under these distracting circumstances. Such commonsense observations—garnered from his own experience—should lead the sociologist to make independent assessments of the functions served by lengthy training, a respected place in university educational programs and participation in conventions.

1. Roth makes no distinction between professionalization as a social-structural variable and professionalism as an ideology. This distinction will be discussed later on in the paper.

Roth (1974:17) accuses Greenwood of not making "independent assessments," and of being a sociological apologist and a lobbyist for "one of America's most anxiously upwardly mobile occupations, social work."

In a less critical vein, Goode (1969) has discussed the "theoretical limits" and obstacles to professionalization which confront upward aspiring "people-serving" occupations such as social work. More generally, and in the context of attempts at "the professionalization of everyone," Wilensky (1964:158) optimistically speculates about social workers as "program professionals" and about the positive association between their administrative authority and their advancing professionalization. In contrast, Haug (1975) considers occupations such as social work in light of "the deprofessionalization of everyone" and projects a "de-professionalized future." Challenging Haug's view, Lopata (1976) foresees "the expertization of everyone" and envisions future social worker/client relations as being more democratic as well as more reliant upon professional expertise.

Despite the foregoing predictions of advancing and retreating professionalization, Bennett and Hokenstad (1973:22) question whether the "professional model" is "at all appropriate for describing the major modes of people working." They propose a revised and de-professionalized conceptualization of social work which is empirically based. In this context, they offer some untested "hunches and predictions" about the future social bases of human service occupations and conclude that,

Due to the possibility for misunderstanding, it should be emphasized that these are empirical predictions, not normative exhortations. They are hypotheses for testing, and they are suggested for professional people working partially because some of the trends are clearly in evidence, but more importantly because they are theoretically entailed in a revised conceptualization of the social basis and the entailed meanings of working people. (Bennett and Hokenstad, 1973:42)

None of the above mentioned authors in their analyses or projections presents empirical data bearing on social workers. The purpose of this paper is to employ the empirical evidence that *is* available to assess the current state of social-worker professionalization and to question the descriptive and predictive validity of professionalization as a variable. We take no position on the issue of whether social work should or should not become more professionalized. Moreover, no attempt is made to predict the future. In fact, much of the "data-base" comes from a 1966 survey of over a thousand

NASW members (Epstein, 1968). These findings are supplemented by the few, more limited studies of social-worker professionalization conducted before and since. In addition, we draw upon relevant theoretical and empirical literature from the sociology of occupations and professions.

Our purpose is to consider the congruence of the existing empirical evidence and the various heuristic models of social-worker professionalization. We approached this paper with the assumption that professionalization was a significant descriptive and predictive variable to be refined only by the specification of qualifying conditions. The empirical analysis suggests, instead, that our conceptualization of social work should be deprofessionalized. In other words, despite their frequent claims to professionalization, their accompanying credentials, and their genuine service contribution, it is perhaps more descriptively valid to consider social workers non-professionals, organizational functionaries, bureaucrats, or agency workers than to consider them "professionals." Some implications for the sociology of social work, the paraprofessional movement, and the delivery of service are then discussed.

SOCIAL WORK AS A NON-PROFESSION

Most social workers consider themselves professionals. Most sociologists of social work seem to agree. Even those who do not have generally considered professionalization to be a valid empirical construct and an important predictor of social-worker attitudes and behavior. In this section the *descriptive* and *predictive* validity of social-worker professionalization is discussed.

PROFESSIONALIZATION AS A POOR DESCRIPTIVE CONCEPT

In recent years, sociologists of the professions have distinguished between the actual and aspirational aspects of professionalization. Vollmer and Mills (1966:viii), for example, conceive of "professionalization" as the process by which occupations attain "certain crucial characteristics," such as those described by Greenwood, which are presumed to be associated with "ideal type" professions, that is, the ministry, law, and medicine. They use the term "professionalism" to refer to "an ideology and associated activities that can be found in many diverse occupational groups where members aspire to professional status." They go on to say,

Professionalism as an ideology may induce members of many occupational groups to strive to become professional, but at the same time we can see that many occupational groups that express the ideology of professionalism in reality may not be very advanced in regard to professionalization. Professionalism may be a necessary constituent of professionalization, but professionalism is not a sufficient cause for the entire professionalization process. (Vollmer and Mills, 1966:viii)

Recognizing that many upward-aspiring occupations never attain "the full character of a profession," Freidson (1971:469) advocates assessment of given occupations' claims to professionalization against the model of organization provided by medicine. Hall (1969:80) cautions that the external symbols of professionalization—for example, codes of ethics, professional associations, training schools—have become "well known to occupational groups that are aspiring to become known as professions." He points out "that the process of professionalization probably is based on much more than what the occupation does in trying to professionalize itself" (Hall, 1969:90). Simply stated, wishing is not enough. Without the benefit of empirical evidence, however, Greenwood (1957) asserts the validity of social work's claim to professional status. How well does the available data concerning social-worker professionalization support his conclusion?

In a highly influential paper, Goode (1957) describes the established professions as having achieved, and the aspiring professions as seeking to achieve, a state of "community of profession." This notion of professional community is implicit in the writings of both proponents and opponents of social-work professionalization. Proponents view the professional community as organized around systematic knowledge and a service ideal. Opponents, on the other hand, view the professional community as organized around a conservative, neutralist ideology (Epstein, 1970a). To operationalize the community concept, Benguigui (1967) has suggested that within an occupational group, the more positive the correlations among various structural measures of professionalization, the more closely the occupation approximates a professional community. This intercorrelational approach to the study of professionalization is also implicit in the empirical research of Hall (1967, 1968, 1969), March and Simon (1958), Snizek (1972), and Fox and Vonk (1973).

In an effort to assess the extent to which social work is a professional community, Epstein (1970a) looked at the intercorrelations among five commonly used structural measures of professionalization. These indexes included a measure of organizational professionalization, a measure of participation in professional activities, and three measures of professional role-orientation. Despite the fact that these measures are generally assumed to be interchangeable indicators of professionalization and that the sample was drawn from what might be assumed to be a highly professionalized population (NASW members with master's degrees in social work), it was found that only two of the ten paired relationships are significantly correlated in a positive direction (Epstein, 1970a:72). Of the two positive relationships, one is very weak (tau-c = .10) and the other may be explained as a consequence of a common item shared by the two positively associated indexes. The absence of strong positive correlations among the various measures of professionalization led Epstein (1970a:73) to conclude, "The evidence presented suggests that social work should not be considered an integrated professional community. Thus, these commonly accepted indexes are not tapping an underlying monotonic structural dimension which can be characterized as professionalization."

Billingsley's (1964b:132–33) study of two social-work agencies produced equally dismal findings for those who assert the existence of a professional social-work community. He indicates that when agency setting is disregarded, there is only "slight" evidence that "persons with a professional orientation are more likely to be . . . active in the professional subsystem." These differences are not statistically significant. Furthermore, when agency setting is considered, the finding is reversed in three out of ten tests of the hypothesis.

Looking at the relationship between structural and attitudinal aspects of professionalization, data from a subsample of social workers in Hall's (1969:82–83) comparative study of eleven occupational groups support his general conclusion "that the assumption of concommitant variation between structural and attitudinal components of professionalization is incorrect." Similarly, Epstein (1970a:74) found no relationship between his five structural measures of professionalization and an attitudinal measure of commitment to a "neutralist ideology of professionalism."[2]

In their paper "Professions in Process" Bucher and Strauss challenge the validity of the community approach to the professions. They suggest that

2. These Likert-like items tested respondents' attitudinal commitment to political neutrality, professional decorum, affective neutrality, and the superiority of professional definitions of client need.

rather than looking at professions as communities, it is more accurate to regard them as "loose amalgamations of segments, pursuing different objectives in different manners, and more or less deliberately held together under a common name at a particular time in history" (Bucher and Strauss, 1961:325).

At the level of the total profession, segments or specialties may engage in struggles to shape the goals and means of the larger profession in line with their own objectives and technologies. Within segments, definitions of appropriate goals and means may serve as the bases of movements for professionalization (Bucher and Strauss, 1961:332–33). In other words, the professionalization of specialties within a profession may institutionalize differences among them. Within the segments themselves, however, one would expect to find the elements of professionalization to be internally integrated.

In a test of the "process model" of social-work professionalization, Epstein (1970b:159–60) analyzes patterns of professionalization within the three major practice "segments" of social work—casework, groupwork, and community organization. The intercorrelations of measures of professionalization within practice segments present more problems of interpretation,

Among caseworkers, for example, none of the measures of professionalization is significantly correlated with another. In fact, within groupwork and community organization agencies there is a statistically significant *negative* correlation between organizational professionalization and worker commitment to a neutralist ideology of professionalism. . . . In addition, those groupworkers and community organizers who are most strongly oriented to their professional peers on the Billingsley measures are least likely to participate in professional conferences, associations, etc. . . . These findings point to the need for future elaboration of the diverse meanings of professionalization. . . . (Epstein, 1970b:160; emphasis in the original)

Finally, Hage and Aiken's study of program innovation in sixteen human service organizations offers indirect evidence of the non-covariation of different measures of social-worker professionalization. Although the authors do not indicate the correlation between their two measures of professionalization—professional training and professional activity—these two measures show different patterns of association with program innovation (Hage and Aiken, 1967:508–09).

The findings presented thus far concern patterns of professionalization *within* social work. Another approach to the empirical assessment of social-work professionalization is to compare the professional characteristics of social workers with those of other occupational groups of professionals, in order to determine social work's relative professionalization. Inclusion of the Wilensky professional orientation index in the Epstein questionnaire made it possible to compare Epstein's sample of social workers with Wilensky's sample of professors, lawyers, and engineers. The results of this comparison indicate that on the Wilensky professionalization measure—a composite index of reference group, job attractiveness, and professional par-

Table 7.1 PERCENT OF PROFESSORS, LAWYERS, ENGINEERS, AND SOCIAL WORKERS MENTIONING EACH GROUP AS THE ONE WHOSE JUDGMENT SHOULD COUNT MOST REGARDING PROFESSIONAL PERFORMANCE

	Professors	Lawyers	Engineers	Social Workers
Professional Colleagues and Associations	81%	51%	18%	17%
Administration, Supervisors, etc.	8%	8%	47%	65%
Students, Clients, and Recipients of Services	9%	43%	34%	19%
N	99	207	184	833

Source: Epstein, 1970a:74.

ticipation items—only 5 percent of the social workers scored "high" in comparison with 51 percent of the professors, 25 percent of the lawyers, and 11 percent of the engineers (Epstein, 1970a:73).

The comparative data concerning reference group orientation of these four occupational groups is reproduced in Table 7-1; the latter presents responses to the *prescriptive* question: "Whose judgment should count most when your overall professional performance is assessed?" Despite the fact that the social work respondents were master's degree social workers and members of NASW, Table 7-1 shows that they were least likely (17 percent) to mention professional colleagues and associations as the preferred arbiters of their professional performance. Social workers were almost as low (19 percent) in their selection of clients as their evaluators. Rather, of the four occupational groups studied, social workers were most likely to say that their supervisors and/or agency administrators *should* count most in evaluating their professional performance (65 percent). While many of these super-visors and administrators may have completed professional training in social work, the findings lead us to question the familiar claim to colleague control exerted by an *external* professional community. Moreover, supervisors' and administrators' familiarity with social work jargon only increases the possi-bility that basically bureaucratic requirements will be presented as though they were expressions of professional norms.

Billingsley's (1964a) study of 110 "professionally trained social case-workers and casework supervisors in two voluntary, non-sectarian, profes-sional casework agencies" demonstrated a similar "bureaucratic orienta-tion." Hall's (1969:81–84) data concerning social workers in one public and two private agencies indicate, rather anomalously, that relative to other oc-cupations social workers scored high in use of the professional organization as a major reference, but low in their belief in colleague control.

The other available bits and pieces of empirical evidence raise addi-tional questions about social work's claim to professional status. In studying the public's image of social work, for example, Kadushin (1958:40) found evidence to support the conclusion that social work's public image is one of a "minor if not marginal profession." In Bailey's (1959:62) study of public attitudes toward various professional helpers, respondents were least likely to choose social workers for help with interpersonal problems. Varley's (1963) study of the "professional socialization" of social work students showed that on values directly related to social work practice, there was no significant difference between beginning and graduating master's degree students. A study of master's degree social workers with advanced certifi-cation (members of the Academy of Certified Social Workers) (Varley, 1966: 87) indicates that this most "professionalized" group of practitioners demonstrates only "a moderate commitment to the service ideal." An anal-ysis of complaints brought before NASW for violations of social work's Code of Ethics between 1965 and 1970 (Witte, 1971:978–79) indicates an average of four complaints a year. When one considers the fact that the membership of NASW averaged close to 50,000 during that period, the au-thor's conclusion that the Code of Ethics affords "modest" protection to the public appears to be a gross understatement.

Finally, a recent study of 152 persons who took the California licensing exam for clinical social workers showed that the only variable positively as-sociated with passing the exam was whether the applicant had himself undergone psychotherapy (Borenzweig, 1977). Training variables such as the "graduate school orientation, clinical or non-clinical emphasis, fieldwork, early work experiences, and the training and credentials of supervisors—did not significantly correlate with passing or failing the examination" (Borenzweig, 1977:175). Describing the examiners (many of whom were "grandfathered" into their licenses) participating in this dubious credentialization procedure, Borenzweig (1977:177) comments:

It was generally known that most examiners held psychoanalytic and offshoot-psychoanalytic beliefs (such as those derived from gestalt psychology, transactional analysis, ego psychology, and the theories of Jung and Reich). It is probable that an applicant who had an allegiance to a perspective similar to that of the examiners and who could "reasonably" defend this allegiance had a greater likelihood of passing his oral exam. The term *reasonably* is emphasized because examiners were instructed to fail applicants considered to be a "danger to the public."

The foregoing is hardly a procedure and a minimal standard to inspire public confidence.

What this diverse empirical evidence suggests is that, despite its professional claims and private practice aspirations, its sociological apologists, its certification procedures, and its attempts at licensing, social work is *not* a profession. In other words, the term "profession," as empirically-oriented sociologists use it or as the general public uses it, does not *describe* social work.

Discussing the characteristics of "the profession of social work" in NASW's *Encyclopedia of Social Work,* Meyer (1971:971) optimistically asserts that professionalism in social work is "in flux." He suggests that this "diversity matches the structural diversity that appears to be emerging and marks, perhaps, a state of continuing professionalization in social work as a more mature profession." Through some rather tortuous logic, Clearfield (1977:29), writing in the *Journal of Education for Social Work,* implies that social-work educators should ignore troublesome "objective" findings and encourage their students to emulate those social workers who have developed a self-image that discounts their negative public image. He states,

However, what is real has less importance than what is perceived to be real. Even if it is not accurate, the perception of a negative self-image is real in its consequences. Indeed, since what other social workers think has an important impact on self-image, the false perception [that social workers have a negative self-image] serves to influence the actual self-image. The task of correcting the perceptions of the self-image is the responsibility of social work education, for it is during the educational process that one most clearly learns to evaluate one's profession. (Clearfield, 1977:29)

Halmos (1971:589) eloquently argues that social scientists who are critical of the "personal service professions" have confused skepticism with scholarly rigor and should endorse more "optimistic" views. For Meyer, Clearfield, and Halmos, each advocating professional status for social workers, it may be functional to ignore the empirical evidence. For those interested in assessing objectively the actual level of social work professionalization, the evidence cannot be ignored.

PROFESSIONALIZATION AS A POOR PREDICTOR

Throughout the history of social work, advocates for and against social-work professionalization have attributed great predictive powers to this dimension. Those who have bothered to assess empirically the impact of social-worker professionalization generally have done this in two ways: (1) by treating professionalization as an independent variable and considering the zero-order correlations between measures of professionalization and certain outcome variables, or (2) by treating professionalization as an intervening variable and considering the partial correlations between other sets of independent and dependent variables, controlling for the effects of professionalization. In this section the *predictive* validity of professionalization is assessed.

Professionalization as an independent variable. Despite the many claims and counterclaims about positive and negative consequences of social-worker professionalization, a review of the literature in this area offers no empirical research linking different degrees of social-worker professionalization with various performance criteria.[3]

Within social work, Baker (1974) reports on NASW's abortive attempts to define the competencies which should be expected of social workers at six

3. This is not unique to social work. Thus, Berg (1975:108–09) describes a study by Freedman of five different occupational settings. Freedman's findings are described as follows: "She found . . . that 'nominal' occupational ladders are developed by employees partly in response to the need to differentiate the positions of personnel of different seniority levels who earn different incomes. These ladders do not reflect skill and related economically significant differences as much as they do simple desires to legitimize distinctions that are too finely drawn to stand up under rigorous examinations of skill differences" (Berg, 1975:109).

different training levels. Commenting on the *Standards for Social Service Manpower* finally adopted by NASW in 1973, she remarks: "The failure of the document as a classification lies in its failure truly to distinguish the functions of each of the six levels, one from the other. The eventual effect is of falling back upon a series of small differences in educational levels as the only real distinguishing factor" (1974:381).

Instead of assessing the relationship between professionalization and competence, empirical studies of social workers assess the links between professionalization and pro-client attitudes, program innovation, and political attitudes. Thus, for example, in a study of non-MSW public welfare workers, Blau and Scott (1963:68) have shown that the more "professionalized" workers, who have a professional reference group orientation and who have had exposure to some graduate courses, are more likely to believe that clients should get more assistance and that agency procedures interfere with service to clients. Elsewhere, Scott (1965:74) has shown that these workers are more concerned with the level of professionalism of their supervisors. A study comparing MSW and non-MSW social workers (Eimicke, 1974:412) indicated that those with master's degrees "were significantly more receptive to clients' rights than those without a degree . . ."

In assessing the findings of the preceding studies, the frequent contradictions between questionnaire responses and actual behavior should be considered. Thus, in a study of public assistance workers, Kroeger compared caseworkers' statements about their grant-issuing behavior and clients' reports of grants received with official records. She found caseworkers' accounts of their own generosity to be greatly exaggerated. Clients' reports of grants received, on the other hand, were quite reliable (Kroeger, 1975:187–88). Moreover, Piven and Cloward (1971:176) describe an HEW study of relief practices in eleven cities in which a *negative* relationship was found between "professional orientation" and the proportion of the poor who actually received AFDC.

In a study of organizational innovation to which we referred earlier, Hage and Aiken test the relationship between two measures of organizational professionalization and the rate of program change. They found a weak, positive correlation between the level of professional training and the rate of program change (r = .14) (1967:508). A stronger positive correlation (r = .37) was found between the level of "extra-organizational professional activities of members" and the rate of program change (Hage and Aiken,

1967:509). This relationship is considerably reduced, however (r = .11), when organizational size is controlled (Hage and Aiken, 1967:516).

Using the same data-base to study social-worker alienation, Lawler and Hage encountered the "paradoxical" finding that professional training reduced alienation, whereas professional activity increased it. Yet when other factors were controlled, the predictive power of the two measures of professionalization did not exceed .20 (Lawler and Hage, 1973:5).

In an area closely tied to social work, Downs (1976) conducted a national study of juvenile correctional institution administrators and found no relationship between staff professionalization and measures of deinstitutionalization—a program innovation. He reports the results of test of the relationship as follows,

Executives were asked the number of professional associations to which they belonged and the number of professional conferences they had attended in the past year. The respective correlations of the two measures of deinstitutionalization are − .03 and .04—almost a perfect lack of association in both cases. The relationship of agency directors to their profession, at least as measured by these two variables, appears to have little to do with how deinstitutionalized their agencies are. It turns out that this nonrelationship is not due to correctional executives' having no impact on agency innovativeness . . . but to the fact that their professional ties are poor indicators of their ideologies and priorities. (Downs, 1976:206)

The relationship between professionalization and conservatism is equally problematic. Cryns (1977) recently found that graduate students in social work scored more conservatively than undergraduate social work students. In his sample of MSW's, however, Epstein (1970a) found no consistent relationships between structural measures of professionalization and social-worker radicalism. Thus, with his total sample he found that professionalization was associated neither with conservative nor with radical conceptions of appropriate strategies of social change. Looking at different "segments" within social work, he found that social workers who identified with various practice methods differed significantly in their endorsement of radical goals and means for social work. However, "professionalization did not intensify the differences among representatives of different practice methods" (Epstein, 1970b:162). Here again, the distinction between professionalization and professionalism is significant. Although structural measures of professionalization produced no consistent conservative effects, those social workers who were committed to a neutralist ideology of professionalism *were* significantly more conservative than those who eschewed this ideology. This was true for the total sample (Epstein, 1970a:75–76) and for each of the practice methods (Epstein, 1970b:161–62).

Rather than clarifying the contingent character of professionalization, these diverse and disparate findings challenge the optimistic belief in the existence and benefits of professionalization. They also contravene the belief held by radical critics that professionalization is conservatizing. What they do suggest is that professionalization, as a structural variable, has little predictable impact.

Professionalization as an intervening variable. The sizeable theoretical literature focusing on organizational/professional interaction in social work traditionally has presented two opposing perspectives. One perspective stresses the conflict between bureaucratic and professional norms (Eimicke, 1974; Finch, 1976; Green, 1966; Litwak, 1961; Wasserman, 1971). The other stresses the complementarity between these elements (Billingsley, 1964a; Cloward and Piven, 1977; Freidson, 1970; Toren, 1969).

The limited empirical research on this topic treats social-worker professionalization as a variable which somehow affects the impact of organizational characteristics on dependent variables such as radicalism and alienation. The findings in this literature indicate that the actual relationships are much more complicated than the theorists would suggest. In Epstein's (1970c:129–30), for example, professionalization—as measured by commitment to the Billingsley professional role-orientation index—neutralized the conservative effects of high organizational rank. It had its most powerful mitigating effect on groupworkers and community organizers.

A similar finding is reported by Eimicke (1974:412) in his study of casework supervisors. Epstein (1970c) also found that the same measure of professionalization *intensified* both the *conservative* effects of bureaucratic orientation and the *radical* effects of a client orientation. In other words, the most conservative social workers in Epstein's sample were high on professional and high on bureaucratic orientation. The most radical social workers were high on professional and high on client orientation (Epstein, 1970b). Looking at the intervening effects of professionalization on the relationship between background characteristics and radicalism, Epstein (1969:186–88) found that professionalization *intensified* both conservative and radical predispositions associated with different sets of background characteristics. He concluded that whatever the explanation for these complex findings, ''it is clear that professional norms and values are sufficiently undefined at this point so as to support both conservative and radical ideologies'' (Epstein, 1970c).

The amorphous character of organizational/professional interaction in social work agencies is demonstrated in Lawler and Hage's work as well. Focusing on social-worker alienation, these authors (1973:5–9) find that the impact of professional education and professional activity are opposed in direction. Moreover, depending on the agency setting under study, each of these measures' association with a measure of powerlessness reverses the direction of its impact.

One way to approach these anomalous and frequently unexpected findings is to develop a series of ex-post-facto hypotheses which articulate the seemingly endless sets of conditions under which to expect one or another set of outcomes. Once this tedious operation has been completed, however, the measures of professionalization in Epstein's and in Lawler and Hage's studies would explain no more than about 5 percent of the variance on the dependent variables. Under these circumstances, the more strategic research decision would be to abandon professionalization as an intervening variable. The wisdom of this decision is further supported by Epstein's (1969) unanticipated discovery that, despite all the radical rhetoric concerning the conservative effects of professionalization, organizational factors and background characteristics were most predictive of social-worker conservatism. Professionalization had little effect on these relationships.

What we are suggesting is that social-work researchers consider abandoning Greenwood's (1957) model of social work as a profession, Scott's (1965) notion of social work as a ''heteronomous profession,'' and Etzioni's (1969) conception of social work as a ''semi-profession'' and first assess the descriptive and predictive power of a totally de-professionalized conceptual model of social work.

IMPLICATIONS FOR SOCIAL WORK

Overall, the limited descriptive and predictive validity of social-work professionalization clearly suggests the need for a more empirically based, de-professionalized model of social work. This approach would reject the normative "professional" model of social work borrowed from the "established" professions and endorsed by advocates of professionalization. It would begin with the assumption that social workers, even those with MSW and ACSW after their names, are simply organizational functionaries whose work-related attitudes and behaviors are similar to those of factory workers, bureaucrats, or any other organizational employees. It would reject the pompous assertions about social-work schooling and "professional socialization." Instead social-work education would be seen as basically a screening and sorting mechanism which, at best, prevents those who are patently disturbed or misanthropic from entering the field and sorts the remaining numbers according to the bureaucratic settings in which they would be most comfortable. It would view claims to social-work professionalization as in fact expressions of social-work professionalism—an *ideology* associated with *aspiration* to professional status rather than as an expression of the central norms of social work as a "professional community."[4] This ideology is often used to unload unpleasant organizational tasks (Emerson and Pollner, 1976; Maslach, Street, 1977) or to justify political apathy (Epstein, 1970a).

An empirically based de-professionalized model would view the paraprofessional movement with equal skepticism—requiring empirical evidence of paraprofessionals' superior effectiveness and efficiency. To date, the limited empirical literature on paraprofessionals is largely descriptive rather than evaluative (Gartner, 1971; Katan, 1974). Finally, an empirically based, de-professionalized model of social work would view claims to professional status and efforts at licensing and other forms of credentialization in a political-economic context, that is, as devices to extend access to resources (Mc-

4. Similarly, in a study of professionalization and unionization among rehabilitation counselors, Haug and Sussman (1971) indicate the ways in which an expressed ideology of professionalism may serve as an altruistic disguise for other motives. Thus, they find a relatively weak correlation between an attitudinal measure of the professionalization of individual counselors' roles and their anti-union attitudes. They also find a weak correlation between counselors' professional participation and their anti-union attitudes. Nearly 65 percent of those who oppose unionization, however, oppose it on the grounds that it is "unprofessional." They (1971:533) comment, "One possible explanation is that the individual who perceives himself as a professional, having taken on the imagery of the role, uses a rhetoric which is basically different from the pro-union occupational holder. Both want the best wages and working conditions for themselves and their colleagues. The latter employs an open dialogue of rights, demands, grievances, needs, and privileges, while the former cloaks his hidden agenda of higher pay and ideal work environment behind the words of service, reward, skill, mystery, and privilege."

Carthy and Zald, 1973), to disengage the poor (Cloward and Epstein, 1967), to benefit from third-party payments and to maintain a competitive edge (Kurzman, 1973).

Naturally, many social workers will reject de-professionalization and the notion that they are bureaucrats (Pruger, 1973) working in bureaucracies (Whatcott, 1974) delivering service (Baker, 1974). Some, in fact, even find the designation "social worker" problematic. Thus, for example, Pollock contends that social workers should consider the negative "implications of the very term 'social worker' for the profession." He comments, "We do not have 'medical workers,' we do not have 'legal workers'; we do not have 'theological workers' or 'educational workers.' The term 'work' has a mechanistic connotation. It does not reflect concern with the increase of knowledge on which the professional function is based, does not employ a concept of professional ethics; in short, it is not a professional term" (Pollock, 1961:111). Specht (1972) even goes so far as to predict that the mere consideration of de-professionalization augurs social work's demise.

Despite the possibility that delicate elitist sensibilities might be disturbed by it, there is much to be gained by de-professionalizing our conception of social work. It would reestablish the legitimacy of social workers doing what they do best and what the public expects of them—locating and providing concrete services. It would help break down, or at least curtail, artificial, credential barriers to social-work employment. It would clarify and demystify the relationship between the techniques social workers employ and the political purposes they serve (Epstein, 1975). It would open the way to identifying, codifying, and teaching the kinds of organizational skills (Pawlak, 1976; Pruger, 1973) that enhance organizational responsiveness to clients and reduce social worker "burn-out" (Maslach, 1976). Finally, an empirically based, de-professionalized conceptual model of social work would enable us to identify more readily those factors which facilitate or obstruct social service delivery.

REFERENCES

Bailey, Margaret B. 1959. "Community Orientations toward Social Casework," *Social Work,* 4:60–66.

Baker, M. R. 1974. "Social Work: A Profession or a Service Delivery System?" *Social Casework,* 55:381–84.

Benguigui, Georges. 1967. "La Professionalization des cadres dans l'industrie." *Sociologie du Travail*, 8:134–43.

Bennett, William S., Jr., and Merl C. Hokenstad, Jr. 1973. "Full-Time People Workers and Conceptions of the 'Professional.' " In P. Halmos, ed., *Professionalization and Social Change*. The Sociological Review Monograph 20. Keele: University of Keele.

Berg, T. 1975. "Licensing of Paraprofessionals: The Visible and Hidden Agendas," *Education and Urban Society*, 8:104–18.

Billingsley, Andrew. 1964a. "Bureaucratic and Professional Orientation Patterns in Social Casework," *Social Service Review*, 4:400–07.

—— 1964b. *The Role of the Social Worker in a Child Protective Agency: A Comparative Analysis*. Boston: Massachusetts Society for the Prevention of Cruelty to Children.

Blau, Peter M., and W. Richard Scott. 1962. *Formal Organizations*. San Francisco: Chandler.

Borenzweig, Herman. 1977. "Who Passes the California Licensing Examinations?" *Social Work*, 22:173–77.

Bucher, Rue and Anselm Strauss. 1961. "Professions in Process," *American Journal of Sociology*, 66:325–34.

Clearfield, Sidney M. 1977. "Professional Self-Image of the Social Worker: Implications for Social Work Education," *Journal of Education for Social Work*, 13:23–30.

Cloward, Richard A. and Irwin Epstein. 1967. "Private Social Welfare's Disengagement from the Poor: The Case of Family Adjustment Agencies." In G. Brager and F. Purcell, eds., *Community Action Against Poverty*, pp. 40–63. New Haven: College and University Press Services.

Cloward, Richard A. and Frances Fox Piven. 1977. "The Acquiescence of Social Work," *Society*, 14:55–63.

Cryns, Arthur G. 1977. "Social Work Education and Student Ideology: A Multivariate Study of Professional Socialization," *Journal of Education for Social Work*, 13:44–51.

Downs, George W. 1976. "Bureaucracy, Innovation and Public Policy." Ph.D. Diss., University of Michigan.

Eimicke, W. B. 1974. "Professionalism and Participation: Compatible Means to Improved Services?" *Public Administration Review*, 34:409–14.

Emerson, Robert M. and Melvin Pollner. 1976. "Dirty Work Designations: Their Features and Consequences in a Psychiatric Setting," *Social Problems*, 23:243–54.

Epstein, Irwin. 1968. "Social Workers and Social Action: Attitudes toward Social Action Strategies," *Social Work;* 13:101–08.

—— 1969. "Professionalization and Social Work Activism." Ph.D. dissertation, Columbia University.

—— 1970a. "Professionalization, Professionalism, and Social Worker Radicalism," *Journal of Health and Social Behavior,* 11:67–77.

—— 1970b. "Specialization, Professionalization, and Social Worker Radicalism: A Test of the 'Process' Model of the Profession," *Applied Social Studies,* 2:155–63.

—— 1970c. "Organizational Careers, Professionalization, and Social Worker Radicalism," *Social Service Review,* 44:123–31.

—— 1970d. "Professional Role Organization and Conflict Strategies," *Social Work,* 15:87–92.

—— 1975. "The Politics of Behavior Therapy." In H. Jones, ed., *Toward a New Social Work.* London: Routledge, Kegan-Paul.

Etzioni, Amitai, ed. 1969. *The Semi-Professions and Their Organization.* New York: Free Press.

Finch, W. A., Jr. 1976. "Social Workers vs. Bureaucracy," *Social Work,* 21:370–75.

Fox, J. W. and J. A. Vonk. 1973. "Reply to Snizek," *American Sociological Review,* 38:392–95.

Freidson, E. 1970. *Professional Dominance: The Social Structure of Medical Care.* New York: Aldine-Atherton.

Freidson, E., ed. 1971. "Professions in Contemporary Society," *American Behavioral Scientist,* 14:467–597.

Galper, Jeffry H. 1975. *The Politics of Social Services.* Englewood Cliffs, N.J.: Prentice-Hall.

Gartner, Alan. 1971. *Paraprofessionals and Their Performance: A Survey of Education, Health and Social Service Programs.* New York: Praeger.

Goode, William. 1957. "Community within a Community," *American Sociological Review,* 22:194–200.

—— 1969. "The Theoretical Limits of Professionalization," in A. Etzioni, ed., *The Semi-Professions and Their Organization.* New York: Free Press.

Green, A. D. 1966. "The Professional Social Worker in the Bureaucracy," *Social Service Review,* 40:71–83.

Greenwood, Ernest. 1957. "Attributes of a Profession," *Social Work,* 2:44–55.

Hage, Jerald and Michael Aiken. 1967. "Program Change and Organization Properties," *American Jouanal of Sociology,* 72:503–19.

Hall, Richard H. 1967. "Some Organizational Considerations in the Professional-Organizational Relationship," *Administrative Science Quarterly,* 12:461–78.

—— 1968. "Professionalization and Bureaucratization," *American Sociological Review*, 33:94–104.

—— 1969. *Occupations and the Social Structure*. Englewood Cliffs, N.J.: Prentice-Hall.

Halmos, P. 1970. *The Personal Service Society*. London: Schocken.

—— 1971. "Sociology and the Personal Service Profesions," *American Behavioral Scientist*, 14:583–97.

Haug, Marie. 1975. "The Deprofessionalization of Everyone?" *Social Focus*, 8:197–214.

Haug, Marie R. and Marvin B. Sussman. 1971. "Professionalization and Unionism: A Jurisdictional Dispute?" *American Behavioral Scientist*, 14:525–40.

Kadushin, Alfred. 1958. "Prestige of Social Work—Facts and Factors," *Social Work*, 3:37–43.

Katan, Joseph. 1974. "The Utilization of Indigenous Workers in Human Service Organizations." In Y. Hasenfeld and R. English, eds., *Human Service Organizations*, pp. 448–67. Ann Arbor: University of Michigan Press.

Kroeger, Naomi. 1975. "Bureaucracy, Social Exchange and Benefits Received in a Public Assistance Agency," *Social Problems*, 23:182–96.

Kurzman, P. A. 1973. "Third-Party Reimbursement," *Social Work*, 18:11–22.

Lawler, Edward and Jerald Hage. 1973. "Professional-Bureaucratic Conflict and Intraorganizational Powerlessness among Social Workers," *Journal of Sociology and Social Welfare*, 1:1–11.

Litwak, Eugene. 1961. "Models of Bureaucracy That Permit Conflict," *American Journal of Sociology*, 67:173–83.

Lopata, Helena Z. 1976. "Expertization of Everyone and the Revolt of the Client," *Sociological Quarterly*, 17:435–47.

March, James G. and Herbert A. Simon. 1958. *Organizations*. New York: Wiley.

Maslach, Christina. 1976. "Burned Out," *Human Behavior*, 5:16–22.

McCarthy, John D. and Mayer N. Zald. 1973. *The Trend of Social Movements in America: Professionalization and Resource Mobilization*. Morristown, N.J.: General Learning Press.

Meyer, Henry J. 1966. "The Effect of Social Work Professionalization on Manpower." In E. Schwartz, ed., *Manpower in Social Welfare*, pp. 66–77. New York: National Association of Social Workers.

—— 1971. "Profession of Social Work: Contemporary Characteristics." In *Encyclopedia of Social Work*, 2:959–72. New York: National Association of Social Workers.

Pawlak, Edward J. 1976. "Organizational Tinkering," *Social Work,* 21:376–80.

Piven, Frances Fox and Richard A. Cloward. 1971. *Regulating the Poor.* New York: Random.

Pollock, Otto. 1961. "Image of the Social Worker in the Community and in the Profession," Social Work, 6:106–11.

Pruger, Robert. 1973. "The Good Bureaucrat," *Social Work,* 18:26–32.

Reissman, Frank. 1977. "Paraprofessionals, Poverty and Politics," *Society,* 14:72–78.

Roth, Julius A. 1974. "Professionalism: The Sociologist's Decoy," *Sociology of Work and Occupations,* 1:6–23.

Scott, Richard W. 1965. "Reactions to Supervision in a Heteronomous Professional Organization," *Administrative Science Quarterly,* 10:65–81.

Snizek, W. E. 1972. "Hall's Professionalism Scale: An Empirical Reassessment," *American Sociological Review,* 37:109–14.

Specht, Harry. 1972. "The Deprofessionalization of Social Work," *Social Work,* 17:3–15.

Street, David. Forthcoming. "Bureaucratization, Professionalization and the Poor." In K. Gronberg, D. Street, and G. Suttles, eds., *Poverty and Social Change.* Chicago: University of Chicago Press.

Toren, Nina. 1969. "Semi-Professionalism and Social Work: A Theoretical Perspective," In A. Etzioni, ed., *The Semi-Professions and Their Organization,* pp. 141–95. New York: Free Press.

Varley, Barbara K. 1963. "Socialization and Social Work Education," *Social Work,* 8:102–09.

—— 1966. "Are Social Workers Dedicated to Service?" *Social Work,* 11:84–91.

Vollmer, Howard and Donald L. Mills. 1966. *Professionalization.* Englewood Cliffs, N.J.: Prentice-Hall.

Wasserman, Harry. 1971. "The Professional Social Worker in a Bureaucracy," *Social Work,* 16:89–95.

Whatcott, W. 1974. "Bureaucratic Locus and Service Delivery," *Social Work,* 19:432–37.

Wilensky, Harold L. 1964. "The Professionalization of Everyone?" *American Journal of Sociology,* 70:137–58.

Witte, Ernest F. 1971. "Profession of Social Work: Professional Associations," *Encyclopedia of Social Work.* 2:972–82. New York: National Association of Social Workers.

EIGHT

Client-Organization Relations:
A Systems Pespective

YEHESKEL HASENFELD

HUMAN SERVICE organizations have been distinguished from other types of bureaucracies by the centrality of client-staff transactions as the core activity in such organizations. Unlike the public of other bureaucracies, the clients in human service organizations not only assume the role of consumers, but also serve as raw material to be worked upon; and occupy a quasi-membership role in the organization (e.g., Hasenfeld and English, 1974; Parsons, 1970; Wheeler, 1966; Lefton and Rosengren, 1966). The essential character of any human service organization will be manifested through the patterned relations between its clients and staff, relations which are the *raison d' être* of the organization. It is not surprising that much of the research on human service organizations focuses on identifying the parameters which determine and shape the transactions between the clients and the organization (for a review of these studies see McKinlay, 1972; Katz and Danet, 1973; Rosengren and Lefton, 1970). In general, such studies fall into two broad categories. First, a long-standing tradition of research, particularly in the health field, looks at the attributes of clients as the major determinants of the use of human services and the role the client will assume. McKinlay (1972) identified three specific research approaches in this category: a) the socio-demographic approach, which explores the effects of such variables as sex, age, race, education, and socio-economic status of the client; b) the socio-psychological approach, which focuses on such client attributes as motivation, perception, and learning; c) the socio-cultural approach, which explores the effects of cultural and social class affiliations, kinship, and friendship networks on the client's role.

Second, a growing body of research focuses on organizational determinants of client-staff relations. These studies examine the effects of such organizational variables as goals (Street, Vinter, Perrow, 1966; Scott, 1969) technology and professional ideology (Perrow, 1965; Rapoport et al., 1960; Strauss et al., 1964), organizational resources (Scott, 1967), and professionalization (Freidson, 1970a; Walsh and Elling, 1968; Cloward and Epstein, 1965). Nevertheless, both categories of research, while advancing our understanding of various facets of human service organizations and their clients, have failed to provide systematic and, most importantly, cumulative knowledge of the parameters that determine client-organization relations.

PROBLEMS IN STUDIES OF CLIENT-ORGANIZATION RELATIONS

I contend that the major reason for the current "state of the art" is a result of the failure to consider *both* client attributes and organizational variables and the interaction between them as determinants of client-organization relations. Thus, for example, numerous studies suggest that clients from low socio-economic background are less likely to initiate service requests; they underutilize services and they terminate their transactions with organizations prematurely (e.g., McKinlay and McKinlay, 1972; McKinlay, 1972). These actions are attributed to cultural factors, socialization patterns, and social network characteristics. In contrast, several studies indicate that the difficulties clients from low socio-economic background experience with human services are attributable to organizational variables, such as professional biases, inappropriate technology (Cloward and Epstein, 1965; Walsh and Elling, 1968), ideological biases (Sjoberg et al., 1963), and the like. Yet, because both sets of variables are not studied simultaneously, one cannot draw systematic conclusions from either set of studies regarding the conditions that affect the relations between lower-class clients and human service organizations. Neither of these research strategies allows the investigator to estimate the relative importance of each set of variables, or to ascertain whether certain interaction effects between specific client attributes and organizational variables account for important patterns of client-staff exchanges.

The problem is not strictly methodological but is also substantive. With few exceptions, to be noted below, most studies lack a theoretical framework or a causal model that interrelates both client and organizational attributes. The difficulties in doing so are obvious. First, one faces the problem of relating two different units of analysis, each of which has distinct structures and processes. Second, there is no apparent efficient way to select the relevant variables from each unit of analysis. Finally, the dependent variable itself—client-organization relations—must be so defined as to be compatible with and appropriate to both units. Nevertheless, a major contention of this paper is that a theoretical framework relating both units of analysis is a basic prerequisite for effective research on client-organization relations, particularly in the human services.

One of the earlier attempts in this direction has been provided by Thompson (1962), who proposed that the interaction between the degree of client discretion and the specificity of organizational control over members will produce differential transaction structures. Carlson (1964) developed a similar typology based on the client's discretion to participate in the transaction and the organizational control over its intake. Wheeler (1966) identified several client-related variables, such as social composition and social context, and several organizational characteristics, such as goals, processing technology, and organization-environment relations as determinants of client careers in socialization setting. Nevertheless, these attempts and other similar ones have been fragmentary and limited in scope. The most systematic effort to develop a comprehensive scheme relating client attributes and organizational variables to transactional outcomes has been conducted by Katz and Danet (1968, 1973). Viewing the staff-client encounter as a social system, they identify its input as consisting of the environment, the organization, and the situation; the throughput as the interaction itself; and the output as consisting of the evaluation of outcome re: 1) manner, 2) procedure, and 3) resources (Katz and Danet, 1973:22). There are several important contributions that such a framework offers. First, it systematically articulates the components of the encounter following the logic of an open system perspective. Second, it identifies more clearly the clusters of variables that shape each facet of the encounter, thus enabling a more systematic ordering and classification of the research on the subject matter. However, the model suffers from several limitations: a) it does not differentiate clearly between client attributes and organizational variables; b) it does not include a finite set of variables and is global in scope; and c) it does not inform on how the variables relate to each other, thus making it difficult to generate specific hypotheses from it.

The model developed here takes off from the work of Katz and Danet (1968, 1973) and attempts to overcome the various limitations cited above. It also adopts the open-system perspective and its logic as a foundation; within this perspective it articulates a common set of client and organization dimensions as determinants of the encounter; and it shows how the model can be used to generate specific hypotheses, linking variables from both systems to elements of the encounter. It should be noted, in this context, that I use the term client to simply denote persons who find it necessary to interact with human service organizations and, therefore, become their raw material. As I shall point out later, such interaction may be either voluntary or involuntary. Moreover, it is not assumed that the services provided by these organizations are always beneficial to the clients. In fact, there may be settings in which clients experience only costs (for example, prison). Finally, the model focuses on clients relating to the organizations as individuals rather than as organized collectivities, since the former is the more predominant mode of interaction with human service organizations.

CLIENT-ORGANIZATION RELATIONS AS INTERACTION OF TWO SYSTEMS

The starting point in the model building is to view both clients and organizations as purposeful and open systems with analogous functional components. That is, clients and organizations as units of analysis share similar system characteristics in the sense that each is an open system with the following characteristics: 1) a cyclic exchange of energy-information through input, throughput, and output; 2) negative entropy; 3) negative feedback; 4) steady state and dynamic homeostasis; 5) differentiation; and 6) selection of goals and means (Katz and Kahn, 1966:19–26; Ackoff and Emery, 1972:31). Client-organization relations are therefore a manifestation of the interaction between the two systems whereby there is an exchange of energy-information between the two which is essential to their self-maintenance and purpose. This is depicted schematically in Figure 8.1 where both elements d and j represent the boundary subsystems of the client and the organization respectively. It should be noted that the interaction is not confined to elements d and j since through the course of interaction other elements from each system do exchange energy-information.

The central proposition that underlies the model is that the values assumed by the elements (that is, subsystems) in each system will determine the characteristics of the interaction between the organization and the client. Therefore, the first task is to identify the elements in each system relevant to the interaction. I will do so by viewing organizations and clients as analogous systems. The second task is to define the components and dynamics of

FIGURE 8.1 Client-Organization Relations as Interaction of Two Systems

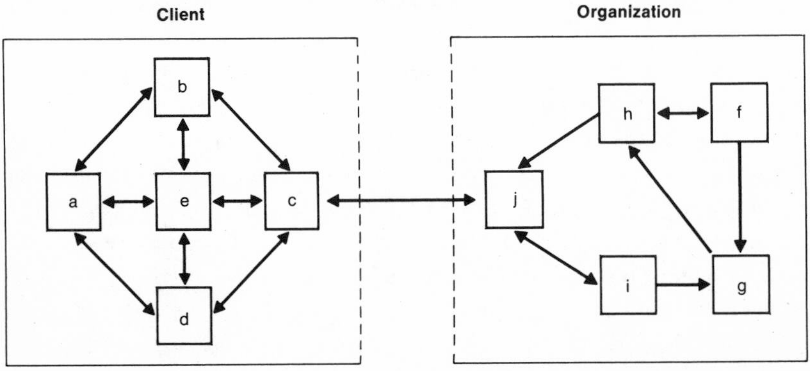

the interaction. This will be done through the use of exchange theory (White, 1974; Blau, 1967).

CLIENTS AND ORGANIZATIONS AS ANALOGOUS SYSTEMS

Following the systems perspective, the client and the organization can each be conceptualized as consisting of a similar set of functional subsystems essential to their self-maintenance and pursuit of objectives. These subsystems can be specified as follows:

a. The boundary subsystem: The set of transactional exchanges at the system boundaries aimed at procurement of needed inputs and disposal of output (Katz and Kahn, 1966:89). For the client, these include affiliations with various social networks and activities to obtain personal resources and social status. For the organization, the subsystem functions to provide raw material, fiscal and manpower resources, marketing of output, and attainment of institutional legitimation.

b. The normative subsystem: The set of values and norms that enable the system to define its purpose and guide its choices. For the client, the subsystem is manifested in his cultural background, personal beliefs, and priority of needs. For the organization, it is expressed through domain consensus and organizational ideologies.

c. The throughput subsystem: The set of activities that transform the input of energy into a specified output. For the client, this is the repertoire of skills and competences needed to perform a particular behavior (Morley and Sheldon, 1973). For the organization, it is the set of technologies used to transform the raw material (Perrow, 1965).

d. The learning and adaptive subsystem: The set of activities that enable the system to monitor and respond to a changing environment through information processing, feedback, and memory. For the client, this is expressed by such processes as perception, learning, and knowledge development (Kuhn, 1974). For the organization, it includes intelligence activities, research and development, and planning.

e. The control and coordination subsystem: The set of activities aimed to manage, control, and coordinate the various components of the system. For the client, it encompasses his decision-making processes, including preference ordering, search behavior, assessment of perceived costs and benefits, and choice based on a "satisficing" principle (Kuhn, 1974). For the organization, this is the managerial component or the decision-making aspect of the organization (Katz and Kahn, 1966) and involves the coordination of organizational components, decisions about major resource commitments, resolution of conflict and coordination of external demands with organizational resources and needs.

THE COMPONENTS OF THE INTERACTION

Viewing organization-client relations as an exchange between two systems suggests that the central issue concerning these relations has to do with the ability of each system to optimize its interests. Put differently, I assume that the client will enter the relationship with the objective of getting needed resources and services and/or minimizing personal costs from the organization; while the organization aims to obtain from the client the resources needed to accomplish its objectives, enhance its self-maintenance, and minimize its costs in doing so. Thus, the ability of each system to obtain a favorable outcome from the exchange will depend on the amount of control each can exercise over the other.

From this perspective, three components of the interaction can be identified, each of which measures a particular facet of the underlying control dimension. The first component of interaction refers to the extent to which each system can control the initiation of the interaction (Carlson, 1964). Clients who have complete control over the initiation of the interaction operate as consumers in the free market, while clients who lack any control are said to be involuntary subjects of organizational action. Similarly, organizations may vary in the degree of control they have over intake. The second component of the interaction refers to the power-dependence relations between the client and the organization. It focuses on the degree to which the two systems are interdependent on each other in order to optimize their respective interests. The third component refers to the norms that govern the interaction, specifically the degree of trust the client and the organization have in each other (Bidwell, 1970). Clearly, these components of the interaction are interrelated and affect one another. For example, when clients do not have control over the initiation of the interaction, the problem of establishing trust between themselves and the organization becomes greater. Similarly, the greater the dependence of the organization on client resources, the more will the organization attempt to induce clients to initiate the interaction. The entire model is presented schematically in Figure 8.2.

DETERMINANTS OF CLIENT-ORGANIZATION INTERACTION PATTERNS

The proposed model attempts to identify systematically *both* the client attributes and the organizational variables which may determine the characteristics of the interaction itself. In this section I will show how the model enables us to generate some specific hypotheses in guiding research and in evaluating existing studies on this subject. In doing so, two basic principles must be kept in mind. First, the cause-effect relations between client and organizational variables and the patterns of interaction are shaped by the exchange of energy-information between the two systems. Thus each system, in the pursuit of its purpose and self-maintenance, attempts to obtain needed

FIGURE 8.2 A Systems Model of Client-Organization Interaction

Subsystem	Client	Client-Organization Interaction	Organization
Boundary	Social affiliations; Personal resources		Resource procurement and output disposal; Social legitimation
Normative	Cultural background; Personal beliefs; Need priorities	1. Initiation 2. Power-dependence 3. Trust	Domain consensus; Ideologies
Throughput	Repertoire of skills and competences		Technologies
Learning and Adaptive	Perception; Learning; Knowledge		Intelligence activities; Research and development; Planning
Control and Coordination	Decision-making processes		Managerial activities

resources and services controlled by the other system at minimal costs to itself. Second, each component of the interaction will be influenced primarily by those subsystems which are functionally relevant to it.[1] What follows are illustrations of the utility of the model in articulating the causal relations among the variables.

INITIATION OF THE INTERACTION

In general, the ability of clients and organizations to control the initiation of the interaction will be a function of their respective goals and values, their other boundary transactions, and their accumulated knowledge and intelligence. Specifically:

The larger the possession of personal resources and the greater the organizational need for client resources, the greater the client control over the initiation of the interaction. Clients who possess many personal resources have a greater choice in the range of organizations they can approach and are less constrained by the costs involved in crossing organizational boundaries. Rushing (1971), for example, noted that rates of involuntary to voluntary commitment to mental hospitals were positively correlated with lower-class positions and unstable marital status, both measures of lack of individual resources. Similarly, Anderson and Anderson (1972) noted a positive relationship between financial security (through personal income or insurance) and utilization of health care services. However, this is a necessary but not a sufficient condition, since the lesser the dependence of the organization on the client's resources, the greater its ability to control its intake (Greenley and Kirk, 1973). Similarly, as the need of the client for the organization's services increases, such need lessens his ability to control the initiation of the interaction. For this reason, for example, personal resources may be relatively unimportant in initiating requests for medical care when facing a serious medical problem (Suchman, 1965).

The greater the congruency between the client's personal beliefs and organizational ideologies, the greater the willingness of both systems to initiate the interaction. Numerous studies have suggested that the failure to use services may be due to the fact that the client's cultural background, belief system, or need priorities are at variance with the predominant value orientation toward clients in the organization. Cloward and Epstein (1965) noted

---

1. Since the control and coordination subsystem intersects all other subsystems, for much of the analysis it will be treated as a constraint.

that the disengagement of family service agencies from the poor was partly due to the middle-class orientation of the professionals, who favored and sought out clients who shared a similar orientation. Similar conclusions were reached by Osofsky (1968) and Strauss (1969). McKinlay and McKinlay (1972) suggested that failure to use free prenatal care services by women of lower socio-economic status might be due to the incompatibility between the need priorities of the women and the objectives of the clinics. Finally, Berkanovic and Reeder (1974) cite several field experiments by neighborhood health care centers which deliberately attempted to increase the cultural congruency of the organizational mode of service delivery. These experiments brought about a significant increase in the use of the centers.

The greater the amount of client knowledge about organizational services and the greater the dissemination of information by the organization, the greater the client's control over the initiation of the interaction. Knowledge of alternative organizational services, quality of services, eligibility criteria, and the like enable potential clients to make choices and to assess the outcome of alternative courses of action. For this reason the client's social network or lay referral system assumes an important role in the initiation of interaction. The more knowledgeable the lay referral system, the greater the effectiveness of the client in selecting appropriate and better quality human services (Freidson, 1961; Kadushin, 1969). In contrast, as shown by Levine and Taube (1970), clients lacking knowledge of the availability of organizational services and the procedures to obtain them were less likely to receive adequate housing-related services. The rise of numerous consumer advocacy groups can be seen in part as an attempt to provide clients with better knowledge of organizational services and thus help them to gain some measure of control over the initiation of transactions with public officials (see, for example, Kahn, 1970). Similarly, I suggest that some of the effectiveness of client rights organizations, such as the National Welfare Rights Organization, in enabling clients to effectively initiate and receive services from public bureaucracies has been due to the bureaucratic knowledge they have provided clients (Cloward and Elman, 1966).

Nevertheless, the client's knowledge is clearly constrained by the willingness of the organization to disseminate and share information about its services. In fact, organizations that wish to control their intake are likely to be highly selective as to the nature of the information they provide and to whom they give it. As Kadushin (1969) points out, psychoanalytic therapists and clinics use a carefully controlled information dissemination process—primarily through persons who are part of the "psychoanalytic system"—to control the flow of "appropriate" patients.

Similarly, one of the most effective mechanisms utilized by human service organizations to control their intake is through the designation of selected referral "gatekeepers" who receive privileged information about the nature of the services offered, and the desired clientele, while the potential clients and other agencies may be kept in ignorance regarding effective referral procedures (Greenley and Kirk, 1973).

It should be noted, in this context, that organizational intelligence activities aimed at identifying environmental developments and changes affecting the supply and demand for services will affect the initiation of client-organization transactions. Organizations sensitive to the changing needs of the population and the developments in other human services can adapt and adjust their own service delivery systems so that congruency between the client's needs and values and the organizational goals is preserved. Moreover, such intelligence activities are also likely to assist potential clients and referring agents by informing them about the actual services offered.

POWER-DEPENDENCE RELATIONS

The power-dependence relations between the client and the organization will determine the ability of each to direct the interaction in a manner congruent with its interests. Paraphrasing Thompson (1967:30), a client is dependent on the service organization: 1) in proportion to his need for resources or for the performances the organization provides, and 2) in inverse proportion to the ability of others to provide the same resources or performances. The same, of course, can be said about the organization's dependence on the client. Interdependence, therefore, implies that both systems control important resources needed by each that cannot be easily obtained elsewhere. The advantage of such a perspective is not only in avoiding the "zero-sum" concept of power relations but also in indicating that each system may exercise power in very specific and delineated areas. The frequently espoused cliché that clients are powerless vis-à-vis bureaucracy may result from the failure to recognize this important fact.

It can be deduced from the paradigm (Figure 8.2) that the power-dependence relations will be determined by the resources or performances available or needed by each subsystem. That is, to carry out its function, each organizational subsystem may need certain client resources or performances, while the client depends on the resources and activities of various organizational subsystems to satisfy his service needs. This further attests to the multidimensionality and complexity of these relations.

For the sake of brevity I will illustrate how the paradigm can be used to generate hypotheses concerning the conditions under which the power-dependence relations between the client and the organization will be characterized as interdependent. It will be assumed, unless otherwise specified, that the clients have a high need for the organization's services, and therefore seek to interact with it.

The more the client provides important resources and/or sources of legitimation to the organization the greater the degree of interdependence between them. Clients may be important suppliers of income, of scarce "raw material," and be important legitimators of the organization's performance and existence. This is aptly demonstrated in the case of private schools (Bidwell, 1970:53–54). Both the study by Clark (1956) of the transformation of the adult education program and that by Zald and Denton (1963) of the changes in the YMCA indicate that as the dependence of these organizations on income generated by clients increased, programmatic changes occurred that reflected more closely clients' demands. An extreme example of organizational dependence on clients as instruments in the solicitation of funds is presented in a study by Scott (1967) of agencies for the blind. In this instance, the dependence on blind children and employable adults to launch effective fund-raising campaigns resulted not only in competition for such clients, but also in the reluctance of such agencies to let these clients exit.

Similarly, organizations may seek out clients who possess the appropriate attributes to ensure success on those performance criteria used by key legitimating units in assessing the organization. For example, vocational rehabilitation programs evaluated on the basis of successful employment placement of clients are likely to avoid clients least attractive to employers and seek out potentially successful cases, resulting in a high degree of interdependence between the rehabilitation workers and "attractive" clients (Krause, 1966).

The greater the match between the technological requirements of the organization and the attributes and behavioral repertoire of the client the greater the interdependence between them. The hypothesis is based on the fact that every human service technology, in order to be operative, requires that clients possess a certain set of attributes and behavioral repertoire. For example, the success of the conventional educational technology is predicated on having pupils with an acceptable level of intelligence, motivation to learn, and a middle-class behavioral repertoire. As a result, there is a high degree of interdependence between teachers and children possessing these attributes, while children lacking them are rejected (Rist, 1970). In the same vein, it has been argued by several writers that psychotherapeutic technologies favor clients who possess middle-class attributes, thus leading to the rejection and disengagement of clients from lower socio-economic status (Cloward and Epstein, 1965; Teele and Levine, 1968; Ryan, 1971). Furthermore, the attributes of the clients and the technological requirements may be such that they necessitate close interdependence between the client and the practitioner in order to achieve successful results. This is analogous to what Szasz and Hollender (1970) term the mutual participation model, as exemplified in the treatment of diabetes mellitus. Henry (1957), in a classic analysis of the Orthogenic School, suggests that extraordinary interdependence between workers and children was achieved because the workers' own personal growth and development was tied to the therapeutic progress of the child.

In the human services there are intimate linkages between service technologies and organizational ideologies and the distinctions between the two are frequently blurred (see, for example, Perrow, 1965). Specifically, organizational ideologies regarding the moral worth of the client, attribution of responsiblity to the client's condition, and beliefs about desired outcomes are major determinants of how staff define their role, how they relate to clients, and how they assess service outcomes. Consequently, the affirmation of these ideologies may often depend on the behavioral and normative responses of the client. Therefore:

The greater the reliance of staff on the client's beliefs and behaviors to affirm service ideologies, the greater the interdependence between them.
Rapoport's study (1960) of the therapeutic milieu clearly demonstrates that the need to confirm this treatment ideology through the attitudes and behavior of the patients resulted in a high degree of interdependence between therapists and patients. Similarly, the study by Scott (1969) shows that workers in agencies for the blind could work only with clients who have ac-

cepted and behaved in accordance with the organization's rehabilitation ideology.

Finally, in this context, it should be noted that the exercise of power by the organization (and the client) is constrained by a normative system that defines the conditions under which such power can be exercised and that is expressed through policy and administrative regulations, law, and professional codes. These in turn may be invoked and enforced when clients perceive inappropriate use of such power. Therefore, the greater the knowledge that clients have of this normative system, the better the likelihood that they could protect themselves from the abuse of power by staff. It is in this sense that one can perhaps explain why clients with bureaucratic competence are likely to have greater success in dealing with bureaucracy (Gordon, 1975). And, as Katz and Danet (1966) have demonstrated, successful appeals to public officials occur when the appeals are addressed to the normative basis upon which the organization rests.

TRUST

Trust is an attitude and a belief about the outcome of the interaction *and* the manner in which it is conducted. That is, client trust in the staff of the organization is a belief in the quality and desirability of their performance and confidence in their methods and mode of conduct (Bidwell, 1970). Concomitantly, the trust that the staff have toward the client is a belief that the client will not abuse the relationship and attempt to exploit it for illegitimate purposes (for example, obtaining drugs for faked symptoms, receiving aid via falsified information). Clearly, without trust the staff cannot hope to gain access to the client's life space and employ intervention techniques that require exposure of the client's private domain, and the client cannot hope to obtain the moral commitment of the staff to respond to his needs. In both instances, each system uses trust as a mechanism of control over the other system. Thus, for example, the greater the client's trust in the organization, the greater its potential control over him.

The establishment and maintenance of trust relations between clients and organizations is an exceedingly complex and vexing issue and beyond the scope of this paper. Rather, I will attempt to show how the paradigm presented here can be used to begin identifying some of the parameters that may set the broad conditions for the emergence of trust. It should be noted that there is a conspicuous dearth of empirical research on this variable, which further limits the scope of this inquiry. Since trust involves beliefs about outcomes and the means to achieve them, it seems that the subsystems most relevant in this context will be the normative, and the throughput. Thus:

The greater the perceived congruency between the client's personal goals and the organization's output goals, the greater the degree of trust between them. For the client, such congruency assures him that the outcome of the organizational intervention in his life will serve his needs and therefore provide him with a positive impetus to put himself in the hands of the staff (Conviser, 1973). Similarly, the organization is less concerned that the client will use it for side transactions (Thompson, 1962). It is partly for this reason that clients express greater satisfaction with fee-for-service medical practice, since in such a system physicians are motivated to foster the congruency between the patient's personal goals and the treatment objectives (Freidson, 1970b:305–06). In contrast, clients who attempt to use emergency rooms for routine medical problems experience considerable mistrust from the medical personnel (Roth, 1972).

Street, Vinter, and Perrow (1966) found that in those correctional settings where staff were more attuned to the personal needs of the inmates, greater trust and positive interaction between staff and inmates developed. And David (1968) found that patients' compliance with doctors' advice (a sign of trust) was partially based on the congruency of values and expectations between them.

An important facilitator of the development of trust relations is the ability of both the client and the organization to control the initiation of the interaction. That is, to the extent to which both systems can select and control the specific systems they interact with, they are able, among other things, to insure that such congruency will be attained. Put differently, trust relations are much more likely to emerge if the relationship is voluntary.

The greater the prestige and reputation of the organization and the more diffused the client's knowledge of the organization, the greater the client's trust in the organization. To the public, the prestige and reputation of the organization are indicators of excellence of the services provided by the organization and of the competence of its personnel—the major ingredients in the establishment of trust (Bidwell, 1970). Yet, much of the potency of the organization's prestige and reputation is based on the fact that it provides diffused and selective knowledge about itself. As clients gain more specific knowledge about the organization through past experiences and the lay and professional referral systems, they are less likely to accept the prestige of organizational staff at face value. Rather, the client is more likely to withhold his trust until concrete actions by staff point to their trustworthiness. Hence, clients who possess technical knowledge about the intervention techniques of the organization are more likely to question the decisions made by staff and to challenge their authority, which is why, argues Freidson (1970b), physicians like to control all communications to their patients.

The more the organizational technology treats the client as a subject and the more the client is capable of active decision-making, the greater the trust between the two. The assumptions about the client incorporated in the human service technology vary along a continuum ranging from the client as a subject to the client as an object. In the former, the client is perceived as a person who can actively participate in decision-making about himself, a person who can control his fate. In the latter, the client is seen as passive and incapable of participating in making decisions about his fate. Howard (1975) reviewed a large body of literature on physician-patient relations and concluded that a humanizing and trusting relationship can emerge only when the patient is treated as a subject rather than as an object (see also, Freidson, 1970b; David, 1968). Studies of the "therapeutic community" model in the treatment of mental patients, in which patients are encouraged to participate actively in decisions about their treatment, also point to increased trust and openness in the relations between staff and patients (see, for example, Jones, 1968).

Similarly, studies of teacher-student interaction patterns, although not measuring trust directly, seem to suggest that when teachers encourage students to participate in decision-making and to make choices in curricular matters, there is greater acceptance of the teachers and improved classroom morale (Larkin, 1975).

For trust to emerge, organizational orientation toward clients as subjects is a necessary, but not sufficient condition. Surely, the client needs to be equipped with the necessary behavioral repertoire that will enable him to become an active participant in the decision-making processes concerning the intervention technology. When the technology sets behavioral expectations for the client which cannot be met, he is likely to experience frustration and to develop mistrust toward the staff. Rapoport (1960) noted this problem in his study of the therapeutic milieu, where patients were expected to participate in decisions for which they lacked competence. Thus, for example, clients who are accustomed to accept passively the authority of officials may react quite negatively and with mistrust when asked to participate actively in decisions about their treatment. Moreover, when patients are unexpectedly asked to participate in decision-making about their course of treatment, they may perceive this as a manipulative device by the organization to ensure compliance rather than a way of sharing the power to decide (Etzioni, 1960).

Finally, *trust will be a function of the interaction between the form of compliance used by the organization in conjunction with its intervention*

Table 8.1 EFFECTS OF CLIENT'S CULTURAL ORIENTATION AND THE ORGANIZATION'S MEANS OF CONTROL ON CLIENT TRUST

Client's Cultural Orientation	Organization's Means of Control		
	Persuasion	Inducements	Constraints
Normative	M	–	–
Utilitarian	+	M	–
Coercive	+	+	M

M = Maintain current level of trust.
+ = Increase level of trust.
– = Decrease level of trust.

technologies and the client's cultural orientation toward compliance. Following Etzioni (1975), one can distinguish among three forms of compliance—normative, utilitarian, and coercive. The organization can use persuasion, inducements, and constraints to achieve each form of compliance respectively (Gamson, 1968). Similarly the client, depending on his socialization, social affiliations, and personal experiences, will develop a cultural orientation toward compliance (that is, how compliance should be achieved) along the same categories. It is clear that trust relations cannot be established under conditions of coercion (for example, prison), but through inducements or persuasion. Assuming that the client's cultural orientation toward compliance may be either normative, utilitarian, or coercive, it is possible to predict the effects on trust of the deployment of the three means of control by the organization, following the principle suggested by Gamson (1968). See Table 8.1.

That is, when the correspondence between the client's orientation and the organization's means of control is along the diagonal, the initial level of trust will remain unchanged, while the interaction between the two below the diagonal will increase trust and above the diagonal will decrease trust, based on the proposition that trust increases with the movement from coercive to normative compliance.

CONCLUSION

This paper attempts to formulate a framework for the study of client-organization relations, based on open system concepts and exchange theory principles. Both the client and the organization are viewed as open systems, each with an analogous set of subsystems. The interaction between the client and the organization is conceived as an exchange of energy—information, whereby each system attempts to obtain needed resources from the other system in a manner that optimizes payoff and minimizes costs. Three major components of the interaction are treated as dependent variables: 1) control over the initiation of the interaction; 2) power-dependence relations; and 3) trust. These variables measure the amount of control that each system exercises over the other. It has been shown how the model can be used to generate specific hypotheses that focus on the interaction between organizational variables and client attributes as predictive of client-organization relations.

Hence, it is believed that a major contribution of the proposed framework is its emphasis on the simultaneous effects of *both* sets of variables on client-organization relations, thereby enabling us to test the relative contribution of variables from each set as well as their interaction effect in explaining variance in these relations. In particular, the utilization of the social exchange theory enables us to generate specific hypotheses about the causal relations between client attributes, organizational variables, and the components of client-organization interaction. Moreover, should these hypotheses prove to be correct, as the review of the literature seems to indicate, they have important implications for the practitioners who are committed to enhance the responsiveness of human service organizations to their clients. The model points to the type of organization variables *and* client attributes that need to be changed in order to increase the congruency between human service organizations and their clients.

Nevertheless, the framework is not without its shortcomings that must receive attention as it is being further developed and refined. First, there must be greater specification of the relevant variables in each of the subsystems. An inherent problem in the use of a systems approach is the high level of abstraction that it forces on the investigator and the use of system dimensions that are too encompassing. Hence, as research continues on the subject, it should be possible to tease out the key variables from each system and develop more specific causal models. Second, the interaction between clients and organizations is viewed from a social exchange theory. Nevertheless there are limitations in such an approach, particularly in its applicability to public organizations. In such organizations, client-staff transactions are more likely to be controlled by universalistic norms that severely constrain the discretion of officials (Kroeger, 1975). Thus, more attention must be given to conditions external to the client and the organization that constrain their exchange relations. Put differently, the social context in which both clients and organizations are embedded will set some definite boundaries as to the structure and the content of their interaction. Thus is must be explicitly defined and incorporated in study of client-organization relations.

REFERENCES

Ackoff, Russell L. and Fred E. Emery. 1972. *On Purposeful Systems.* Chicago: Aldine-Atherton.

Anderson, O. W. and R. M. Anderson. 1972. "Patterns of Use of Health Services." In H. E. Freeman, S. Levine, and L. G. Reeder, eds., *Handbook of Medical Sociology,* Englewood Cliffs, N.J.: Prentice-Hall.

Berkanovic, Emil and Leo G. Reeder. 1974. "Can Money Buy the Appropriate Use of Services?" *Journal of Health and Social Behavior,* 15:93–99.

Bidwell, Charles E. 1970. "Students and Schools: Some Observations on Client Trust in Client-Serving Organizations." In W. R. Rosengren and M. Lefton, eds., *Organizations and Clients,* pp. 37–69. Columbus, Ohio: Charles E. Merrill.

Blau, Peter. 1967. *Exchange and Power in Social Life.* New York: Wiley.

Carlson, R. O. 1964. "Environmental Constraints and Organizational Consequences: The Public School and Its Clients." In *Behavioral Science and Educational Administration,* pp. 262–76. Chicago: National Society for the Study of Education.

Clark, Burton R. 1956. "Organizational Adaptation and Precarious Values," *American Sociological Review,* 21:327–36.

Cloward, R. A. and R. M. Elman. 1966. "Advocacy in the Ghetto," *Transactions:* 27–35.

Cloward, R. A. and I. Epstein. 1965. "Private Social Welfare's Disengagement from the Poor: The Case of Family Adjustment Agencies. In M. Zald, ed., *Social Welfare Institutions*. New York: Wiley.

Conviser, Richard H. 1973. "Toward a General Theory of Interpersonal Trust," *Pacific Sociological Review*, 16:377–99.

Cumming, Elaine. 1968. *Systems of Social Regulation*. New York: Atherton Press.

David, M. S. 1968. "Variations in Patients' Compliance with Doctors' Advice: An Empirical Analysis of Patterns of Communication," *American Journal of Public Health*, 58:279–86.

Etzioni, Amitai. 1960. "Interpersonal and Structural Factors in the Study of Mental Hospitals," *Psychiatry* 23:13–22.

—— 1975. *A Comparative Analysis of Complex Organizations*. New York: Free Press (revised and enlarged edition).

Freidson, Eliot. 1961. *Patients' View of Medical Practice*. New York: Russell Sage Foundation.

——1970a. "Dominant Professions, Bureaucracy, and Client Services." In W. R. Rosengren and M. Lefton, eds., *Organizations and Clients*, pp. 71–92. Columbus, Ohio: Charles E. Merrill.

—— 1970b. *Profession of Medicine*. New York: Dodd, Mead.

Gamson, William A. 1968. *Power and Discontent*. Homewood, Ill.: Dorsey.

Gordon, K. L. 1975. "Bureaucratic Competence and Success in Dealing with Public Bureaucracies," *Social Problems*, 23:197–208.

Greenley, James R., and Stuart A. Kirk. 1973. "Organizational Characteristics of Agencies and the Distribution of Services to Applicants," *Journal of Health and Social Behavior*, 14:70–79.

Hasenfeld, Yeheskel, and Richard A. English, eds. 1974. *Human Service Organizations*. Ann Arbor: University of Michigan Press.

Henry, Jules. 1957. "Types of Institutional Structure." In M. Greenblatt, O. J. Levinson, and R. H. Williams, eds., *The Patient and the Mental Hospital*, pp. 73–90. New York: Free Press.

Howard, Jan. 1975. "Humanization and Dehumanization of Health Care." In J. Howard and A. Strauss, eds., *Humanizing Health Care*, pp. 57–102. New York: Wiley.

Jones, Maxwell. 1968. *Beyond the Therapeutic Community*. New Haven: Yale University Press.

Kadushin, Charles. 1969. *Why People Go to Psychiatrists*. New York: Atherton Press.

Kahn, Alfred J. 1970. "Perspectives on Access to Social Services," *Social Work*, 15:95–101.

Katz, Daniel, and Robert Kahn. 1966. *The Social Psychology of Organizations*. New York: Wiley.

Katz, Elihu, and Brenda Danet. 1966. "Petitions and Persuasive Appeals: A Study of Official-Client Relations," *American Sociological Review*, 31:811–22.

—— 1968. "Communication between Bureaucracy and the Public: A Review of the Literature." Hebrew University at Jerusalem. Mimeo.

—— 1973. *Bureaucracy and the Public*. New York: Basic Books.

Krause, A. Elliot. 1966. "After the Rehabilitation Center," *Social Problems*, 14:197–206.

Kroeger, Naomi. 1975. "Bureaucracy, Social Exchange, and Benefits Received in a Public Assistance Agency," *Social Problems*, 23:182–96.

Kuhn, Alfred. 1974. *The Logic of Social Systems*. San Francisco: Jossey Bass.

Larkin, Ralph W. 1975. "Social Exchange in the Elementary School Classroom: The Problem of Teacher Legitimation of Social Power," *Sociology of Education*, 48:400–10.

Lefton, Mark, and William R. Rosengren. 1966. "Organizations and Clients: Lateral and Longitudinal Dimensions," *American Sociological Review*. 31:802–10.

Levine, Jack, and Gerald Taube. 1970. "Bureaucracy and the Socially Handicapped: A Study of Lower Status Tenants in Public Housing," *Sociology and Social Research*, 54:209–19.

McKinlay, John B. 1972. "Some Approaches and Problems in the Study of the Use of Services—An Overview," *Journal of Health and Social Behavior*, 13:115–52.

McKinlay, J. B., and S. M. McKinlay. 1972. "Some Social Characteristics of Lower Working Class Utilizers of Maternity Care Services," *Journal of Health and Social Behavior*, 13:369–81.

Morely, Eileen, and Alan Sheldon. 1973. "Work Systems and Human Behavior: Toward a Systems-Theoretic Approach." In F. Baker, ed., *Organizational Systems*, pp. 141–50. Homewood, Ill.: Irwin.

Osofsky, Howard J. 1968. "The Walls Are Within: An Exploration of Barriers between Middle Class Physicians and Poor Patients." In I. Deutscher and E. J. Thompson, eds., *Among the People: Encounters with the Poor*, pp. 239–58. New York: Basic Books.

Parsons, Talcott. 1970. "How Are Clients Integrated into Service Organizations?" pp. 1–16, in W. R. Rosengren and M. Lefton, eds., *Organizations and Clients*. Columbus, Ohio: Charles E. Merrill.

Perrow, Charles. 1965. "Hospitals: Technology, Structure, and Goals." In J. March, ed., *Handbook of Organizations*, pp. 910–71. Chicago: Rand McNally.

Rapoport, R. N., R. Rapoport, and I. Rosow. 1960. *Community as a Doctor*. London: Tavistock.

Rist, Ray C. 1970. "Student Social Class and Teacher Expectations: The Self-Fulfilling Prophecy in Ghetto Education," *Harvard Educational Review*, 41:411–51.

Rosengren, William R., and Mark Lefton, eds. 1970. *Organizations and Clients*. Columbus, Ohio: Charles E. Merrill.

Roth, Julius A. 1972. "Some Contingencies of the Moral Evaluation and Control of Clientele: The Case of the Hospital Emergency Service," *American Journal of Sociology*, 77:839–56.

Rushing, W. A. 1971. "Individual Resources, Societal Reaction, and Hospital Commitment," *American Journal of Sociology*, 77:511–25.

Ryan, William. 1971. *Blaming the Victim*. New York: Pantheon.

Scott, Robert A. 1967. "The Selection of Clients by Social Welfare Agencies: The Case of the Blind," *Social Problems*, 14:248–57.

—— 1969. *The Making of Blind Men: A Study of Adult Socialization*. New York: Russell Sage Foundation.

Sjoberg, G., R. A. Brymer, and B. Farris. 1966. "Bureaucracy and the Lower Class," *Sociology and Social Research*, 50:325–37.

Smith, C. G., and J. A. King. 1975. *Mental Hospitals*. Lexington, Mass.: D. C. Heath.

Smith, Dorothy E. 1965. "Front-Line Organization of the State Mental Hospital." *Administrative Science Quarterly*, 10:381–99.

Strauss, A. L. 1969. "Medical Organization, Medical Care and Lower Income Groups," *Social Science and Medicine*, 3:143–77.

Strauss, A., L. Schatzman, R. Bucher, D. Ehrlic, and M. Sabshin. 1964. *Psychiatric Ideologies and Institutions*. New York: Free Press.

Street, David, Robert D. Vinter, and Charles Perrow. 1966. *Organization for Treatment*. New York: Free Press.

Suchman, E. A. 1965. "Stages of Illness and Medical Care," *Journal of Health and Social Behavior*, 6:114–331.

Szasz, Thomas, and Marc H. Hollender. 1970. "The Basic Models of the Doctor-Patient Relationship." In H. W. Polsky, D. S. Claster, and C. Goldberg, eds., *Social System Perspectives in Residential Institutions*, pp. 119–31. East Lansing: Michigan State University Press.

Teele, James E., and Sol Levine. 1968. "The Acceptance of Emotionally Disturbed Children by Psychiatric Agencies." In S. Wheeler, ed., *Controlling Delinquents*. New York: Wiley.

Thompson, James D. 1962. "Organizations and Output Transactions," *American Journal of Sociology,* 68:309–24.

—— 1967. *Organizations in Action.* New York: McGraw-Hill.

Walsh, J. L., and R. H. Elling. 1968. "Professionalization and the Poor: Structural Effects and Professional Behavior," *Journal of Health and Social Behavior,* 9:16–28.

Wheeler, Stanton. 1966. "The Structure of Formally Organized Socialization Settings." In O. G. Brim and S. Wheeler, eds., *Socialization After Childhood,* pp. 51–116. New York: Wiley.

White, Paul E. 1974. "Resources as Determinants of Organizational Behavior," *Administrative Science Quarterly,* 19:366–76.

Zald, Mayer N., and Patricia Denton. 1963. "From Evangelism to General Service: The Transformation of the YMCA," *Administrative Science Quarterly,* 8:214–34.

NINE

Exposing the Coercive Consensus: Racism and Sexism in Social Work

FELICE DAVIDSON PERLMUTTER AND
LESLIE B. ALEXANDER

THE RELATIONSHIP between social movements and public policy forms a dynamic system in which the actions of each affect the actions of the other (Freeman, 1975). This discussion will address one aspect of the relationship, focusing largely on a description of the rise and potential impact of several selected social movements which provide a direct response to racism and sexism within traditional social service agencies.

The essay will be divided into two parts. Part I, based on a review of data available in the social work literature from 1960 to the present, will attempt to provide a preliminary assessment of the extent of racism and sexism within the social services, in terms of ideology, practice theory, and manpower utilization.

Part II will provide a preliminary assessment of the rise and potential impact of selected self-help social movements within the social service sector, whose birth in the late 1960s is at least in part a reaction to racism and sexism within traditional social welfare agencies. Beginning with the Welfare Rights Movement (WRO) in the mid-1960s, self-help movements of clients have proliferated at an amazing rate ever since. Those of particular interest to this essay—the racial and ethnic, the women's, and the gay movements—have arisen not only because of the more favorable climate created by federal civil rights, poverty, and affirmative action policies and programs, but also because of the continued pervasiveness and intransigence of racism and sexism within traditional social service settings.

DEFINITION OF CONCEPTS

Before proceeding further, several terms will be defined as they are used in this discussion. These include: (1) the social services, (2) ideology, (3) practice theory, and (4) manpower utilization.

The term *social services* is limited to the general or personal social services, as described by Kammerman and Kahn (1976). These include family and child welfare services, social services for the young and old, social care for the handicapped, frail, and retarded, information and referral services, and community services. Although other professionals and categories of workers are involved, these are the services, both identified with social work and in which social work serves as the core profession (Kammerman and Kahn, 1976).

Ideology refers to the predominant belief systems embedded within and informing the development and delivery of social services. Ideologies are composed of, hence closely interrelated with, values and reflect value preferences. Just as values are often ambiguous and inconsistent, so too, then, are ideologies. Ideology influences the range of facts to be observed, the importance attached to those facts, and offers prescriptions for action in relation to those facts.

Ideologies can be understood only in relation to the particular values which inform them, which reflect conceptions of what is deemed desirable or worthy for a particular group—what ought to be promoted and protected rather than treated with indifference. Values do not emerge fullblown, but are formed and reformed in a dialogue with the larger environment. Burton Clark's (1961) distinction between secure and precarious values is germane here. To him, secure values are those which are clearly defined in behavior and strongly established in the minds of many. Precarious values, on the other hand, are less well defined and not well grounded in a firm social base. Social movements are often developed with an interest in protecting and promoting precarious values. For example, the elimination or reduction of racism and sexism represent precarious rather than secure values in social welfare and are the direct concern of the self-help groups under discussion in the latter part of this essay.

In this essay, *practice theory* refers to the dominant model(s) of casework or direct practice in the delivery of social services. Such a limited focus seems justified, since social casework has been historically, and direct service continues to be, the core of professional activity.[1]

Manpower utilization in service delivery is operationalized as an analysis of the composition of boards, staff, and professional associations.

PART I: RACISM AND SEXISM IN THE SOCIAL SERVICES

IDEOLOGY

A rhetoric exists in the social work profession which suggests that the profession's values embody only the most noble of society's values and indeed transcend them. This was the dominant theme through the 1950s (Boehm, 1958) and is even suggested in the 1970s. For example, a Task Force of the National Conference on Social Welfare (*Roles for Social Work in Community Mental Health Programs* 1975) discusses the unique ideology of the profession, which is characterized as less therapeutic and more prevention oriented, less concerned with the individual than with broad social and community systems. Other writers today, however, such as Carol Meyer (1970), present a much less sanctimonious, more realistic picture. According to Meyer: "As an institution of society, social work has reflected the best and the worst movements of thought in that society; it can do no more" (1970: 14).

The ideology of social work, in fact, has always reflected the liberal humanitarian values of the developing welfare state in this country, which, as Harold Wilensky (1965) aptly describes, remains a "reluctant" and only partially developed welfare state. Although the twin goals of eliminating racism and sexism have become more important on the liberal humanitarian agenda within the last decade, their position still remains somewhat precarious, even within the liberal mainstream, including social work. It is our con-

---

1. Although direct services now appear to be a smaller proportion of all social workers' activities, more students are trained for direct service (including group work as well as casework) than for broader social service functions, such as planning and administration (Meyer and Siegel, 1977). In spite of growing interest in a "macro" focus, which includes community organization, policy, and administration, "the modal image of the professional social worker as reflected in NASW membership statistics is that of a direct service worker who provides casework, perhaps supplemented with group work and some community activities, in a psychiatric or medical setting or in a family or children's agency" (Meyer and Siegel, 1977: 1073).

tention that the attitudes and practices regarding the elimination of racism and sexism have been particularly intractable and have changed less dramatically than might appear on the surface.

With regard to *racism*, a number of reasons which relate to ideological considerations have been offered which attempt to explain the fact that the data relevant to all aspects of race have been somewhat fugitive in social work, as in all fields. Most convincing is the suggestion that, given the liberal-humanitarian values embedded within the social service system, it is assumed without question that the system is color-blind and non-discriminatory. A related belief is that problems of minorities are merely facets of larger social problems; for example, housing and child welfare problems are seen as related to social class (for example, low income), rather than ethnic or racial factors (O'Reilly, 1969). Kahn (1976: 28) relates the declining interest in ethnic, cultural, or sectarian content to increasing professionalization in the 1950s: "Functional expertise superseded ethnic or cultural content."

In the wake of the "rediscovery" of poverty and the Civil Rights Movement of the 1960s, however, the liberal tradition did move somewhat to the left, reflecting, to some extent, a consensus in advance of that which fostered the development of the income maintenance programs of the 1930s (Leiby, 1971). While it is true, as Titmuss (1968) pointed out, that the War on Poverty reflected values similar to the 1834 Poor Law Reforms, such as an emphasis on redemption through work, and a residual concept of poverty, rooted in individual pathological explanations, nevertheless, at the same time, the War on Poverty and Great Society Programs also reflected a rising emphasis on the value of equality of opportunity and on the rights of public beneficiaries (Dorsen, 1971).

In spite of some evidence of ideological movement to the left, exemplified by the Great Society Programs, there was still meager attention paid to the issues of race and ethnicity at either a theoretical or practice level in the social work literature of the 1960s. Although the concept of institutional racism had been identified by Carmichael and Hamilton in 1967, the analysis of race in terms of unequal power distribution and use had not yet pervaded professional thinking to any extent. A general assimilationist-integrationist or melting-pot program orientation continued. In fact, by 1970, the number of articles dealing with race and ethnicity could still be counted on both hands (Kolodny, 1969).

According to one author, social welfare as an institution, and many social workers, could be characterized as adopting an attitude toward blacks and the ghetto best described as philanthropic colonialism, which comprised the twin assumptions of cultural underdevelopment and clinical or psychological damage (Miller, 1969).

If there was any question about social work's tenuous relationship with the black community in the late 1960s, the white reader of *Social Work* was impassionately and directly cautioned by Saunders (1969: 87–88):

For those of you who believe you have successfully extricated yourself from the slave/master syndrome and have decided to enter the black sea, remember that you are in unfamiliar surroundings. Roll a bit with the washing tide; ask, do not tell. To paraphrase, can you honestly expect to be the master in another man's home? Leave your middle-class standards, values, and moral judgments at your own place of abode. They are not welcome here. . . . Can you think black? This, I believe, is the key to the locked iron gates of the ghetto. Once inside, your primary function is not to change the man, but to help him effectively change his environment. . . .

Although, in the 1970s, both the National Association of Social Workers (NASW) and the Council on Social Work Education have established special task forces on minorities, and a slow, yet steadily expanding literature on the importance of ethnicity and racial differences among minority groups has developed (see, for example, Cafferty and Chestang, 1975; Street, 1977), we would still argue that, just as in the larger society, the ideology of racism still doggedly persists in the 1970s in the social services—less uncritically and blindly perhaps, but still as a cogent force, nonetheless.

Regarding *sexism,* there was really no identifiable ideological thrust promoting women in social work until the 1970s, when the women's movement and federal affirmative action policies became viable and active forces on the larger political scene. Before the 1970s, popular stereotypes of the social worker were almost exclusively female—whether as cold snooper, Lady Bountiful, or motherly healer. However, women were ultimately considered less desirable or capable than men to serve in upper management positions. Wilensky and Lebeaux (1958: 323) tap the prevailing sentiment well:

It is when she becomes a supervisor with male subordinates that her troubles may begin. There is a norm still prevalent in American culture which says:

"Women should not be in authority over men of roughly the same social class and age." Further, the next step up is likely to be blocked for the female supervisor, because of the notion that women are not good risks for top administration. The rationale goes like this: if they marry, they may quit; if they do not quit, they may have difficulty getting along with their husbands, since it is still thought that women should not exceed their husbands in status and authority. In addition, the active, aggressive entrepreneurial behavior needed to develop professional and community contacts and to gain access to men of power—both essential for agency survival—is often deprecated for women.

As a further attestation to the second-class ideological status of women in social work, Arnulf Pins (1963) outlined six major points for easing the personnel crisis and improving recruitment into the profession. The fourth point urged that recruitment should be selective for certain groups, including those with high undergraduate records, individuals with an upper socio-economic background, and men. Women, as a separate category, were not deemed worthy of special recruitment efforts. Although similar attitudes, staffing patterns, and salaries were common in all professions at the time, social work was one of the few professions in which women were both in the majority numerically and had the lead in terms of professional training. It was also one of the few professions which claimed as central values a belief in the dignity of each individual and equality of opportunity.

In spite of the fact that many of the profession's pioneers were women, including Jane Addams, Mary Richmond, Lillian Wald, and the Abbott sisters, as were many of the profession's leading theoreticians, including Virginia Robinson, Antoinette Cannon, Bertha Reynolds, Gordon Hamilton, Helen Harris Perlman, Florence Hollis, Grace Coyle, and Gertrude Wilson, securing professional status remained a key concern of the 1960s. As long as women predominated, the prevailing belief was that only marginal professional status could be attained. As described by Kadushin (1958: 40), and accurate for the 1960s as well:

. . . the prevalent feeling is that women ought not to compete with men for occupational status. This expresses itself in a tendency to resist free entrance of women into occupations dominated and controlled by males and to derogate occupations dominated by women. The prestige of social work is, therefore, adversely affected because it identified as a women's profession.

Although stark inequities disfavoring women continue in many facets of administrative practice in social work in the 1970s, there is, at least, some evidence of a shift at the ideological level. In 1973, the NASW Delegate Assembly added the Equal Rights Amendment and the elimination of sexism, in addition to that of poverty and racism, to other legislative priorities. A Committee on Women's Issues was also established within NASW, and the entire November 1976 issue of *Social Work* was devoted to women. In addition, an observer of any recent conferences including social workers will not fail to find the discussion of practice issues relating to women's problems and women's rights on the agenda.

PRACTICE THEORY

In order to implement a commitment to science, casework had been founded on a medical model, which persisted throughout the 1960s. This model focused on the world in linear terms, thereby resulting in a "trained incapacity for seeing the world in systemic terms. . . . The model appeared to give priority to understanding the individual, and environment was viewed as a 'linear appendage' '' (Germain, 1970: 20). This model also tended to direct attention to presumed individual deficits, which must be understood, treated, and, it was hoped, cured. An inherent bias persisted, favoring the individual rather than the situation as the primary source of the problem. The "cause" of problems was seen as rooted deep within the psyche, with environmental factors taking a decidedly back seat. This resulted in a tendency to equate economic and other environmental difficulties with personal failure or misconduct.

Not only did the prevailing model tend to define problems as largely intrapsychic, it was also a culture-bound, rather inflexible model, most applicable to middle-class clientele (Cloward and Epstein, 1967). The narrow clinicalism failed to take into account the varying needs and lifestyles of people of different social classes, races, and ethnic groups, implying a melting-pot philosophy.

In addition, as has been amply documented recently (Schwartz, 1973; Kravetz, 1976), stereotypical views of female development, traditional sex-role standards, and anti-female bias in certain personality theories provided the theoretical framework for much of the practice theory taught in casework until the mid-1970s. Traditional and monolithic views of marriage and the family, which did not reflect the variety existing in those forms even in the 1960s, were also taught, and guided practice (Kravetz, 1976). Only recently have such sexist models been challenged, and then, largely by female social work students!

Although it is impossible to gauge the extent to which changes in theoretical models of direct service have actually impacted day-to-day practice in the field, there is some evidence, reflecting a loosening of the rather monolithic model of casework predominant in the mid-1960s. These changes were in response to a number of different pressures, all of which challenged casework's effectiveness, efficiency, and relevance—particularly in relation to low-income clients. Not only was there evidence provided by Cloward and Epstein (1967) that casework systematically excluded those persons most in need of help and had gradually disengaged from the poor, there were also critics who suggested that social work methodology, focused largely on a case-by-case approach, was at best inefficient and perhaps even harmful (Briar, 1967, 1973). Finally, there was growing evidence that traditional casework was not effective, even when properly applied to persons disposed to use it (Meyer et al., 1965).

How, then, did the traditional casework model change? First, there was growing interest in family and transactional models of treatment and in socio-behavioral techniques. There was also growing interest in short-term treatment and the spread of experimentation and evaluation within that mode (Reid and Shyne, 1969).

In addition to broadening the theoretical base from the traditional psychodynamic to other modes, there was also interest in expanding the functions of casework beyond the therapeutic or clinical function. Both of these—the broker and the advocate functions—had historical roots in the casework practice of an earlier day (Briar, 1967, 1973) and were particularly relevant to the immediate needs of low-income clients. In addition, particularly through the experiences of the Mobilization for Youth Program in the early 1960s, it became clear that in order to be relevant for the poor, there had to be a strong emphasis on concrete, practical, immediate services —such as small loans of money, legal aid, escort service, baby sitting, and job counseling (Weissman, 1969), rather than an emphasis only, or primarily, on "relationship" services.

In the seventies, the traditional caseworker of the 1940s and 1950s would find herself or himself in a rather strange and topsy-turvy practice world indeed, as the models of direct practice in the 1970s do demonstrate somewhat more variety, flexibility, and recognition of clinical uncertainty rather than orthodoxy. Most recent efforts to reconceptualize professional practice models have included the following features: "A view of human phenomena through a systems perspective, an emphasis on institutional and environmental structures, and the identification of various 'target systems' as the loci for professional intervention'' (Gittelman and Germain, 1976: 601). The importance of concrete services has been restored to an important position within all of these schemas (Meyer, 1970; Pincus and Minahan, 1973; Goldstein, 1973; Goldberg and Middleman, 1974; Siporin, 1975).

MANPOWER UTILIZATION

In spite of the fact that the data on race, in particular, is fugitive and piecemeal in the social service literature, it is possible to pull together trends on both the racial and sexual composition of agency boards, staff, and professional associations.

Findings on Race. There is little data on the racial composition of *agency boards.* A study done in the 1950s of welfare planning through the Indianapolis Community Chest only incidentally mentioned the role of the Blacks or any other minorities in the community welfare system. A few authorities, such as Robert Morris, Martin Rein, and Whitney Young, decried the lack of minority representation in health and welfare planning structures (O'Reilly, 1969). The studies which did provide information on board composition confirmed that agency boards were dominated by the economic elite of the community; powerful representatives from business, medicine, and the law, which, in the 1950s and 1960s, precluded Blacks and other minorities (Seeley et al., 1957; Willie et al., 1964; Holloway et al., 1963).

A 1967 survey of five national agency boards revealed that the average board had 38 members, with an average of 1.5 Blacks per board (O'Reilly, 1969). A 1965 survey of board members of voluntary and public agencies in the Metropolitan Boston area showed that 60 percent had no nonwhites on their boards, 24 percent had one non-white board member and 7 percent had two or more (Hackshaw, 1971). A study of the effect of OEO funds on 16 voluntary agencies in Pittsburgh from 1960 to 1967 indicated that only minimal movement had taken place in terms of Black representation on the agency boards (Lambert et al., 1970). Finally, Mayor Richard Hatcher of Gary, Indiana, reported in 1970 that "there has never been anything approaching a third of the members of the board of the United Fund who represent minority groups in the community" (Hackshaw, 1971: 1066). Only in Community Action Agencies were the community representatives on boards similar in class and racial composition to their constituencies and generally well-integrated into their respective communities (Fainstein and Fainstein, 1974).

With regard to *staffing patterns*, earlier reports on staff composition in various areas of social work failed to provide information on the racial composition of agency staff. For example, neither the 1965 manpower report of the Department of Health, Education, and Welfare—*Closing the Gap in Social Work Manpower*—nor the Council on Social Work Education's report of the same year on social work education and manpower—*Social Work Education and Social Welfare Manpower: Present Realities and Future Realities*—provided any information on race (O'Reilly, 1969).

Later studies disclosed miniscule Black representation in higher staff positions. For example, a 1968 study of decision-making positions in Chicago revealed that of 1,088 policy-making positions in federal, state and local government, only 5 percent were held by Blacks. This was in spite of the fact that Blacks made up 20 percent of the county's population. In welfare agencies, only 5 of the 135 directors of large and medium welfare agencies were Black (Hackshaw, 1971).

Similar trends were also found in two separate and extensive national studies, carried out under the auspices of the National Assessment of Juvenile Corrections at the University of Michigan. One, a national survey of juvenile correctional facilities, including institutions, group homes, and day treatment centers, revealed the following. To quote: "The assumption that few members of minority groups reach decision-making positions is confirmed. . . . Even though only 1 in 2 juvenile offenders was white, 5 out of 6 top executives were white. It should also be noted that minority executives tended to run disproportionately small units" (Vinter, 1976:55). Even more striking disparities were found in the second survey, involving an extensive national study of juvenile courts. Although the survey of juvenile courts revealed a referral rate for white youth of 7 per thousand as compared with 19 per thousand for non-white youth, the racial characteristics of court staff did not reflect similar racial ratios. Rather, all five occupational subgroups of court staff studied were overwhelmingly white, including 94 percent of the judges; 89 percent of the administrators; 93 percent of the probation supervisors; 89 percent of the line probation officers; and 86 percent of the detention supervisors (Sarri and Hasenfeld, 1976).

While the proportion of Black personnel varied in other agencies studied, a different and very interesting pattern occurred in the Billingsley and Giovannoni (1972) study of eight adoption agencies in four cities—Los

Angeles, New York, Chicago, and Philadelphia—agencies which, in 1968—69, were serving the largest number of Black children in those cities. There were Black personnel in higher administrative and supervisory positions, but relatively few at the operating level. For example, the executive director and director of casework at Spence-Chapin in New York were both Black, but the rest of the staff was almost entirely white. In the New York public agency studied, the administrator and three-fifths of the supervisory personnel were Black, but the line staff were, again, predominantly white (Billingsley and Giovannoni, 1972).

In trying to fathom these counter-trends, the authors point out that perhaps the explanation was simply that the adoption field at one time attracted more Blacks than now. Because there were no data on employment patterns among Black social workers, it was difficult for them to sort out whether the pattern reflected career patterns of Black social workers or agency hiring practices.

A trend similar to that noted by Billingsley and Giovannoni in the adoption field was also noted by Vargus (1977: 1); she reports that "of all the professions outside of Theology, Social Services and Education probably have the largest number of minority administrators." At the same time, both Vargus and Bush (1976) identify some of the peculiar psychological stresses and strains experienced by these minority administrators, many of whom are moved very quickly into administrative positions without the requisite experience.

Exclusionary patterns at top levels were also noted in senior faculty positions in schools of social work. A 1968 study by the Council on Social Work Education revealed that in 46 schools reporting minority faculty, there were 114 Black members out of a total of 1,065. Of this number, only 18 of 684 were full or associate professors (Hackshaw, 1971).

NASW, the professional association, has made solid attempts to combat racism and sexism within its own ranks, particularly among top leadership positions. In addition to the 1973 Delegate Assembly's adding the Equal Rights Amendment and the elimination of sexism to the elimination of racism and poverty as legislative priorities, there have been changes in the national leadership, both elected and appointed. As of 1970, the national leadership was 74.7 percent male and 86 percent white. In 1976, it was 50 percent female and 30 percent minority (Mahaffey, 1976). Both a Women's and a Minority Task Force have also been established within NASW.

What meager evidence does exist, however, suggests that the record on both racism and sexism is somewhat less laudable in rank and file NASW membership. Based on a sample of 32,706 members in 1975, 14.5 percent of the total membership was minority, with a high of 7.6 percent for Blacks, and a low of .7 percent for Puerto Ricans, and .3 percent for American Indians (NASW, 1975). This contrasts with a total minority membership in 1968 of 9.5 percent (Stamm, 1969).[2]

Although minorities continue to join NASW, separate national associations by ethnic group are also needed. The Association of Black Social Workers, organized in 1969, is the largest and the one founded earliest. The formation of this Association was representative of a movement in the late 1960s among the other Black professionals, including doctors, psychologists, and educators, to form their own separate associations. This Association, dedicated to monitoring the racist social welfare system, to social action, and to education, was founded because of the belief that the dominant professional group was not an adequate or suitable spokesman for Black social welfare (Sanders, 1970).

Only in one sector of the social work manpower pool did a truly different picture emerge; these noticeable changes in racial representation were effected by the poverty program, through the tremendous growth of the paraprofessional or New Careers movement within social work and other human service professions (Council on Social Work Education, 1967; Grosser et al., 1969; Pearl and Reissman, 1965). It came in the form of a change in the racial composition of staff at the lowest level of the hierarchy and, again, was true only in large public agencies. Family service agencies, for example, still considered among the elite of casework agencies, rarely hired paraprofessionals to do direct service. In 1972, about 100,000 people worked as social service aides, the majority of whom were lower-class, ethnic-minority women (Schindler, 1977). Job advancement, however, remains a serious cause of concern for aides, since, for the most part, there is no long-range career ladder, nor are these ladders adequately articulated in most states. As a result, salaries and upward mobility tend to be limited.

Findings on Sex. While the data are sporadic, there are some indications that women were represented on *agency boards* in the early 1960s only if they happened to be wives of rich businessmen or industrialists (Wilensky

2. Interestingly, no information was routinely collected on racial composition of NASW membership until 1972, according to Tia Pratt, Membership Development Coordinator, NASW National Headquarters.

and Lebeaux, 1958). Not until reports from the studies of the Target Area Organizations (TAO) in the Community Action Program was high female involvement found. In fact, the major role women played in urban minority political movements represents a major deviation from the typical pattern found in the United States (Fainstein and Fainstein, 1974).

The sexual distribution of the *staffing* patterns of social welfare workers in 1960 was also interesting. Using the 1960 Bureau of Labor Statistics (BLS) data, the ratio of men to women among social welfare workers in the early 1960s was 40 to 60, compared with a 30 to 70 ratio in 1950. In the early 1960s, women outnumbered men in direct service positions by more than two to one. Whereas men held only 48 percent of the executive positions in 1950, by 1960 they held 58 percent. This was true in spite of the fact that a considerably higher proportion of women than men in supervisory and executive positions had completed graduate school preparation (Baker, 1965).

From a feminist perspective, salary data were equally depressing. The 1960 BLS study indicated a $7,020 median salary for men who had completed professional education, as compared with $5,000 for men who had completed only a Bachelor's degree. The median salaries for women in the identical categories were $6,340 and $4,350, respectively. The NASW study revealed an even larger differential—a $7,700 median for men and a $6,600 median for women (Baker, 1965).

Through the late 1960s, the status of women in the profession continued in much the same direction as reported earlier. Most professional social workers (about two-thirds) continued to be female, with men largely found in top administrative positions and women in direct service and line supervisory positions. Forty percent of male NASW members reported administration as their primary task, while only 20 percent of the women did. There was also evidence that men had more rapid career advancement than women and that men consistently earned $1,000 to $1,500 more per year than women. Men also dominated the deanships and were the top officers and chairmen of the important professional associations (Meyer, 1971).

Again, in the 1970s, women, as a group, do not seem to have fared well. In spite of the fact that the social service work force continues to be predominantly female (63 percent), a study by the Committee on Women's Issues of the National Association of Social Workers found that ". . . women comprise a very small percentage of the decision-making body in social work. . . . Of the 868 agencies surveyed, 141, or 16 percent, were directed by women in 1976'' (NASW News, April 1977: 12). Data from the national assessment of juvenile correctional facilities, mentioned earlier, revealed a similar pattern. To quote: "Executives are preponderately male in all program types. The few females are found only in coed or all-female programs . . . where they are still outnumbered by males" (Vinter, 1976: 57).

Furthermore, clear salary differences favor men at the casework, administrative, and teaching levels. Although some of the differences are related to marital status and parenthood, gaps can, by no means, be totally accounted for by family characteristics (Fanshel, 1976).

However, it should also be noted that some progress has been made with regard to sexism. Whereas in 1970, the national leadership in NASW was 25.3 percent female, in 1976 it was 50 percent female. In addition, positive trends are found in the leadership positions in schools of Social Work; although fewer than 15 percent of the deans are women, there is a steady increase in this area (Schools of Social Work, 1975). However, women are still underrepresented in top faculty positions; for example, in 1973, 63 percent of the full and associate professors were men (Ripple, 1974).

In conclusion, the data regarding sexism and racism suggest that the field of social work has not made great strides on either dimension, and that, contrary to the rhetoric in the profession, social work is not distinctive from the larger system in which it is embedded.[3] In fact, in the early 1970s, the necessity for, and proliferation of several social movements, which often developed alternative forms of service outside the mainstream social service network, attests to the intransigent quality of racism and sexism within traditional social work agencies.

PART II: RISE AND POTENTIAL IMPACT OF SELECTED SELF-HELP MOVEMENTS

Before describing the rise and potential impact of selected self-help movements on racism and sexism in the social services, it is instructive to examine first the case of WRO, which began in the wake of the Civil Rights Movement and the War on Poverty (Piven and Cloward, 1977). WRO was really the first of the constituent or self-help movements to impact the service delivery system to any degree since the time when older people had

3. This assertion was empirically supported in a study of social workers in Community Mental Health Centers (Perlmutter, 1977).

been involved in the California Institute of Social Welfare many years earlier (Steiner, 1971). WRO is also important because the movement represented an external challenge to the ideological underpinnings of public welfare and set a precedent in the use of client power to shift not only ideology, but also practice.

Although composed primarily of Blacks and women, racism and sexism were not the focus; WRO represented an oppressed, lower-class group, seeking to get its welfare entitlements. WRO's power and effectiveness resulted from its group activity and pressure, since clients, as individuals, are generally powerless to command benefits from government or even private agencies, particularly if they are poor or stigmatized. This is especially true in the case of public bureaucracies which are free of market constraints and which, in the case of public welfare agencies, have a monopoly over services. However, a slightly different way of viewing the impact of WRO administratively is to consider this movement as an organized expression of an enforcement agency's clientele. As noted by Selznick (1949), because of long and intense association, these types of agencies often gradually identify with their clientele and become captured or co-opted by them; policies and regulations may change as a result.

Certainly in the instance of welfare departments, which were stormed by WRO groups, entitlements were granted, rules were relaxed, not only out of fear, but also out of sympathy with the rights and needs of the organized recipients. In fact, WRO, in addition to creating visibility and wider community support for its campaigns, experienced its greatest success at the local level, in many instances co-opting the welfare bureaucracy. Because its focus was on extracting all they were legally entitled to from the system, such co-option was permissible. When peaceable co-optation was not forthcoming, the fear that WRO might spark public disorder also resulted in concessions being granted (Steiner, 1971). This can still be seen: a phone call to the welfare department by WRO or the arrival of even a small number of WRO members at the office is generally enough to wrest entitled benefits from the system.[4]

4. This assertion is based on discussions by the authors with various staff at local welfare offices in Philadelphia. It should also be noted that WRO was much less successful as a national voice for welfare reform. Although Cloward and Piven (1966), as the ideologues of the movement, spoke in terms of larger political aims—for example, of "overloading" the welfare system and causing its demise—these revolutionary ideas met with little success. Rather, WRO had its roots and success in the moderate ideologies of self-help, local autonomy, collective action, and the importance of ethnic separatism (Cloward, 1968; Piven and Cloward, 1977).

While the predominant movements of the 1960s centered around civil rights and the opposition to the war in southeast Asia, some of the prominent movements of the early seventies centered more around nationalism and ethnic consciousness, Women's Liberation, and gay rights. The expansion of the latter movements "paralleled the civil rights movements of ethnic minorities and women and the Office of Economic Opportunity programs that heightened the concepts of community participation and 'consumerism' " (Katz, 1977: 1,254). Maximum feasible participation, then, extended not just to the poor, but to all those underrepresented or stigmatized in society.

Particularly in the case of self-help movements within the social services, these movements also represented extreme dissatisfaction with established institutions, with the rhetoric that so much was being spent for services, when, in fact, so few real services were delivered (Derthick, 1975; Morris, 1973; Bell, 1973), and with traditional professional methods of delivering services, which often discriminated against the poor and other minorities, and in which there were often great discrepancies between client and professional perspectives of the client's problems (Mayer and Timms, 1970). There was, then, on the part of clients, a growing dissatisfaction with and questioning of the value of professionalism for clients by the early 1970s (Haug and Sussman, 1969).[5]

Thus, during this period, "many social and cultural forces converged to produce a critical re-evaluation of personal beliefs, lifestyles and group affiliations among significant sections of the population" (Katz, 1977: 1254), which had an impact on the ideological base of social welfare.

The use of a social movement analysis (Katz and Bender, 1976) for understanding these groups seems appropriate. As such, then, these groups are best understood as somewhat unstable, emergent phenomena, evolving spontaneously in reaction to a shared feeling of dissatisfaction with the status quo; there is some feeling of relative deprivation. It is our view that self-help groups are particular kinds of social movements—those in which, according to Turner and Killian (1972) participation orientations, or personal change, predominates over either value or power orientations. However,

5. According to Haug and Sussman (1969: 156), professional autonomy is questioned when "(1) the expertise of the practitioners is inadequate, (2) their claims to altruism are unfounded, (3) the organizational delivery system supporting their authority is defective and insufficient, or (4) the system is too efficient and exceeds the appropriate bounds of its power."

within the WRO, the women's groups, among the gays, and in the case of self-help groups among poor minorities, a social action or reform orientation is seen, albeit less dominantly.

Specifically, these self-help groups have developed a variety of alternative services, with both a concrete and a counselling focus.[6] For WRO, the issue has not really been providing social services per se, but rather providing access to services and entitlements (Steiner, 1971). For the women's movement, the rape services have offered an array of alternative approaches (Rudnick, 1975). A similar pattern of alternatives has come from the gay movement (National Gay Task Force, 1976; Lee, 1972; Forrester, 1976); racial and ethnic minorities have been a powerful counterforce as well (Fainstein and Fainstein, 1974; Perry, 1976).

We would argue that these self-help movements have affected the ideological orientations of social welfare and have stimulated some questioning and change to occur both in professional practice and in manpower utilization.

From our analysis of service patterns over time, it seems clear that there were tremendous service gaps for such groups mentioned above, or if services did exist, that they were inappropriate to the needs of the group in question. Consequently, in the Black community there was a proliferation of autonomous community organizations developed on self-help patterns, with "a focus on articulating intervention strategies and engaging in action programs directed at meeting the needs of blacks" (Perry, 1976: 210). The requirement for new practices in social welfare was clearly called for among the numerous ethnic minorities within various welfare settings. For example,

6. In relation to the whole question of values, it is unmistakable that self-help movements are within the individualistic tradition, so prevalent in this country. Katz's (1977: 1,256) contention in this regard—that self-help groups today reveal a distinct polarity in response to the individualistic ethos, with social and individual change being of equal strength—seems debatable. Certainly in the movements we will examine, there is some emphasis on social change, but individual concerns do dominate. In the case of the women's, gay, and lower-income minority social service movements, it is the actual preoccupation with social service or participation orientations which is seen as deflecting attention from the social change aims of the larger political movements from whence all of these self-help movements derive (Fainstein and Fainstein, 1974: 49–50; Freeman, 1975). In the social movement literature, this transformation into largely participation-oriented groups is regarded as conservatizing (Turner and Killian, 1972; Messinger, 1955). Such service orientations among the women's, gay, WRO, and self-help groups among poor racial and ethnic minorities have been a subject of much debate and some factionalization both within the larger movements from which these particular self-help groups were spawned, as well as within the self-help groups themselves.

Dohen (1971) discusses a new role for the Juvenile Court, appropriate to the local ethnic context, as she focused on the Puerto Rican community.

Finally, there has been a slow, but growing recognition of the importance of ethnicity and the diversity of services needed by different minority groups in society (Cafferty and Chestang, 1975). According to one author, this requires not only a reconceptualization of traditional services, but the development of alternate or parallel services as well (Brown, 1974).

Similarly, Forrester et al. (1976) document numerous ways that gays, both as clients and as workers, have been discriminated against in traditional service agencies. Specifically, there has been a tendency to view homosexuality as *the* major problem to be "cured," with lack of attention to other pressing problems the client may present, or to the need for services other than those of a therapeutic nature.

In addition to satisfying serious unmet needs, another extremely important function of self-help movements is to educate and sensitize the wider professional community to their needs, so that the mainstream organizations can modify some of their own services (Abarbarel, 1976). A cogent example of this process was offered in a panel discussion at the National Conference of Social Welfare, 1977. One social work clinician discussed the impact of the women's movement on her work with abused and battered wives. Although she herself was female, prior to the women's movement her work with clients focused on psychological premises of sadomasochism; her approach has been completely changed as a result of the women's movement, as she now focuses on the immediate reality needs. A second example is provided by Eunice Evans, Director of Program Management Services, United Services Agency, Wilkes-Barre, Pennsylvania, who reports that the women's movement has had a definite impact on her agency's planning of services for "battered women" and child abuse cases (March 30, 1977).

Several other effects of the movement groups can be noted. First, mainstream professionals can refer clients to such self-help groups; second, such self-help groups may screen mainstream professionals for referral purposes. Such action has taken place in the case of gays in Philadelphia, where various gay self-help groups will give a prospective client a list of professionals in the wider community who have been screened as being appropriate therapists for gays.[7]

7. Conversation with Joan DeForrest, Director of Community Services, Eromin Center, Philadelphia, May 5, 1977.

The great danger, of course, is that self-help movements will become co-opted by professionals and ultimately lose their distinctive character (Katz, 1977). Yet there is no question that the recent flowering of these groups is of intense interest to professionals (Katz and Bender, 1976).[8] It should be noted that self-help movements have varied tremendously in their relationship to professionalized services and to individual professionals. While some, such as Synanon, refuse professional help as a matter of principle (Katz, 1977), the particular groups discussed in this section have generally accepted the assistance of professionals on a limited and carefully screened basis.

Thus, it seems clear that the activity of self-help movements is critical, particularly in the case of highly stigmatized groups of clients. Not only do they provide needed and appropriate services, but they also alert the wider professional community to the ideological issues involved. Such sensitizing may cause changes in the mainstream service delivery system, both in the broadening of its manpower pool, as well as in its redefinition of relevant services.

CONCLUSIONS

We have tried to document, on the one hand, that in spite of some gains, racism and sexism still doggedly persist in the social services. On the other hand, we have also tried to describe the rise of selected self-help groups, which have geared themselves specifically to problems of racism and sexism in the traditional social services.

It is our view that those shifts, which have occurred in the social services and which are moving them to be more responsive in their manpower utilization as well as more flexible and more accountable to the populations they serve, are, in part, a result of the tremendous growth, visibility, and impact of the self-help movements of the 1970s. Because of their particular relevance to the issues of sexism and racism within the administration of the social services, these movements have been, and continue to be a vital force, impacting the total system, including ideology, practice models, and, ultimately, manpower utilization.

While data in the field of social work practice are very sparse in gen-

8. Note that the entire September/October 1976 issue of *Social Policy* is devoted to self-help groups.

eral, it is a particular problem vis-à-vis race and sex. Because the data are so incomplete, Fanshel (1976) makes several good suggestions for future research on women in social work, such as logitudinal studies following recent graduates from schools of social work; a more thorough scrutiny of the decision-making process in agency hiring practices; and a comparison of sex-based differentials in social work with other professions. Because the data on the minority composition of the social work labor force are equally sparse, we urge that the implementation be extended to include minorities as well.

In addition, detailed case studies of the variety of self-help movements within the social service sector need to be developed and offer a virtually untouched research area: only then will the intricacies and dynamics of the interrelationship between social service movements and social service policies and practices be better understood. We hope that this essay has provided a preliminary stimulus in that direction.

REFERENCES

Abarbarel, Gail. 1976. "Helping Victims of Rape," *Social Work,* 21:478–82.

Baker, Mary R. 1965. "Personnel in Social Welfare," *Encyclopedia of Social Work,* 15:532–40. New York: National Association of Social Workers.

Bell, Winifred. 1973. "Too Few Services to Separate," *Social Work,* 18:66–77.

Billingsley, Andrew and Jeanne Giovannoni. 1972. *Children of the Storm: Black Children and American Child Welfare.* New York: Harcourt, Brace, Jovanovich.

Boehm, Werner. 1958. "The Nature of Social Work," *Social Work,* 3:10–18.

Briar, Scott. 1967. "The Current Crisis in Social Casework." In *Social Work Practice,* pp. 19–33. New York: Columbia University Press.

—— 1973. "Effective Social Work Intervention in Direct Practice: Implications for Education." In *Facing the Challenge: Plenary Session Papers from the 19th Annual Program Meeting,* pp. 17–30. New York: Council on Social Work Education.

Brown, June. 1974. "Can Social Work Education Prepare Practitioners to Continue to Contribute to a Cogent Challenge to American Racism?" In *Black Perspectives on Social Work Education: Issues Related to Curricu-*

lum, Faculty, and Students, pp. 1–12. New York: Council on Social Work Education.

Bush, James A. 1976. "The Minority Administrator." Unpublished paper.

Cafferty, Pastora San Juan and Leon Chestang, eds. 1975. *The Diverse Society.* New York: National Association of Social Workers.

Carmichael, Stokeley and Charles Hamilton. 1967. *Black Power.* New York: Random House.

Clark, Burton R. 1961. "Organizational Adaptation and Precarious Values." In A. Etzioni, ed., *Complex Organizations: A Sociological Reader,* pp. 159–67. New York: Holt, Rinehart, and Winston.

Cloward, Richard A. 1968. "The War on Poverty: Are the Poor Left Out?" In C. Waxman, ed., *Poverty: Power and Politics,* pp. 159–70. New York: Grosset and Dunlap.

Cloward, Richard and Irwin Epstein. 1967. "Private Social Welfare's Disengagement from the Poor: The Case of Family Adjustment Agencies." In G. Brager and F. Purcell, eds., *Community Action Against Poverty: Readings from the Mobilization Experience,* pp. 40–63. New Haven: College and University Press Services.

Cloward, Richard and Frances Fox Piven. 1966. "A Strategy To End Poverty," *The Nation,* May 2:510–17.

Council on Social Work Education. 1967. *Personnel in Anti-Poverty Programs: Implications for Social Work Education.* New York: Council on Social Work Education.

——1975. *Schools of Social Work with Accredited Master's Degree Programs.* New York: Council on Social Work Education.

Derthick, Martha. 1975. *Uncontrollable Spending for Social Service Grants.* Washington, D.C.: Brookings Institution.

Dohen, Dorothy. 1971. "A New Juvenile Court Role in an Ethically Controlled Community Agency," *Social Work,* 16:25–29.

Dorsen, Norman, ed. 1971. *The Rights of Americans.* New York: Pantheon Books.

Fainstein, Norman I. and Susan S. Fainstein. 1974. *Urban Political Movements: The Search for Power by Minority Groups in American Cities.* Englewood Cliff, N.J.: Prentice-Hall.

Fanshel, David. 1976. "Status Differentials: Men and Women in Social Work," Social Work, 21:448–54.

Forrester, Randal G., James Huggins, and Barbara K. Shore. 1976. "Effective Functioning for Homosexuals and Other Sexual Minorities." In *Social Welfare Forum, 1976,* pp. 221–30. New York: Columbia University Press.

Freeman, Jo. 1975. *The Politics of Women's Liberation*. New York: David McKay.

Germain, Carel. 1970. "Casework and Science: A Historical Encounter." In R. Roberts and R. Nee, eds., *Theories of Social Casework*, pp. 5–32. Chicago: University of Chicago Press.

Gittelman, Alex and Carel B. Germain. 1976. "Social Work Practice: A Life Model," *Social Service Review*, 50:601–09.

Goldberg, Gail and Ruth Middleman. 1974. *Social Service Delivery: A Structural Approach to Social Work Practice*. New York: Columbia University Press.

Goldstein, Howard. 1973. *Social Work Practice*. Columbia, S.C.: University of South Carolina Press.

Grosser, Charles, William E. Henry, and James A. Kelly. 1969. *Non-Professionals in the Human Services*. San Francisco: Jossey-Bass.

Hackshaw, James O. F. 1971. "Race and Welfare." In *Encyclopedia of Social Work*, 16:1065–68. New York: National Association of Social Workers.

Haug, Marie and Marvin Sussman. 1969. "Professional Autonomy and the Revolt of the Client." *Social Problems*, 17:153–61.

Holloway, Robert G., Jay W. Artis, and Walter E. Freeman. 1963. "The Participation Patterns of Economic Influentials and the Control of a Hospital Board of Trustees," *Journal of Health and Human Behavior*, 4:88–98.

Kadushin, Alfred. 1958. "The Prestige of Social Work: Facts and Factors," *Social Work*, 3:37–43.

Kahn, Alfred J. 1976. "Service Delivery at the Neighborhood Level: Experience, Theory, and Facts," *Social Service Review*, 50:23–56.

Kamerman, Sheila B. and Alfred J. Kahn. 1976. *Social Services in the United States*. Philadelphia: Temple University Press.

Katz, Alfred H. 1977. "Self-Help Groups." In *Encyclopedia of Social Work*, 17:1254–60. New York: National Association of Social Workers.

Katz, Alfred H. and Eugene I. Bender. 1976. *The Strength in Us: Self-Help Groups in the Modern World*. New York: New Viewpoints.

Kolodny, Ralph L. 1969. "Ethnic Cleavages in the United States," *Social Work*, 14:13–23.

Kravetz, Diane. 1976. "Sexism in a Woman's Profession," *Social Work*, 21:421–27.

Lambert, Camille J. and Leah R. Lambert. 1970. "Impact of Poverty Funds on Voluntary Agencies," *Social Work*, 15:53–61.

Lee, Ronald. 1972. "Mental Health and Gay Liberation." In *Social Welfare Forum, 1972*, pp. 295–303. New York: Columbia University Press.

Leiby, James. 1971. "Social Welfare: History of Basic Ideas." In *Encyclopedia of Social Work*, 16:1461–76. New York: National Association of Social Workers.

Mahaffey, Maryann. 1976. "Sexism and Social Work," *Social Work*, 21:419.

Mayer, John E. and Noel Timms. 1970. *The Client Speaks: Working Class Impressions of Casework.* New York: Atherton Press.

Messinger, Sheldon. 1955. "Organizational Transformation: A Case Study of a Declining Social Movement," *American Sociological Review*, 20:3–10.

Meyer, Carol. 1970. *Social Work Practice: A Response to the Urban Crisis.* New York: Free Press.

Meyer, Henry J., Edgar F. Borgotta, and Wyatt C. Jones. 1965. *Girls at Vocational High: An Experiment in Social Work Intervention.* New York: Russell Sage Foundation.

—— 1971. "Profession of Social Work: Contemporary Characteristics." In *Encyclopedia of Social Work*, 16:959–71. New York: National Association of Social Workers.

Meyer, Henry J. and Sheldon Siegel. 1977. "Profession of Social Work: Contemporary Characteristics." In *Encyclopedia of Social Work*, 17:1067–81. New York: National Association of Social Workers.

Miller, Henry J. 1969. "Social Work in the Black Ghetto: The New Colonialism." *Social Work*, 14:65–76.

Morris, Robert. 1973. "Welfare Reform 1973: The Social Services Dimension," *Science*, 181:515–22.

National Association of Social Workers. 1975. *Manpower Data Bank Frequency Distributions.* New York: National Association of Social Workers.

NASW News. 1977. "Survey Indicates Social Work Women Losing Grounds in Leadership Ranks," *NASW News*, 22:12.

National Conference on Social Welfare. 1975. *Roles for Social Work in Community Mental Health Programs.* Task Force Report.

National Gay Task Force. 1976. *Gay Community Services: Directory and Source Book.* New York: National Gay Task Force.

O'Reilly, Charles T. 1969. "Race in Social Welfare." In R. Miller, ed., *Race, Research, and Reason: Social Work Perspectives*, pp. 88–97. New York: National Association of Social Workers.

Pearl, Arthur and Frank Reissman. 1965. *New Careers for the Poor*. New York: Free Press.

Perlmutter, Felice D. 1977. "Social Workers as a Source of Community Orientation for Community Mental Health Centers." Paper presented at the Council on Social Work Education Annual Meeting.

Perry, Lorraine. 1976. "Strategies of Black Community Groups," *Social Work*, 21:210–15.

Pincus, Allan and Anne Minahan. 1973. *Social Work Practice*. Itasca, Ill.: F. T. Peacock.

Pins, Arnulf M. 1963. *Who Chooses Social Work, When and Why?* New York: Council on Social Work Education.

Piven, Frances Fox, and Richard Cloward. 1977. *Poor People's Movements: How They Succeed, How They Fail*. New York: Pantheon Books.

Reid, William J., and Ann W. Shyne. 1969. *Brief and Extended Casework*. New York: Columbia University Press.

Ripple, Lilian, ed. 1974. *Statistics on Graduate Social Work Education in the United States: 1973*. New York: Council on Social Work Education.

Rudnick, Patricia. 1975. "The Rape Movement: A Social Movement Analysis of a Philadelphia Case Study." Master's thesis, Bryn Mawr College.

Sanders, Charles L. 1970. "Growth of the Association of Black Social Workers," *Social Casework*, 51:277–84.

Sarri, Rosemary and Yeheskel Hasenfeld, eds. 1976. *Brought to Justice? Juveniles, the Courts, and the Law*. Ann Arbor: University of Michigan, National Assessment of Juvenile Corrections.

Saunders, Marie Simmons. 1969. "The Ghetto: Some Perceptions of a Black Social Worker," *Social Work*, 14:84–88.

Schindler, Ruben. 1977. "Profession of Social Work: Aides." In *Encyclopedia of Social Work*, 17:1060–66. New York: National Association of Social Workers.

Schwartz, Mary C. 1973. "Sexism in the Social Work Curriculum." *Journal of Education for Social Work*, 9:65–70.

Seeley, John R. et al. 1957. *Community Chest: A Case Study in Philanthropy*. Toronto: University of Toronto Press.

Selznick, Philip. 1949. *TVA and the Grass Roots: A Study in the Sociology of Formal Organization*. Berkeley: University of California Press.

Siporin, Max. 1975. *Introduction to Social Work Practice*. New York: Macmillan.

——1976. *Social Policy*, 7:Entire Issue.

Stamm, Alfred. 1969. "NASW Membership: Characteristics, Deployment, and Salaries," *Personnel Information*, 12:33–45.

Steiner, Gilbert Y. 1971. *The State of Welfare*. Washington, D.C.: Brookings Institution.

Street, Loyd. 1977. "Minorities." In *Encyclopedia of Social Work*, 17:931–46. New York: National Association of Social Workers.

Titmuss, Richard. 1968. *Commitment to Welfare*. London: George Allen and Unwin.

Turner, Ralph H. and Lewis M. Killian. 1972. *Collective Behavior*. 2d ed. Englewood Cliffs, N.J.: Prentice-Hall.

Vargus, Ione. 1977. "The Minority Administrator." Unpublished paper.

Vinter, Robert D., ed. 1976. *Time Out: A National Study of Juvenile Correctional Programs*. Ann Arbor: University of Michigan, National Assessment of Juvenile Corrections.

Weissman, Harold H., ed. 1969. *Individual and Group Services in the Mobilization for Youth Experience*. New York: Association Press.

Wilensky, Harold L. 1965. "The Problems and Prospects of the Welfare State." In H. L. Wilensky and C. H. Lebeaux, *Industrial Society and Social Welfare*, pp. v–lii. 2d ed. New York: Free Press.

Wilensky, Harold L. and Charles H. Lebeaux. 1958. *Industrial Society and Social Welfare*. New York: Russell Sage Foundation.

Willie, Charles V., Herbert Notkin, and Nicholas Rezak. 1964. "Trends in the Participation of Business Men in Local Volunteer Affairs," *Sociology and Social Research*, 48:289–300.

III PRESCRIPTIVE STRATEGIES

TEN

Some Issues in the Evaluation of Human Services Delivery

PETER H. ROSSI

THE MAIN message of this paper is that evaluations of human services delivery systems are difficult to accomplish to the satisfaction of either evaluators or the professionals and administrators responsible for the design and operation of the systems.[1]

Going beyond merely the reporting of troubles, this paper elaborates the issue in two ways: First, it attempts to provide an understanding of why human services are so hard to evaluate satisfactorily, reviewing in the process both the nature of human services delivery systems and characteristic evaluation approaches. Second, it proposes an evaluation strategy that is designed especially for human services and that attempts to make possible more satisfactory evaluations.

Many activities go under the name of evaluation, ranging from offhand opinions, through news reporters' haphazard investigations, to social science research efforts as rigorous as the current state of the art in basic social science permits. For the purposes of this paper, I want to restrict the term evaluation to the application of current state-of-the-art social science re-

1. The preparation of this paper was aided by a grant from the Russell Sage Foundation "Measuring the Delivery of Public Services," whose assistance is gratefully acknowledged. The comments of several colleagues, Wayne Alves, Richard Berk, and Huey Chen, on an earlier draft were most helpful in sharpening the paper at several points.

search methods to the assessment of whether given social policies can achieve or are achieving their intended aims. This restriction excludes those evaluating activities that do not pretend to be social science and those that pretend but do not succeed at it. Admittedly, such characterizations are judgment calls, but ones upon which I am sure we would all mainly agree. I also exclude researches that do not attempt to assess the success of programs in fulfilling their goals and are hence purely descriptive accounts. Policy analyses are also excluded on the grounds that they do not involve primary research activities.[2]

As we shall see in a later section of this paper, this definition of evaluation research does cover a wide range of activities, including research that attempts to discern what the goals of a program are, monitoring activities that seek to ascertain how a program is operating, process or formative evaluative activities, as well as impact assessments and field experiments.[3]

If there is any empirical law that is emerging from the past decade of widespread evaluation research activities, it is that the expected value for any measured effect of a social program is zero. In short, most programs, when properly evaluated, turn out to be ineffective or at best marginally accomplishing their set aims. There are enough exceptions to prevent this empirical generalization from being phrased as the "Iron Law of Social Program Evaluation," but the tendency is strong enough to warrant placing bets on evaluation outcomes in the expectation of making a steady but modest side income.

The disappointments that have arisen from the results of program evaluations have led, on the one hand, to a reconsideration of programs and, on the other hand, to a reconsideration of evaluation research as an activity. Neither reassessment has led to much progress up to this point. It is apparently the case that evaluation research does not lead immediately to radical improvements in social programs. Nor does the failure of evaluation research to find positive effects of programs lead to its being discarded as an approach. Indeed, one can make the case that nothing succeeds like failure, a paradox whose resolution rests on the understanding that it is composed of

2. Policy analysis may be viewed as the application of social science theory along with the results of social science research to the examination of policy alternatives. Properly undertaken, policy analyses assume that alternative policies have been evaluated and that their effectiveness values are known.

3. For a more detailed description of these research activities, see Rossi and Wright (1977).

half truths. Thus, some believe that evaluation results reflect reality while there is nothing wrong with evaluation research methods. Others believe the exact opposite. Each camp partially neutralizes the other with the result that there is widespread skepticism both about social programs and about evaluation research. Yet so far we cannot do without either.

ON THE NATURE OF HUMAN SERVICES DELIVERY SYSTEMS

The tertiary sector of our economy has been growing at a faster pace than any of the other sectors. Our affluent society apparently has mastered the problems involved in primary extraction and in the manufacture of finished product and has turned of late to putting the finishing touches on the "quality of life." This fine tuning of our social machinery involves the extension of existing human services and the invention of new forms of such services. Through government agencies and private entrepreneurs we now channel a considerable portion of our GNP into providing services that depend essentially on the delivery outside market mechanisms of some sort of "product" to clients through the use of more or less trained intermediaries. The essential aspect of human services is that the mode and content of the delivery itself is the product that is being delivered. Thus education is the interaction between students and the schools, the primary aspect of which is the activity of the classroom. Similarly, job counselling is the contact between a counsellor and a client and the product is the content of these encounters. Of course, there is more to human services than human interaction in face-to-face encounters: Schools consist of physical structures in which the schooling takes place, textbooks, writing implements, audio-visual aids, and so on. Similarly, job counselling may involve the use of aptitude tests, pamphlets, and audio-visual displays.

The essential premise of human services systems is that there are pockets of deficiencies in our social structure that can be corrected through such encounters, or that naturally occurring processes accompanying human development can be speeded up or made more efficient with the use of human services delivery. We know that without formal schooling children will grow into adults and acquire some degree of verbal language skills. We also know that some families alone could rear children who are literate and who have basic mathematical and other skills. But, the family as an institution is not very good at imparting such skills: Without the public educational system, the disparities among families in these respects would tend to exacerbate inequalities in skills and knowledge while at the same time lowering the average levels of skills and knowledge below those seemingly required by our need for a relatively literate and knowledgeable labor force. Public education is simply more efficient than the family in aiding young children to develop the necessary skills and knowledge.

What is apparently very clear with respect to education is not as clear in the cases of other types of human services. Thus, we do not have any institutions that are universally found in all societies that are concerned with the detection of crime or with the rehabilitation of prisoners who are released to freedom. Nor do we expect that unemployed persons will have on hand all the skills that would make it easy for them to get other jobs or that their families and friends will have all the information on hand that will make the transition back into the labor force as easy as possible.

Furthermore we recognize that there are gross inequalities among individuals and households in their abilities to deal successfully with the world about them. Although money cannot buy everything, the rich and the powerfully connected can buy many things on the open market that make life easier. The poor, those disadvantaged in some respect, or those whose skills and aptitudes are deficiently below normal all apparently need help or they will sink further down to new lows in depravity. Obviously, here is where human services come to the rescue.

It should be noted that there are two aspects to those problems of deficiencies in individuals and households. On the one hand, a deficient human being or household lacks or is deprived of experiences and/or resources that are essential to adequate functioning. Thus, according to this view, everyone should have a chance at a reasonable job or a reasonable chance to recover from an illness or injury. In short, we hold to concepts of *social minima* for units of our society. On the other hand, a society with deficient individuals and households suffers some disabilities because of those pockets of deficiency. An unrehabilitated released felon will commit additional crimes. An unemployed man is not contributing to the GNP. There is an underlying concept of a societal minimum, a minimum level of functioning for the society.

Corresponding to these two aspects of the problem of deficiencies in individuals and households, there is a duality that, on the one hand, expresses concern for individual suffering under deprivations, and, on the other hand, concern with social control. Thus an unrehabilitated prisoner is deemed to be a potentially unhappy person and also someone who is a menace to social order. In this conception of deficiencies, both society and the deficient individual or household have at least parallel if not identical interests: An unemployed person wants a job and the society wants to have a low level of unemployment or underemployment. Fix one and you fix the other. It should be noted that there are some areas where the parallelism is not so obvious. Certainly, society may want a low crime rate, but some professional criminals might have little interest in being rehabilitated to follow occupations that are less interesting and remunerative. This duality becomes expressed with particular force in some human services delivery systems where the interests of clients and the interests of society diverge sharply.[4] We will return to this theme again in this paper.

The establishment of a human services delivery system rests upon a number of critical assumptions:

1) that there are deficient individuals or households whose deficiencies prevent optimal functioning and whose presence in the society presents problems to the society.
2) that either the deficiencies can be corrected or functioning can be changed so that individuals and households can function "normally" through the use of some sort of human services "treatment."
3) that the human services "treatment" can be delivered uniformly and widely through the training of delivery personnel and their embeddedment in an organization.
4) that there are no serious conflicts of interests between the social control goals of human services and the goals of clients.

The evaluation of human services delivery systems ordinarily takes place around points two and three. There is little doubt in conventional establishmentarian views that there are deficient individuals and households in our society. Of course, there are some skeptical voices: Some challenges have been made to IQ measures, for example, on the grounds that they measure not individual deficiencies but subgroup deprivation, and others

---

4. This duality is closely related to that involved in the provision of public goods. It makes little sense for any individual to pay taxes unless paying taxes is made compulsory for all, since the marginal utility for any individual of the majority of public services is very small.

have asserted that valid subcultural differences are alternative explanations for what appear to be pockets of deficiency. Perhaps the major challenge to the first assumption listed above comes from radical interpretations of our society that recognize the existence of deprived and deficient individuals and households but ascribe causality to the malfunctioning of the society. Of course, the radical viewpoints and subcultural interpretations do not find their way into evaluative activities.

Little or no attention has been paid to designing or carrying through evaluations that question the fourth assumption on the above list. The utilitarian heritage of our liberal social philosophy equates—at least in the long run—the utility for an individual with social utility. However, in the case of some social programs this identity of interests is not clear. For some persons of low educational attainment and correspondingly low repertory of job skills, getting a job may not be better than remaining on welfare, as many of the mothers enrolled in the WIN program were to learn. The WIN program that attempted to move welfare mothers into the labor force assumed that a low-paying job would appear more attractive to mothers of young children than remaining on the welfare rolls.

The main thrusts of evaluation center around assumptions two and three. It is assumed that there is some way in which these deficiencies in individuals and households can be corrected (or compensated for) through treatments and that such treatments can be delivered effectively to clients with reasonable cost-to-benefit ratios. While few evaluations center around the fourth assumption, it can be shown that this assumption when violated in fact plays an important role in the failure of human services delivery systems.

THE FAILURE OF TREATMENTS

Assuming that pockets of deficiency exist, then whether a treatment can be devised that will reduce the size of such pockets depends clearly on whether or not the conditions generating the deficiencies are properly understood. In short, treatment depends on the existence of a valid model of how the deficiency is produced and/or maintained. Thus, if a model of black unemployment differentials sees the high unemployment rate among blacks as due to a lack of skills that match current labor market demand, then a reasonable treatment to apply is vocational training. Obviously, if the model is not valid, then vocational training will fail as a treatment. Or if the model underlying the design of a prison is that criminals are members of a criminal subculture, then the design might minimize contact among prisoners and emphasize lofty sermons on the straight life. Clearly such a treatment is likely to fail.

An infinity of models may be devised that will seemingly generate such deficiencies as poverty, crime, unemployment, illiteracy, and the corresponding treatments may also be seen as almost infinite in number. Indeed, the same model may lead to quite different treatments depending on whether one emphasizes one or another part of the model. Thus a production function model for public education might lead one to emphasize school inputs to learning or emphasize family inputs, the first treatment leading to heavier investment in teachers, schools, or teaching methods, while the second leading possibly to child-rearing instruction for parents.

Furthermore, every treatment can be shown to "work" in the sense that after experiencing the treatment, some of the deficient persons or households will improve. The problem here is that the social world is highly stochastic, with individuals and households moving from state to state with probabilities that are significantly large. Thus, poor individuals and households are quite likely to cross the poverty line if left untreated and some portion of those who are treated will also cross the line and appear to have been affected by the treatment. While the old are not going to get young over time, the opposite process appears to make young adult criminals into more law abiding older adults. Men and women who never finished high school on time often manage to get their diplomas later in life. Some persons who have received vocational training will have higher wage rates after training, but so will their counterparts who have not taken training but who are just a few months older. In short, "spontaneous remission" is characteristic of these deficiencies.

Finally, it is difficult to separate the treatment from the manner of delivery. Human services treatments that are given by exceptionally devoted persons are probably efficacious as often because of the devotion expressed in the delivery as because of the treatment. Individual tutoring of children has always seemingly worked for the rich who have been able to hire skilled and devoted teachers as tutors. Any brand of therapy wielded by a devoted psychotherapist is probably as good as any other brand of psychotherapy. However, the same treatment administered by the indifferent and unskillful may fail to have any impact. The *delivery* of human services treatment is critically important in their effectiveness, a theme that is treated at length in the next section of this paper. Before proceeding, however, it is important to point out that treatments can fail in the first place because they are inappropriate to the problem, because they have been generated by an invalid model of the phenomenon in question. They can also fail because the treatment itself has been poorly specified and in fact indistinguishable from its mode of delivery.

THE FAILURE OF DELIVERY SYSTEMS

Assuming for the moment that an efficacious and theoretically valid treatment has been devised, then the next question is whether it can be delivered on a large scale. A related problem is whether the delivery system devised for the treatment either negates the treatment or transforms it into something else. The delivery system is of special importance in human services because the ultimate delivery point is a human being whose needs may be such that they work at cross purposes to appropriate delivery.

A few examples of how delivery systems can fail may be appropriate at this point:

THE PROBLEM OF THE NON-PROGRAM

This is the case where a delivery system has been set up or an existing system has been designated as a deliverer, but no treatments are delivered. Lest the reader believe that these are rare instances, it turns out that there are many examples, as follows:

> A network of advisors was set up to provide advice to new MDs sent out to rural areas to help the doctors become accustomed to their new (and presumably strange) environment. Evaluators sent out after a year or so of the program discovered that the advisors rarely contacted the doctors after the first visit. Apparently, advisors (who kept on receiving their stipends) discovered, as did the doctors, that no advice was needed or wanted or appropriate.[5]

> The Office of Education's attempt to find out exactly what new educational services were delivered to children in schools in poor neigh-

5. The author cannot cite a public reference for this example, since knowledge of it stems from a consulting relationship with the organization that contracted to deliver the services.

borhoods under Title I of ESEA have been repeatedly frustrated by the inability of local educational authorities to describe their Title I activities in any detail (McLaughlin, 1975).

Attempts to decriminalize alcoholism and to use the police to bring alcoholics into treatment centers in Washington, D.C., and Minneapolis have found that when the police stopped arresting people for public drunkenness they did not necessarily scoop them up and bring them to treatment centers. Police get credits for arrests but not for ambulance service.

THE PROBLEM OF CREAMING

Although the world is stochastic, it is also lawful. Hence a delivery system can simulate success by delivering treatments to individuals or households who are most likely to rise spontaneously out of their deficient state. In any event, some examples follow:

In the first years of the Job Corps, screening methods employed tested for "poverty," eliminating those whose families were too affluent, and for "potential," eliminating those who seemed "unlikely to benefit from the treatment."

FHA guarantees for mortgages, originally proposed as a means of helping the poor to purchase homes, became a subsidy for the middle class as FHA administrators took care to give loans only to those who had good credit ratings.

Fellowships for graduate study, proposed as a move to bring more talent into fields of particular national importance, are given out competitively, assuring that those who would go into a field anyhow because of interest and aptitude are subsidized (Davis, 1962).

A Planned Parenthood Clinic set up in the early fifties on the South Side of Chicago found itself so swamped with clients drawn from the students at the University of Chicago that it never saw fit to start an outreach program to reach the blacks of the South Side.

THE PROBLEM OF DELIVERY NEGATING TREATMENT

Here the problem is that the mode of delivery operates in such a way as to negate the treatment. Some examples follow:

Case workers in a state public welfare system were found to have developed a classification of "good" clients and "bad" clients, the former to whom they offered all the options for payments allowable under regulations and the latter to whom they gave payment options only when asked for specifically. "Good" clients were those who presented themselves as suppliants and expressed gratitude easily for help proferred, while "bad" clients were those who demanded payments as a matter of right.[6]

A negative income tax experiment, sparked in part by a desire to test a system that did not have a demeaning means test, developed a system of monthly family income reports that kept closer track of participating family earnings than any public welfare system (Rossi and Lyall, 1976).

An experiment that was to test the effectiveness of group counselling in prison used prison guards as group leaders (Kassebaum et al., 1971).

There is some evidence that the contract learning experiments were sabotaged by the school systems in which they were conducted, with the consequence that the treatment was delivered in only a subset of the thirteen schools originally contracted for (Gramlich and Koshel, 1975).

THE PROBLEM OF UNCONTROLLED TREATMENT VARIATION

Here the problem is that discretion on program implementation left to the front-line delivery system is so great that treatments vary in significant ways from site to site. This variation exists especially when the treatment itself is a form of delivery with the content of services to be delivered left to local delivery systems to determine. Some of the best examples can be found in the early programs of the Office of Economic Opportunity:

The Community Action Program left considerable discretion to local communities to engage in a variety of actions, constrained only by the requirement that there be "maximum feasible participation" on the part of poor citizens. As a consequence, it is almost impossible to document what the CAP programs in fact did.

A similar lack of content definition also characterized the Model Cities Program.

Project Head Start gave money to local communities to set up preschool teaching projects for underprivileged children. Programs started

6. These generalizations stem from observations made of caseworker-client transactions in four Massachusetts public welfare offices during the summer of 1976.

had a variety of sponsoring agencies, differing coverages, varying content, and so on. To evaluate Head Start is to evaluate a program that is so heterogeneous in essential respects that it cannot be called *a* program at all.

THE PROBLEM OF RITUAL COMPLIANCE

Here the problem lies in the lack of commitment to a program on the part of a front-line delivery system with the result that minimal delivery of the program occurs. The treatment is not negated, it is simply watered down almost to the point of non-existence.

In an effort to assure more contact between professors and their students, a state legislature mandated semester reports from each professor with detailed "contact hours" counts to be entered. A considerable professorial effort went into stretching every potential contact opportunity into a contact hour. Thus there were more advisees reported than there were students to be advised.

To comply with affirmative action directives, university departments often place ads in national professional publications for positions already informally filled, announcing the selection officially only when replies to ads have been received and the resulting applications rejected.

THE PROBLEM OF OVERLY SOPHISTICATED TREATMENTS

Here the problem arises from the fact that some treatments that might work well in the hands of highly trained and highly motivated deliverers are put in the hands of a mass delivery system whose training and motivation is considerably less. In short, there is a considerable difference between pilot and production runs of sophisticated treatments.

Thus, although many educators have come forth with teaching methods that have worked well within their experimental classrooms and schools, the adoption of such teaching methods in ordinary school systems have not proved very successful. (In part this is a problem of the delivery being part of the treatment.) Computer-assisted learning and individualized instruction, for instance, are examples of techniques that seem to do less well away from the centers where they were developed.

THE PROBLEM OF CLIENT HETEROGENEITY

A treatment that works well with one type of client may not work well with another. This problem is especially acute if the pilot tests of a treatment are done with a special population and then applied in a production run with a quite different client population.

In the New Jersey-Pennsylvania Income Maintenance Experiment ethnicity turned out to be one of the characteristics distinguishing subgroups with different work effort responses: Black households increased their work effort under a guaranteed income plan; whites decreased, and Puerto Ricans showed no significant work effort effect (all compared with controls who were not on payment plans) (Rossi and Lyall, 1976).

Efforts to replicate failed to duplicate the early somewhat spectacular finding that pre-school children could be taught effectively using electric typewriters. Apparently middle-class pre-school children were aided by the method, especially in the skilled hands of its originator, while lower-class children were unable to benefit similarly from the treatment.

THE PROBLEM OF CLIENT REJECTION OF TREATMENT

Here the problem stems from rejection of the treatment by potential clients with the result that the treatment cannot be delivered to the extent desired.

The Housing Allowance Experiments currently underway have experienced participation rates considerably below (30–40 percent) full coverage of eligible population groups (Carlson and Heinberg, 1977), despite apparently obvious advantages to potential participants.

Community Mental Health Centers designs to provide outpatient treatment to clients in need find that it is difficult to get potential clients to come to the centers. Even patients conditionally discharged from state mental hospitals, who have been assigned to centers as a condition of their discharge, often do not appear at centers for their treatments.

The litany of delivery problems outlined above has its roots in the fact that human services delivery cannot be made operator-free. Rules for deliverers can be developed which seemingly take discretion out of the hands of operators, but the proliferation of rules itself can be seen as one of the sources of operator discretion. Thus the manuals governing (in principle) the work of a caseworker in the Massachusetts Public Welfare Department are close to a foot thick, more than anyone can be expected to know intimately. Hence there is considerable variation from caseworker to caseworker, from local office to local office, and from season to season, in which rules are enforced and which provisions of the manual are in fact used.

Another way of putting this problem is that human services treatments are insufficiently robust and are unable to survive mishandling on the part of delivery systems. Even seemingly robust treatments in the form of transfer payments can become transformed in the course of being administered by a delivery system.

Often enough insufficient attention is paid to the problem of motivating human services operators to deliver treatments as specified. Thus in the case of the Washington, D.C., and Minneapolis decriminalization of public drunkenness, no thought was given to motivating the police on the beat to escort drunks to the alcoholism treatment centers. Similarly, the contract learning experiments made no attempts to lower the seeming threat to jobs of regular teachers by allowing private contractors, in effect, to compete with their regular classes.

Another source of difficulty may lie in the professionalization of some of the deliverers of human services. It is of the essence of a professional occupation that incumbents function with minimal supervision, the assumption being that professionals need little supervision because their training fits them to make appropriate discretionary decisions about the content, pacing, and outcome of their work. When professionalization is added to immunity from market and price effects, then a delivery system may be particularly difficult to affect by administrative directives mandating changes in delivery practices. Thus, my colleagues and I found in a comparative study of fifteen major metropolitan areas that police practices and public welfare agency practices were more subject to variation from place to place than were the practices of educators (Rossi et al., 1974). Indeed, it was possible to predict more closely how police behaved toward black residents (as reported by blacks themselves) on the basis of policies professed by police chiefs and mayors than it was to predict how teachers behaved toward their pupils on the basis of pronouncements of mayors and school superintendents. The behavior of caseworkers in public welfare agencies fell in between, but resembled more the case of the police than the case of public education.

The current issues surrounding the cost of medical care and its quality also illustrates how difficult it is to establish some modicum of control over a highly professionalized delivery system. Despite the proliferation of hospital planning councils, hospitals still tend to build more beds than they need and to install expensive equipment the use of which scarcely justifies the investment. Serious abuses exist in the over-use of surgery and in the wholesale prescribing of tranquilizing drugs and antibiotics in cases where such treatments are clearly not indicated. A peer review system functions only when the abuses are flagrantly obvious.

These findings indicate that we need an engineering counterpart to the "pure" social sciences. An academic mechanical physicist can design a bridge according to a new concept, but it is an engineer who selects the materials, prepares the site, and works out the details of how the new design should be implemented. Insufficient attention has been paid to the development side of "research and development" activities in the social sciences.[7] We need to devise ways in which we can test various production forms of a treatment in which the characteristics of delivery systems are taken into account and to develop treatments robust enough to survive considerable mishandling.

A STRATEGY FOR EVALUATING HUMAN SERVICES DELIVERY SYSTEMS

In this section I propose a strategy for evaluating human services delivery systems that takes into account the characteristics of such systems described in previous sections. Before doing so, however, it is important to point out that only those human services delivery systems (or any social program, for that matter) can be evaluated whose intended aims are delimitable, measurable, and not inherently contradictory. For example, a program that is designed to increase the quality of life in America cannot be evaluated until specific content is given to the phrase "quality of life," a difficult, if

7. The R&D centers funded by the Office of Education, although not very successful as a group in either research or development were in principle a step in the right direction. They were intended as centers in which effective educational treatments would be developed and then tested in cooperation with school systems until an effective diffusable system could be worked out. Some of the reasons for the poor performance of the R&D centers are given in Rossi (1976).

not impossible task. Incompatible goals are also a contradiction of evalua-
bility: Thus a pre-school educational program that is designed to serve all
segments of the class structure and at the same time decrease the gap in
learning between classes is probably contradictory in its aims and hence cannot be evaluated.[8]

Assuming human services programs that have definite, non-contradic-
tory, and measurable goals, there are three points at which the treatments involved can be evaluated (and should be evaluated): 1) the question may be
raised whether the treatment *is effective* in achieving its goals, given the
most favorable delivery method; 2) can the treatment be delivered by a delivery system that can reach the appropriate target population at reasonable
cost levels, while maintaining the integrity of the treatment; and 3) can a
given delivery system, in principle, deliver a treatment at a level of quantity
and quality necessary to assure a reasonable level of effectiveness and one
that will be accepted by the target population?

Note that as far as evaluation is concerned, these three questions are interlocking ones. A treatment that has been found to be ineffective on the
first level cannot be evaluated as successful on the second and third levels.
Similarly, a treatment that is judged effective on some pilot basis may fail to
be effective in practice because it cannot be delivered either by the best of
all possible delivery systems or by the usual mass delivery system that an
enacted program would use.

This nested quality of the three evaluation questions strongly suggests
that an effective evaluation strategy ought to be based on a progression of
evaluative activities proceeding from an attempt to answer positively the
first question, and so on through all three.

IS A TREATMENT EFFECTIVE?

A treatment in principle is effective to the extent that the treatment
flows from a model of the phenomenon in question that is a valid reflection
of the processes involved. Thus a treatment for juvenile delinquency based

8. There are two types of contradiction possible: First, some goals are logically incompatible in the sense that the achievement of one goal makes it logically impossible to achieve
another goal (e.g., reducing payments to unemployed persons, *ceteris paribus*, and maintaining
the purchasing power of the unemployed). Second, some goals are empirically incompatible in
the sense that achieving one goal empirically implies diminishing the ability to achieve another.
The example given in the text is that of empirical incompatibility.

on a model of delinquency in which brain injury is the causative agent is likely to fail because the underlying model is faulty.[9] An effective treatment should be effective, at minimum, under delivery circumstances that are most favorable to effectiveness and, at maximum, be effective no matter what the form of delivery.

These considerations lead to a first step in an effective strategy of evaluation concerned with testing the effectiveness of a treatment under maximum favorable conditions, or under a varying set of conditions of delivery sufficiently diverse that it becomes possible to separate the effectiveness of a treatment from its mode of delivery. Indeed, the evaluative activity variously called "process evaluation" or "formative evaluation" is often most appropriate to this task.

It should also make sense that treatment evaluations at this stage should be small scale, "pilot" studies that maximize internal validity—in this case, the ability to make strong statements about the effectiveness of the treatment. Carefully designed randomized experiments would be particularly appropriate, assuming that the treatments lend themselves to laboratory or field experimentation, an issue to which we will turn in a later part of this section. If the treatment is one that can vary in amount of intensity and one that can be delivered by a number of techniques that appear a priori to be roughly equally appropriate, then a pilot experiment could be designed that would vary level of treatment and delivery technique simultaneously. The end result of such a more elaborate pilot phase would be more useful knowledge about appropriate levels of treatment and the most effective modality of delivery.

A good example of the type of design suggested above can be found in the Kassebaum, Ward, and Wilner (1971) study of group counselling with prison inmates into which several levels of treatment and technique were integrated into a randomized design. One may reasonably question whether the treatments varied enough in levels from one experimental condition to another and whether there was sufficient variation in the techniques of deliv-

---

9. If the treatment is frontal lobotomy, the treatment is likely to be successful in the sense that it cures delinquent behavior, but also "cures" (or eliminates) other types of behavior as well, including much of the behavior forms that allow the individual to function normally in the society. A treatment that is effective must not only eliminate the condition in question but also not impose other deficiencies upon the individual. Untoward side effects must also be avoided, a point that may often be overlooked.

ery,[10] but the general outline of the design remains a good one and particularly appropriate to the issue addressed in this section.

It should be noted that randomized controlled experiments in human services delivery are relatively rare. The major field experiments in social programs of the past decade typically center around the delivery of transfer payments as treatments rather than human services as typically defined. The five negative income tax experiments involve payments to poor and near-poor families that are conditioned upon their earnings. The current experiments on housing allowances for poor and near-poor families also use transfer payments as treatments in some experimental groups that are conditional upon improvements in their housing. The health insurance experiment currently under way also involves federal subsidies on a sliding scale for full coverage medical and hospital insurance. Finally, the Department of Labor financed experiment providing simulated unemployment compensation payments to prisoners released from state prisons is another example of the use of money payments as a treatment.

Of course, it is an oversimplification to regard the payments in such experiments as the treatments. In fact, the treatments consist not only of the payments but of all the contacts between the paying organizations and families in the experimental groups. In the negative income tax experiments, monthly reports of earnings were required as a condition for eligibility and some discretionary powers were given to persons who computed payments.

Nevertheless, it is fair to say that transfer payments are at the core of the treatments studied in the major field experiments because payments appear to be robust treatments that can be standardized and delivered in relatively fixed ways compared to such treatments as parole supervision, job counselling, and the like. Such experiments are easier to interpret, since one can be more certain that the treatments were delivered—checks can be traced, amounts can be ascertained. In contrast, whether parole supervision of any sort actually took place is problematic, and parole supervision can range in intensity from brief superficial contacts between a parole officer and

10. The question whether an experiment of this sort tested a sufficiently wide range of the treatment is one that can always be raised post facto when results are found that indicate that treatments had no discernible effect. The question is whether the advocates of the treatment and its potential users agree a priori that the range of treatment covers what they consider to be a reasonable test of the treatments' effectiveness. As a matter of strategy, I would suggest that such treatments exceed the range of reasonable treatment levels, anticipating the criticism that the trial of the treatment was unfair in the range of treatments tested.

a parolee to more intensive encounters. It is instructive to note that the one negative income tax experiment in Gary, Indiana, that tried to introduce social services as an additional treatment in one of the experimental conditions failed to implement that treatment. It was simply too difficult to standardize sufficiently the social services rendered, to deliver the services in a systematic way, and to get client acceptance of such services.

This suggests that designing human services delivery experiments according to classical randomized designs will be very difficult, a task that is sure to tax the ingenuity of experimental design experts and social service professionals. For unless the treatment can be made more or less standard and delivered in a standard way, the interpretation of experimental results will be difficult, if not impossible.

CAN THE TREATMENT BE DELIVERED?

A treatment that survives the tests suggested above using a randomized design has to be considered next from the point of view of an appropriate delivery system. If the delivery techniques have been varied in the pilot experimental phase, some knowledge about effective delivery has also resulted from this phase. Such results, however, are not to be trusted entirely. A treatment that works well within an experimental context with personnel specially trained by an advocate of the treatment may fail in the field when an attempt is made to use personnel and organizations that cannot match the dedication and skill of the group that has run the randomized experiment. In short, the next task is to test the external validity of a treatment, its ability to be transferred into the "real" world of existing organizations.

A few precedents for such delivery system testing can be cited. The Follow Through Planned Variation evaluations of the Office of Education (Cline, 1975) were intended to perform this function for a variety of compensatory learning techniques, but the execution was flawed. The idea behind the evaluation was to get several school systems each to choose one of several teaching methods, to implement those innovations within the school systems, making provision for reasonable controls within schools. Since there were to be several school systems testing each method, it was hoped that information would be generated on the relative effectiveness of the different teaching methods and on the relative effectiveness of variations in the delivery systems. The evaluation failed because treatments were varied in unsystematic ways when implemented.

A second example is the so-called "Administrative Experiment" designed to test the ability of local authorities to administer a housing allowance program (Carlson and Heinberg, 1977). Local communities were asked to bid for designation as a demonstration for a housing allowance program in their cities. Eight successful bidders were chosen from among competing cities. Agencies within the cities varied from place to place—in some cities the program was administered by separately established agencies, in other cities by an already established housing authority or planning department. Cities were chosen to represent a spread in size and region, although none of the very large metropoli were among the group. Unfortunately, the administrative demonstrations were not monitored carefully enough nor with sufficient attention to problems of valid inferences about relative effectiveness so that at the present time it is not possible to make statements about how effective the delivery systems were.[11]

A third example is the Transitional Aid Research Project of the Department of Labor. In a pilot randomized experiment in Baltimore, the Department of Labor (U.S. Department of Labor, 1977) found that in providing payments resembling unemployment compensation payments to prisoners released from the Maryland state prisons, those who received payments were less often arrested for property crimes in the year following their release. The pilot experiment was run by a dedicated researcher, Dr. Kenneth Lenihan, who recruited a staff of counsellors, payment clerks, and so on. Currently the Department of Labor is funding two additional large scale randomized experiments in the states of Georgia and Texas, in which state agencies administer the payment plans and collect data on released felons. Up to this date, the experimental design appears to have been implemented correctly and payment systems are operating well within the two states. The purpose of the larger scale experiment was both to replicate the Baltimore experiences of Kenneth Lenihan and to test whether or not existing state agencies can administer such payments in a way that would retain their effectiveness. The administration of the plan and the collection of research

11. It should be borne in mind that one of the motivations of the Department of Housing and Urban Development in funding the administrative "experiment" was to buy political support and time while two very well designed randomized experiments were being run. A demand experiment is testing the effectiveness of the treatments in bringing about an increase in the quality of housing occupied by families under allowance payment plans. A supply experiment should test the responses of local housing markets to the existence of payment plans by increasing the supply of acceptable low cost housing rather than raising prices on existing housing.

data on the released felons are being monitored carefully by the Department of Labor and a set of subcontractors.

The Department of Labor's Transitional Aid Research Project provides an excellent example of research designed to test whether existing delivery systems can function effectively in delivering a treatment that is known to be effective. One might have wanted a few more replications, possibly ones in which different state agencies administered the program and which covered some of the largest metropolitan areas, but the appetites of researchers are well known to be insatiable.

IS A TREATMENT BEING DELIVERED?

Assuming that a treatment passes with flying colors the tests described in A and B above, there is still the question whether, when implemented as statutory program with appropriate coverage, treatments are in fact being delivered in appropriate ways. To answer this question requires the setting up of monitoring systems that measure and assess treatment delivery.

To the extent that the human services treatment delivered is some interpersonal transaction between a deliverer and a client, the measurement of delivery is rendered extremely difficult and expensive. To the extent that there is some observable, relatively objective outcome of the delivery the task of monitoring becomes that much easier and less expensive. For example, it is possible to obtain fairly accurately counts of how many clients have been served by a family planning agency and how many intra-uterine devices have been inserted (or how many other types of contraceptive methods have been prescribed, such as pills or diaphragms). Similarly, AFDC client loads can be counted, authorized payments summed and averaged, and other quantitative indices defined and computed. What is difficult to measure is the style and content of contraceptive advice given in client visits or whatever counselling takes place in the caseworkers' contacts with AFDC applicants. Were clients treated with due regard for their human dignity? Was the advice appropriate to the client? Did the counselling given resemble closely enough what the program designers had intended to be given? These essentially qualitative aspects of client-deliverer contacts are difficult to measure at an acceptable level of cost.

The remarks made above are not to be taken as meaning that quantitative measures of client-deliverer contacts are not important. Indeed, one can learn a great deal about how human services are being delivered by considering such relatively simple indices as client loads, socio-economic composition of client populations, counts of specific service delivered, and so on. For example, in the routine monitoring of hospitalizations in a New England state, it was discovered that in one of the hospitals an extraordinary number of appendectomies were being conducted. Further investigation brought to light the fact that one surgeon was contributing almost all of the surplus appendectomies being conducted in that hospital. The fact of inquiry led to the hospital setting up a peer review committee that subsequently disciplined the offending doctor. Or, a comparison across states in the per capita state prison populations brings to light some startling inter-state differences in criminal justice systems, some states moving prisoners quickly through their systems and others retaining prisoners for longer terms. Such "epidemiological" studies of the functioning of delivery systems can be very valuable for understanding the gross features of the delivery system, for pinpointing problems in functioning in some cases for laying the basis for an evaluation of effectiveness.[12]

An accounting system that is run by the delivery system itself is clearly the least expensive way of monitoring, although subject to the possibility of generating self-serving statistics. A reporting system that is useful both to the delivery system and to outside monitors is obviously desirable, since such a system tends to motivate the deliverers to maintain its quality. Thus, in the juvenile court system of Connecticut a reporting system was devised that served both as the data base for a monitoring operation and as the basic file on each juvenile brought through the system. The forms used were developed through extensive consultation between a central research and evaluation staff, case workers, and the juvenile courts. The quality of the resulting data appears to be high as a consequence.

Monitoring the more qualitative aspects of human services delivery is a more difficult and expensive task. Yet there are some good examples: Albert

---

12. Two outstanding examples of the use of existing records in extremely creative ways ought to be cited here: First, Phillips Cutright and Frederick S. Jaffe (1977) used counts of clients served in family planning clinics in groups of counties throughout the country to evaluate clinic effectiveness by relating such counts to subsequent birthrates. Secondly, the Vera Institute (1977) traced a large sample of felony arrests through to the final dispositions of each case, providing excellent accounts of the circumstances under which plea bargaining is used and the kinds of cases which are brought finally to trial. The Vera Institute researchers also conducted intensive studies of subsamples of cases, interviewing the state's attorney, and defense attorneys in these cases in order to obtain an understanding of the decision processes used.

J. Reiss (1971) placed observers in police patrol cars who filled out systematic observers reports of each encounter between the police and citizens in a sample of duty tours. In a now classic study of a state employment service, Peter M. Blau (1955) sat in as an observer as clients were interviewed as they registered in the agency.

"Windshield" surveys have been devised to measure the cleanliness of streets in various neighborhoods as a measure of the effectiveness of street cleaning and garbage removal crews. In some of the studies, streets were compared against "standardized" photographs indicating extremely, moderately, and poorly cleaned streets, and the streets were rated according to their resemblances to the standard photographs.

Considerable effort has gone into the measurement of human services delivery systems through interviews with clients (or potential clients). Thus my colleagues and I analysed interviews with samples of black residents in fifteen major metropolitan areas that asked about instances of police brutality either experienced directly or known about, as well as satisfaction with the services of neighborhood stores, schools, and public welfare offices (Rossi et al., 1974). In the New Jersey-Pennsylvania Income Maintenance Experiment, participants were asked about their knowledge of the payment plans they had experienced in an effort to discern whether correct knowledge about the plans experienced affected their labor force responses (Rossi and Lyall, 1976).

Direct observation of deliverer-client contacts are obviously expensive and, in addition, unwieldly as a research operation. It is also not clear to what extent the presence of observers affects the ways in which human services are delivered. Reiss (1971) informs the readers of his monograph that the police in the patrol cars soon became accustomed to having observers around, but this observation can only be an impression.

Client interviews are cheaper and are potentially quite useful. It is important that such interviews not rely simply on global assessments of delivery system behavior (for example, how satisfied are you with your case worker?), but also provide quite specific information on the content and utility of contacts. For example, it is probably more useful to know whether the deliverers address clients by their first or last name than it is to know the clients' assessment of how politely they have been handled. Similarly, it is more important to know whether a policeman stopped and frisked an arrestee than it is to know whether he thinks the police "are doing a good job."

This paper has devoted so much space to the topic of monitoring ongoing programs out of the conviction that such activities are extremely important in the assessment of the effectiveness of human services delivery. A treatment that is not being delivered or is being delivered in a defective way obviously cannot be effective, although correct delivery is not any guarantee of effectiveness. The same ingenuity that has brought social science research to its present state of competence in other areas, if focused on the problem of program monitoring, should result in effective and informative monitoring operations. A monitoring system is useful not only for evaluation but also for correcting administrative faults. A human services systems administrator who does not know whether his program is operating as designed is obviously an inefficient administrator who has to operate largely in the dark.

IS THE PRODUCTION RUN OF A PROGRAM EFFECTIVE?

The final question is whether a treatment that has been proven effective in a tightly designed pilot experiment and has been shown to be delivered correctly and efficiently by a delivery system is in fact having its intended effects when implemented as a matter of social policy. Presumably a treatment that has survived the previous hurdles should be effective, but not necessarily. Many intervening events can lead to ineffectiveness as an enacted social policy. Specification error (or erroneous models) in the original experiment may have misled the investigator into mistaking a correlated effect for a real one. Historical shifts may have made an appropriate model into an inappropriate one. For example, the unemployed in times of high unemployment may contain a different mix of population types than the unemployed in times of low unemployment. Or women seeking birth control information in a period of high fertility may be quite different (and have different needs for treatment) than women who come to birth control clinics in a period of low fertility. It is also possible that the pilot experiment inadvertently creamed the target population of clients. And so on.

An ongoing social program that is functioning at its intended coverage and funding cannot be evaluated through the use of the more powerful research designs. In particular, randomized experiments ordinarily cannot be used since the construction of a control group through randomization will mean depriving some individuals or households of treatments to which they would otherwise be entitled by law. Hence such programs usually can be evaluated only by quasi-experimental methods. It should be pointed out that the success of quasi-experimental methods depends very heavily for its utility on a valid understanding of the causal processes underlying the phenomenon in question. Thus, if we want to evaluate the effectiveness of family planning programs in reducing fertility rates, we clearly have to know something about what affects fertility in order to hold constant in our statistical models those factors that affect fertility in the absence of a family planning program.

There are essentially two broad types of quasi-experimental designs that are appropriate to the evaluation of ongoing programs:

Correlational Designs Based on Cross-Site Program Variation. Our nested forms of government provide a useful source of variation in program delivery. Thus we can anticipate that in some states and in some local communities a program will have excellent coverage and in other places be so slight as to be almost non-existent (and sometimes, in fact, non-existent because of the failure of states and local governments to opt for the program). Thus at the present time our public welfare system is hardly uniform across states and sometimes within states. Some public welfare programs are extremely generous (for example, in New York and Massachusetts) and other are penurious beyond belief (as in Alabama and Mississippi). Coverage may vary from state to state, with the more generous states in this respect covering not only families whose heads are unemployable but also heads that are employable. In some places, efforts are made to publicize the welfare program eligibility requirements in order to obtain as large a coverage as possible of the eligible population; in other states, public welfare eligibility requirements are held almost as state secrets.

This variation from place to place in the intensity and coverage of treatments provides a means for evaluating effectiveness. Simply put, treatment levels that are heavy and broadcast widely among eligible populations should produce more effects than treatment levels with the opposite characteristics, *ceteris paribus*. Thus, Cutright and Jaffe (1977) in their analysis of the effectiveness of the family planning program essentially examined the fertility rates of groups of counties that had programs with wide coverage with the fertility rates of groups of counties with opposite program characteristics, holding constant county characteristics known to be related to fertility (for example, age composition or socio-economic level).

The phrase *ceteris paribus* is, of course, the obstacle to be overcome.

Hence the stress on a priori understanding of the phenomenon in question.[13] Previous knowledge about what causes inter-area variation in fertility made it possible for Cutright and Jaffe (1977) to make other things equal statistically. It is questioning of that knowledge in the Coleman report that produced the controversies surrounding its interpretation, with the economists claiming that Coleman had mis-specified his model of how individuals varied naturally in their educational achievement levels (Mosteller and Moynihan, 1972).

Time Series Designs Based on Variation Over Time. The second approach to the evaluation of ongoing programs rests on the existence of variations over time in the extent and intensity of treatments. Thus changes in the level of treatment obviously occur at the start of a program, the change going from zero to an initial delivery level, and changes in policy often produce variations in the amount and coverage of treatments over time.

A change in one or both respects should produce a change in a desired effect, *ceteris paribus* if the treatment is effective. Thus in a time series analysis of the effect of the Massachusetts 1974 gun control law, Deutscher (1977) found that crimes in which firearms were used declined significantly after the gun control law went into effect. His analysis took into account the long range trends in such crimes in Massachusetts by constructing a model that fit such trends and extrapolating that model to cover the period after the gun control law went into effect. Similar analyses have been made of the effect of changes in our national labor relations laws on the incidence of strikes, and of the changes in speed limits on traffic deaths.

The ability to undertake time series analyses depends, obviously, on the existence of accurate measurements of intended program effects taken over a relatively long period of time. Thus deaths from traffic accidents, reports of crimes committed and known to the police, the incidence of industrial strikes, and fertility measures are all examples of measures for which relatively long and reliable time series exist. For other types of intended effects for which time series are not available, longitudinal analyses cannot be taken.

The technical issues surrounding the use of cross sectional and time series designs have been dealt with at length in other publications (Hibbs, 1976). One need only summarize in the context of this paper: A variety of

13. The issues involved in specification errors have been thoroughly reviewed in Cain (1975).

statistical models are available that when appropriately employed in connection with valid substantive models can produce firm evaluations of ongoing programs.

CONCLUSION

This paper has attempted to provide a generalized characterization of human services and a detailed account of some of the difficulties in evaluating the effectivenss of such services. It pointed out that the critical feature of human services is that they are highly operator-dependent and difficult to standardize. Hence, it is always problematic whether a treatment is being delivered as designed, whether the mode of delivery is adding some unintended treatment to the basic one, and finally whether a treatment can be delivered in a reasonable way at all by the typical human services organization.

The paper also sets forth a strategy for the evaluation of human services treatments. A progressive series of tests are suggested, starting with a tight experimental design for the evaluation of the effectiveness of a treatment under the best possible mode of delivery, through a final evaluation through correlational designs of the effectiveness of a human services program that has been enacted into social policy.

Although the paper stresses the boobytraps and pitfalls that lie in the way of someone wishing to evaluate human services treatments, it is not intended to advocate an avoidance of this area of social science research. Rather, by pointing out some of the difficulties, it is hoped that the paper has presented a challenge to some of the more ingenious research designers to try their hand at this rather difficult game.

REFERENCES

Blau, Peter M. 1955. *Dynamics of Bureaucracy*. Chicago: University of Chicago Press.

Cain, Glen G. 1975. "Regression and Selection Models to Improve Non-Experimental Comparisons." In C. A. Bennett and A. A. Lumsdaine, eds., *Evaluation and Experiment*, pp. 297–317. New York: Academic Press.

Carlson, Davis B., and John D. Heinberg. 1977. *How Housing Allowances Work*. Washington: Urban Institute.

Cline, M. G. 1975. *Education as Experimentation: Evaluation of the Follow Through Planned Variation Model*. Cambridge: Abt Associates.

Cutright, Phillips, and Frederick S. Jaffe. 1977. *Impact of Family Planning Programs on Fertility: The U.S. Experience*. New York: Praeger.

Davis, James A. 1962. *Stipends and Spouses*. Chicago: University of Chicago Press.

Deutscher, John. 1977. "The Massachusetts Gun Control Law." Paper presented at 1977 LEAA Evaluation Conference.

Gramlich, Edward M., and Patricia P. Koshel. 1975. *Educational Performance Contracting*. Washington: Brookings Institution.

Hibbs, D. A., Jr. 1976. "On Analyzing the Effects of Policy Interventions: Box-Jenkins and Box-Tiao vs. Structural Equation Models." In D. L. Heise, ed., *Sociological Methodology*. San Francisco: Jossey-Bass.

Kassebaum, Gene, David Ward, and Daniel Wilner. 1971. *Prison Treatment and Parole Survival*. New York: Wiley.

McLaughlin, Milbrey W. 1975. *Evaluation and Reform: The Elementary and Secondary Education Act of 1965/Title I*. Cambridge: Ballinger.

Mòsteller, Frederick and Daniel P. Moynihan. 1974. *Evaluating Educational Opportunity*, New York: Basic Books.

Reiss, Albert J. 1971. *The Police and the Public*. New Haven: Yale University Press.

Rossi, Peter H. 1976. "Assessing Organizational Capacity for Educational R&D in Academic Institutions," *Educational Researcher* (April 1976), 5:3–10.

Rossi, Peter H., Richard A. Berk, and Bettye K. Eidson. 1974. *The Roots of Urban Discontent*. New York: Wiley-Interscience.

Rossi, Peter H. and Katharine Lyall. 1976. *Reforming Public Welfare*. New York: Russell Sage.

Rossi, Peter H. and Sonia R. Wright. 1977. "Evaluation Research: An Assessment of Theory, Practice and Politics," *Evaluation Quarterly* I:5–52.

U.S. Department of Labor. 1977. *Unlocking the Second Gate*. Washington, D.C.: Government Printing Office, R&D Monograph Number 45.

Vera Institute of Justice. 1977. *Felony Arrests: Their Prosecution and Disposition in New York City's Courts*. Vera Institute of Justice Monograph. New York: Vera Institute of Justice.

ELEVEN

Toward a Paradigm of Middle-Management Practice in Social Welfare Programs

RINO PATTI

THE CENTRAL purpose of this paper is to present a paradigm of social welfare administration that systematically relates management roles and activities to the developmental requirements of social service programs. This is not a particularly novel idea. There is a substantial body of literature that attempts to describe and explain the dynamics of organizational growth and development over time and suggests the types of leadership patterns that are likely to be most functional at each stage (Lowi, 1971; Starbuck, 1965; Downs, 1967; Perrow, 1961; Hasenfeld & English, 1974; Katz & Kahn, 1966). There is also a rather extensive theoretical and empirical literature, variously referred to as contingency and situational management, which postulates that leadership styles and patterns will be variably effective depending on contingencies in the work situation, such as the personal characteristics and attributes of subordinates, the nature of the task, and the interpersonal climate (Filley et al., 1976; Mintzberg, 1973; Carlisle, 1973). A related body of theory suggests an appropriate fit between the internal structure (vertical and horizontal differentiation, roles, and so on) of an organization and the nature of its technology and environment (Perrow, 1970; Thompson, 1967; Burns & Stalker, 1961). This paper builds on each of these perspectives by attempting to make an explicit link between management behavior and organizational processes in the context of stages of development.

This paper is prompted, in part, by a need to define some of the characteristic issues and problems that confront social welfare organizations so that practitioners and theoreticians in the field may be in a better position to purposively select knowledge and technology from the management sciences. During the last decade, in the face of severe criticism from high level funding and policy making groups, social agencies have sought to rationalize their administrative practices. A host of management technologies developed largely in other fields have been eagerly sought and often indiscriminately adopted to quell critics and regain credibility (Patti, 1975). In the process, too little attention has been given to whether the purposes of social agencies would be well served by techniques imported from other fields and ideological contexts. The glitter and promise of these management innovations has begun to fade somewhat and the assumption that management technology can be straightforwardly transferred between sectors with very different social missions is being increasingly questioned. In many ways, therefore, this is an opportune time to examine the administrative needs of social welfare agencies from the inside out—asking first what needs and problems require attention; next, what values and objectives should be pursued; and, finally, what management tools seem best suited to furthering these ends.

DEFINITIONS AND ASSUMPTIONS

In this paper a social program will be defined as the subsystem of a larger organization responsible for pursuing a limited set of objectives subservient to the goals of the host agency. It is the locus of specialized activities and expertise and the vehicle through which an organization delivers services to its clients.[1]

Operationally, programs take the form of projects, departments, bureaus, or sections. Some typical examples include the social service department of a hospital, the day treatment program in a community mental health center, the child protective services unit of a county welfare department, and the rehabilitation division of a juvenile corrections institution.[2]

1. In this discussion we shall be concerned only with programs that provide services directly to clients. There are, of course, other kinds of programs that provide staff services (e.g., planning, personnel), but these will not be addressed here.

2. In some instances, a program may be virtually coterminous with an agency. This is often the case with small, relatively new organizations established to provide a specialized service in response to a recently recognized community need. Centers for runaway youth, home

The structural characteristics of programs vary with the size and complexity of the host agency. Generally, however, they will have no more than three distinct administrative levels, corresponding to front-line staff, supervisors, and the program director. Most of the program's resources are likely to be tied up directly or indirectly in the provision of services to clients. Staff support services like planning, training, and evaluation are usually provided by other units or by external funding and planning bodies. Program administrators seldom relate directly to the governing board of an agency, but it is not uncommon for them to have advisory committees to consult on priorities, service delivery problems, and the like. Finally, program staff will ordinarily be in fairly intense and continuous interaction with one another over time. Tasks tend to be highly interdependent so that disruptions in work flow or breakdowns in coordination are likely to affect the entire staff.

This paper is based upon the assumption that social service programs typically evolve through three stages of development corresponding to design, implementation, and stabilization.[3] Each of these stages is characterized by a relatively predictable set of structural attributes that cumulatively set it off from the others. Moreover, in what follows we suggest that there are certain tasks and issues associated with each phase which, if unresolved, can have serious negative consequences for the subsequent development of the program. Movement between stages is not necessarily linear, although observation and experience suggest that the developmental process is directional. Finally, although it is only possible to speculate at this point, it seems reasonable to estimate that programs typically move through a developmental cycle in three to five years.[4]

In the discussion that follows, we shall be principally concerned with the administrative behavior of those at middle echelons in the organizational

---

health care agencies, halfway houses, and alternative programs for delinquent youth are common examples.

3. This scheme follows rather closely the one employed by Hage and Aiken (1969), though in describing each of the stages we shall also draw heavily from the work of several other authors who have attempted to describe the developmental cycle of programs and organizations (Tripodi et al., 1971; Perlmutter, 1969; Mogulof, 1967; Lyden et al., 1969; Downs, 1967).

4. Among other things, it appears that the rate at which a program develops is greatly influenced by the timing of program evaluations and the funding cycle. Other variables that no doubt affect the length of the developmental cycle are the specificity of the authorizing policy, the degree to which the program approximates or diverges from prior practice, and the extent to which constituents and supporters agree about its purposes and objectives.

hierarchy who carry day-to-day responsibility for single social service programs. Little attention has been given to middle-management on the theory, it seems, that there is nothing substantially unique about what administrators do in this context. The assumption appears to be that when one learns what is involved in being an executive, the principles and techniques need only be adapted at lower levels. This is a questionable assertion because, while there are similarities, there is also evidence to suggest that the configuration of administrative activities and their relative importance at upper and middle management levels vary significantly (Mintzberg, 1973:109–14; Petit, 1975:65–84). The author's research on the activity patterns of managers at several administrative levels in social welfare organizations strongly confirms this position (Patti, 1977).

Persons operating at this level in the agency hierarchy are called by a variety of titles, but in this presentation we will use the generic designations program manager, director, and administrator. Managerial personnel at this level are often recruited from within the organization. Some have had prior supervisory and administrative experience, but more often than not they have not had formal academic preparation for management. In most cases, such persons will have received their basic professional preparation in direct services. Many will have had extensive experience as front-line practitioners.

In conceptualizing administrative practice, we draw heavily from the work of Mintzberg (1973) and Sayles (1964). Both describe management in terms of roles and activities rather than functions, which is the more common approach. Additionally, in both instances the conceptual frameworks employed are derived from extensive empirical analyses of what managers actually do. Descriptive categories developed in these studies are quite similar, but for the sake of convenience we shall employ the formulation employed by Mintzberg (1973). Managerial behavior, according to Mintzberg, is encompassed in three interdependent role sets as follows:

I. Interpersonal Roles
   a. Figurehead[5]
   b. Leader
   c. Liaison

5. We have not dealt with the figurehead role in this presentation since the activities involved here seem to be more commonly associated with upper level management.

II. Informational Roles
   a. Monitor
   b. Disseminator
   c. Spokesman

III. Decisional Roles
   a. Entrepreneur
   b. Disturbance Handler
   c. Resource Allocator
   d. Negotiator

In general, these role sets are thought to be inextricably linked. Interpersonal roles, which fall to the manager largely by virtue of status, put him or her in a position to collect and process information that is in turn utilized for decision making purposes. Thus, all administrative roles form a gestalt such that failure to perform in one area is likely to impair role performance in the other areas as well.

Mintzberg and Sayles do not attempt to make any systematic connection between managerial roles and stages of program development. However, Mintzberg recognizes that certain roles take on somewhat greater importance as the organization moves through periods of change and stability. The next section of this paper attempts to elaborate this notion in the context of social service programs.

STAGES OF PROGRAM DEVELOPMENT: CHARACTERISTICS, ISSUES, AND MANAGERIAL ROLES

This section will outline an approach to social program administration wherein the roles and activities of managers vary in response to the program characteristics and administrative issues associated with stages of development. Each stage of program development is briefly described in terms of its major developmental tasks, relations with the environment, internal structure, and patterns of service delivery. Administrative issues, problems, and dilemmas that frequently emerge during a given stage are then discussed. Finally, clusters of managerial roles that are likely to take on particular importance in a developmental context are identified. Table 11.1 summarizes the main points.

In presenting this general model of program administration we will be more concerned with identifying and describing critical variables than

Table 11.1 MANAGEMENT PRACTICE IN STAGES OF PROGRAM DEVELOPMENT: STAGES, ISSUES, AND ROLES

Stages of Program Development	Critical Administrative Issues	Central Managerial Roles
Design	—Obtaining support of organizational leaders —Reconciling diverse interest & expectations of various factions among agency superiors —Mediating the preferences & expectations of superiors & subordinates, maintaining loyalty & commitment of program staff	Liaison Monitor (external) Disseminator Enterpreneur
Implementation	—Reducing program vulnerability (e.g., building support, establishing exchange relationships) —Avoiding premature evaluations —Reducing resistance of other organizational units —Maintaining balance between centralization & decentralization of authority	Spokesman Negotiator Leader Resource Allocator
Stabilization	—Handling staff resistance to change —Preventing the tendency to goal displacement & ritualism —Maintaining links between agency policy & program operations	Leader Monitor (internal) Disturbance Handler Entrepreneur (change agent)

suggesting causal relationships among them. Neither will we attempt to offer a presecriptive or normative theory of management. An effort is made to argue that certain management roles take on greater or lesser importance at various stages of development, but this is somewhat short of suggesting that the performance of these roles and attendant activities will result in more effective program performance. Too little is yet known about what makes for successful management in social welfare to permit the development of such a prescriptive model.

PROGRAM DESIGN

Program design is the pre-service stage of development which normally commences after an agency policy or directive has been formulated authorizing the establishment of a program and setting its general goals and purposes. More often than not this mandate will be in the nature of a recognized need for a new service and a statement regarding th general behaviors and conditions to be changed. The major developmental task in this phase is to translate this mandate into a working program plan which indicates the specific outomes to be sought, the services to be employed to bring them about, and the resources (that is, persons, money, facilities, authority) necessary.

During the design phase, the program staff, particularly the manager, are likely to be heavily dependent on superiors for information, support, and legitimacy. If the staff has been recruited from within the organization and has had a hand in identifying the need which prompted the new program, its dependence may not be as pervasive. Nevertheless, in most instances staff members will require clarification regarding policy intent, availability of resources, and permissible parameters of program operation. Organizational superiors,[6] for their part, are likely to maintain a rather tight tether during this preliminary phase, especially if the program represents a major departure from existing policy. Beyond this, however, one can anticipate that agency elites will have a disproportionate influence at this stage of development because of their ability to secure and provide resources and their knowledge of community expectations (Perrow, 1961).

Relations with other units of the host organization will ordinarily be af-

6. Throughout this discussion the terms superiors, elites, and leadership will refer to the person or persons to whom the program manager is accountable. Under various circumstances this could be a top-level executive (e.g., assistant director), the head of the agency, or the governing board.

fected by the way in which the new program is perceived, whether as a rival for resources or jurisdiction or both (Downs, 1967:9). To the extent that established units anticipate a potential threat to their domain or resources, they may withhold full and complete cooperation until the effects of the new initiative on their operations are clear. If, on the other hand, a new program is perceived as augmenting or complementing existing functions, the reception is likely to be more positive.

The internal structure of a program at this point tends to be relatively simple. First, the staff will generally consist of a small group who have been chosen or self-selected because of their prior interest in, or commitment to, the ideas represented in the new program. Initially at least, there will tend to be a relatively high level of agreement regarding the group's purposes, as well as some willingness to submerge temporarily individual differences and idiosyncratic needs in the interest of getting the new venture established. The types of power utilized by the program director and the compliance responses of staff at this stage are likely to resemble what Etzioni (1964:64–65) refers to as a normative-moral configuration, since subordinates tend to be committed to the value of the program and are prepared to make sacrifices in the interest of bringing it to fruition. Second, at this stage the program staff is confronted with essentially novel problems with indeterminant solutions. While the manager may be more experienced or expert in matters pertaining to these problems, he or she is seldom in a position to impose decisions unilaterally and tends to be heavily dependent on subordinates for information, ideas, and initiatives. Although there may be attempts to define discrete areas of responsibility, or to formalize relationships, the need for spontaniety and freedom of exchange make it difficult to maintain this structure. Thus, at this stage programs will tend to be characterized by relatively fluid, informal interpersonal relationships, where participatory decision making is the prevailing mode and where roles are situationally defined by problem specific expertise rather than administrative level or formally designated areas of responsibility.

Several issues typically arise during the design phase that require the attention and deliberate response of the program administrator. The first of these grows out of the fact that in order to have some reasonable chance for success a new program must have the support of organizational superiors. This would seem to follow from the fact that it was they who originally recognized the need for the program and authorized its establishment. Yet experience suggests that between the time a program is mandated and the operating plan has been developed, several things can occur to effectively undermine this support base.

In the course of designing a new program, the program staff must often turn its attention to the needs and interests of external constituents, such as, other agencies, consumers, and community leaders. Not uncommonly, the program manager finds that in order to gain acceptance and legitimacy, the new program must reflect the concerns and priorities of these groups as well as those of organizational elites. The cumulative effect of these accommodations can give rise to a program design that differs substantially from that originally envisioned. This is perhaps most likely to occur when the external constituencies of agency leaders are distinctly different from those of the program administrator. Thus, a program which is originally thought responsive to the priorities of a legislative or funding group may, when tailored to the needs of a potential consumer group, serve a much different set of interests. The short term interests of the program administrator would seem to argue for reconciling this dilemma in favor of superiors, but this choice may have negative residual effects when the program moves into the implementation phase.

To this point we have treated the organizational superiors as a monolith. In fact, it is not unusual for agency leaders to be quite divided regarding the need for a program, its relative priority on the organizational agenda, and so on (Weiner, 1964:109–10). Not all components of the leadership will have equal power to affect the flow of resources to the new program, but each is likely to try to influence the direction of the program in a way that is compatible with its own self interests. The issue frequently confronting the administrator then is whether to align with the interests of one faction and risk alienating others, or to seek to be responsive to the widest possible array of expectations. The latter course is likely to dictate a program design pitched at a level of generality in order to avoid conflict, while the former allows for greater specificity regarding program objectives, technology, and resources, but runs the risk of engendering opposition. A choice in either direction may entail opportunity costs at some point in the future, so the manager's decision is a critical one.

Another issue that arises with some regularity during the design phase is the strain between program logic and organizational reality. As previously noted, the staff will often be composed of persons with a high commitment to and/or expertise in the program area. They will frequently view their assignment as an opportunity to build a program that reflects the best of professional and technical knowledge and/or one that promotes deeply held personal values and ideals. This set of dynamics often gives rise to an optimal program plan (as viewed by program staff) that has its own internal logic but little correspondence to what is, in fact, possible or acceptable in a large organizational context. The program manager then, is confronted with the task of mediating the preferences and expectations of both superiors and subordinates, while maintaining credibility in both camps. The issue is how to forge a plan superiors can support on the one hand, and at the same time maintain the loyalty, commitment, and morale of those who will ultimately implement the design.[7]

Managerial roles represent a complex and interdependent gestalt. At each stage of development the manager is likely to engage in the performance of all the roles mentioned earlier. It is not my intent to deny this reality in what follows, but rather to argue that in a given stage of program development a certain cluster of roles will take on special importance, both in terms of the time that is given to them and their salience to achieving the tasks and resolving the issues that arise.

The role cluster that appears to dominate the manager's concerns during the design phase consist, respectively, of *liaison, monitor, disseminator,* and *entrepreneurial* roles. The liaison role is the cornerstone of managerial responsibility during the design phase, inasmuch as it involves establishing contact with a network of groups and organizations in the environment that control or infuence the flow of resources to the program and consume its services. The primary purpose of these role activities is to gain visibility for the program and its administrator and to develop linkages that can subsequently be used for more instrumental purposes. The manager joins associations, makes speeches and other public appearances, attends conferences, seeks and holds introductory meetings with the heads of other programs both within and outside the organization, writes letters and distributes announcements, and so on. These liaison activites are largely of symbolic importance

7. I am grateful to Ian Cox for pointing out that during the design phase, the program manager probably has more leverage to bargain with agency superiors for concessions and favors than at any other point in the program's history. The comments above emphasize the mediating function of the manager. Clearly, however, the manager also serves as an advocate for the program in the decision process, attempting to protect the integrity of the proposal and to maximize its innovative potentials.

when viewed by themselves, however the contacts established create conditions that enable the manager to carry out other roles crucial in the design phase.

The monitor role entails activities oriented to seeking, collecting, and processing information about the program's environment. Here the manager functions largely as a student and researcher, talking to experts and knowledgeable actors, reading reports and analyses, digesting agency manuals, conducting surveys, and the like. At least five aspects of the program's environment will require attention: the policy environment, incuding particularly the priorities of funding and policy-making groups; the host agency, including the preferences, interests, and functional domains of agency leaders and other program heads and the loci of formal and informal power; community agencies, incuding the clients they serve, the services provided, the extent of potential competition for consumers, personnel resources, and funds; the client population, including their problems and needs, services preferences, and impediments to service access; and the extant technology, that is, available techniques and methods for achieving program objectives, evidence regarding the comparative efficacy of alternative modalities, the resources necessary to implement alternatives and associated costs.

Information from all these sources is vital if the manager is to mold the program in terms that will ultimately be acceptable to its varied constituencies. It is seldom that a program design can reconcile the preferences and ideas that emerge from these quarters, but the manager must nonetheless attend to this array of inputs if he or she is to be aware of the alternative designs available and the tradeoffs that each requires.

The manager, however, is not simply a passive recipient of information. He or she also assimilates, orders, and sets priorities for the data collected, and ultimately disseminates it to subordinates. In his or her role as disseminator, the manager links the external world to internal program operations through a variety of activities, such as personal conferences, staff meetings, memoranda, and circulating reports and documents. The information may be disseminated as directives, as advice, or simply as information to be considered by subordinates as they perform their design tasks.

The entrepreneurial role is also part of that cluster of roles that become particularly salient during the design phase. Here the manager is engaged in deciding upon the nature of the program to be recommended to superiors. Specific programmatic objectives are formulated, an implementation plan set forth, resource needs projected, and budget estimates assigned. This decision-making activity normally occurs in the context of rather intense interaction with staff, with each subordinate attempting to maximize his ideas and preferences in the program plan. It is in this role that the manager engages the program staff with its own set of preferences, values, and information and seeks to reconcile internal program logic with external realities. With or without the concurrence of staff, the manager ultimately approves the final design and presents it to superiors for their authorization. The process of advocacy and justification is likely to vary depending on the magnitude of the program and its potential impact for other operating units in the host agency, as well as the organizational leaders' prior involvement in the design activity. In most instances, however, modifications will be required since superiors are unlikely to be able to anticipate the implications of a new program before they have had a chance to see it fully laid out. Since the manager is likely to have a considerable investment in the plan proposed and a sense of obligation to subordinates, he or she will often try to minimize the changes proposed and to gain the most favorable authorization possible.

PROGRAM IMPLEMENTATION

During the implementation phase, the program plan is translated into operating reality. Organizational leaders have signed off on the program and funds have been allocated for some initial period which permit the acquisition of personnel, materials, and facilities. The major developmental task at this stage is to demonstrate that there is in fact a need for the proposed program, that clients will use the services provided, and that such services show at least the potential for meeting the objectives envisioned.

Whereas organizational leaders were the dominant environmental influence during the design phase, at this point other groups take on increasing importance. Horizontal relationships both within and without the host organization become especially critical. Earlier contacts with functionally related units and organizations that focused on soliciting support now become subjected to the test of daily operations, where the constraints of time, the press of limited resources, communication problems, and personality conflicts can undo the most carefully formulated agreements. These problems are particularly vexing for the new program because of its substantial dependence on established units in the service network for visibility in the community, a flow of clients, timely responses to referrals, and so on. Indeed, serious obstacles to interorganizational cooperation can often paralyze a new program or threaten its very existence. Consequently, during the implementation phase a program will often undertake a number of programmatic and procedural changes intended to facilitate relationships with agencies in the horizontal network and to reduce any threat that it may represent.

Programs entering this stage must contend with the problem of integrating an influx of front-line practitioners into the organizational structure. In the design phase, as we noted, the core staff is likely to have some particular interest in, or commitment to, the mission of the new program. The new staff, by contrast, most of whom will be recruited at lower administrative levels, will tend to be much more calculating regarding involvement in the program and will probably not share the enthusiasm of the founding group. Moreover, in some instances where program staff is drawn from among existing agency employees, loyalty to former units or investment in previous behavior patterns may constitute a drag on the implementation process.

The existence of a substantially enlarged and heterogeneous (in terms of motivation) program staff tends to increase the prospects of disagreement over program objectives and methods of procedure and the concomitant need of superiors to control and supervise subordinates. Thus, before a program moves very far into the implementation stage, the program administrator is likely to formulate job descriptions and rules to guide behavior, establish reporting systems, and create a supervisory hierarchy in order to monitor staff performance and insure compliance. In some instances, as Hage and Aiken (1969:101–02) point out, program administrators may solicit the participation of lower level staff members in activating the program in order to elicit cooperation and increase their sense of "ownership." But this too may be problematic insofar as staff influence threatens to alter the original conception of the program.

In any case, efforts to bring greater consistency and predictability to program operation at this point will be substantially limited by the newness of the program. Even the most rigorous and far-sighted program designs will be unable to anticipate all the contingencies that are likely to arise, and program personnel will find it necessary to experiment with and adapt prescribed methods as they confront unplanned-for situations. A degree of ambiguity, confusion, and uncertainty usually prevails until patterns of service delivery become established. Until that occurs, the use of mechanisms to ensure more reliable and consistent performance among subordinates will be less than successful.

Service delivery in the implementation phase tends to be heavily conditioned by the need of the program to establish a clientele. It is not uncommon for a new program to have relatively few takers initially, even when the need for the services offered has been amply documented. The tendency, therefore, is to provide a broad and flexible array of services in order both to respond to clients seeking help and to attract others in the target population (Rosengren, 1970: 121–22). Whereas the original design may have called for a rather specific kind of service provided to a select group, many new programs find it necessary to relax these expectations in order to attract their allotment of clients. Among other things, this start-up period may involve experimentation with various modes of service and means of easing client access.

As the foregoing discussion has implied, a major administrative issue during the implementation phase is how to contend with and, it is hoped, reduce the program's vulnerability, so that it may reach what Downs (1967: 9) refers to as its "initial survival threshold." At a time when resources are insufficient to meet the demands of well-established programs, let alone underwrite those coming into existence, the specter of curtailment or termination is particularly real. New programs, therefore, as perhaps never before, are allowed little grace period to become established and the push to develop a distinctive area of competence, a clearly identified clientele, and external support becomes a central preoccupation.

In the most general sense, the acute vulnerability of new programs arises from the fact that they are likely to have few beneficiaries. The benefits anticipated by various constituencies are still in the nature of unfulfilled promises. Relatively few clients will have received services, and other agencies, though perhaps supportive of the program's potential, are not likely to commit full support until some kind of exchange relationship has been established instrumental to the achievement of their own purposes. In an attempt to consolidate sources of support, beginning programs often fall prey to the temptation of initiating contacts on a broad front. This may be appealing in the short run, when resources are being under utilized and the program is attempting to stimulate a demand for its services. In the long term, however, this often creates a dilemma. If, on the one hand, the program attempts to honor commitments made to diverse groups, it runs the risk of diffusing its efforts and attenuating its effectiveness. On the other hand, a move to impose some priority on multiple demands can be seen as a violation of initial commitments which may engender ill will among potential allies and supporters.

A second major administrative issue concerns the criteria against which the program is to be evaluated (the types of evidence decision makers will consider sufficient to justify continued funding). Is it sufficient for a program to show that its services are reaching the target population in anticipated numbers, that appropriate staff have been recruited and trained and are operating in a reasonably efficient manner? Or must it, in addition, provide evidence that the problem it was originally created to address has in fact been reduced or ameliorated in the desired direction? Despite some indication that outcome evaluation may be premature during the implementation phase (Tripodi et al., 1971: 55–59; Mogulof, 1967), agency directors, governing boards, and funding groups often press for evidence that programs are achieving their objectives even while such programs are in the process of becoming established. The dilemma for the program manager grows out of his or her inability to refuse cooperation in this type of evaluative endeavor (Tripodi et al., 1971: 15), while at the same time prematurely exposing the program to a test of its effectiveness. Unfortunately, managers often fail to appreciate this risk, only to find when the evaluation has been completed that the vulnerability inherent in the implementation phase has been accentuated by a finding of null or negative program effects.[8]

A third issue common to implementation is internal organizational resistance. New programs of any magnitude will almost inevitably affect the operations of other units in the host agency. This issue is likely to emerge first in the design phase, as noted above, but it is only when a program swings into operation that its full implications for other parts of the agency become apparent (Hage & Aiken, 1969: 100–01). At the very least, a new program is likely to require changes in the routines of other units, to press for the adoption of new rules and procedures, and to make competing de-

---

8. This issue underlines the importance of setting forth realistic program objectives and a timetable for their accomplishment as part of the design. Unfortunately, during the design phase many program administrators are too ready to accept objectives imposed by superiors or external funding groups, either out of a desire to win support or because of a naïve optimism about what the program can accomplish.

mands on staff support resources. In addition, new programs often command a disproportionate share of attention from organizational leaders, thereby threatening to gain greater influence. To the extent that existing units are in a position to impede the development of the new program, their resistance will become a major issue. To avoid problems that this can create, the emerging program must often reduce its demands on the system or attempt to enlist the authority of superiors. The former strategy may result in postponing or compromising the original intent of the program. The latter can, of course, precipitate intense conflict and will often elicit more subtle forms of resistance.

Finally, the program manager, as suggested earlier, must contend with the issue of how to distribute authority in his or her unit. The relative uncertainty confronting a new program and the necessity to maintain flexibility in relation to external expectations would seem to argue for a relatively decentralized and informal program structure. In many instances, however, this choice may be constrained by the nature of the host organization. For example, in a parent agency characterized by a steep hierarchy and a plethora of rules and regulations, a new program often comes under some pressure from leaders and other units to conform to this style. If, as well, the new program is staffed by organizational members who have previously worked under a centralized regimen, a work environment that emphasizes discretionary worker behaviors and decentralized authority may require more of an adjustment than some are willing or able to make. Finally, even when decentralization is not at variance with the norms and procedures of the host agency, interpersonal conflict arising from inadequate coordination, unclear role boundaries, and differential performance expectations may necessitate placing more authority in the hands of the program director.

Several managerial roles take on special significance during the implementation phase. The four we shall focus upon are *spokesman, negotiator, leader,* and *resource allocator.* The first two roles in the cluster are critical for dealing with the program's vulnerability to external forces, while the latter two address matters of internal organization.

The spokesman role, which builds on the liaison relationships established earlier, requires that the program administrator act as an expert informant to interested and influential groups in the program's environment, including superiors and those in the horizontal network. Activities include providing periodic verbal and written reports, describing and interpreting the program both within and without the agency, issuing press releases, appearing on TV and radio, and so on. Although the activities are similar in many ways to the disseminator and liaison roles played during the design phase, their purpose is likely to be quite different. Earlier the manager was receiving information to transmit back to the program for its internal planning use. This continues to occur, but now the emphasis tends to be on disseminating information about the program in order to inform and persuade various publics regarding the need for, and credibility of, the new venture.

The negotiator role also involves dealing with the environmental field, but in a somewhat different way. Here the program manager engages in activities that are concerned with establishing the terms of the exchange with other units and organizations whose cooperation is important to achieving objectives. The problems to be addressed, as we suggested earlier, are myriad and include, for example, the kinds of clients to be referred and received, response time, conflicts in service objectives, the overlapping of services, competition for clients, and so on. Many of these relationships are with other agencies over whom the manager has no formal authority and negotiations tend to be heavily influenced by the fact that participants will be primarily concerned with protecting and furthering the short-term interests of their own programs. As a result, these relationships are often marked by considerable tension and conflict. Nevertheless, the failure to reach a *modus vivendi* can often be so costly in terms of reduced program effectiveness that the program manager usually has little choice but to continue to search for mutually acceptable solutions. The primary medium through which these differences are resolved is trading, wherein two parties agree to exchange resources (for example, jurisdiction, prestige, time) in a way that protects the integrity of their respective programs and yet facilitates cooperation (Tropman, 1974: 148–50). The negotiating role takes on central importance in the manager's responsibility as he or she addresses the resistance of other units in the host organization as well as parallel programs in the community. It is also critical to establishing the conditions under which the new program will be evaluated, insofar as what is to be evaluated and the cooperation of staff in this venture are negotiable resources. Both of these, as mentioned earlier, are major issues in the implementation phase.

The leader role is without doubt the most ubiquitous and most difficult to define of all managerial responsibilities. The activities that comprise it are crucial in every stage of development, but we single it out here because of its vital contribution in creating the structure and climate of new program units. Several aspects of this role are particularly critical in the implementation period. The first involves recruiting, selecting, and socializing new staff members. At no other point in the program's history are these activities likely to be so important, since the initial cohort of staff will do much to shape the fundamental character and substance of the service delivery system. Their past experience, competencies, and motivation will determine, in large part, the limitations and potential of the program.

A second component of the leader role consists of directing, supervising, and consulting activities with subordinates. Here, too, the leader role is critical because there are likely to be relatively few rules and precedents to inform subordinate behavior. Thus, in day-to-day interaction with staff, the manager in effect elaborates, refines, and adapts the original program plan to address the multitude of events and problems that were unanticipated. Cumulatively, these interactions set the tone and direction of the program, clarify roles, establish a division of labor and modes of cooperation. These norms and operating guidelines tend to become rather quickly institutionalized as the staff seeks some framework for dealing with the rather considerable areas of ambiguity and uncertainty that confront them. The legacy of these early leadership behaviors is likely to have a discernible impact on the tasks structure of the program for some time beyond the implementation phase.

A third aspect of the leader role involves authority relations between the manager and his or her subordinates. Here the manager sets a pattern that cues the staff on such important matters as how much discretion will be allowed in the performance of tasks, the circumstances under which staff participation in administrative decisions will be allowed, and the extent to which the manager will tolerate negative feedback.

Closely related to the leader role is that of resource allocator, wherein the manager makes decisions regarding how personnel and materials are to be distributed to various aspects of the program's operation. The budgeting process is the most visible exercise of this role, but program administrators seldom have final authority for such decisions. Rather more important are those actions which interpolate budget categories and translate them into program priorities, such as the assignment of workers to service tasks, the distribution of training and consultation funds, the provision or withholding of staff support services, the timing and sequencing of various program activities, and so on. The resource allocation role becomes especially critical during the implementation phase for two reasons. First, it is through these activities that the manager adapts and tailors the program to emerging environmental contingencies. Second, experience suggests that program plans are often more ambitious than available resources allow, thus requiring the manager to make choices that were either not envisioned or were avoided as the design was being developed. These choices often become policy.

The leader and resource allocator roles give shape and direction to a program at precisely a time when it is likely to be most susceptible to disorganization. The manager's success in developing a coherent service delivery capability will be a necessary, if not sufficient, basis for building a more stable and predictable environment for the program. In some ways this is the most demanding period for the program administrator, because whatever his or her natural predisposition, it is vital that both internal operations and external relations be closely monitored and actively cultivated. Inattention to either arena can unnecessarily prolong the implementation phase and the vulnerability inherent in it.

PROGRAM STABILIZATION

The point at which a program achieves a degree of autonomy from its external environment is also likely to mark the beginning of its stabilization phase. Among other things, autonomy means "the extent to which a [program] possesses a distinctive area of competence, a clearly demarcated clientele or membership, and an undisputed jurisdiction over a function, service, goal, issue or cause. . . . Autonomy gives an organization a reasonably stable claim to resources and thus places it in a more favorable position to compete for those resources" (Clark & Wilson, 1961: 158).

As the program enters this stage, there is no longer any serious ongoing question about its continuance. It has established a steady clientele, it is likely to enjoy some credibility in the community service network, and has probably developed a rapprochement with other programs and units in the host organization. Continued funding at or near present levels, while by no means a certainty, tends to be assumed. To the extent that funding continues to be an issue, the concern tends to focus on avoiding cutbacks and/or acquiring additional resources for program expansion. By this stage, in short, the program has become institutionalized, a permanent fixture on the organizational scene.

The major developmental tasks during stabilization are achieving greater internal rationality and efficiency and maximizing services in the interests of program goal attainment. Relationships with the environment, while a matter of continuing importance, are no longer as acute and pervasive a concern as previously. This is likely to be the case for two reasons. First, since the need for, and efficacy of, the program have by some criteria been generally decided, organizational leaders are not likely to be as intimately involved. The major thrust becomes the refinement and intensification of services, matters which agency leadership must of necessity delegate to internal specialists. Program staff, consequently, develop an increasing monopoly over information and expertise necessary to comprehend operations. Second, at this point the program is likely to be engaged in some mutually useful reciprocity with other units in the agency as well as organizations in the community.

The stabilization phase is usually marked by an increasingly elaborate internal structure. Rules and procedures are formalized to codify past experience, increase efficiency, and assure greater consistency. As staff members become more knowledgeable about the clients they are serving, additional needs are recognized and specializations requiring their own kind of expertise emerge within the program to meet them. Increased specialization, combined with growth in the number of program staff, in turn, requires greater attention to coordination and a concomitant increase in the number of supervisory staff. The supervisory staff, in addition to coordinating the work of subordinates and reconciling differences between them, also increasingly assumes the task of socializing new members to ensure continuity.

By this point in a program's history a fund of experience and conventional wisdom (if not empirical evidence) has developed about those kinds of services best suited to clients' needs. The program tends to develop clearer priorities about those clients who are thought to be most benefited. Thus, it is likely to focus on a more select group of consumers and to provide them with a more intense and long-term service than was the case during the implementation phase (Rosengren, 1970: 122–25; Perlmutter, 1969: 471).

Unless a program is burdened with a legacy of unresolved problems and issues from previous phases, it should, at this point, be at the peak of its performance capability. Staff members are likely to be experienced, service technologies refined and tailored to the needs of identifiable client groups, and rules and procedures formulated to handle routine matters. Ideally, the energies of the program staff at this stage can be more fully directed to the attainment of programmatic goals since the struggle to gain permanent status in the organizational family has, by and large, been won and survival is no longer a paramount concern. Ironically, however, the very attributes and processes that create the potential for effectiveness also contain the seeds for several disabling organizational conditions. Herein lies the major administrative challenge for the manager: how to maintain the capability of a mature program and at the same time avoid the dysfunctions that can seriously undermine these capabilities. This issue has several related aspects.

A stabilized program usually has a cadre of experienced staff with a substantial investment in current modes of operation. Such persons, who often occupy senior practice or supervisory jobs, have probably been instrumental in promoting and gaining the acceptance of certain innovations, developing operating procedures, and institutionalizing practice technologies. Their "sunk costs" in existing program arrangements are likely to be substantial, and their own power, security, and convenience contingent upon maintaining things much as they are. Senior staff often play an important role in defending the program against hasty and ill-conceived changes and thereby help to maintain continuity (Klein, 1969). At the same time such persons can often resist needed change or effectively undermine it once it is initiated. For programs that operate in a rapidly changing policy environment, this can become a serious problem. Thus the program manager, who is often in no position to avoid the imposition of internally imposed change, is confronted with the delicate task of complying with directives while at the same time dealing with staff resistance in a way that does not undermine the morale and commitment of those who may be among the program's most valuable personnel resources.

Rules, regulations, job specifications, and performance standards are the hallmark of a stabilized program. Frequently, they constitute the distillation of previous successful experience and represent means for ensuring consistent and predictable program responses to recurrent situations. Among other things, they help to establish and maintain stable patterns of interaction among staff, staff and clients, superiors and subordinates, to make expectations explicit, and to facilitate work flow and coordination. To be sure, these aspects of formal structure are often seen as limiting and cumbersome, but without them ambiguity, frustration, and conflict can become debilitating.

Over time, however, several problems often occur. Rules, job specifications, and the like take on an existence of their own divorced (or at least apparently so) from the purposes they were originally created to serve. Program administrators and organizational leaders tend to attach considerable importance to subordinate compliance since this promotes reliability and, in one sense at least, eases the task of monitoring. Under these circumstances, rule observance can become a measure of performance in its own right. To this extent, the staff often comes to perceive the formal structure as an end rather than a means for achieving program objectives. The literature is replete with analyses of this phenomena. Suffice it to say that the manager who is not alert to the potential for goal displacement and ritualism during the stabilization phase and who fails to address the dynamics that give rise to it runs the risk of seeing program capabilities seriously eroded.

The program manager, as we noted earlier, is at the intersection between service delivery and administrative decision making. Much of his or her responsibility is to mediate between these often distinct organizational subcultures, while maintaining credibility in both. Performing this function necessarily involves living with marginality and a degree of dissonance. Over time, it is not unnatural for most program managers to attempt to reduce this discomfort by becoming more solidly aligned with either subordinates or superiors. Experience suggests, especially if the manager is upwardly mobile, that it is usually the latter with whom he or she is likely to become strongly identified. This can have unfortunate consequences, because to the extent that staff members perceive the administrator as an instrument of organizational leadership, they are likely to be extremely selective in the amount and kind of information they provide. The manager, accordingly, usually begins to lose touch with day-to-day operations and this tends to further reduce his or her credibility with the program staff. This can, of course, occur at any stage of development, but the danger is greatest during stabilization, when front-line practitioners tend to be more self-sufficient because of their experience and informal group relationships. Ultimately, the manager who loses contact with his or her program will be unable to represent its interests effectively and, perhaps more importantly, will be unable to ensure that organizational policies have some meaningful relationship to program implementation.

Four management roles have particular salience to the developmental tasks and administrative issues that emerge during the stabilization phase. These are, respectively, *leader, monitor, disturbance handler,* and *entrepreneur.*

The leader role continues to occupy a central place in the manager's responsibility during this period, but the configuration of activities is likely to be somewhat altered. Less attention, for example, will be given to staffing, defining and organizing tasks, and establishing norms and procedures, and increasingly more to motivating and encouraging staff performance, handling grievances, acting as an intermediary and arbitrator between subordinates in conflict, and dealing with staff resistance to change. The manager is also likely to devote attention to advocating increased resources for his or her program and/or attempting to mediate or ward off directives and policy changes from organizational leaders that threaten to disrupt the stability that has been established.

The monitoring role was discussed earlier in connection with the design phase of development. There, it will be recalled, we emphasized activities tailored to scanning the program environment for information that would inform internal planning. By virtue of his or her interface to the host organization and other organizations in the service community, the program manager continues to receive, process, and transfer information to subordinates. In addition, however, at this stage the program manager is likely to become more heavily involved with monitoring internal operations. This will occur because of the increased complexity of the program, the need for greater coordination and the necessity of accounting to superiors for program performance. Activities typically involve making inquiries of subordinates and/or their supervisors in regular or ad hoc meetings, analyzing data generated by the information system, and receiving complaints and comments from consumers and heads of other departments or agencies. The purposes of this internal monitoring activity are generally twofold: to ensure that the program continues to operate smoothly or to detect variations in work flow or output that may require corrective attention; and to determine, based on information received from the environment, whether program objectives, priorities, or in-service patterns need to be altered. Thus, through monitoring activity, the program manager develops a base of information that is at once useful in maintaining program operations and, where necessary, changing them in response to environmental shifts.

Information obtained through monitoring activity provides the necessary basis for the performance of yet another role that is critical in the stabilization phase, that is, disturbance handler. This role involves activities aimed at resolving disruptions and addressing crises in program operations. Conflict among subordinates, a complaint received from a client, or a precipitous resignation, are examples of occurrences that erupt from time to time and require some immediate intervention from the manager. Other kinds of problems are less emergent, but often more serious, such as an older worker's failure to keep abreast of developments in his or her method, workers prematurely closing cases that are defined as undesirable, intake workers or receptionists interpreting agency policies too narrowly. These kinds of problems develop over time so that the manager ordinarily has an opportunity to respond in a more thoughtful and deliberate fashion. By the same token, such problems are often symbolic of more fundamental dysfunctions such as goal displacement.

Finally, in response to either internal problems, external changes, or both, the manager will often become involved in the change agent role (entrepreneur). Much of what is done in this capacity resembles the activity profile of the entrepreneurial role described during the design phase. However, one of the major differences at this stage is that the manager must contend with a staff whose investment in the prevailing program is likely to be substantial. Change nearly always threatens routine and often results in the redistribution of privilege, power, and influence. Unless the manager can look to a considerable change in staff composition, he or she will be constrained by the values, preferences, and interests of those who occupy current positions. New program objectives and altered patterns of service can, of course, be unilaterally imposed, but the prospects of succesful implementation are likely to be rather poor under these circumstances. Assuming, then, that the manager has some control over the magnitude and rate of change to be introduced, he or she will often opt for a more incremental approach characterized by considerable staff participation in an effort to reduce resistance (Stein, 1961).

CONCLUSION

The formulation presented in the preceding discussion must necessarily be considered tentative. Although it seeks to build on several existing strands of organizational and administrative theory, there is as yet little empirical research that specifically addresses management practice in the context of emergent social welfare programs. Several areas of inquiry seem worth pursuing at this point in order to fill out and refine this paradigm. First, while a good deal of attention has been given to what Starbuck calls the "metamorphosis model" of growth and development (Starbuck, 1965: 489), very little of this has been particularized to social welfare agencies and even less to programs or sub-units of such organizations (Gillespie et al., 1976; Bernard, 1975). Descriptive studies that systematically trace the structural and interpersonal changes that occur as programs evolve over time and the environmental conditions associated with the rate and magnitude of these changes would provide a much firmer base on which to build a model of program administration. Second, the few available studies that look at what managers in social welfare agencies do have given little or no attention to how activity patterns vary over time. Many managers are intuitively aware of how roles change as programs emerge, and it would seem worthwhile to try to capture this experience, even if the studies conducted are retrospective in nature. Since it is not uncommon for program managers to be involved in a complete developmental cycle in a relatively short period of time, this population would appear to be a particularly useful source of information on this question. Finally, research on effective or successful management in social welfare is practically nonexistent (Steger et al., 1973). The conceptual and methodological problems in conducting such research are formidable, but a useful point of departure might be an examination of managerial behavior in relation to program development tasks such as those outlined earlier. Such studies might focus, for example, on the methods used by program administrators to gain the support of leaders for program innovations, to elicit support and cooperation from units in the horizontal network, to establish contact with client populations, and so on. These inquiries would not address the ultimate question regarding causal relationships between managerial behavior and program effectiveness, but they would appear to be a useful first step in that direction.

Even this brief list suggests a rather substantial agenda for future research and our hope is that this paper will help to stimulate and inform that effort. In the meantime, managers will continue to deal with the complex task of guiding programs through the developmental process. With the benefit of past experience and conventional wisdom, many of them are able to anticipate and make the role changes required as programs unfold. In many instances, however, the transition between stages of development is marked by an extended period of administrative trial and error during which the manager finds that previously successful behaviors are no longer functional to the needs of the program. The personal and organizational crises associated with these transitions are often costly for the administrator, the program, and ultimately, for clients. An awareness of the inevitability of program development and an ability to assess the characteristics and requirements associated with successive stages should provide managers with a framework for assessing their capabilities and deliberately preparing themselves to address the new challenges that lie ahead.

REFERENCES

Bernard, Sidney. 1975. "Why Social Service Delivery Programs Fail," *Social Work,* 20:206–11.

Burns, T., and G. M. Stalker. 1961. *The Management of Innovation.* London: Tavistock.

Carlisle, Howard. 1973. *Situational Management.* New York: Amacon.

Clark, Peter, and James Wilson 1961. "Incentive Systems: A Theory of Organizations," *Administrative Science Quarterly,* 6:129–66.

Downs, Anthony. 1967. *Inside Bureaucracy.* Boston: Little, Brown.

Etzioni, Amitai. 1964. *Modern Organizations.* Englewood Cliffs, N.J.: Prentice-Hall.

Filley, Alan, Robert House, and Steven Kerr. 1976. *Managerial Process and Organizational Behavior.* Glenview, Ill.: Scott Foresman.

Gillespie, David, Dennis Mileti, and Ronald Perry. 1976. *Organizational Response to Changing Community Systems.* Kent, Ohio: Kent State University Press.

Hage, Gerald, and Michael Aiken. 1969. *Social Change in Complex Organizations.* New York: Random House.

Hasenfeld, Yeheskel, and Richard English. 1974. *Human Service Organizations.* Ann Arbor: University of Michigan Press.

Katz, Daniel, and Robert Kahn. 1966. *The Social Psychology of Organizations.* New York: Wiley.

Klein, Donald. 1969. "Some Notes on the Dynamics of Resistance to Change: The Defender Role." In G. Watson, ed., *Concepts for Social Change.* Washington, D.C.: National Training Laboratories.

Lowi, Theodore. 1971. *The Politics of Disorder*. New York: Basic Books.

Lyden, Fremont, George Shipman, and Morton Kroll, eds. 1969. *Policies, Decisions and Organization*. New York: Appleton-Century-Crofts.

Mintzberg, Henry. 1973. *The Nature of Managerial Work*. New York: Harper & Row.

Mogulof, Melvin. 1967. "A Developmental Approach to the Community Action Idea," *Social Work*, 12:12–20.

Patti, Rino. 1975. "The New Scientific Management: Systems Management for Social Welfare,"*Public Welfare*, 33:23–31.

—— 1977. "Patterns of Management Activity in Social Welfare," *Administration in Social Work*, 1:5–18.

Perlmutter, Felice. 1969. "A Theoretical Model of Social Agency Development," *Social Casework*, 50:467–73.

Perrow, Charles. 1961. "Analysis of Goals in Complex Organizations," *American Sociological Review*, 26: 856–66.

—— 1970. *Organizational Analysis: A Sociological View*. Belmont, Calif.: Brooks-Cole.

Petit, Thomas. 1975. *Fundamentals of Management Coordination*. New York: Wiley.

Rosengren, William. 1970. "The Careers of Clients and Organizations." In W. Rosengren and M. Lefton, eds., *Organizations and Clients*, pp. 117–35. Columbus, Ohio: Charles E. Merrill.

Sayles, Leonard. 1964. *Managerial Behavior*. New York: McGraw-Hill.

Starbuck, William. 1965. "Organizational Growth and Development." In J. March, ed., *Handbook of Organizations*, pp. 451–533. Chicago: Rand McNally.

Steger, Joseph Richard Woodhouse, and Robert Goocey. 1973. "The Clinical Manager: Performance and Management Characteristics," *Administration in Mental Health*, 1:76–81.

Stein, Herman. 1961. "Administrative Implications of Bureaucratic Theory," *Social Work*, 6: 14–21.

Thompson, J. D. 1967. *Organizations in Action*. New York: McGraw-Hill.

Tripodi, T., P. Fellin and J. Epstein. 1971. *Social Program Evaluation*. Itasca, Ill.: F. E. Peacock.

Tropman, John. 1974. "Conceptual Approaches to Interorganizational Analysis." In F. Cox, J. Erlich, J. Rothman, and J. Tropman, eds., *Strategies of Community Organizations*, pp. 144–58. Itasca, Ill.: F. E. Peacock.

Weiner, Hyman. 1964. "Social Change and Social Group Work Practice," *Social Work*, 9:106–12.

TWELVE

Conceptual and Technical Issues in the Management of Human Services

ARNOLD GURIN

INTEREST IN the management of human services is growing and is reflected in a number of significant trends. At all levels of government, managers are being appointed to direct human service programs. Rapid expansion is taking place in educational programs designed to train such managers. These include: programs of public management in business schools, graduate programs of public policy, and specializations in policy and/or administration in a number of professional schools of education, public health, and social work, among others. Underlying such developments is a general climate of opinion that the human services are not well managed and are in need of improvement.

The conventional wisdom of the 1970s is embodied in such gems of succinct knowledge as: "'Social programs don't work''—''You can't solve problems by throwing money at them''—''There is no free lunch.'' These are in sharp contrast with the slogans of the 1960s such as: "the great society''—''the war on poverty''—and ''we shall overcome.'' Since each decade considers its wisdom superior, it is not surprising that the current climate is viewed as the reaction of hard-headed realism to romantic illusions. It is at least equally probable, however, that the truths of the 1970s will turn out to be as faulty as the assumptions that underlay the 1960s may have been, although in different ways. The human services are in the eye of these turbulent and shifting winds. They were the major vehicles of the Great Society and are the prime targets of the current reaction. I shall not try to deal with the reasons for this reaction. That is an important but separate subject. The general nature of the reaction is clear. A deep skepticism as to the efficacy of intervention and a consciousness of the scarcity of economic resources are among the major components.

It is not altogether clear, however, just what diagnosis is being made nor what set of alternatives is being considered. The summary statement that "social programs don't work" conceals a wide range of perspectives, prejudices, and evaluations. In order to evaluate the evaluations, it is necessary to sort out several different levels of critique. At least three very different kinds of statements are implied: a) the programs are faulty in their basic conception—their goals are wrong or unrealistic, or immoral, or what not; b) the goals may be all right, but the specific policies and programs employed are faulty—the wrong instruments are being used; c) the goals and even the program designs may be valid, but the ways in which they are pursued are faulty—the problems lie in the area of implementation, administration, or management. The cry for better managers of social programs, which suggests that the diagnosis lies in the third area and focuses on implementation, is misleading. As often as not, the assertion that social programs need better managers is based on the assumption that at least the design of programs and perhaps even their underlying conceptions and goals are faulty and need correction.

We have a choice here. One can accept this formulation and deal with problems of the management of human services in a very broad frame of reference that encompasses policy formulation and program development as well as implementation. Or one can sort out the issues and render unto other areas what belongs to them, reserving the term management for the narrower activities that we associate with implementation. My own approach will be to avoid issues of definition but to deal with the broader field. My concern is not with whether we call something management, or, for example, policy analysis, but to identify issues that fall into distinctive spheres of activity and yet are mutually interdependent in many ways. Thus, if one restricts management to the more narrow issues of implementation, one must still deal with the policy framework in which this implementation is to take place, how it comes about, what role "management" does or does not play in that process, and what effects variations in policy have upon the content and form of management activities.

My first point is that the largest and most serious problems that affect the human services are at the level of policy and program design rather than management in the narrow sense. There has been ample documentation of the policy shortcomings of the programs of the 1960s—confusion of objectives, unwarranted expectations from programs ill-designed to meet their ostensible objectives, as well as faulty conceptualizations of the problems to be addressed. Even in regard to problems that might seem to lie more clearly in the sphere of management narrowly defined, it takes relatively little analysis to reveal the close interrelationship betwen policy and management issues. The public assistance system, commonly known as the "welfare mess," is caught in management problems that derive from its fragmented and contradictory policies. It would be easier to avoid fraud and ineligibility in a system based on family allowances or negative income tax than in one based on individualized investigations and a large element of investigator discretion. Problems of managing the bookkeeping and payments under Medicaid, let alone costs, are a function of the private enterprise fee-for-payment system on which Medicaid is based. The examples could be multiplied extensively.

POLICY ISSUES

It is therefore necessary to consider a number of issues of social policy that set the framework for the administration of social programs.

The central conclusion, it seems to me, that can be derived from the studies that have been done on various aspects of the Antipoverty Program of the 1960s is that there was a substantial gap between the stated objectives and the programs that were supposed to achieve them. That message is reinforced by the latest collection of evaluations issued by the Institute for Research on Poverty under the title *A Decade of Federal Antipoverty Programs* (Haveman, 1977). In his introductory article, Robert Haveman reports that while there is some indication that poverty has been reduced, at least in absolute terms, that has occurred through direct income transfers rather than as a result of the services included in the antipoverty programs. Henry Levin (1977) concludes that the expenditures on remedial educational programs of various kinds cannot be shown to have made any impact on poverty. Parenthetically, he goes on to point out that these negative findings can be explained, equally plausibly, by any extant theory, from genetic determinism to a Marxist critique of the basic economic system, so that the experiments have not even helped to settle theoretical arguments. In two cases where there is evidence of positive findings, legal services and community action, there were values involved other than a direct impact on poverty— greater access to the law in one case and to the political process in the other (Hollingsworth, 1977; Peterson and Greenstone, 1977).

As the studies show, the antipoverty program was the result of many interacting forces. Different actors had different objectives and were making different assumptions as to the relationship between their objectives and the proposed programs. But one aspect of that melange was undoubtedly what has come to be called the "service strategy"—namely, that certain human service programs could make an impact on the reduction of poverty. That is not the first time a service strategy has been enacted in that way. It was embodied earlier in amendments to the Social Security Act that authorized an expansion of social services in the public welfare system on the grounds that such services would be instrumental in removing recipients from the welfare rolls. The backlash against rising costs of social services may be attributed at least in some part to that disappointed hope.

The evidence is thus ample, if any proof were needed, that human services are limited in the objectives that they can achieve and that they are not themselves able to make up for the deficiencies in other major systems. What kind of problem does this pose for the administrator of a human service organization? Insofar as public relations is part of the responsibility of the administrator, there is at least a public relations problem. Administration must be concerned with the way in which the objectives of the organization are projected and with the realism of the promises being made. Political expediency may dictate the limits of honesty, but then one needs at least to know what the risks are in backlash and retribution. More broadly, this suggests that it is a function of administration to be concerned with policy analysis, one major aspect of which is to trace the connections between alternatives and objectives. This means that the objectives as well as the possible efficacy of proposed human service programs need to be analyzed in relation to the other systems on which they depend. If a service program is designed to improve the employability of individuals, it must take into account the availability of employment opportunities. In the human services area, more than in many fields, there are close linkages among service systems, such as employment, health, welfare, and income maintenance. Administration therefore cannot escape participation in the kind of policy analysis that points to the impacts of these interactions on what the given organization can or cannot do.

Perhaps this issue is captured best in the phrase "cure or care" that Robert Morris (1975) has used. One of the problems that confounds management of the human services—and this is a problem at the policy level—is the commingling within those services of commitments to curing and to caring. It is very difficult for a variety of reasons, both humanitarian and economic, to make clear-cut distinctions between those functions. The humanitarian motivations that should underly the human services argue for maximizing the ability of all people to realize their potentialities and to overcome the handicaps that may stand in their way. Other cultural attitudes impede the easy acceptance of a burden for social care unless there is convincing proof that "cure" is not attainable. The dilemma is hard to resolve but it cannot be avoided. Policy analysis needs to deal with objectives and with expectations that relate actions to objectives. Choices do have to be made, with, it is hoped, a maximum of opportunity for review and correction. Management takes over from policy analysis at the point where the functions are clarified and translates those expectations into a means of bringing them about, through organizational structure, allocation of human and other resources, establishment of performance standards, evaluation, and the like.

I shall return a bit later to other aspects of the relationship between policy analysis and management but let me turn now to some more substantive issues.

The most general issues that arise in grappling with a policy framework for the human services are issues of efficiency and equity and the trade-offs between the two. Efficiency relates to the optimum use of resources for the production of goods and services, whereas equity refers to the distribution of goods and services. In the policy field and especially in social policy, the emphasis has been, traditionally, on distribution. From Lasswell's early definition of policy science in terms of who gets what to the work of Titmuss (1974) and his followers in both England and America, the major concern of social policy has been equity, especially for the least advantaged who experience greatest difficulty in obtaining access to resources. However, there has been growing pressure upon the human services to take account of efficiency as well. This takes the form primarily of concern with costs, which are a growing constraint upon all social programs. Policy in the human services can no longer ignore the realities of costs and their impact on the efficiency of other sectors of the economy and on the economy as a whole.

Efficiency criteria are also involved in the choice of mechanisms for implementation of social policy, with the options including the private market, subsidies, and direct government provision, among others. The argument for greater use of the private market as a mechanism has been advanced primarily by economists out of their tradition as against the social welfare-social work tradition that goes back to the New Deal tenet that public money should be administered by public agencies. While the argument is advanced in terms of efficiency, it is far from clear that greater efficiency is assured through one method or another, so that there is ample room for policy debate on those grounds. In truth, there is a very substantial ideological ingredient in this debate as there is in all policy debates. The bias of economic analysis, indeed its whole structure, is rooted in the centrality of consumer choice. In those terms, the rationale for public service becomes a residual one. It is to be used only as much as inescapably necessary to make up for deficiencies in the operation of the market or where the nature of the goods, like national defense, cannot be purchased by the consumer on his own to the exclusion of others. There are very few goods that are by definition public goods and almost any kind of human service can be organized along market lines if one holds that value to be the one to maximize (Steiner, 1970). Nor is equity necessarily sacrificed, since equity can be achieved and in the view of many economists can be achieved best by income transfers that accomplish the desired distribution of income without interfering with consumer choice.

As an aside, it is interesting to note that the current positions taken by economists circle back to a traditional stance held with great fervor by the social welfare reformers of an earlier day. It was one of the tenets of the public welfare leaders in the thirties to urge cash relief rather than relief in kind in the name of the dignity and right to self-determination of the relief client. For a variety of reasons having to do more with political expediency than intrinsic merits, there has grown up a considerable battery of means-tested benefits in kind, such as food stamps, rent allowances, and of course medical care, the largest of all. At this stage it is the economists rather than the social welfare leaders who are emphasizing the maximization of freedom of choice on the part of the welfare client.

Be that as it may, the debate on the issue of market mechanisms is important because it forces explicit evaluation of alternatives in relation to values of both equity and efficiency. Ideological principles, either on the side of the sovereignty of consumer choice or in favor of public administration of public funds, are no longer sufficiently persuasive. In the planning of human service programs, there are many options available but as yet relatively little systematic evidence as to what mix of market or nonmarket mechanisms will produce a greater volume of service, equality of treatment, consistent quality of service, or lowest cost within those constraints. These issues are of course at the heart of the current deliberations regarding a program of national health insurance. One option being advocated is to provide an insurance benefit to everyone in the population, leaving it to the individual to shop for his medical care. All of the analytic techniques available to project answers to questions of equity and efficiency will be brought to bear in an attempt to make a proper choice, and they will of course not be adequate.

A third aspect of policy development (the first two being who benefits and what mechanism should be used) has to do with the process whereby policy is formulated. This is essentially the political dimension. It involves on the one hand the issue of participation in decision-making and the power relationships among decision-makers. It also involves the impact on the polity of the road taken in a given policy, just as efficiency considerations involve the impact of a human services policy on the economy. Given our political system, some degree of consensus is a sine qua non for social policy, and the negotiation of consensus is an essential element of policy formation. The cultivation of consensus is also an essential element for the maintenance of social programs after they have been initiated. Wildavsky (1971), among others, has warned that policy analysis that ignores the requirement of workable political agreement cannot be effective.

POLICY AND ADMINISTRATION

We thus move quickly from the area of policy to the area of administration. In regard to all of the above issues, the answers are not given but involve a process of negotiation among decision makers who bring to bear a combination of value preferences and rational judgments in their selection of policies. Policy is never settled for all time but involves a continuous process of negotiation in which management is necessarily engaged.

It is at this point that the evolving field of policy analysis has much to contribute to administration. While there is no firm definition of policy analysis, it clearly represents an attempt to deal with economic and political variables in a systematic way and in a context of decision making. It raises and answers such questions as who will benefit from a number of alternatives, and who will lose; what will be the consequences of various alternatives for other values and interests that relevant actors in the policy-making process may represent; what are the sources of support and opposition for various alternatives, how strong are they, and to what extent and through what means are they subject to modification? The policy analysis approach can be built into the management of a human service organization in a variety of ways. It becomes a way of helping to decide among the alternatives available to the administrator. But, perhaps even more importantly, it points to ways in which the information and experience of the organization can be utilized to inform the ongoing policy-making process in which the work of the organization is embedded. Thus, to take an obvious example, the data gathered by the organization in a routine way can be so designed as to maximize the information available as to who benefits and who loses from various policy alternatives.

The growing interest in implementation reflected in the policy literature is based on the recognition that an adequate policy analysis needs to take into account the means whereby the policy will be carried out. At the same time, for the reasons already stated, the field of administration, concerned as it is with implementation, is inevitably involved as well in policy formulation and development. There are nevertheless two kinds of distinctions that can be made. One has to do with level. On a continuum from policy to implementation, there is clearly a larger component of policy at echelons of management that are closer to the level of overall responsibility. For example, the CAMS program developed by Lynn and Seidl (1977) in HEW was labeled a Cooperative Agency Management System, but it was really, as the description makes clear, primarily an instrument of policy planning designed to serve the Secretary of HEW and geared very much to the budget. The people involved in that planning process were heads of agencies and top level officials close to the Secretary. The framework for the process was a "planning guidance memorandum" developed by the Secretary stating overall objectives and priorities. The term "cooperative" in the title refers to participation in an intensive planning process by these top level officials. The efforts were directed primarily to the Office of Management and Budget and Congress. It dealt with the external relationships of HEW rather than with problems of internal control.

Another distinction has to do with role differentiation between the analyst and the decision maker. The role of the policy analyst is clearly a staff function. It may be a very limited role involving no more than the provision of data and the development of a series of alternatives or it may extend to the formulation of recommendations. However, even when analysts make strong recommendations, they do not have responsibility for the actual decisions, and there is a significant break in continuity between the analyst and the decision-maker. The essence of management on the other hand is responsibility for decision-making whether done directly or by delegation.

MANAGEMENT

Let us turn now to the functions of management in a more narrow sense. Assuming that an organization is in a position in regard to mandate and resources where it can reasonably be expected to perform its prescribed functions, what are the basic tasks of management and what are the special characteristics of those tasks in the human service organization?

In the profit sector, the overall purposes of organizations are sometimes described as survival, growth, and profit. These criteria are somewhat applicable to the human service organization, but with important differences. In most instances, survival is certainly an objective, unless the organization is defined clearly as a temporary ad hoc sort of program with very delimited functions. The institutional as opposed to residual conception of social welfare makes survival a legitimate manifest function as well as a latent one. The same might be said of growth, given the gaps between defined needs to which service programs are committed and the extent of utilization in most areas. However, there are clearly some areas in which growth is not a socially desirable objective, as in the case of services that are expected to reduce the prevalence of problem behavior conditions. Under such circumstances, growth can be perceived as an index of failure rather than success. Profit is by definition not a purpose of public or voluntary agencies. However, the human service agency, while not seeking profit, is certainly concerned with the costs for units of service and with maximizing the ratio of volume and/or quality of service to cost of service. The considerations that go into profit maximization are largely applicable to that task.

In outlining the content of the administrative process and the tasks of the administrator we generally resort to laundry lists on which we try to impose a conceptual framework. They can be grouped into a number of broad categories, such as determination of objectives, information processing, and task performance. Under objectives, I include both internal and external components of the organization and their interaction. This would include all the processes whereby the organization influences and is influenced by its constituencies. We assume that in most instances there are multiple constituencies and multiple objectives and that it is the ongoing task of the administrator through coordinating and planning mechanisms to bring these into an effective working relationship, the criterion for effectiveness being task performance. What is meant by information processing is self-evident except to note that it covers a very wide gamut, from ongoing determination of needs that the organization is trying to meet to monitoring its impact upon those needs. Task performance presents all kinds of problems of definition and measurement, but the organization must come to terms in one way or another with the requirement that it define its product or products and demonstrate that they have in fact been produced.

Human service organizations experience great difficulty in dealing with all three of these administrative components and are looking for help. Serious investments are now being made in an attempt to develop a field of specialization in the administration of human service organizations. The search is for theoretical frameworks and practice principles, which, in combination with methods, skills, and techniques in which people can presumably be trained will help to develop competence and thereby result in the improvement of the performance of human service organizations. Such a specialization is necessarily the product of borrowings from other fields whose concepts and methods have somehow to be applied to policy issues, program designs, modes of intervention, relevant information concerning population groups, and similar specific content in the human services.

In considering the sources from which borrowings can take place, two fields are obvious sources for adaptations to the human services. These are business administration and public administration. In both instances, the paradigms that have governed those fields are now subject to challenge and their interest in human services is a reflection of pressures within the respective fields. The traditional model of the firm as a single-minded instrument for the maximization of profit is an oversimplified one in today's society. Multiple objectives are not the monopoly of public organizations but are evident in the corporation as well. Especially important are the constraints that stem from a growing number of sources, such as governmental regulation and pressures of community and interest groups, let alone labor union demands. The traditional model of hierarchical authority is also subject to challenge, as up-to-date business managers learn organizational theory, a popular subject in business schools, and try to implement notions of job enrichment and human relations principles. The field of public administration, in turn, shifted some years ago from an emphasis on the formal aspects of government structure and management to an emphasis on policy and has given rise to a new network of educational programs that have policy analysis as the core methodological area.

It should be noted that both business administration and public administration are applied fields. They are not in themselves well-defined disciplines, certainly not free-standing ones. The elements of theory and methodology that comprise their subject matter have been borrowed from a number of disciplines in the eclectic fashion that is prevalent in social welfare and other human service areas. In extending their programs to the human services, schools of business and public administration are using approaches that were developed through the adaptation of various disciplines to problems in business and government. Those earlier processes of adaptation can provide some useful models for the various programs in human service management that are now appearing on the scene.

The parallels are particularly strong in the field of public administration. A recent description of public administration could easily be used to describe the state of affairs in social welfare or human services administration. Public administration, writes Waldo (1975:223) is "not and cannot be a 'discipline,' much less a sub-discipline. . . . No single discipline, as these are now constituted and named, provides the knowledge base for preparation of such careers. No single discipline even comes close; instead, many disciplines and foci now contribute and should contribute."

Such contributions are drawn from politics, economics, organization theory, social psychology, and management science. These are the same sources that are reflected in the programs of business schools and are the sources from which social work and other professions draw in developing a specialization in the administration of human services. The combinations in which they appear vary, with economics and management science playing a larger role in business administration, and political science figuring more prominently in applications to public administration. In none of these fields is there any overall integrated theory. Most would probably agree with Waldo (1975) that there cannot be, although an interesting proposal in that direction has been advanced by Wamsley and Zald (1973) through the use of organizational theory as a framework for interrelating political and economic variables. Their scheme is based on a division, derived from organizational theory, between environmental structure and process and internal structure and process. That division, crossed against political and economic elements in public administration, provides them with four quadrants into which to classify the functions and activities of the field. Admittedly this is a preliminary attempt and it is only a taxonomical base for a theory so that its usefulness remains to be seen.

In regard to all of the sources of borrowing, there are problems, not only of translation and adaptation, but of the state of knowledge itself. In almost every area that is relevant to the administration of human service agencies, available knowledge is limited and ambiguous.

Human service agencies find most congenial to their objectives and environment what is frequently referred to as the "human relations approach to industry." Indeed, most of the administration courses in schools of social work until recently dealt almost exclusively with issues of personnel management, especially in regard to relationships between the professionals and the bureaucracy. It would be comforting if there were by this time a secure body of knowledge supporting the tenets of the "new management." But the evidence is inconclusive and contradictory, as recent reviews of the "Theory Y" concept have shown, and it is not at all clear that so-called "humanistic" management, as characterized by a high degree of decentralization, is reflected in superior performance or even in higher morale. There are too many other variables (Gibson and Teasley, 1973; Morse and Lorsch, 1970).

Similar frustrations await us in regard to task performance. An extensive literature is available on organizational effectiveness. In a recent review, Scott (1977) has indicated the great difficulty in identifying generalizable propositions that can guide action. This literature, together with an equally extensive one on the relationships between organizations and their environments, points in the direction of what is now being called a "contingency" approach. That is a way of saying that the state of the art in the study of organizations, and therefore of administration and management, does not permit the development of "if . . . then" propositions, but that generalizations of a much more limited character must be settled for. These generalizations must be tied to "contingencies" or contexts that differ in very important ways in different kinds of organizations.

Many of the conceptual issues that have been touched upon in this quick review come to a focus around the technical tasks of applying quantitative analytic methods to management problems in the human services. Battle lines have been drawn on this issue in ways that are not particularly helpful. Advocates of program budgeting and cost-benefit analysis argue that quantification is essential in order to make specific and explicit both what is being done, let alone accomplished, and what consequences may be expected from designated alternatives (Rivlin, 1970; Capron, 1967). On the other hand, experiences such as the PPB push under the Johnson administration have given rise to scathing criticisms, such as those of Wildavsky (1971) and Hoos (1972). Although one can quickly agree with Hoos (1972:177) that we should reject "the technical approach that confuses management of an enterprise with management of its record-keeping," this does not obviate the need for adequate and efficient management of the record-keeping. More importantly, it does not deal with the question of how those who are managing the enterprise can obtain the kind of information they need in order to make wise decisions.

What seems promising in the current attempts to adapt management science to the human services is the use of quantitative analytic methods, computer-based where warranted by the size of the operations, to link information systems with planning and evaluation. In the Department of Mental Health of Massachusetts, for example, research had been until recently a completely separate function. Planning was virtually nonexistent as an organized process and data processing was something quite distinct and also quite inadequate. Not only have these functions been brought together, but they have been redefined. Both data processing and evaluation are now structured in conscious relationship to decision-making around budget and program.

The theme of relating evaluation research to decision making is one that is beginning to appear in the literature as a possible direction for the future (Edwards et al., 1975). It is designed to overcome the limitations that have impeded the usefulness of both approaches—evaluation because it was not always relevant to the decision that had to be made, and decision-making because it was not adequately informed by research data.

Decision analysis is beginning to appear as a tool in human services administration. The appeal is natural, since it is a methodology that is built on subjectivity, a commodity found in great abundance in the human services. Decision analysis provides techniques for translating intuitive preferences and values into manipulable quantitative terms. It does not overcome subjectivity but merely makes it more explicit. Boiled down to its essentials and greatly simplified, decision analysis proceeds as follows:

A decision has to be made between two alternatives (taking the simplest possible case). Two kinds of situations may exist: a) the consequences of a decision can be calculated with certainty; or b) the consequences of a decision are uncertain. Under the first condition, there is no problem if the decision involves only one attribute. Then, clearly, all that is left is to make the calculations and to choose the alternative that gives the best result. But if the decision involves an objective that has two attributes, then it becomes necessary to calculate how much of each attribute is gained or lost under each alternative. The problem for decision-making is to decide upon a trade-off between results—how much of a desirable consequence makes it worth while to tolerate how much more of one undesirable consequence? This makes it necessary for the decision maker to specify what ranges of results he is ready to tolerate in regard to the various attributes and also to express his preference for one group of results over another.

The same process applies to situations where the consequences are uncertain. Here, however, the calculations are based not on the results which we are sure will take place, but rather on the *probabilities* of their taking place. The decision maker therefore needs to deal not only with his preferences but with his attitudes toward risk. The analyst can help him to identify these attitudes and to translate them into quantitative terms that will reveal to him what he would have to do to translate these attitudes into action, whereas the researcher, one hopes, can help to inform his estimates of probabilities.

How difficult all of this is is reflected in the work undertaken by Edwards, Guttentag, and Snapper (1975) for the Office of Child Development.

Their analysis generated long lists of objectives and program proposals. Even after these were boiled down to a manageable number, participants in the process were asked to make numerical judgments both as to the importance of an objective and as to what contribution they would expect a particular program to make toward that objective. The numerical values they assigned to these items were on a ratio scale, so that the respondents were expected to be able to give a precise weighting to their relative judgments in these matters. Whether much more can be said for so elaborate and in some ways so unreal an approach than that it makes people think a little harder is a real question. Certainly the process would be made more useful if the degree of subjectivity in estimating probabilities could be reduced by data.

Aside from the adaptations of quantitative analytic methods, many of the technical problems in the management of human service organizations would seem to revolve around structural organization of the service delivery system and deployment of staff. While that is more familiar ground for human service administrators, the experience has not been a very satisfactory one. The major reason for our dissatisfaction is the absence of a service delivery model that would provide the basis for an organizational structure. The recent experience in Britain is instructive in this regard. On the basis of the Seebohm reform of the social services, local communities established a new type of social service department in which were combined a number of functions that had been under separate departments previously. These departments were organized on the basis of certain conceptual models reflecting the purposes of the reform, the basic idea of which was that there be a generic front-line service at the neighborhood level, backed up by specialized resources. It was possible under those circumstances to develop modules of staff units for a given size of population within neighborhoods.

The specification of the objectives and content of the delivery service should be coming from the social welfare specialists. How to relate those judgments to the efficient allocation of resources and how to implement that relationship through administrative structure and process is a critical area for future development. Here and there some interesting beginnings can be perceived.

Miller and Pruger (1975, 1976), in a series of papers, have tried to apply the methods of microeconomics to the study of social agencies. They divide social agency functions into two broad categories—maintenance and change. The major function of a maintenance agency is to provide equality of treatment, whereas the major function of a change-oriented agency is to bring about change. In each case, this objective provides the basis for managerial decisions in regard to the distribution of workload and allocation of manpower funds. The central notion is that worker time is a scarce commodity and that its use should be measured against the value received. In the case of the maintenance organization, the managerial problem is to save as much money as possible from eligibility and assignment functions so that more can be spent on providing the actual services. It is possible to reach an optimum point where an additional dollar spent on eligibility and assignment (distribution) functions does not achieve enough equity to balance the loss in using that money for services. In the people changing organization the problem of optimization is to assure that each additional dollar spent on a given program will yield the same amount of change as a dollar spent on another program. That is, each program should receive not the same amount of dollars but the amount of dollars needed to achieve an equivalent result. Otherwise, large quantities of resources may be being used to achieve negligible results while others are being neglected. From this analysis, they derive proposals for the organization of program units and caseloads which they are planning to test in field experiments.

CONCLUSION

My overall conclusion is that the development of management approaches in the human services is still at a relatively primitive stage and that we should learn to walk before we run. There are major hurdles to overcome before the human services can deal more adequately with problems of efficiency. Partly they are philosophical and psychological problems, involving the necessity for a shift in the value orientations of professionals who have been trained to focus on the quality of the service rendered as the primary measure of both effectiveness and equity. Partly they are problems of a more cognitive character, involving modes of verbalization and patterns of thought. The shift to a quantitative mode of thinking is a particular barrier. With these difficulties to overcome, it seems a dubious approach to try to introduce into most human service agencies complex systems analysis techniques the efficacy of which is uncertain at best and the language of which maximizes the difficulties of communication. There are many more limited approaches that are more immediately responsive to felt needs on the part of the agencies.

At this stage the major contribution that the various fields of management can make to the human services is to provide sensitizing concepts and methods that can help administrators and their staffs to think about their problems in somewhat different ways. For example, the notion of marginal benefits and costs can be a powerful dynamic in the administrative process in a human service organization. The tendency in most such agencies is to focus on overall total results or activities as related to total costs, in order to arrive at a cost per unit. It is much different to ask the question—what benefit will be obtained if an additional dollar is spent in one way as against another? Only when the question is formulated that way can administration come to grips with choices of priority and evaluation of effectiveness. Another sensitizing concept is the notion of "satisficing" which is so prevalent in modern administration theory. This suggests to the administrator the usefulness of thinking through both objectives and constraints. In situations where many different pressures must be kept within a working balance, the notion of "satisficing" points not to the one optimal solution but to a range of acceptable solutions that can be evaluated in relation to the political forces impinging upon the organization.

Another positive approach is to think carefully about variables not only in the kinds of organizations being dealt with but perhaps more importantly in the kinds of problems being addressed. Some organizations are very large and have major logistical problems that need to be solved in a way that routinizes processes which should be routinized and that preserves scarce time and talent for judgments that cannot be routinized. Any human service organization that fails to avail itself of the technology available to deal with such problems is subject to valid criticism for poor management. Most of the problems of management are not that clear cut. Every organization needs to process information, but careful consideration needs to go into the decision as to the purposes for which information is to be used and the benefits to be derived in relation to cost. For some organizations, the manager's concern should be focused primarily on environmental relationships, for others on internal management. Or different problems may become primary at different times. The growing body of knowledge that helps us to understand the manager's job has become subtle and sophisticated enough to help, again in a sensitizing way, to draw lessons that can be applied to the specific problems of given human service agencies in particular places at particular times.

This leads to the conclusion that the stance appropriate to the current state of knowledge is one of experimentation and search rather than one of application of knowledge from one field to another. The messages being transmitted from all of the relevant fields today are that applications are limited, results are inconclusive, and situational and contextual factors play a major role. Practical experience points in the same direction. Even in the business field, there has been great difficulty in utilizing systems analysis and similar approaches. In the human services, there are many case studies of failures. The problems of translation are substantial. They call certainly for giving full and careful consideration to the specifics of the human services, which means not only the philosophy and value system of those services, but at least equally the specific policy and programmatic issues involved in those services. Beyond this, what is needed is collaboration between human service specialists who know the substantive field and experts in the methodologies that can be brought to bear upon appropriate problems. This is not a matter of applications from one field to another but rather of developing the languages and processes of administration that can take root indigenously within the human services.

The final word I borrow again from the field of public administration. It is a warning from Don Price (1975:242) who says that "it is all too easy for (public administration) to put emphasis on specific, narrow skills and to neglect the more difficult but less definable, perhaps less teachable, skills that constitute the application to unmanageable problems of wisdom as well as techniques." The key words are "unmanageable" and "wisdom."

REFERENCES

Capron, William M. 1967. "Cost-Effectiveness Analysis for Government Domestic Programs." In T. Goldman, ed. *Cost-Effectiveness Analysis,* pp. 131–39. New York: Praeger.

Edwards, Ward, Marcia Guttentag, and Kurt Snapper. 1975. "A Decision-Theoretic Approach to Evaluation Research," In E. Struening and M. Guttentag, eds. *Handbook of Evaluation Research,* 1:139–81. Beverly Hills, Calif.

Gibson, Frank K., and Clyde E. Teasley. 1973. "The Humanistic Model of

Organizational Motivation: A Review of Research Support," *Public Administration Review*, Jan.–Feb.: 89–96.

Haveman, Robert H., ed. 1977. *A Decade of Federal Antipoverty Programs*. New York: Academic Press.

Hollingsworth, Ellen Jane. 1977. "Ten Years of Legal Services for the Poor." In R. Haveman, ed., *A Decade of Federal Antipoverty Programs*, pp. 285–314. New York: Academic Press.

Hoos, Ida R. 1972. *Systems Analysis in Public Policy: A Critique*. Berkeley: University of California Press.

Levin, Henry M. 1977. "A Decade of Policy Developments in Improving Education and Training for Low-Income Populations." In R. HAveman, ed., *A Decade of Federal Antipoverty Programs*, pp. 123–88. New York: Academic Press.

Lynn, Lawrence E., Jr., and John M. Seidl. 1977. "Bottom-Line Management for Public Agencies." *Harvard Business Review*, Jan.–Feb.:144–53.

Miller, Leonard, and Robert Pruger. 1977. "The Two Activities of Social Services: Maintenance and People Changing." Berkeley, University of California School of Social Work. Mimeo.

—— 1977. "The Division of Labor in a Perfect People-Changing Agency." *Administration in Social Work*, Summer: 171–85.

Morris, Robert (with Delwin Anderson). 1975. "Personal Care Services: An Identity for Social Work," *Social Service Review*, 2:157–75.

Morse, John J., and Jay W. Lorsch. 1970. "Beyond Theory Y." *Harvard Business Review*, May–June:61–68.

Peterson, Paul E., and J. David Greenstone. 1977. "Racial Change and Citizen Participation: The Mobilization of Low-Income Communities through Community Action." In R. H. Haveman, ed., *A Decade of Federal Anti-Poverty Programs*, pp. 241–78. New York: Academic Press.

Price, Don K. 1975. "1984 and Beyond: Social Engineering or Political Values?" In F. Mosher, ed., *American Public Administration: Past, Present, Future*, pp. 233–52. University, Ala.: University of Alabama Press.

Rivlin, Alice M. 1970. "The Planning, Programming, and Budgeting System In the Department of HEW: Some Lessons from Experience." In R. Haveman and J. Margolis, eds., *Public Expenditures and Policy Analysis*, pp. 502–17. Chicago: Markham.

Scott, W. R. 1977. "Effectiveness of Organizational Effectiveness Studies." In P. G. Goodman, J. M. Pennings and Associates, *New Perspectives on Organizational Effectiveness*, pp. 63–95. San Francisco: Jossey-Bass.

Steiner, Peter O. 1970. "The Public Sector and the Public Interest." In
    R. Haveman and J. Margolis, eds., *Public Expenditures and Policy Analysis*, pp. 21–58. Chicago: Markham.
Titmuss, Richard M. 1974. *Social Policy: An Introduction*. New York:
    Pantheon.
Waldo, Dwight. 1975. "Education for Public Administration in the Seventies." In F. Mosher, ed., *American Public Administration: Past, Present,
    Future*. University, Ala.: University of Alabama Press.
Wamsley, Gary L. and Mayer N. Zald. 1973. *The Political Economy of
    Public Organizations*. Lexington, Mass.: D. C. Heath.
Wildavsky, Aaron (with Bill Cavala). 1971. "The Political Flexibility of Income by Right." Wildavsky, ed., *The Revolt against the Masses and
    Other Essays on Politics and Public Policy*. New York: Basic Books.

THIRTEEN

The Social Political Process
of Introducing Innovation
in Human Services

ANDRÉ L. DELBECQ

I WOULD LIKE, in this paper, to present my clinical reflections in answer to
a question I am often asked by service providers: "Given the vast proliferation of literature on organization change, organizational development,
needs assessment, program planning, and so on, can you summarize process
diagnostics and guidelines which are both theoretically defensible as well as
useful to practicing administrators in human services?" I think the answer to
this question is yes. I think it is possible to make some seminal points about
"politicking" change through human service organizations in a single
paper. If I can do so, then we can ask what implications these processes
suggest relative to service delivery systems.

Let me make one last introductory remark. We all know from current
organization sociology that some organizations are more likely to innovate
than others. That is, organizations which are more differentiated, professional, less formalized and centralized, in turbulent environments, and so
forth, are more likely to innovate (Terreberry, 1968; Hage and Aiken, 1967;
Mohr, 1969). This is important information from a macro perspective. On
the other hand, from the standpoint of the service provider seeking to play
the advocate role in fostering a program innovation in his or her own organization, it is often less helpful. Most service providers would like to have a
sense of how to advocate change without divorcing their organization, even

if it is but average, neither polar in terms of being organic or mechanistic in personality, somewhat ambivalent as regards formalization and centralization, and lacking venture management structures. A focus on process, then, should be helpful to the social service professional or administrator who is willing to enter the innovation race under less than ideal structural conditions. I will try to suggest how on a temporary, situation-specific basis, structures and processes might be introduced to increase innovation. These processes are often institutionalized in organizations where high rates of innovation prevail, but generally are less clearly understood in the crusty bureaucracies you and I live with.

In summary, the focus of this paper is in two concerns: 1) what sensible process guidelines can be set forth for the professional or administrator who is going to play the "advocate" role in trying to introduce an innovation into a human service organization; 2) what are the implications of trying to institutionalize these roles within human service organizations?

DEFINING INNOVATION

The term "innovation" as used in this paper refers to recommendations for new or revised programs that are qualitatively different from the present *status quo* in the organization. Innovation is not equated with "invention" in that the critical features of the recommended program may already exist in science or other organizations. Thus, the emphasis is on newness of the proposed program to the organization. Nonetheless, we are concerned with recommendations that imply some conceptual reorientation among key organizational actors and have some impact on existing organization structures or processes.

DIAGNOSING PLANNING COMPLEXITY

Figure 13.1 presents a number of variables that increase the complexity of planning for innovations. High agreement across a diverse body of social science literature suggests that increased complexity with respect to these variables will make innovation more difficult (Delbecq, 1974).

Number of Groups. As one increases the number of groups involved in the innovation, idea generation increases, but the probability of adoption declines (Delbecq, 1974). Assuming that a representative structure in some

FIGURE 13.1

Easy to Deal With		Difficult to Deal With
one group	◄—— *Number of Groups Affected* ——►	multiple groups
no conflict with existing value system in terms of awareness, priority, and intensity of concerns	◄—— *Degree of Value Agreement* ——►	major conflict with existing value system in terms of awareness, priority, and intensity of concerns
no reorganization required	◄—— *Impact on Organizational Structure* ——►	significant reorganization required
no change in resource allocation pattern required	◄—— *Impact on Resource Allocation* ——►	significant change in resource allocation pattern required
within existing technological tradition in terms of comprehension of causation and sophistication of technology	◄—— *Technical Difficulty* ——►	radical change from existing technological tradition in terms of comprehension of causation and sophistication of technology

form emerges to guide planning for innovation, as you enlarge group size, you increase problems of coordination and communication, increase formation of opposing factions, increase disagreement, and decrease consensus. Stalemate or unduly prolonged decision processes are often the result of a large number of groups involved in the innovation (Aiken and Alford, 1970a and b).

Degree of Value Agreement. To the extent that values are in conflict, difficulties similar to those just cited for enlarged group size emerge. The two variables are highly interrelated, of course, since enlargement of group size often implies the confrontation of multiple value sets (Clark, 1968; Crain and Rosenthal, 1967).

Impact on Organization Structure. To the extent that the innovation will require "reorganization," whether in the sense of changes in structural arrangements, power distributions, or role realignments, the innovation will be more difficult to plan for and implement (Becker and Whisler, 1967; Delbecq, 1974; Knight, 1967; Menzel, 1960).

Impact on Resource Allocation. To the extent that the innovation cannot be funded through slack resources, or through outside sources, innovation will likewise be more difficult (Wilson, 1966).

Technical Difficulty. To the extent that the innovation is at variance with existing modalities of treatment or services and requires new learning and training, the innovation process becomes more complex (Evan and Black, 1967).

So what? Isn't this conventional wisdom? I am not so sure. John Bryson and I are presently engaged in a research project at the University of Wisconsin to answer whether this *is* conventional wisdom, even for "wise and experienced" planners. Ninety planners have been exposed to two planning situations differing in complexity. Preliminary analysis suggests considerable differences between planners with respect to which of these complexity variables they are sensitive to and what strategic choices they make under varying conditions. For the moment, let me simply make two statements:

1: SOCIAL SERVICE PROFESSIONALS AND ADMINISTRATORS ARE GENERALLY NOT TRAINED TO DIAGNOSE PLANNING COMPLEXITY WHEN ADVOCATING A PROGRAM INNOVATION.

My empirical data and clinical experience suggest that personnel in the human services tend to be quite adroit *"ex post"* in explaining the difficulties they encountered in planning for innovation. Unfortunately, they seldom diagnose these difficulties *prior* to undertaking the innovation.

2: SOCIAL SERVICE PROFESSIONALS AND ADMINISTRATORS OFTEN DO NOT MAKE STRATEGIC CHOICES IN ORDER TO "SIMPLIFY" INNOVATION EFFORTS.

For example, with respect to group size, there is a "high participation" ethic in the human service field. This often leads to coordinative boards or decision bodies connected with innovative programs of exhorbitant size (12-15-30). Yet, there are a number of strategic alternatives to enlarging the size of a planning or coordinative group associated with innovation. One can: 1) make better use of needs assessment techniques as a substitute for overly large client participation (Delbecq, 1976a); 2) make clear choices about types of participation, that is, decision sharing, consultation, information giving, and liaison, as opposed to rolling all forms of participation into a single decision structure or process (Delbecq, 1976b); 3) begin with smaller decision bodies during pilot phases and enlarge participation during demonstration and technological transfer stages. The point is that the degree and form of participation (and subsequently the size of coordination and decision-making groups) can often be decreased as one strategic choice to simplify innovation planning.

Likewise, strategic choices can be made with regard to the other variables. For example, regarding value differences, controversial programs can be piloted in fairly benign settings, where value agreements among early innovators protect innovations until organizational experience and evaluation evidence provides data around which new attitudes on the part of more hostile groups can be formulated. With regard to organizational disruption, during pilot phases situations with resource richness and slack should be sought as a test site. With regard to technical complexity, the pilot site should be chosen where personnel are sufficiently sophisticated to cope with technical complexity. In a later phase of the innovation process, diffusion resources can be garnered for technical training and support to minimize these difficulties.

The point of all of this is to indicate that the average service provider has his or her eyes on the technical character of the "innovation," not on the social-political processes which surround the adoption and early organizational experiences with the innovation. As a consequence, he or she does not make careful choices aimed at simplifying the introduction of innovation, even where possible.

Figure 13.2 suggests two other areas of diagnosis with respect to planning complexity (Bryson, 1976). While Figure 13.1 focused on complexity with respect to those with whom one must "plan for and with" in fostering innovation, Figure 13.2 focuses upon the resources of the planning or advocate group itself.

An obvious question is the fit between the difficulties anticipated when diagnosing the elements in Figure 13.1, and the resources available to the advocates as implied in Figure 13.2. Obviously, the less benign the conditions as analyzed in Figure 13.2, the less heroic the undertaking appropriate as analyzed in Figure 13.1. We are all painfully aware of situations where staff size, elite support, time and money to plan for—let alone implement— the innovation have been far too modest. Skimpy resources assure failure not because of the inadequacy of the technical character of the innovation, but rather due to the mismatch between planning complexity and the resources of the advocate group.

With this modest incursion into the territory of innovation complexity, we can turn to a review of planning processes.

A PROGRAM PLANNING MODEL FOR HUMAN
SERVICE INNOVATION (PPM)

The planning process model given here was developed by me and Andrew Van de Ven a number of years ago (Delbecq and Van de Ven, 1971; Van de Ven and Koenig, 1976). The purpose of presenting the model here is not to "prescribe" a process. It is rather to review typical process phases compatible with the many process models available in the innovation literature (Zaltman et al., 1973). Having done so, we can later suggest contingent complexity conditions that lead to the relative emphasis or deemphasis of individual process phases. More importantly, this review of the character of processes underlying innovation advocacy will suggest important role and structural implications for the human services.

However, the review of the PPM processes will be cast in terms of a

FIGURE 13.2

Easy to Deal With		*Difficult to Deal With*
ample time available ←	—Time Available—	→ severe time constraints
ample money available ←	—Money Available—	→ severe money constraints
established coalitions and stability in the organizational network ←	—Coalition Development—	→ non-existent coalitions and turbulence in the organizational network
organization has major power, authority, and responsibility, plus a history of success ←	—Character of Lead Organization—	→ organization has little power, authority, and responsibility, plus a history of failure
large and skilled ←	—Character of Planning Staff—	→ small and unskilled

"normative" approach as a parsimonious means of suggesting more effective as opposed to less effective approaches to each phase assuming conditions of planning complexity.

ORGANIZATIONAL INNOVATION MANAGING
LARGE-SCALE CHANGE

PHASE 1. Initial Mandate (Securing agreement about the planning purpose)

PHASE 2. Problem Exploration (Assessing client or user needs)

PHASE 3. Knowledge Exploration (Searching for solutions to needs)

PHASE 4. Proposal Development

PHASE 5. Program Design   5. Evaluation Design

PHASE 6. Program Implementation   6. Evaluation Feedback
         Pilot studies
         Field test
         Direct implementation

PHASE 7. Program Transfer (Replicating successful projects)

PHASE 1: INITIAL MANDATE

Phase 1 of the Program Planning Model is securing a mandate with organizational elites regarding the purpose of the innovation and the processes that should be followed in carrying out the innovation (Delbecq, 1974; Delbecq and Filley, 1974; Rogers and Shoemaker, 1971; Van de Ven and Delbecq, 1972). While this would seem to be a common sense first step, many advocates for change proceed directly to designing a new program, Step 5, without first having entered into negotiation with elites.

Why does it matter? Well, to begin with, there is the well-documented relationship between elite support and innovation adoption (Friedman, 1973; Hage and Dewar, 1973). Indeed, since structural research does not focus upon process, the case is probably understated. Elites, after all:

Pay unusual attention to innovation in terms of "management by exception";

Sit at the information nexus with respect to environmental information and are thus astute in terms of anticipating intergroup conflict;

Control whatever slack funds may be available, thus must direct resources to the innovation;

Must legitimate projects, and even unleash rewards and sanctions to obtain cooperation with new programs;

Play a key boundary spanning role among resource controllers, innovation advocates, and groups impacted upon by innovation.

However, while elites are critical to the success of innovation, they are also besieged with requests for support. Unless they can be co-opted early into an active role in planning for the innovation, any request for support at a later phase is treated as "just one more item in the hat." If one is to believe the recent work of Mintzberg et al. (1976), it is seldom that elites will expend extraordinary energy at any single moment relative to a single decision, particularly innovation that is an "exception." Further, it is not politically critical if the proposal is rejected, but it is often politically risky if the proposal is accepted.

That being the case, early dialogue with elites *prior* to any requests for support can be an important precondition for innovation. The outcome of the mandate between elites and the advocates of innovation should include a shared understanding with respect to:

Value and timeliness of the innovation being considered;
Groups who should be involved in designing the innovation;
Planning steps and sub processes;
Form, frequency, and timing of feedback regarding planning for innovation;
Level of resources to be devoted to planning the innovation.

Out of this dialogue should come a shared diagnosis in terms of the complexity variables mentioned earlier. It is not unusual for innovation proposals to fall on the deaf ears of elites, because the timing of the proposal is out of phase, key provider groups working in related areas were not co-opted, the project was scaled too large or too small, and so on.

A second outcome incorporated into the mandate should be agreement concerning subsequent phases of the planning process to be discussed later in the paper.

Finally, the innovation effort should begin with the appointment of a coordinating committee composed of elite representatives with proper authority to oversee the planning processes and to review key decisions at interim points prior to requesting formal approval of the proposal. The coordinating committee should be composed of a decision set intermediate in size (5–7) and be representative of those groups who must ultimately "approve" the final decision, thus providing a basis for a coalition of sponsorship larger than the original advocate group. This is the beginning of both co-optation and reconnaissance.

In summary:

The initiation of planning for innovation often includes a mandate negotiated with elites encompassing a shared diagnosis of the general objectives of the innovation, agreement regarding the complexity of the planning context, the resources required by the planning group, the general processes and timetable to be followed in planning for the innovation, and the formation of a coordinating committee which enlarges the basis of sponsorship for the innovation.

Finally, we can ask what methods "advocates" might use to obtain this mandate to proceed with planning for an innovation. Again, there is considerable agreement in the literature. Endorsement, alliances, opinions, judgments are all weaker bases for attention getting than indicative evidence of either a potential threat to the organization's legitimacy or domain or potential opportunities for organizational prestige and profit (Achilladelis et al., 1971; Utterback, 1971, 1973a and b, 1974). In the absence of such evidence, preferably presented in simple information displays, obtaining the mandate may have to await the next Phase, Problem Exploration. The difficulty of reversing these steps, however, is that the cost and processes of problem exploration are then the financial and energy burden of the advocate group which may lack planning funds.

PHASE 2: PROBLEM EXPLORATION

The second phase in the Program Planning Model is to assess the nature of the client's or user's needs. The basic premise is quite simple: Organizations respond to either threats or opportunities with respect to serving clients within their domain. That is, an opportunity to increase the number of clients (and presumably resources), program effectiveness, or client satisfaction is appealing. Loss of clients, failure to serve or treat clients successfully, or client dissatisfaction can be a threat. The purpose of this step is to make the potential threat or opportunity "real" to members of the organization, particularly elites.

There are some important attributes to the nature of the evidence one presents to organizational elites that increase the probability of their supporting a program innovation. First, the evidence must be unmanipulated. This would suggest that it is firmly based on client needs as defined *by clients* rather than opinions offered by provider advocates for new programs of interest to professionals (Turner, 1969; Utterback, 1971, 1973 a and b). Numerous techniques are available to facilitate this attribute. (Modestly, I would mention that the Nominal Group Technique which I developed is a helpful protocol for this purpose—(Delbecq et al., 1975.)

Second, the evidence should suggest the range of differences among clients. Hard sell attempts to lump all clients into a "typical" client stereotype are increasingly suspect.

Third, an honest estimate of the immediate client population that *will* take advantage of services, as opposed to the potential market that *might* take advantage of a service program, is important. Overestimation of client potential is a major cause of program failure and elite cynicism.

The evidence should be presented in a combination of both qualitative, descriptive scenarios (which make clients "real") and quantitative distributive data (which makes the degree of need real). To make the distributive data "living," interspersing field reports and interview information with more "objective" statistical indicators is important (Delbecq et al., 1975).

Finally, it is also important that a sense of public "expectations" with respect to the character of new services be tapped through hearings or public meetings, so that later solutions do not fall prey to local biases or attacks by public advocacy groups. Public sentiment can often sabotage well-formulated technical proposals.

In other words, Problem Exploration is aimed at consciousness raising, dialogue, and education. It is not simply "evidence." Since individuals interested in a particular client problem are often seen as vested in any resources directed or redirected to a new program, we can see the advantage of the coordinating committee organized in Phase 1. The committee can serve to testify both to the objective character of the processes followed in Problem Exploration and to the unmanipulated evidence presented at the conclusion of this phase. In the end, however, unless there is elite agreement regarding the importance of the problem, it is largely futile to proceed to solution design.

In summary, in a political sense, the outcome of Phase Two, Problem Exploration, should be:

Documentation of unmet client needs, reviewed and agreed upon by elites, as either an important potential source of resources or as a potential threat to organizational legitimacy or domain if the organization does not respond.

A qualitative as well as quantitative understanding of the character of client needs, indicating a shared tension.

The belief by all reviewers that the needs assessment evidence obtained in problem exploration is an unmanipulated statement of user group needs.

PHASE 3: KNOWLEDGE EXPLORATION

Innovation in the sense of "creative" new programs does not follow automatically from problem understanding. There is a great deal of evidence that decision-making with respect to solution search, even when one becomes aware of new problems, is not only "satisfying," it is "incestuous." Many professionals, planning for program change (despite training in decision-making), tend to reach to prior experience, prior approaches, or modest distortions of old answers in dealing with new problems, as opposed to really engaging in search behavior (Mintzberg et al., 1976). As a consequence there is one predominant *prescription* with respect to solution development: don't talk to either yourself or your immediate colleagues until after search behavior.

Empirically, high rates of innovation tend to be the product of organizations with high degrees of differentiation and professionalism. The explanation offered is that such organizations contain individuals who are "cosmopolitans" and serve as boundary spanners to the broader world of professional and scientific insight (Liefer, 1974; Liefer and Delbecq, forthcoming).

First, with the knowledge explosion, it is unlikely that any organization will possess within its own staff the necessary competence to encapsulate "knowledge" about the new program under study. Second, it is far more expensive to invent than to adopt; more expensive to engage in trial and error learning than to share experience. Third, the most successful form of unfreezing is the confrontation of a variety of heuristic clues—both from professionals with prior experience and from related scientific perspectives (Utterback, 1974).

While this is old stuff in decision theory, it is not normal staff behavior for non-cosmopolitans except under conditions of failure or severe stress (Greiner, 1970; Cyert, and March, 1963). The normative message is clear enough. If physicians should be expected to take complete medical histories, innovators should be expected to engage in an orderly search for critical solution components *prior* to proposal development, including understanding multidisciplinary perspectives and talking to organizations who have tried related programs in other settings.

The predominant instrumentality is the telephone, and the process is to move from nominations of potential resource people gleaned from calls to cosmopolitans (in funding, provider, and professional organizations) to follow-up conversations with specific resource people. The sifting and winnowing of this external information is shown to be a more important contributor to change than the conventional literature search, which is often a form of inverse plagiarism wherein we cite authors who agree with us (Utterback, 1971; Mintzberg et al., 1976). Indeed, the literature often becomes interpretable only after interpersonal conversations placing articles, reports, and so on into appropriate contexts.

There is clear evidence that a search behavior Phase underlies many successful innovations. There are also clear prescriptive protocols available that suggest how to engage in external information searches (Delbecq et al., 1975). In the end, however, the legitimacy, creativity, and potential technical quality of innovation proposals often depends more on the degree of search behavior, than on the amount of (local) problem solving. In summary, the outcome of Phase 3, Knowledge Exploration, should be:

A broad search of solution-relevant information from sources external to the professionals planning the innovation in order to: increase innovativeness of the program design, decrease time required for solution development, increase the technical legitimacy of the proposal, and provide learning from earlier related adoptions.

PHASE 4: PROPOSAL DEVELOPMENT

Klein has suggested that many proposals are not adopted because the authors of the proposal are unwilling to repeat with reviewers the long processes from which their thinking has emerged (Delbecq, 1974; Klein, 1967; Michael, 1973). The warning, of course, is that proposal development should proceed through two stages: a preliminary informal review of the concepts and approach as a basis for learning and dialogue; and only later, the development of a formal proposal that is the basis for the "decision to adopt." The error is to proceed to the second step without first developing

the concepts underlying the proposal in dialogue with elites who must ultimately "approve" the innovation (Delbecq, 1974).

The usual method to facilitate informal review is a draft document that
chronicles the careful planning process undertaken within the guidelines of
the original mandate. The document itself should be a concept paper, not a
proposal. It should be written in outline form and utilize clear illustrations
and data summaries. It should *crisply* highlight goals based on problem exploration and solution features based on knowledge exploration. It should
show how the coordinating committee and project staff have incorporated
cosmopolitan knowledge and experience into an approach tailored to the
local situation. This combination of a historical perspective along with a
clear statement of needs and solution strategies is far more important than
the conventional "theoretical justification." Finally, the document should
contain endorsements of the key constituencies involved in the planning effort to date (Delbecq, 1974).

None of these characteristics negate the characteristics of proposals
conventionally discussed as leading to "adoption" in the planning literature,
such as relative advantage, flexibility, and technical quality (Brief et al.,
1976). What this approach adds is simply the overt recognition of the processes through which the proposal has emerged.

More important, however, is that a "draft" is a vehicle for dialogue (in
contrast with a proposal which advocates often try to sell). Shared excitement emerges from discussions of flexible, emerging concepts, not ratifica-
tion of crystallized positions. The importance of this dialogue is that it
removes the stigma of self-serving advocacy, enlarges the basis of sponsorship, and demonstrates that while client and professional concerns have
been incorporated into the thinking of the advocate group, the concept is still
flexible. There is a clear desire to incorporate the perspective of elites and
funders.

It is at this point that the planning process returns to the decision set
whence the original mandate was received, to fully incorporate elite concerns easily lost in the suboptimization inevitable when concentrating on
client and professional perspectives. Elites in responding to a concept paper
can often suggest concerns that may be only loosely attended within the
draft document: for example, organizational conflicts that may only now
become clearer as the adumbrations of the innovation emerge; resources that

can be pooled to support the program concept; implementational arrangements that will minimize organizational disruption (Brief et al., 1976).

The key point is that the advocate group must be willing to enter into a serious dialogue with elites with respect to innovation proposals, focusing not only on strengths of the emerging program innovation, but also upon modifications that would improve the concept. This underscores the importance of making the concept paper an early draft and keeping the attitudes of the advocate group flexible and not yet closed on the final design. (Elsewhere I have written at length about meeting formats and group processes that can be utilized to structure this discussion—(Delbecq et al., 1975).

The outcome of the proposal review process should be agreement concerning the conditions that must be met to obtain a formal adoption decision, the level of resources needed and available, agreements among those who must cooperate with implementation, and a shared sense of excitement about the forthcoming formal proposal. In summary,

Preliminary review of proposals allow for the accommodation of valid objections, incorporation of features that strengthen the proposal, increase organizational accommodations and readiness, and create a coalition of support in preparation for formal adoption decisions.

PHASE 5: PROGRAM DESIGN

Only now should the advocate group proceed to write the formal proposal. Recent evidence in fields such as management science suggests that fully twenty percent of the time and energy for planning for innovation should *precede* proposal development. (In the lexicon of planners, this is, often called the "feasibility study" stage.) It is only at this point that the advocate group can settle into the task of formulating a proposal document that is communicable, technically of high quality, clear in terms of relative economic advantage, providing realistic assessments with respect to administrative and organizational requirements, and incorporating an appropriate evaluation design (Van de Ven and Koenig, 1976). Since the characteristics of any proposal beyond these general features are specific to the types of services being planned for, I will discuss implementation strategies and the problem of technological transfer before suggesting some broad issues which this discussion of the planning processes underlying program innovation suggests.

PHASE 6: PROGRAM IMPLEMENTATION

Three generic implementation strategies can be mentioned as proto-
types: pilot studies, demonstration studies, and direct implementations. I
will comment on each strategy to indicate the subtleties of choice implicit in
each.

Pilot Studies. Where knowledge of causation is limited in the sense that
one is dealing with a new and untested service or treatment, where organization traditions are inconsistent with the innovation, where resistance is high
either due to value incongruence or technological unfamiliarity, and where
the organizational and staffing requirements require "learning," the prototype implementation strategy is the pilot study. These criteria are diagnostics
too often overlooked by enthusiastic advocates of new programs. In the entrepreneurial fervor of belief in the innovation, it is easy for the advocate
group to generalize their convictions that their program innovation will meet
enthusiastic embrace throughout the delivery system. Yet, as we all know,
resistance to change under these conditions is great, and probabilities of success not assured (Delbecq, 1974; Michael, 1973; Rogers and Shoemaker,
1971). Pilots allow innovators to "debug" programs, make use of formative
as opposed to summative evaluation strategies (Scriven, 1967), provide objective evidence of worth, and particularly provide an opportunity for organizational learning so that the necessary skills, support systems, and protocols necessary to incorporate the innovation can be made explicit
(Delbecq, 1974).

The three most often reported reasons for failure of program innovations are: 1) a lack of anticipated client interest, 2) disillusionment because
anticipated benefits were not matched by performance, and 3) organization
disruption was greater than expected. Pilots allow the innovation to be tested
with a minimum of risk and a maximum of support. It is also often possible
to build into pilots types of technical assistance, consulting, and staff learning which would be too expensive in larger implementation strategies. As a
result, organization learning takes place which allows more realistic predictions to be made, fitting levels of aspiration more closely to program performance. Principle: *The risks are greatest by starting too big, not too small.*

Demonstrations: Demonstrations, by contrast, are aimed at showing
that innovations already piloted can be effective under "normal" conditions.
The purpose of the demonstration, however, is not focused simply on the or-

ganizations chosen as the demonstration sites, but rather upon a network of organizations for which the demonstration is aimed at influencing. It is important, therefore, that the demonstration be the property of "future adopters" in the network, not simply the demonstration sites.

Tactics which will increase this sense of ownership by the organization network would include: 1) formation of a study committee or coordinating committee within the network for purposes of overseeing the demonstration; 2) selection by the committee (not advocates) of demonstration sites, including an appropriate range of "typical" organizations (this is in contrast to placing demonstrations in elite or benign organizational sites); and 3) providing for participant-observers (chosen from later adopters) to play an active role in the demonstrations, perhaps in terms of shared staffing and funding (Delbecq, 1974).

Obviously, this approach to demonstrations is riskier than locating a single demonstration in an enthusiastic organization, and often must be predicated on a prior pilot. In addition, successful demonstrations following this model should incorporate sufficient technical assistance and consulting services to the demonstration organizations. Further, they should allow for organizational learning by incorporating a design that contains two evaluation periods. Two iterations provide for organizational learning and the possibility for the new program to stabilize. This allows formative evaluation in period one and summative evaluation in period two.

Sophisticated demonstrations, then, imply that the prototype is indeed ready for transfer into the real world of average organizations. This means that pilots must develop not only technological feasibility, but the necessary learning materials to train staff in these later adopting demonstration organizations.

Direct Implementation. This of course is seldom a strategy normatively desirable for purposes of innovation. The necessary conditions:

causation understood
hierarchical and professional support high
process simple
implementation skills available
well-developed training and implementation materials
ample technical assistance
compliance standards clearly worked out so that designs are not distorted

Since these conditions seldom prevail, direct implementation is a fool's strategy for introducing innovation. Nonetheless, we have all known some "Kamikaze" innovators.

PHASE 7: PROGRAM TRANSFER

The final chapter in the innovation scenerio is technological transfer and diffusion. The conditions for direct implementation listed above must be in place. In addition, start-up support in the form of financial and technical assistance, inducements and rewards, and elite mandates and support are necessary. The difficulty here is that those involved in pilots or demonstrations are seldom interested in "going on the road" and training new organizations. This implies that technological transfer is a new and formidable task requiring the codification of the lessons learned in the demonstrations into systems and training for later adopting organizations. Structurally, this often means the transfer of the "new" program to old-line functional units. We need not belabor here the difficulties of the transition between these stages of program evolution, nor the fact that much innovation in social services never *is* transferred, benefiting only the original demonstration sites and having virtually no broad scale impact on social service delivery in general.

CONTINGENT CONDITIONS

The above innovation story expressed as a normative model is, of course, subject to considerable variability. Phases often overlap, are in alternate sequences, and receive varied degrees of attention. Space does not permit a complete discussion of the relative importance of planning phases in the form of a contingent model. A sense of contingencies, however, can be briefly sketched.

Elites. The term "elite," used as a general term in the previous model, was used in the tradition of Hage & Dewar: "Those who actively participate and influence decisions." (Hage and Dewar, 1973). Contingently:

> In centralized organizations, elites tend to occupy hierarchical, positional roles;
> In decentralized professional organizations, elites tend to include provider opinion leaders;
> In situations where clients are well informed and have access to and can choose among multiple providing organizations, clients will be included among elites.

The key point is that the definition of who "elites" are differs for varied innovation projects.

Political Complexity. In situations we can summarize as politically complex (that is, a large number of groups affected and value fragility), Phase One (Securing a Mandate) and Phase Four (Proposal Review) receive greater attention.

Technical Complexity. In situations where knowledge is the primary barrier to innovation, Phases Two (Problem Exploration) and Three (Knowledge Exploration) are more emphasized. Further, early in the history of the technology underlying a new program, problem-centered investigation is more important. Under this circumstance, Problem Exploration creates "relative advantage" to the organization since sponsorship of a program which meets unmet needs can result in both new resources and enlarged clientele. Knowledge Exploration is more important late in the history of a program's technology, where improvement of processes allows for cost reduction. This creates relative advantage in that the organization can be more *efficient* than competitors.

Organizational Complexity. Where program innovation requires considerable restructuring, training, and so on, Phases six and seven become keystones. Staffing patterns, support, and feedback systems are of relatively greater importance.

The normative PPM model, outlined earlier, then, is simplistic, since it assigns equal weight to Political, Technical, and Organizational complexity, a rare circumstance. Nonetheless, this simplified review of processes underlying innovation brings us to some broad issues around which this paper concludes.

ISSUES FOR INNOVATION IN SOCIAL SERVICES DELIVERY

The above discussion of the social political processes of introducing innovation in human services suggests three critical issues: 1) the need for training in social planning; 2) the structural requirements for supporting innovation; 3) the problem of subsidiarity (decentralization).

TRAINING IN SOCIAL PLANNING

To those who are familiar with the literature on social planning and organization innovation, this review of change processes is old stuff. But to many administrators, professionals, and providers in human service, the gamesmanship of innovation processes is not only vague, but each attempt involves trial and error suffering. Additional training in social planning might decrease failure rates, or at least increase the learning rate. Further, since elites play such a critical role, this training is not only called for at the pre-entry level, but is an important second career and executive educational agenda for administrators in human services.

Program and project management is a specialized managerial role in organizations having high rates of innovation in the private sector. There seems to be less recognition of these positions or roles in human services. Training of managers for varied roles associated with the advocacy and management of innovation requires considerable theoretical rigor as well as experience. We need to recognize in human services, even as in engineering and commercial organizations, that the management of innovation is a specialized role that should become a career path. I should add that the placement of individuals trained in social planning should not be exclusively into planning departments. Rather, I see it as even more critical that we recognize project management as a staff function, which should often support line administration. This issue of training staff for organizational roles and career paths associated with experimental projects, which is only now beginning to stabilize in the private sector, must be thought through in human services.

ORGANIZATIONAL STRUCTURES

While one can move innovation processes through a crusty bureaucracy on an ad hoc basis, organizations with higher rates of innovation eventually adopt some form of matrix structure (overlapping project and program management with functional departments). How will this development emerge in human service organizations?

There are diseconomies of scale when implementing matrix structures in small organizations. Size and resource requirements for effective project management are such that not all delivery organizations would qualify. I suspect this will require organizational specialization within service providing networks. Some organizations will need to be provided differential resources to carry out developmental planning and demonstration procedures.

Further, innovation aimed at network change and technological transfer will require interorganizational cooperation and large scale funding. This implies the evolution of interstitial projects at the network level, rather than placing demonstrations under the aegis of single providing organizations.

Given the lack of slack in most human service organizations for supporting developmental endeavors, how will slack be created? Through consortium arrangements?

SUBSIDIARITY (DECENTRALIZATION)

Finally, since the innovation game is complex, expensive, and time consuming, priorities with respect to innovation will have to be carefully determined. Yet I am uneasy that presently much innovation is "federally mandated" through existing grant arrangements. Such a pattern is not without risks. There is little evidence of stimulating adequate innovation rates through central planning in the private sector. Rather, innovation flourishes under conditions of decentralization and subsidiarity in planning and project design. This being the case, how can we provide venture capital and sufficient resources from a central level, but at the same time, decentralize design and demonstration of new programs at the network level?

REFERENCES

Achilladelis, B., P. Jervis, and A. Robertson. 1971. *Report on Project SAPPHO to the Science Research Council: A Study of Success and Failure in Innovation.* Sussex, England: University of Sussex, Science Policy Research Unit.

Adams. S. 1953. "Status Congruency as a Variable in a Small Group," *Social Forces,* 32:16–22.

Aguilar, F. J. 1967. *Scanning the Business Environment.* New York: Macmillan.

Aiken, M., and R. R. Alford. 1970a. "Community Structure and Innovation: The Case of Urban Renewal," *American Sociological Review,* 35:650–65.

—— 1970b. "Community Structure and Innovation: The Case of Public Housing," *American Political Science Review,* 64:843–64.

Aiken, M., and J. Hage. 1968. "Organizational Interdependence and Intraorganizational Structure," *American Sociological Review,* 33:912–30.

—— 1971. "The Organic Organization and Innovation," *Sociology,* 5 (Jan.).

Aleshire, Robert A. 1970. "Planning and Citizen Participation: Costs, Benefits and Approaches," *Urban Affairs Quarterly,* 5 (4).

Arnstein, S. R. 1969. "A Ladder of Citizen Participation," *Journal of the American Institute of Planners,* 35 (5).

Back, K. W. 1951. "Influence through Social Communication," *Journal of Abnormal and Social Psychology*, 46:9–23.

Barnes, L. B. 1967. "Organizational Change and Field Experiment Methods." In V. Vroom, ed., *Methods of Organizational Research*." Pittsburgh: University of Pittsburgh Press.

Barnett, H. G. 1953. *Innovation: The Basis of Culture Change*. New York: McGraw-Hill.

Bass, B. 1970. "When Planning for Others," *Journal of Applied Science,* 6 (2).

Bean, A., R. D. Neal, M. Radnor, and D. Tansik. 1973. "Structure and Behavioral Correlates of the Implementation of Formal OR/MS Projects: Success and Failure in U.S. Business Organizations." Paper presented at a research conference on "The Implementation of OR/MS Models: Theory, Research and Application" at the Graduate School of Business, University of Pittsburgh.

Becker, S. W., and F. Stafford. 1967. "Some Determinants of Organizational Success," *Journal of Business,* 40 (Oct.).

Becker, S. W., and T. L. Whisler. 1967. "The Innovative Organization: A Selective View of Current Theory and Research," *Journal of Business,* 40 (Oct.).

Blake, R. R., and J. S. Mouton. 1961. "Comprehension of Own and Outgroup Positions under Intergroup Competition," *Journal of Conflict Resolution,* 5:304–10.

Bolan, R. S. 1967. "Emerging View of Planning," *American Institute of Planners Journal,* 13 (July).

—— 1969. "Community Decision Behavior: The Culture of Planning," *American Institute of Planners Journal,* 35 (Sept.).

—— 1971. "The Social Relations of the Planner," *Journal of the American Institute of Planners,* 37 (Nov.).

Bolan, R. S., and R. L. Nuttall. 1975. *Urban Politics and Planning*. Lexington, Mass.: D. C. Heath.

Brandner, L., and B. Kearl. 1964. "Evaluation for Congruence as a Factor in Adoption Rates of Innovations," *Rural Sociology,* 29:288–303.

Brief, A. P. 1974. "Toward a Theory of Planned Social System Change: An Empirical Analysis of Adoption Behavior," Ph.D. dissertation, University of Wisconsin.

Brief, A. P., A. L. Delbecq, and A. C. Filley. 1974. "An Empirical Analysis of Adoption Behavior." Paper presented at the 34th Academy of Management Meeting, Seattle, Wash.

Brief, A. P., A. L. Delbecq, A. C. Filley, and G. P. Huber. 1976. "Elite

Structure of Attitudes: An Empirical Analysis of Adoption Behavior,"
Administration and Society, 8 (2).

Bryson, J. M. 1976. "Participation in Public Sector Program Planning Projects." Madison: University of Wisconsin, Department of Urban and Regional Planning. Manuscript.

Burke, E. 1968. "Citizen Participation Strategies," *Journal of the American Institute of Planners,* 34 (5).

Burns, T., and G. M. Stalker. 1961. *The Management of Innovation.* London: Tavistock.

Campbell, D. T., and J. C. Stanley. 1963. *Experimental and Quasi-Experimental Designs for Research.* Chicago: Rand McNally.

Carroll, J. 1967. "A Note on Departmental Autonomy and Innovation in Medical Schools," *Journal of Business,* 40 (Oct.).

Carter, C., and B. Williams. 1957. *Industry and Technical Progress: Factors Governing the Speed of Application of Science.* London: Oxford University Press.

Clark, R. D., and E. P. Willems. 1969. "Risk Preferences as Related to Judged Consequences of Failure," *Psychology Reports,* 25 (Dec.).

Clark, T. N. 1967. "Power and Community Structure: Who Governs, Where and When?" *Sociological Quarterly,* 8:291–316.

—— 1968. "Community Structure, Decision-Making, Budget Expenditures and Urban Renewal in 51 American Communities," *American Sociological Review,* 33:576–93.

Collins, B. E., and H. Guetzkow, eds. 1964. *A Social Psychology of Group Processes for Decision Making.* New York: Wiley.

Corwin, R. G. 1969. "Patterns of Organizational Conflict," *Administrative Science Quarterly,* 14:507–20.

—— 1972. "Strategies for Organizational Innovation: An Empirical Comparison," *American Sociological Review,* 37:441–54.

Costello, T. W., and S. S. Zalkin, eds. 1963. *Psychology in Administration: A Research Orientation.* Englewood Cliffs, N.J.: Prentice-Hall.

Crain, R. L., and D. B. Rosenthal. 1967. "Community Status as a Dimension of Local Decision Making," *American Sociological Review,* 32:970–83.

Crain, R. L., E. Katz, and D. B. Rosenthal, eds. 1969. *The Politics of Community Conflict: The Fluoridation Decision.* Indianapolis: Bobbs-Merrill.

Cummings, L. 1965. "Organizational Climates for Creativity," *Academy of Management Journal,* 8.

Cummings, L., and M. O'Connell. 1972. "Organization Innovation: A

Conceptual Framework." Working Paper, University of Wisconsin.

Cyert, R., and S. March, 1963. *A Behavioral Theory of the Firm.* Englewood Cliffs, N.J.: Prentice-Hall.

Dalton, G. W. 1970. "Influence and Organizational Change." In N. Schwitter, ed., *Organizational Behavior Models.* Kent State University, Bureau of Economics and Business Research.

Davis, J. H. 3d. 1969. *Group Performance.* Reading, Mass.: Addison-Wesley.

Delbecq, A. L. 1974. "Contextual Variables Affecting Decision-Making in Program Planning," *Decision Sciences,* 5 (4).

—— 1976. "The Nominal Group as a Needs Assessment Technique for Qualitative Understanding of Client Concerns," in Roger Bell, Martin Sundell, Joseph Aponte and Stanley Murrell, *Need Assessment in Health and Human Services,* Proceedings of the Louisville National Conference, University of Louisville, pp. 217–230.

—— 1976. "The Management Decision Making Within the Firm: Three Strategies for Three Types of Decision Making," in Karl O. Mayrusen, *Organizational Design: Development and Behavior,* pp. 361–72. Glenview, Ill.: Scott Foresman.

—— forthcoming. "Negotiating Mandates Which Increase the Acceptance of Evaluation Findings Concerning Demonstration Findings in Human Services," Reprint Series, Center for Evaluation Research, School of Social Work, University of Wisconsin, Madison, Wisconsin, 1977.

Delbecq, A. L., and A. C. Filley. 1974. *Program Management in a Matrix Organization: A Case Study.* Madison: University of Wisconsin, Bureau of Business Research and Service.

Delbecq, A. L., and A. H. Van de Ven. 1971. "A Group Process Model for Problem Identification and Program Planning," *Journal of Applied Behavioral Science,* 7 (4).

Delbecq, A. L., A. H. Van de Ven, and D. H. Gustafson. 1975. *Group Techniques for Program Planning.* Glenview, Ill.: Scott Foresman.

Delbecq, A. L., V. A. Schull, A. C. Filley, and A. J. Grimes. 1969. "Matrix Organization, A Conceptual Guide to Organizational Variation." Madison: University of Wisconsin, Bureau of Business Research.

Department of the Army. 1975. *Digest of Water Resources Policies.* Washington, D.C.: Office of the Chief of Engineers.

Derr, C. 1972. "Conflict Resolution in Organizations: Views From the Field of Educational Administration," *Public Administration Review,* 32:495–501.

Dexter, Lewis. 1970. *Elite and Specialized Interviewing.* Evanston, Ill.: Northwestern University Press.

Dubey, Sumati N. 1970. "Community Action Programs and Citizen Participation: Issues and Confusions," *Social Work*, 15 (1).

Edelman, M. 1964. *The Symbolic Uses of Politics*. Urbana: University of Illinois Press.

Engelsen, R. E. 1976. "Cedar-Riverside," *Practicing Planner*, 6 (2).

Evan, W. M. and G. Black. 1967. "Innovation in Business Organizations: Some Factors Associated with Success or Failure of Staff Proposals," *Journal of Business*, 40.

Fagance, Michael. 1975. "The Planner and Citizen Participation," *Planning and Administration*, 2 (2).

Ference, T. P. 1970. "Organizational Communications Systems and the Decision Process," *Management Science*, 17 (2).

Filley, A. C. 1975. *Interpersonal Conflict Resolutions*. Glenview, Ill.: Scott Foresman.

Filley, A. C. and R. J. House, eds. 1969. *Managerial Process and Organizational Behavior*. Glenview, Ill.: Scott Foresman.

Fliegel, F. C., and J. E. Kivlin. 1966. "Attributes of Innovations as Factors in Diffusion," *American Journal of Sociology*, 72:235–48.

Fliegel, F. C., J. E. Kivlin, and G. S. Sekhon. 1968. "A Cross-Cultural Comparison of Farmers' Perceptions of Innovation as Related to Adoption Behavior," *Rural Sociology*, 33:437–49.

Flinn, W. L. 1970. "Influence of Community Values on Innovativeness," *American Journal of Sociology*, 75:983–91.

French, J. R. P., Jr. 1944. "Organized and Unorganized Groups Under Fear and Frustration," *University of Iowa Studies in Child Welfare*, 20:409.

Friedmann, J. 1966. "Planning as Innovation: The Chilean Case," *Journal of the American Institute of Planners*, 32.

—— 1967. "A Conceptual Model for the Analysis of Planning Behavior," *Administrative Science Quarterly*, 12:225–52.

—— 1973. *Retracking America*. Garden City, N.Y.: Anchor.

Galbraith, J. K. 1973. *Economics and the Public Purpose*. Boston: Houghton Mifflin.

Greenstone, J. D., and P. E. Peterson. 1968. "Reformers, Machines and the War on Poverty." In J. Wilson, ed., *City Politics and Public Policy*. New York: Wiley.

Griener, L. E. 1967a. "Antecedents of Planned Organization Change," *Journal of Applied Behavioral Science*, 3.

Griener, L. E. and L. B. Barnes. 1970. "Organization Change and Development." In M. Dalton et al., eds., *Organization Change and Development*, pp. 213–228. Homewood, Ill.: Irwin.

Gribbins, R. E. 1975. "An Investigation of the Responsiveness of Multi-

Specialty Group Practice Physicians to Change. Ph.D. dissertation, University of Wisconsin.

Griffiths, D. E. 1964. "Administrative Theory and Change in Organizations." In M. Miles, ed., *Innovation in Education*. New York: Teachers College Press.

Gross, N., J. B. Giaguinta, and M. Bernstein. 1971. *Implementing Organizational Innovations: A Sociological Analysis of Planned Educational Change*. New York: Basic Books.

Hage, J. 1974. "A Longitudinal Test of an Axiomatic Organizational Theory." Paper presented at the 8th World Congress of Sociology, Montreal, Canada.

Hage, J., and M. Aiken. 1967. "Program Change and Organizational Properties: A Comparative Analysis," *American Journal of Sociology*, 72:503–19.

—— 1970. *Social Change in Complex Organizations*. New York: Random.

Hage, J., and R. Dewar. 1973. "Elite Values versus Organizational Structure in Predicting Innovation," *Administrative Science Quarterly*, 18:279–90.

Hall, R. H. 1972. *Organizations: Structure and Process*. Englewood Cliffs, N.J.: Prentice-Hall.

Hall, R. J., S. E. Haas, and N. J. Johnson. 1967. "Organizational Size, Complexity and Formulation," *American Sociological Review*, 32:903–12.

Hanchey, J. R. 1975. *Public Involvement in the Corps of Engineers Planning Process*. Fort Belvoir, Va.: U.S. Army Engineer Institute for Water Resources.

Havelock, R. G. 1970. *Planning for Innovation through Dissemination and Utilization of Knowledge*. Ann Arbor, Mich.: Institute for Social Research.

—— 1973. *The Change Agent's Guide to Innovation in Education*. Englewood Cliffs, N.J.: Educational Technology Publications.

Hawley, A. H. 1963. "Community Power and Urban Renewal Success," *American Journal of Sociology*, 68:422–31.

Heberlein, T. A. 1976. *Principles of Public Involvement*. Madison: University of Wisconsin-Extension.

Heinicke, C., and R. F. Bales. 1953. "Developmental Trends in the Structure of Small Groups," *Sociometry*, 16:7–38.

Horwitz, M., and D. Cartwright. 1953. "A Projection Method for the Diagnosis of Group Properties," *Human Relations*, 6:397–410.

House, R., H. Tosi, J. Rizzo, and R. Dunnock. 1967. *Management Devel-*

opment: Design, Evaluation and Implementation. Ann Arbor: University of Michigan Bureau of Industrial Relations.

Hyman, H. H., and P. B. Sheatsley. 1947. "Some Reasons Why Information Campaigns Fail," *Public Opinion Quarterly*, 11:411–23.

Janis, I. L. 1959. "Decisional Conflicts: A Theoretical Analysis," *Journal of Conflict Resolution*, 3:6–27.

Johnson, D. L., and I. R. Andrews. 1971. "Risky-Shift Phenomenon Tested with Consumer Products as Stimuli," *Journal of Personality and Social Psychology*, 20:382–85.

Joynt, P. 1973. "The Program Planning Model: Process Analysis." Unpublished paper, University of Wisconsin.

Kaluzny, A., J. Veney, and J. Gentry. 1974. "Innovation of Health Services: A Comparative Study of Hospitals and Health Departments," *Health and Society* (Winter).

Katz, D., and R. L. Kahn. 1966. *The Social Psychology of Organizations*. New York: Wiley.

Kaufman, J. L. 1976. "The Planner as Interventionist." Paper presented at the "Planning: Challenge and Response" Conference Sponsored by the Center for Urban Policy Research, Rutgers University, New Brunswick, N.J.

Kelley, George. 1976. "Seducing the Elites: The Politics of Decision-Making and Innovation in Organizational Networks," *Academy of Management Review*, 1 (3).

Kirton, M. J., and G. Mulligan. 1973. "Correlates of Managers' Attitudes Toward Change," *Journal of Applied Psychology*, 58.

Klein, O. C. 1967. "Some Notes on the Dynamics of Resistance to Change: The Defender Role." In G. Watson, ed., *Concepts for Social Change*. Washington, D.C.: National Training Laboratories.

Knight, K. 1967. "A Descriptive Model of the Intra-Firm Innovation Process," *Journal of Business*, 40 (Oct.).

Kotter, J. P., and P. L. Lawrence. 1974. *Mayors in Action: Five Approaches to Urban Governance*. New York: Wiley.

Lawrence, P., and J. Lorsch. 1967a. "Differentiation and Integration in Complex Organizations," *Administrative Science Quarterly*, 12:1–47.

—— 1967b. *Organization and Environment*. Cambridge: Harvard Press.

Leavitt, H. J. 1962. "Management According to Task: Organizational Differentiation," *Management International*, 1 (Jan.–Feb.).

Liefer, R. 1974. "Boundary Spanning Activity and Boundary Spanning Personnel: A Conceptual Model." Paper presented at the 17th Annual Conference of the Midwest Academy of Management, Kent State University.

—— 1975. "An Analysis of the Characteristics and Functioning of Interorganizational Boundary Spanning Personnel. Ph.D. dissertation, University of Wisconsin.

Liefer, R. P., and A. L. Delbecq. forthcoming. "Organizational/Environ-
mental Interchange: A Model of Boundary Spanning Activity." *Academy
of Management Review*.

Machiavelli, Niccolo. 1950. *The Prince and the Discourses*. New York:
Modern Library.

Maier, N. R. F., ed. 1970. *Problem Solving and Creativity in Individuals
and Groups*. Belmont, Calif.: Brooks/Cole.

Mansfield, E. 1963. "Size of Firm, Market Structure and Innovation,"
Journal of Political Economy, 71:556–76.

March, J. G., and H. A. Simon. 1958. *Organizations*. New York: Wiley.

Margulies, N., and J. Wallace. 1973. *Organizational Change: Techniques
and Applications*. Glenview, Ill.: Scott Foresman.

Menzel, H. 1960. "Innovation, Integration and Marginality: A Survey of
Physicians," *American Sociological Review*, 25:704–13.

Michael, Donald. 1973. *On Learning to Plan and Planning to Learn*. San
Francisco: Jossey Bass.

Mintzberg, H., D. Raisinghani, and A. Theoret. 1976. "The Structure of
'Unstructured' Decision Processes," *Administrative Science Quarterly*,
21:246–75.

Mohr, L. 1969. "Determinants of Innovation in Organizations," *American
Political Science Review*, 63:111–26.

Mytiner, R. D. 1968. *Innovation in Local Health Services*. Arlington, Va.:
U.S. Department of Health, Education and Welfare.

Nedd, A. N. B. 1971. "The Simultaneous Effect of Several Variables on
Attitudes toward Change," *Administrative Science Quarterly*, 16:258–69.

Normann, R. 1971. "Organizational Innovations: Product Variation and
Reorientation," *Administrative Science Quarterly*, 16:203–15.

Nutt, P. C. 1974. "Design Methods Research: An Experimental Comparison of the Effectiveness of Planning Procedures." Ph.D. dissertation, University of Wisconsin.

—— 1976. "The Merits of Using Experts or Consumers as Members of
Planning Groups: A Field Experiment in Health Planning," *Academy of
Management Journal*, 19 (3).

Oppenheim, A. N., ed. 1966. *Questionnaire Design and Attitude Measurement*. New York: Basic Books.

Palumbo, D. J. 1969. "Power and Role Specificity in Organization
Theory," *Public Affairs Review*, 29 (May–June).

Pateman, C. 1970. *Participation and Democratic Theory*. Cambridge, England: Cambridge University Press.

Pelz, D. C., and F. M. Andrews. 1966. *Scientists in Organizations*. New York: Wiley.

Perrow, C. 1967. "A Framework for the Comparative Analysis of Organizations," *American Sociological Review*, 32:194–208.

Pressman, J., and A. B. Wildavsky. 1973. *Implementation*. Berkeley: University of California Press.

Price, J. L., ed. 1968. *Organizational Effectiveness: An Inventory of Propositions*. Homewood, Ill.: Irwin.

Pugh, D. S., D. J. Hickson, C. R. Hinings, and C. Turner. 1968. "Dimensions of Organization Structure," *Administrative Science Quarterly*, 13:65–105.

—— 1969. "The Context of Organization Structure," *Administrative Science Quarterly*, 14 (March).

Ragan, James F., Jr. 1975. *Public Participation in Water Resources Planning: An Evaluation of the Programs of 15 Corps of Engineers Districts*, Fort Belvoir, Va.: U.S. Army Engineer Institute for Water Resources.

Rogers, E. M., and F. F. Shoemaker. 1971. *Communication of Innovations: A Cross-Cultural Approach*. New York: Free Press.

Rosener, J. B. 1975. "A Cafeteria of Techniques and Critiques," *Public Management*, 57 (12).

Sanders, J. T. 1961. "The Stages of a Community Controversy: The Case of Fluoridation," *Journal of Social Issues*, 17 (4).

Schroeder, G., ed. 1953. *The Growth of Major Steel Companies*. Baltimore: Johns Hopkins University Press.

Scriven, M. 1967. "The Methodology of Evaluation," in *Perspectives of Curriculum Evaluation*, pp. 39–83 (AERA Monograph Series on Curriculum Evaluation, No.), Chicago: Rand McNally.

Shaw, M. 1971. *Group Dynamics*. New York: McGraw-Hill.

Shull, F., André L. Delbecq, and L. L. Cummings, eds. 1970. *Organizational Decision-Making*. New York: McGraw-Hill.

Shull, F., and A. Delbecq. 1965. "Norms, A Feature of Symbolic Culture: A Major Linkage Between the Individual, Small Group and Administrative Organization." In W. Gore and J. Dyson, eds., *The Making of Decisions: A Reader in Administrative Behavior*. Glencoe, Ill.: Free Press.

Stagner, R. 1969. "Corporate Decision-Making: An Empirical Study," *Journal of Applied Psychology*, 53:1–13.

Stoner, J. A. F. 1968. "Risky and Cautious Shifts in Group Decisions: The

Influence of Widely Held Values," *Journal of Experimental Social Psychology*, 4:442–59.

Tannenbaum, P. H. 1955. "The Indexing Process in Communication," *Public Opinion Quarterly*, 19:292–302.

Terreberry, S. 1968. "The Evolution of Organizational Environments," *Administrative Science Quarterly*, 12:590–613.

Thompson, J. D. 1967. *Organizations in Action.* New York: McGraw-Hill.

Thompson, J. D., and A. Tuden. 1959. "Strategies, Structures, and Processes of Organizational Decision." In J. D. Thompson et al., eds., *Comparative Studies in Administration.* Number 1. Pittsburgh: University of Pittsburgh Press.

Thompson, V. A. 1965. "Bureaucracy and Innovation," *Administrative Science Quarterly*, 10:1–20.

Torrance, P. E. 1955. "Perception of Group Functioning as a Predictor of Group Performance," *Journal of Social Psychology*, 42:271–82.

Trumbo, D. A. 1961. "Individual and Group Correlates of Attitudes toward Work-Related Change," *Journal of Applied Psychology*, 45:338–44.

Turner, R. H. 1969. "The Public Perception of Protest," *American Sociological Review*, 34:815–31.

U.S. Department of Transportation. 1976. *Effective Citizen Participation in Transportation Planning, Volume I; Community Involvement Processes, and Volume II: A Catalogue of Techniques.* Washington, D.C.: Federal Highway Administration.

Utterback, J. M. 1971. "The Process of Technological Innovation Within the Firm," *Academy of Management Journal*, 14.

—— 1973a. "Successful Industrial Innovations: A Multivariate Analysis." Paper presented at the Southeastern Regional Meeting of the Institute of Management Sciences. Atlanta, Georgia.

—— 1973b. "Factors Affecting Innovation in Industry and the Diffusion of Technology." Unpublished paper.

—— 1974. "Innovation in Industry and the Diffusion of Technology," *Science*, 183 (Feb.).

Van de Ven, A. H. 1973. *An Applied Experimental Test of Alternative Decision-Making Processes.* Kent, Ohio: Kent State University, Center for Business and Economic Research Press.

Van de Ven, A. H., and A. L. Delbecq. 1972. "A Planning Process for Development of Complex Regional Programs." Paper delivered at the 67th Annual Meeting of the American Sociological Association, New York.

Van de Ven, A. H., and R. Koenig. 1976. "A Process Model for Program Planning and Evaluation," *Journal of Economics and Business*.

Van Meter, D. S., and C. E. Van Horn. 1975. "The Policy Implementation Process: A Conceptual Framework," *Administration and Society,* 6 (4).

Walker, J. L. 1969. "The Diffusion of Innovations among the American States," *American Political Science Review,* 63: (Sept.).

Williams, J. M. 1973. "The Ecological Approach in Measuring Community Power Concentration: An Analysis of Harley's MPO Ratio," *American Sociological Review,* 38 (April).

Wilson, J. Q. 1966. "Innovation in Organization: Notes toward a Theory." In J. Thompson, ed., *Approaches to Organizational Design.* Pittsburgh: University of Pittsburgh Press.

Zaltman, G., R. Duncan, and J. Holbeck. 1973. *Innovations and Organizations.* New York: Wiley.

Zand, D. E. 1972. "Trust and Managerial Problem Solving," *Administrative Science Quarterly,* 17:229–39.

FOURTEEN

Conclusions

GRAPPLING WITH the contemporary issues confronting human service organizations necessitates a continuous dialogue among policy makers, social welfare administrators, social work educators, and social scientists. It is through such interchange that issues can be sharpened, different viewpoints can be critically appraised, theoretical formulations can be pitted against experience, and research can be evaluated. That has been the primary objective of this volume—to present the most recent theoretical and research findings on the critical issues facing these organizations and to suggest endeavors of study, research, and policy formulations for the future. In this context we attempt to highlight some of the differing viewpoints that were raised in the discussions and comments on the various papers, and thus sensitize the reader to the diversity and richness of the ideas that emerged.

Both Morris and Lescohier and Aldrich raised serious questions about the desirability of centralized planning and integration of services. As was noted by others, the rhetoric of better services through coordination and integration may simply signal a latent objective by policy makers to reduce actual commitment of resources to social services and to increase political and fiscal control over them. Nevertheless, Carter and others cogently noted that much of the impetus for centralized planning in the 1960s was in part motivated by the ineptitude, resistance, and outright hostility of local units to engage in social reforms. Examples were brought from the experiences of the various anti-poverty legislation and programs in the sixties, in which the federal government directly intervened at the local level to foster the development of new local programs, by-passing local governmental bodies such as municipal and state governments. The resistance of many of these governmental bodies to anti-poverty programs stemmed from their reluctance to accept social reform that often challenged their own legitimacy, their desire to control the flow of the new resources to meet their own vested interests, and perhaps even more from differences over political values about the rights of constituent groups to design and control services which they received. In short, the assumption that increased autonomy in decision making by local social services agencies and by constituent groups will foster innovation and responsiveness was challenged. At the same time those who are quick to conclude that the social welfare innovations of the 1960s failed must recognize that the majority of these programs were tried for too short a time to overcome the problems associated with the liabilities of newness. Recent experiences in many states with the programs mandated by the Juvenile Justice and Delinquency Act of 1974 have indicated that some of the models of the 1960s have utility today. Later Cox noted that the community action and legal services programs provided models that had had viability in other countries.

In contrast, it was proposed by Selassie that it is necessary to have a positive intervention of central authority in the affairs of local service networks in order to ensure that minority groups have fair access to societal resources. He pointed to a series of studies by Lovelace and Thomas (1974), which suggest that throughout the recent history of the United States central interventive strategies have been used successfully to deal with problems associated with economic development and improved utilization of natural resources. Examples are the Tennessee Valley Authority and the Public Works Administration. Thus, Selassie concluded that while the participation of local governmental authorities and elected officials ensures a more realistic determination of local needs, the retention of enforcement and control by the central authority increases the probability that local demands do not undermine nationally valued goals. Nevertheless, as several discussants noted, full acknowledgement must be given to the fact that centralized governmental intervention generates in its wake large and rigid public bureaucracies, which over time often tend to follow Michel's "iron law of oligarchy."

If one follows a developmental approach to social policy formation and administrative organization, it is possible to argue that at certain times in the development of macro-social policy centralized government intervention and control is necessary to introduce fundamental change and to maintain the integrity of complex policy implementation when there may be substantial disagreement among various sub-groups within that society about those policies. At the same time centralized structures have within themselves the seeds of rigidity and stagnation so that there must be a plan for subsequent decentralization and increased local autonomy. Kaufman (1971) has ably analyzed these phenomena and proposed several recommended strategies for large organizations. The principal unsolved problem appears to be accurate prediction of the point at which inflexibility is likely to become problematic so that alternative structures can be designed and implemented, along with a determination of more effective means for achieving the desired change. Given the great variation among the fifty states in the administration of human services, it is clear that there are ample opportunities for further research and experimentation in this area (Downs, 1976).

This issue received further consideration in the proposal of Janowitz and Suttles for the development of a multi-tiered structure of the community by linking social blocs to voluntary organizations and the latter to aggregated metropolitan systems. As noted by Knoke, their model is based on two implicit assumptions: a) Communities are said to be responsible insofar as their rights are balanced with obligations to maintain the social order to become self-governing without coercion from the state; b) Communities become responsible when they accept limits on the demands which they can make of the larger society and when they develop an awareness and acceptance of the competing needs of other social groups. Yet, these two assumptions may vary independently of each other. Thus, promotion of self-governance may have the effects of decreasing concern for the larger social good. Rather, it is quite conceivable that social blocs will simply pursue their own self-interests at the expense of other groups without self-control and restraint. The big city ward-based political machines exhibited many of the characteristics of the reform proposed by Suttles and Janowitz, and in fact blocked major reforms (Banfield and Wilson, 1963; Lineberry and Fowler, 1967). Others also noted the pessimism that has resulted from the limited ability of local action groups to initiate reforms and that such groups often mobilize *against* reform rather than *for* it. The proposed model of community reconstitution by Janowitz and Suttles, therefore, may have the unanticipated consequence of giving formal recognition to narrowly-based political claims in negotiations with public bureaucracies which have largely insulated themselves from such parochial pressures. Knoke further suggested that this proposal overlooks some positive aspects of metropolitan fragmentation for service delivery. He pointed to the research of Ostrom and Bish to indicate that increased efficiency, responsiveness, and innovation were possible when agency jurisdictions overlap and compete (Bish, 1971; Bish and Ostrom, 1973; Ostrom, 1974). Both theory and empirical evidence suggest that a variety of political units and coordinating mechanisms can handle the diversity of public goods, services, and individual preferences better than consolidation of control into unitary hierarchies that lack competitive incentive to respond to citizen demands. Such a perspective on urban governance implies that community groups will be more successful in negotiating modification of bureaucratic practices when they face alternative service providers among which to choose.

Perrow's paper implies that discussions on the merits of rationality and centralized planning may be secondary to a far more central issue, namely, whose interests do human service organizations serve. Perrow suggested that these organizations serve the interests of the elites and only marginally the interests of the clients. It was acknowledged by many that regardless of one's acceptance or rejection of this assertion, such issue should become a major focus of research in human service organizations. For example, Studt pointed out that the entire parole system, rather than being set up to assist in "reforming" criminals, was actually designed to protect governors from political embarrassment in dealing with the flood of pardon pleas and to relieve overcrowding in prisons (Studt, 1972). Clearly, one can find numerous similar examples in the human services where the interests of groups other than clients assume predominance in shaping the objectives of these organizations. Yet, can one blame the failure of these organizations on powerful external interests? Studt suggested that some of the failures may also be attributed to a) the eagerness of professionals to promise too much; b) the lack of a technology that emphasizes individualizing activities by and for clients; c) the inability to link the self-interests of the staff with the needs of clients; and d) by viewing clients as "raw material" and passive subjects. Others also noted that many human service organizations do reflect important if not exclusive commitments to the welfare of clients and that these commitments should not be construed as simply marginal. In this context, it was pointed out that a major responsibility of the professionals in human service organizations is to actively engage the clients in the service giving process (Sarason, 1972). Such mutually supporting interaction can assure that the interests of clients are less likely to be relegated to a minor position in the organization.

Shifting the focus to the internal structure and management of human service organizations, Litwak proposed that most organizations pursue multiple tasks ranging from routine to non-routine. To advance organizational effectiveness, he argued that each type of task necessitates a different work structure ranging from bureaucratic to human relations. Much of the discussion focused on the need to test empirically the proposed models before administrators adopt them as prescriptive guidelines. In his commentary Knoke noted that Litwak's conceptualization of the mega bureaucracy was a promising approach at this time to bridge the distinctions between intra- and inter-organizational analyses. Many state level human service organizations are mega bureaucracies which have such loosely defined authority systems that they more closely resemble a congerie of organizations than a unitary collectivity. Problems of communication, coordination, competition, and control appear very similar to those of inter-organizational networks. Comparative analysis of intra- and inter-organizational complex role structures by methods such as "blockmodeling" (White, Boorman and Breiger, 1976; Boorman and White, 1976) should go a long way toward answering Paul White's question: "Do they require separate conceptualizations?" (White, 1974). Knoke suggested that Litwak's emphasis on ideal types of organizational structure and complex structuring of various organizational variables hampered the empirical testing of his ideas. Rather, one may wish to focus on the empirical relations among the variables themselves to ascertain whether they in fact form the structural types assumed by Litwak. For example, it is not clear whether the increased professionalization in the human services has not affected their structure independently of the tasks to be performed. In fact, Epstein and Conrad argue that the professionalization of social work has served as a screen to obscure the real tasks performed by social workers, has created a myth about the effectiveness of social work technologies, and has generated goal displacement.

Several discussants raised questions about the empirical validity of the findings presented by Epstein and Conrad and the extent to which these support their conclusions. It was noted that the ideal type of a profession used by Epstein and Conrad, against which social work is evaluated, is not upheld even vis-à-vis the more traditional professions such as medicine and law. On a substantive level, Pawlak mustered considerable amounts of information to suggest that the professionalization of social work was accompanied by a great deal of activity of knowledge building, a much stronger client orientation, and the enforcement of professional standards. In particular, he advocated that we adopt a developmental perspective on the professionalization of social work, recognizing that it is still in its infancy as compared to the more established professions. With such a perspective, there are indications that social work has made significant strides, particularly at the corporate level, in advocating and lobbying for the rights of clients, and in developing adjudicatory mechanisms to handle an increasing number of complaints of violations of professional ethics. Yet, as several discussants pointed out, the question still remains whether these and other activities may not have a self-serving function for social workers to gain prestige and recognition in their competition with other helping professions. It is apparent that rigorous research is needed on this subject, particularly in identifying the actual tasks performed by social workers, the conditions under which these tasks are carried out, and on the profession-bureaucracy strains.

In this context, of key importance is the study of the interaction between clients and staff of human service organizations, an issue addressed by Hasenfeld in his paper. As was noted by him and others, the key dimension in client-organizations relations centers around the question of control, namely, the conditions under which clients can exercise control over the organization in order to optimize their benefits and minimize costs and vice versa. Lerman cogently pointed out.that one should not tend to assume that all human service organizations do in fact provide a "service." In the correctional system, for example, one may talk about organizations providing "disservices." Even the concept of client may hide the fact that the person so labelled might be coerced into such a status and that its consequences are disproportionately negative. Put differently, the rise of the welfare state through the expansion of social services has also expanded the boundaries and potential targets of coercive control, as the state requires more and more people to accept "services." Lerman suggested that we have created a combined welfare and control state. Thus, with the increasing intervention of human service organizations in people's lives there is an urgent need to consider the basic rights of "clients" and their protection. These rights include not only the frequently mentioned right to claim services, but also the right to refuse to become an involuntary recipient of service, or at least the right to demand humane care in the least restrictive environment.

The issue of the civil rights of clients, particularly of ethnic minority origins, was one of the foci of the paper by Perlmutter and Alexander. It goes without saying that social welfare institutions, as many other organizations, are likely to reflect societal biases, prejudices, and discriminatory practices toward ethnic minorities, members of lower socio-economic groups, and women. What pressures were brought upon those institutions to eliminate discrimination in their hiring practices, service ideologies, and population served, and how successful were these? While Perlmutter and Alexander suggested that the pressures emanated from the efforts of various civil rights groups within the social service arena and were of significant success, other discussants took exception to this view. Figueira-McDonough noted that there is considerable evidence to at least suggest that some of the changes were due to external policies imposed on social service agencies by legislative, judicial, and regulatory agencies rather than a product of the social movements. For example, a study by Housner (1977) indicated that minority representation on boards of public health agencies was directly related to the existence of anti-discriminatory legislation. Figueira-McDonough cited studies by Kanter (1977a, 1977b) and Rosenbaum (1976) on the position of women and minorities in organizations that suggest that strong discriminatory practices in hiring and promotion still exist. Similarly there is a large body of literature that indicates that human service organizations still exclude many potential clients, particularly of low socio-economic backgrounds, from their services through a variety of implicit and latent intake and cooling out procedures. Moreover, the apparent progress that the authors document is based mostly on documentation from within the social services, and thus may be subject to highly self-serving biases. When one examines data collected independently of these organizations the picture becomes distinctly less optimistic. In fact, as Figueira-McDonough noted, reexamination of the evidence might well indicate a greater diversity within each period and a less regular temporal progression with respect to the ideological and practice aspects of social work. There was wide consensus that considerably more systematic research must be conducted in order to assess the state of non-discrimination in social service agencies, and that active pursuit of this objective must continue vigorously. For example, frequent statements are made about discrimination in the delivery of services to clients on the basis of race, sex, or ethnicity. Yet, differential presence of clients in welfare caseloads does not indicate selective allocation of benefits.

One can only establish that institutionalized racism exists if the population in need is properly identified and compared with the population served. Examination of eligibility criteria also can indicate which sectors of the population tend to be excluded from service programs. Knowledge of operational rather than formal screening criteria is crucial as many studies have shown.

As some of the administrative practices in the human services were examined, the paper by Rossi raised the issue concerning the role of the social scientist in evaluating social welfare policies; certainly the blind acceptance of value free models and pure type experimental methodological approaches is no longer acceptable, although it is still widely practiced. Mott argued that scientists must be far more sensitive to the critical role of the evaluator in studying and changing social values and policies. He further suggested that the scientist-evaluator inevitably must consider whether the social policies being implemented in the program he or she is evaluating are compatible with major societal priorities. That is, he challenged the assertion that the function of evaluation is to assess whether a social program achieves its intended aim, since the aim itself may be undesirable or inhumane. Moreover, its formulators may have not intended it to be fully implemented in the first place, since they are guided by various political considerations. Thus, in Mott's words, "the evaluators are put in the position of attempting to make the mythical silk purse out of the sow's ear and it rarely works." Had there been such self-examination by evaluators in prior years, perhaps some of the major programmatic blunders might have been prevented or at least alleviated.

The papers by Patti and Gurin advocate considerable caution in the application of management tools and techniques to human services. The developmental administration model proposed by Patti drew much support from the social welfare administrators, such as Likins. She noted that this model raises some important issues for administrators, such as how to recruit managers who can handle the differential tasks in each phase of program development and how to train managers to shift from one set to another set of skills at the various stages of program development. Yet, some discussants voiced concern that the model may underestimate the impact of the external environment in shaping program development, let alone alter its sequence. Thus, it is not unlikely, for example, that under legislative or executive pressures to launch a program, the entire developmental process might be truncated.

While Patti is concerned with "creeping technicism in social welfare administration," Gurin, in contrast, points to numerous developments in the field of scientific management that provide stimuli for experimentation in the administration of human service organizations. In many respects, the paper by Delbecq follows the position advocated by Gurin. Through the culling of a large body of studies on innovation in industrial organizations, Delbecq is able to extract a general, yet detailed prescriptive model of innovation applicable to human service organizations. Admittedly this is a value free model; it does not raise concerns about the nature of the innovation itself, nor does it purport to pass judgment on the process itself. Several discussants raised questions on this very issue. Studt, for example, questioned whether, following the model, one is more likely to get innovative services designed by administration rather than by joint efforts of staff and clients. Others raised the possibility that "playing the innovation game" may result in serious goal displacement and subversion of original service objectives. Studt also argued that before an innovation is selected or implemented, the receiving organization should be studied in its current operation, since that organization will be modified by the innovation. An objective data-based profile should be prepared, she asserted, followed by an assessment of what is likely to occur when the particular innovation is attempted. Activities of related units may also be disturbed and, if not dealt with, they can jeopardize the new innovation. Given these activities one can then obtain the necessary commitments of the participants on a realistic basis. Delbecq's model allows for these activities, although less explicitly.

Also emphasized was the need for creativity and initiative where the individual worker and clients grapple together with real-life problems. Too often service programs are designed at the administrative level to solve problems at that level but not in service delivery to clients. Recent experience with "services integration designs" in several states clearly illustrates the latter phenomena. Studt proposed an alternative innovation model directed specifically toward enhanced service delivery. Her model incorporated the following elements: 1) a staff-client pool of human resources jointly assigned responsibility for creating a new service program; 2) a flexible role system that allocated leadership according to task and competence; 3) a structure for problem-identification; 4) mechanisms for conflict resolution within and between units; and, 5) plans for evaluation with incorporate study of both process and output (Goldenberg, 1971 and 1973; Sarason, 1972).

In the same vein, Cox raised a general concern about the applicability of management tools developed in the private sector to human service organizations, since these tools are designed for the enhancement of survival, growth, and profit. Similarly, he argued that one cannot separate management from policy and that the substance of both is predicated on the prevailing ideologies of the political party in power, as is clearly the case, for example, in Australia. Therefore, it is doubtful whether management tools for human services can be devoid of underlying values and ideologies. In fact, there may be a danger that adoption of such tools may make these ideologies implicit rather than explicit and prevent their debate in public.

Cox disagreed with Gurin about strategy and timing for management development in the human services. He decried contemporary pessimism and asserted that the need for action was urgent from his perspective as a state-level administrator. Perhaps surprisingly, the problems that he enumerated from his Australian experience were not substantially different from those of welfare administrators in the United States. He advised social scientists, policy makers, and administrators in the United States to look again to events in the human services in the 1960s, particularly to those areas where positive gains had been achieved. It was also noted that political factors contributed as much to the difficulties which many of these programs encountered as did their intrinsic characteristics. The problems addressed in the 1960s will continue to plague post-industrial societies for the remainder of the century in all likelihood; yet some act as if they could be avoided today in the management of human services. Cox further noted that prevailing management approaches fostered unnecessary bureaucratic hierarchies. These, coupled with professional status hierarchies, produce overly complex organizational processes and structures. He concurred with Morris and Lescohier, and several others, that services integration has been only a fantasy ideal given a great deal of lip service. He asserted that effective service integration should reflect the attainment of quality services centered on, and developed for and with the consumer/citizen in the context of the local community. It was also noted that integration of services at the local community level may well conserve scarce resources, since local voluntary efforts would develop more readily and because services generally cost less provided within normalized contexts rather than in large bureaucratic super-structures that devote much effort only to custody, control, and organizational maintenance.

This volume was the product of a joint effort by a group of social scientists, social welfare administrators, and social work educators who prepared a series of papers related to critical issues in management and service delivery in human service organizations. They met together to analyze and critique each others' theoretical formulations, findings, and recommendations. The focus was directed primarily to those sectors that provide public and private social services, but many of the issues and proposals are applicable to all human service organizations. Out of these efforts and similar work of others it is hoped that the future direction of social policy administration will be forthcoming. We urgently need to design and deliver social services relative to consumer needs and expectations. The difficulty of that challenge is as great with respect to political factors as is the knowledge limitation. It is quite clear that solutions from the business and industrial sectors have limited applicability with respect to some of the more profound problems of human service organizations as both Cyert (1975) and Drucker (1973 and 1977) have noted.

Many lament the rapid growth of the human services and their seemingly contradicting effects on United States society in recent years; yet, like other post-industrial societies, all indicators point to continuing growth in future years. At the same time it must be recognized that we are approaching a crisis because of our inability to continue to fund programs enacted by legislators, given the present level of economic growth and the present modes of service delivery, which continue to produce rapidly escalating costs with little or no increase in effectiveness of service. Related to this phenomenon is an often ignored characteristic of the American welfare establishment, namely, that it no longer serves only the poor, sick, deviant, or handicapped. In the past quarter century a cross-section of persons from all social classes have become recipients of various human services (for example, social security, medical care, mental health, substance abuse, child abuse and welfare, and programs for the elderly). Many observers have argued that the middle class rather than the poor have been the greater beneficiaries of the new social service programs, even when various income transfers are included. Because of this shift, there is a strong demand for more social services by the middle classes, often at the expense of the poor. Such demand is coupled with an apparently increasing belief that entitlements to these services must in some ways be earned. Therefore, there has been a tendency to place greater importance on various social insurance mechanisms rather than to assert that these services are a right to be made freely available to all persons in need. As a result, the young and the poor in particular are in greater jeopardy than they were in the past of being denied social services as a matter of right. Certainly the social values and priorities of the majority will become clearer in the latter part of this century as the United States attempts fundamental changes in health and welfare policies and programs. The challenge for the effective management of the human services could never be greater.

REFERENCES

Banfield, Edward C., and James Q. Wilson. 1963. *City Politics.* Cambridge, Mass.: Harvard University Press.

Bish, Robert L. 1971. *The Public Economy of Metropolitan Areas.* Chicago: Markham.

Bish, Robert L., and Vincent Ostrom. 1973. *Understanding Urban Government: Metropolitan Reform Reconsidered.* Washington, D.C.: American Enterprise Institute for Public Policy.

Boorman, Scott A., and Harrison White. 1976. "Social Structure for Multiple Network Role Structures," *American Journal of Sociology,* 81 (May):1384–96.

Cyert, Richard. 1975. *The Management of the Non-Profit Organization.* Lexington, Mass.: D. C. Heath.

Downs, George. 1976. *Bureaucracy, Innovation and Social Policy.* Lexington, Mass.: D. C. Heath.

Drucker, Peter. 1973. "On Managing the Public Service Institution," *The Public Interest,* 33 (Fall):43–60.

—— 1977. *The Unseen Revolution: How Pension Fund Socialism Came to America.* New York: Harper and Row.

Goldenberg, Ira. 1971. *Build Me a Mountain: Yough, Poverty and the Creation of Settings.* Cambridge: MIT Press.

Goldenberg, Ira, ed. 1973. *The Helping Professions in the World of Action.* Lexington, Mass.: Lexington Books.

Housner, Tony. 1977. "Are Health System Agency Boards Representative of Minorities and Women?'' Paper presented at the Research Symposium on Social Indicators of Institutional Racism-Sexism, Los Angeles, Calif., April.

Kanter, Rosabeth. 1977a. ''Some Effects of Proportions on Group Life: Skewed Sex Ratios and Responses to Token Women,'' *American Journal of Sociology*, 82 (March):965–90.

—— 1977b. ''Access to Opportunity and Power: Measuring Racism-Sexism inside Organizations.'' Paper presented at the Research Symposium on Social Indicators of Institutional Racism-Sexism, Los Angeles, Calif., April.

Kaufman, Herbert. 1971. *The Limits of Organizational Change*. University, Ala.: University of Alabama Press.

Linebury, Robert, and Edmund Fowler. 1967. ''Reformism and Public Policy in American Cities,'' *American Political Science Review*, 61 (Sept.):701–16.

Lovelace, Barry, and Nicholas Thomas. 1974. ''Regional Structure and Regionalism within the States.'' In Selma J. Mushkin, ed., *State Aids for Human Services in a Federal System, Part II*. Washington, D.C.: Georgetown University Public Services Laboratory.

Ostrom, Vincent. 1974. *The Intellectual Crisis in American Public Administration*. University, Ala.: University of Alabama Press.

Rosenbaum, James E. 1976. *Making Inequality*. New York: Wiley.

Sarason, Seymour. 1972. *Creation of Settings and Future Societies*. San Francisco: Jossey Bass.

Studt, Elliot. 1968. *C-Unit: Search for Community in Prison*. New York: Russell Sage.

—— 1973. *Surveillance and Service in Parole*. MR-166. Los Angeles: UCLA Institute of Government and Public Affairs.

White, Harrison C., Scott Boorman, and Ronald Breiger. 1976. ''Social Structure from Multiple Networks I, Blockmodels of Roles and Positions,'' *American Journal of Sociology*, 81 (Jan.):730–80.

White, Paul. 1974. ''Intra- and Inter-organizational Studies: Do They Require Separate Conceptualizations?'' *Administration and Society*, 6 (May):107–52.

APPENDIX

List of Participants

Howard Aldrich
Associate Professor
Institute of Labor and Industrial Relations
Cornell University

Leslie B. Alexander
Assistant Professor
Graduate School of Social Work and
Social Research
Bryn Mawr College

Lisle Carter, Jr.
Chancellor
Atlanta University

Ian Cox
Director-General of Community Welfare
South Australian Department for Community Welfare

André L. Delbecq
Director
Center for Evaluation Research,
Training and Program Development
School of Social Work
University of Wisconsin-Madison

Irwin Epstein
Professor of Social Work
School of Social Work
University of Michigan

Josefina Figueira-McDonough
Assistant Professor
School of Social Work
Michigan State University

Arnold Gurin
Maurice B. Hexter Professor of Social Administration
Florence Heller Graduate School for
Advanced Studies in Social Welfare
Brandeis University

Yeheskel Hasenfeld
Associate Professor
School of Social Work
University of Michigan

Morris Janowitz
Distinguished Service Professor
Department of Sociology
University of Chicago

David Knoke
Associate Professor
Department of Sociology
Indiana University

Paul Lerman
Professor
Graduate School of Social Work
Rutgers University

Vera J. Likins
Commissioner of Public Welfare
State of Minnesota

Eugene Litwak
Professor
School of Social Work
Columbia University

Robert Morris
Kirstien Professor of Social Planning
Florence Heller Graduate School for
Advanced Studies in Social Welfare
Brandeis University

Paul Mott
President
Mott and MacDonald, Inc.
Washington, D.C.

Rino Patti
Professor
School of Social Work
University of Washington

Edward Pawlak
Professor
School of Social Work
University of Tennessee

Felice Davidson Perlmutter
Professor and Research Associate
School of Social Administration
Center for Policy Research
Temple University

Charles Perrow
Professor
Department of Sociology
State University of New York at Stony Brook

Arnulf Pins
Chairman, Grant Committee
The Louis and Samuel Silberman Fund

Peter H. Rossi
Professor
Social and Demographic Research Institute
University of Massachusetts

Rosemary Sarri
Professor
School of Social Work
University of Michigan

Seyoum Selassie
Visiting Assistant Professor
School of Social Welfare
University of Wisconsin-Milwaukee

Samuel J. Silberman
President
The Lois and Samuel Silberman Fund

Elliot Studt
Professor Emeritus
School of Social Welfare
University of California at Los Angeles

Gerald D. Suttles
Professor
Department of Sociology
University of Chicago

Darrel Vorwaller
Principal
Peat, Marwick, Mitchell and Company
Chicago, Illinois

Index

ABT Associates, 32
Abbott sisters, 212
Accessibility (of HSOs), 34-35
Accountability, 8, 25; local, 67; social, 88-90, 92-93, 94, 99
Adaptiveness: in decentralized systems, 65-66
Addams, Jane, 212
Adjudicative principles, 145-49
Administration; developmental, 15-16; of social programs, 40, 266-85, 289-308, 347, 348; of new social programs, 262-88; and policy analysis, 295-97; business, 298-300; public, 298-300, 306; *see also* Management
Administrators, 61, 265, 269-70, 274; accountability of, 67; and service goals, 109; objectives of, 112-14; relationship with staff, 116; and decision making, 126-27; minority, 217; and innovation planning, 312-14
Aiken, Michael: and Robert Alford, 68; and Jerald Hage, 169, 174-75, 264n
Aldrich, Howard, 13, 51-79, 340
Alexander, Leslie B., and Felice D. Perlmutter, 15, 207-31, 346
Alford, R., 10, 12
Alford, Robert, and Michael Aiken, 68
Allied Services Act, 24, 31, 33
Analysis: units of, 52-54; interorganizational, 155; *see also* Policy analysis
Anderson, O. W., and R. M. Anderson, 192
Anderson, R. M., and O. W. Anderson, 192
Arendt, Hannah, 80n
Association of Black Social Workers, 218
Authority, 57; centralized, 27, 53, 154, 155; at local level, 52; as resource, 59-60; manipulation of, 75; delegation of, 126-27; in

new social programs, 277; *see also* Centralization
Autonomy, 4, 6, 280; organizational, 59-60; professional, 222n; local, 341, 342

Bailey, Margaret B., 171
Baker, M. R., 173
Banfield, Edward, and Morton Grodzins, 51
Barnard, Chester, 112
Beatrice, Ellen, 40
Benefit payments, 55, 294-95, 346
Benguigui, Georges, 167
Bennett, William S., Jr., and Merl C. Hokenstad, 165
Berg, T., 173n
Bergunder, Ann, Roland Warren, and Steven Rose, 4, 113
Berkanovic, Emil, and Leo G. Reeder, 193
Billingsley, Andrew, 168, 171; and Jeanne Giovannoni, 216-17
Bish, Robert L., 343
Blacks: and social work, 211, 215-18; professional associations of, 218; self-help groups of, 223; *see also* Discrimination; Racism
Blau, Peter M., 123, 135, 157-58, 256; and W. Richard Scott, 174
Block grants, 24, 27
Borenzweig, Herman, 172
Boston, Mass., 215
Boundary relations, 188, 190-94, 267-72
Bryson, John, 312
Bucher, Rue, and Anselm Strauss, 168-69
Buell, Bradley, 132, 133
Bureaucracy: monocratic, 123-30, 136, 157; human relations structures of, 130-36; mega, 154-56; *see also* Organizations